POLITICAL PHILOSOPHY AND TIME

POLITICAL PHILOSOPHY

AND TIME

By JOHN G. GUNNELL

WESLEYAN UNIVERSITY PRESS
Middletown, Connecticut

BP
638
G82

Library of Congress Catalog Card Number: 68–16009
Manufactured in the United States of America
FIRST EDITION

TO MY MOTHER AND THE MEMORY OF MY FATHER

All politics imply a certain idea of man.

Paul Valéry

We create time as an idea or notion and do not begin till much later to suspect that we ourselves are time, *inasmuch as we live.*

Oswald Spengler

CONTENTS

PREFACE

THIS work is an inquiry into the nature of political vision and its relationship to conceptions of time and history. Although the principal focus is on the emergence of political philosophy as a distinct intellectual activity and on the problem of social order as it appears in Plato's dialogues, significant portions of the book are concerned with symbolization, the conceptualization of time, myth, the Hebrew prophetic tradition, and pre-philosophic Greek thought. The early chapters are not intended to represent an investigation of the genesis of Plato's thought. The primary purpose in these chapters is to consider alternatives to, and analyze continuities and contrasts with, the answers to the problems of human order and historical existence formulated by political philosophy. In the concluding chapter, an attempt is made to point briefly and tentatively through the Western tradition of political philosophy toward the continuing interplay between ideas of time and political order.

This book, or at least its initiation, was the result of a deep uneasiness about current studies in the history of political philosophy, in terms of both purpose and approach. Whether it accrues to its favor or stands as a defect, this work seeks neither to justify or condemn the ideas with which it deals nor to commend or deprecate any trend in the development of political thought or action. The intention is neither to determine a moment of truth in the tradition nor to discover a point at which the tradition went astray. The substantive problem which provided the orientation for this study was that of making intelligible what appeared to be a recurring pattern of attitudes toward time and history on the part of political philosophers, and any passion attaching to this work is either a passion for explanation or the result of a sense of wonderment in the face of the creative minds of Plato and his named and nameless predecessors. In addition, an important concern was with what might be termed a methodological problem, growing out of a dissatisfaction with narrow approaches to the study of the history of political theory which have produced a proliferation of interpretations and reinterpretations insulated from scholarship in other disciplines. Much of the literature in this field has been a curious mixture of intellectual history and social philosophy with little attention to the process through which the transformation of political symbols takes place. One of the principal aims of this study was to make at least a provisional attempt to develop an approach which would overcome this deficiency. This approach, which can be best characterized as a theory of symbolic forms, derives from several aspects of contemporary philosophy and has, it is hoped, some importance not only for the exploration of the history of ideas but for problems of explanation in the social sciences as well.

This manuscript was completed before the publication of Gilbert Ryle's speculative and stimulating reconstruction of Plato's intellectual life and the chronology of his writings, and consequently no attempt has been made to deal with the implications of his conclusions for certain arguments presented in the following pages.*

I am grateful to Professors Norman Jacobson and Sheldon Wolin of the University of California, Berkeley, and Professor Louis O. Mink, Jr., of Wesleyan University for reading the manuscript and offering helpful suggestions; and I am especially indebted to Professor Robert Brumbaugh of Yale University, whose detailed comments on two drafts of this work were invaluable. To Norman Jacobson I also owe a unique intellectual debt which is not easily articulated and can be appreciated only by those who have benefited from his teaching. My wife assisted in the preparation of an early version of the manuscript, and her patience with the demands of scholarly activity has been a constant source of support. Finally, I wish to acknowledge the aid of the librarians and clerical staff of the Graduate School of Public Affairs, State University of New York at Albany, and particularly Miss Addie Ballone, who typed the final draft.

JOHN G. GUNNELL

Albany, New York
September, 1967

* Gilbert Ryle, *Plato's Progress* (Cambridge: Cambridge University Press, 1966).

POLITICAL PHILOSOPHY AND TIME

I

INTRODUCTION

It cannot be stressed enough that the key to a
fundamental understanding, not only of man, but of
the world as well, is to be sought in the relation
between creativity and symbolic reality.

Erich Neumann

Man, in the end, is alarmed by the idea of
time, and unbalanced by incessant wanderings
between past and future.

Isak Dinesen

Symbols and Society

THE assumption which governs the following study is that man, above all else, is *"animal symbolicum"*[1] and that this conception incorporates and transcends any idea of human being as *animal rationale, animal politicum, animal socialis, homo loquens, homo sapiens,* or *homo faber.* While symbolization is related to these various levels of activity, *"the invention of representative symbolization was the great discovery, the decisive event in the evolution of man,"* for "the evolution of symbolic worlds is identical with the creation of a human 'universe,' in contrast to the Uexküllian 'ambient' (*umwelt*) of animals, which is predetermined by their innate, anatomico-functional organization."[2] Man uses signs not merely to indicate objects or as signals but as a medium for representation and conception; while signs stand for things "symbols are not proxy for their objects, but are *vehicles for the conception* of objects . . . and *it is* the conceptions, not the things, that symbols directly 'mean.' "[3] In a sense an "image" of the world may be said to exist on all levels of organic life, but "it is this ability to proliferate and elaborate the image into a symbolic universe that is the peculiarity and glory of

man."[4] To distinguish man in terms of this activity, which Susanne
Langer has characterized as the "symbolic transformation of experience," is to expand the idea of reason beyond what is usually understood
as "rationalism" or "rationalistic" thought; it may be said that "rationality is the essence of mind, and symbolic transformation its elementary
process."[5] But if symbolization is to be taken as the principal activity of
thought, it must be understood as encompassing not only more than logic
and discursive or analytic reason but more than speech and language in
the narrow sense. Discursive speech and thought are merely special instances of symbolic activity which also extends to what may be understood as "presentational" languages such as ritual and art.[6]

   "Signs and symbols . . . are among the means by which man tries to
come to terms with his manifold experiences of transcendency."[7] For
man reality is what is presented to him in his symbols, and there is no
penetrating beyond symbols to a more ultimate datum; the factual
world is given in the symbolic. Man is continually in the process of creating a virtual reality which forms the boundaries of his activity.

> The various symbolic forms—myth, language, art, and science
> —constitute the indispensable precondition for this process. They
> are the true media—which man himself has created—by virtue of
> which he has been able to separate himself from the world, and in
> this very separation, to bind himself closer to it. This feature of
> mediation characterizes all human knowledge. It is also distinctive
> and typical in all human action.[8]

Only in terms of symbolic forms does the world take shape, and there
can be "no standpoint from which a closed whole of Being would be
surveyable, nor any sequence of standpoints through whose totality
Being would be given even indirectly."[9] Since it is only through man and
his symbols that reality finds expression, man as the symbol-maker is
the "shepherd of Being."[10] Although a symbol is not autonomous and always points beyond itself to the "encompassing" realm which surrounds
every symbolic horizon, it must be understood that "symbolic forms are
not imitations, but organs of reality"; they do not simply constitute perspectives but the "finite provinces of meaning upon which we bestow the
accent of reality" and which comprise our vision of both the natural and
social world.[11] The creation of symbols provides man with an orientation
within the universe and gives meaning to that universe.

> Here there emerges, as the fundamental feature of all human exis-
> tence, the fact that man is not lost within the welter of his external
> impressions, that he learns to control this sea of impressions by giv-
> ing it ordered form, which, as such, stems in the final analysis from
> himself, from his own thinking, feeling, and willing.[12]

This order produced through symbolic forms is never definitive, because
"the description of reality is essentially inexhaustible."[13] But it is through
the creation of these forms that man orders his experience, orients himself
both individually and socially, and organizes for action; action and the
objectified products of action can be explained and understood only in
terms of these symbols by which a society defines and justifies itself.

A convergence of symbolic forms gives rise not only to collective
representations constituting a vision of the universe but to particular
systems of social relations. Society presents itself essentially as a symbolic crystal.

> Human society is not merely a fact, or an event, in the external
> world to be studied by an observer like a natural phenomenon.
> Though it has externality as one of its components, it is as a whole
> a little world, a cosmion, illuminated with meaning from within by
> the human beings who continually create and bear it as the mode
> and condition of their self-realization. It is illuminated through an
> elaborate symbolism, in various degrees of compactness and differ-
> entiation—from rite, through myth, to theory—and this symbolism
> illuminates it with meaning in so far as the symbols make the in-
> ternal structure of such a cosmion, the relations between its mem-
> bers and groups of members, as well as its existence as a whole,
> transparent for the mystery of human existence. The self-illumina-
> tion of society through symbols is an integral part of social reality
> . . . and one may even say, its essential part.[14]

But herein lies one of the great problems of social order: the co-ordination and integration of symbolic forms. Each symbolic form and particular configuration of symbols tends to produce an autonomous vision of
reality and mode of existence or "form of life."[15] "In other words, there
are different universes of discourse—let us say the poetic, the scientific,
the religious, and perhaps the metaphysical—and these universes have
different symbolic forms."[16] The greater the proliferation of symbolic
forms, the greater the competition between symbols and universes of dis-

course, the more difficult it is to maintain an integrated collective vision in which individuals and groups do not exist "worlds apart."[17] Yet in these very tensions may be found the key to understanding social change and intellectual creativity.

Symbolic forms, as modes of symbolization, not only place limits on the elaboration of a symbolic universe but enter into the constitution of that universe. For example, the rise of modern science as a symbolic form with its accentuation of the poles of observer and observed created a situation in which the physical world came to be viewed not as a symbolic order in which the mind actively participated, but as an independent external reality.[18] The very power of symbolization carries with it the danger of hypostatization and reification—an idolatry which distorts the nature of symbolization by concealing the participation of the mind in the phenomena. In this regard it must be recognized that phrases such as the "history of political theory" are often misleading. Just as the history of science is sometimes viewed as a progressive penetration of a natural world understood as a fixed and independent datum and as a cumulative process of gaining knowledge of this datum rather than a series of "paradigms" or symbolizations of physical reality which inform scientific activity,[19] there is a tendency to treat the history of political and social thought as a succession of ideologies or perspectives on basically the same phenomena, and this has obscured the extent to which "the field of politics is and has been, in a significant and radical sense, a created one."[20]

The conception of the world provides the limits of action within it, and social action and systems of social relations not only are "permeated with ideas about reality" but "are expressions of ideas about reality."

> Our idea of what belongs to the realm of reality is given for us in the language that we use. The concepts we have settle for us the form of the experience we have of the world. . . . The world *is* for us what is presented through these concepts. That is not to say that our concepts may not change; but even when they do, that means that our concept of the world has changed too.[21]

What must be continually stressed is the primacy of language and communication for the perception of the world, and this means not only the content of communication but its form. The transition from an oral to a written tradition and more recently the ascendancy of electronic media were transformations not only in modes of communicating symbols but in the manner in which reality was perceived and in which social relations were organized.[22] In the end "only where there is language is there world," and

> words and language are not wrappings in which things are packed for the commerce of those who write and speak. It is in words and language that things first come into being and are.
>
> . . . .
>
> Naming does not come afterward, providing an already manifest essent with a designation and a hallmark known as a word; it is the other way around.[23]

It is because man is *animal symbolicum* that communication becomes "the universal condition of man's being. It is so much his comprehensive essence that both what man is and what is for him are in some sense bound up with communication."[24] The symbolic faculty differentiates man from the natural order and makes possible a cultural world which in turn is the condition of historical existence.

In the mythic vision of the ancient world, man, in a sense, enjoyed a perfect orientation. The orders of existence were conceptually undif-ferentiated, and the myth performed the functions of thought which would eventually devolve into a series of symbolic forms ranging from art to metaphysics. With the collapse of the myth, the orders of existence could never again be reintegrated in their former compactness, and the orientation of man and society could only emerge from a co-ordination of symbolic forms. Man could never again become simply part of the order of natural things, and no one set of symbols could encompass the mani-fold of his experiences. This does not mean that the movement of con-sciousness is an irreversible path from unity to complexity and differen-tiation, for it may be the case that in the contemporary age the West may be returning to a compactness of existence in which

> we have extended our central nervous system itself in a global em-brace, abolishing both space and time as far as our planet is con-cerned.
>
> . . . .
>
> . . . Electric technology now begins to transform the visual or eye man back into the tribal and oral pattern with its seamless web of kinship and interdependence.[25]

New symbolic forms or modes of understanding emerge to cope with new dimensions of experience. Each advance in thought from art to quantum mechanics has been in terms of an expansion of consciousness and the development of new symbolic forms to deal with the differentiated areas of experience; "it is a peculiar fact that every major advance in thinking, every epoch-making new insight, springs from a new type of symbolic transformation."[26] The historical order of the development of symbolic forms in the West may be tentatively expressed as a progression from ritual to myth to language to art to philosophy and science, and this corresponds to the differentiation of consciousness since "for each new problem that it encounters it constructs a new form of understanding."[27] Symbolic transformation, however, entails more than the development of successive symbolic forms. Creative transformation takes place within the various forms in terms of a reordering of symbols which produces new configurations and meanings and consequently a new orientation. But at times transformation within a form is not adequate, and, as in the case of political philosophy at various periods with regard to its ability to meet the demands of orientation, a form may be subordinated to or its symbols assimilated in another if the crisis in experience is so grave that, for example, political symbols are no longer meaningful.

It is the transformation of symbols within various forms and the effect of these symbols on modes of activity which give rise to the history of philosophy, art, science, religion, and politics. The transformation which occurs within forms when one orientation or view of reality or configuration of symbols gives way to another, and consequently to a different system of action, as well as the emergence of new symbolic forms themselves can best be understood as a "revolutionary" rather than an incremental process. When modes of thought and action which are informed by a particular orientation or arrangement of symbols come up abruptly against "anomalies" in experience or problems which cannot be encompassed by existing symbols and forms of understanding, it may require a re-evaluation of the prevailing "paradigms" or assumptions about reality which govern activity. Social action changes when the images which orient and justify it no longer meet the demands of life and when such demands create new commitments or when the vision of creative individuals confronts operative assumptions and introduces new symbols and forms which subvert existing images. These tensions may in the end produce the need for a choice which proves to be a choice between different views of reality and consequently "between incompatible modes of community life," whether it is a community of science or the wider community of politics and society.[28]

Symbolic forms do not exist independently; they tend to overlap and penetrate one another. Political philosophy can never be clearly distinguished from the complementary forms of philosophy, art, and science. On the other hand, various forms may compete as guides to orientation and as a vision of man's place in the world such as the conflict between religion and the idea of the political at the end of the Middle Ages. Yet although the development of symbolic forms may be discerned historically and although they may complete with one another for the authority to order society, they do not supersede one another; for example, discursive reason or philosophy is not in any absolute sense a higher mode of thought. Since symbolic transformation is the fundamental activity, conceptual reason presents itself as only one type of language for the symbolic expression of experience. The presentational language of art remains the irreducible instrument for expressing certain experiences of existence and often adumbrates the breakdown of old symbols or the emergence of new meanings.

It is not a condition peculiar to the modern age "that the old metaphysical questions were shown to be meaningless" and that man "had come to live in a world in which his mind and his traditions of thought were not even capable of asking meaningful questions, let alone of giving answers to its own perplexities,"[29] for such a crisis in thought and action is precisely the condition of all significant symbolic transformation. That the plight of the modern age is acute in this respect cannot be doubted; the exhaustion of the vitality of the old metaphysics is evident. But the break with the past is certainly no more overwhelming than the conditions of thought and existence which accompanied the dissolution of the ancient myth or the collapse of Christian universalism.

When the symbols in terms of which a society or civilization has oriented itself in the world and articulated its historical existence no longer encompass the experience and needs of thought and action, new symbols arise in the differentiated conciousness of those creative individuals who most acutely suffer the loss of meaning and search for a new orientation. These symbols, which in the beginning have reality only in the psyche, become the vehicle of a new truth of existence which opposes the old symbolic configurations and forms of understanding. At first discursive language may be inadequate for the task of expressing new symbols, just as in the original sequence of the development of symbolic forms philosophy did not rise immediately from the ruins of the myth. It is often through the presentational language of art that a symbolic crisis and transformation first become apparent. Language is the medium for articulating new symbolic patterns, and it was as true for Plato as it is for Heidegger that "language . . . is the house of Being."[30] Concern with language must be an ultimate concern, since it is through language that a world is gained. Language is not merely a tool which man uses in the same sense that he uses other tools, and no amount of analysis of the contextual uses and purposes of words in everyday life can in the end reach *the* purpose for which language is creatively employed.

It is through the transformation of language and meaning that new symbols find expression, but new symbols do not arise by effecting a complete break with the past, which must ultimately limit and provide the ground of transformation. The transformation first occurs through a creative recasting and manipulation of the old symbols, just as art as a conscious and differentiated activity first emerged from a selection and manipulation of mythic symbols. Also new symbols are meaningful only when they are grounded in the existential situation of an age, and it is here that the problem of relevance is encountered. Yet despite the fulfillment of the criterion of relevance, or rather precisely because of it, new symbols and forms constitute a threat to a social order which has appropriated and objectified the old symbols and organized itself for action in accordance with them. It is in this potential undercutting of a tradition and a social style, the network of meanings which constitutes a society, that new symbols enter the public realm and thought touches action, and it is at this point that the recasting of symbols produces a new vision of order and man's place in the world.

Political Philosophy and Historical Existence

DURING the late Bronze Age, the palace cities of the Peloponnesos, under the leadership of Mycenae, assembled a huge labor force and began the construction of a wall that was to span the Isthmus of Corinth and seal off the peninsula. The wall was not completed, and within a century the flourishing Mycenaean civilization was annihilated. Although the precise significance of this undertaking and the meaning attached to it by the participants must remain obscure, it may be assumed that the threat which inspired the cities to league together in this effort was that great movement of peoples which swept down from the north across the eastern Mediterranean and Asia Minor at approximately 1200 B.C. Before the wall was completed, the Dorian hordes had swelled around the very walls of Mycenae, and the king watched helplessly from the citadel as the territory was devastated. At the unfortified city of Pylos, the palace was razed and fired, and its contents were destroyed with a deliberate vehemence. Although the Dorian invasion subsided momentarily and the seemingly impregnable fortress at Mycenae survived for a time as an island of order, the destruction of the Bronze Age culture was complete in little more than four generations. The last concerted act of the dying civilization was the desperate plundering raid across the Aegean which Homer glorified in the *Iliad* and which formed the boundary of the historical memory of classical Greece. Disorder had bred disorder, and even in the Homeric epic the siege of Troy may be sensed as a doomed venture and an overture to chaos. With the disintegration of a culture contained within what had appeared as the divine and imperishable space of the city, the Attic world descended into time; the collapse of Mycenae was the beginning of a journey "between past and future."

Man first existed in space, but he first became aware of himself in time. Thinking is an activity performed in time, for it is only in terms of time that thought becomes conscious of itself. The discovery of the self and the experience of temporality occurred simultaneously since it is the self that posits, separates, and mediates the dimensions of past and future. The consciousness of both time and the self were in turn tied to the breakdown of the archetypal existence under the form of the cosmological myth which characterized the great civilizations of the ancient world. But the condition of timelessness and selflessness in the mythic Weltanschauung was supported by a static social order; myth and society were reciprocally sustaining. It is unnecessary to establish causal relationships between the consciousness of the self, the consciousness of human time, and the dissolution of the mythic mode; these were contiguous experiences which in turn were bound to the loss, or the threat of the loss, of an ordered social space. The consciousness of the self and its temporal plight emerged with the loosening of the bonds of social order, and in turn it was only through this differentiated consciousness that the rise and fall of social order and eventually the existence of mankind under the form of history became a datum of experience.

Despite symbolic transformations of the idea of the self and the meaning of time, the crucial transition occurred when the atemporal existence which characterized the mythic mode disintegrated. With the dissolution of the unity of the myth and the initial differentiation of the orders of existence with their respective temporal dimensions, there emerged a search for a new vision of order, the appearance of conscious speculation on man's home in the world. Creative thought took place both within the mythic mode and subsequent to it; the difference is in the consciousness of the activity. The moment that the eternal present of the primordial time of the myth was lost, a sense of temporal distance intruded into the psyche, and this inner distance, which was the foundation of the awareness of the self and its unique life, furnished the ground of conscious speculation. With the eclipse of the myth, the self became an object of reflection and the inner distance or time became not only a condition of thought but a problem of existence.

The concern here is with time as a condition of thought and form of existence as distinguished from the myth. Together, the static space of the ancient world and the atemporal perspective of the myth supported man in his sojourn on earth, encompassing him and sustaining him like the embryonic fluid. With the collapse of this space and the dissolution of the mythic vision came the entrance into time which gave birth to the consciousness of a distinctively human condition. The contrast between these modes may be illustrated by Isak Dinesen's parable of the fish.

> Man can move in one plane, and is tied to the earth. Still the earth supports him only by the narrow space under the soles of his two feet; he must bear his own weight and sigh beneath it. He must, so I gathered from the talk of my old fisherman, climb the hills of the earth laboriously; it may happen to him to tumble down from them, and the earth then receives him with hardness.
>
> We fish are upheld and supported on all sides. We lean confidently and harmoniously upon our element. We move in all dimensions, and whatever course we take, the mighty waters out of reverence for our virtue change shape accordingly.

We have no hands, so cannot construct anything at all, and are never tempted by vain ambition to alter anything whatever in the universe of the Lord. We sow not and toil not; therefore no estimates of ours will turn out wrong and no expectation fail. The greatest amongst us in their spheres have reached perfect darkness. And the pattern of the universe we read with ease, because we see it from below. . . .

I shall further—this time for my own sake—in the wise and proven manner of the fish, pass lightly over the fact that man, although fallen and corrupted, once more succeeded, by craft, in coming out on top.

It does, however, remain open to doubt whether, through this apparent triumph, man obtained true welfare. How will real security be obtained by a creature ever anxious about the direction in which he moves, and attaching vital importance to his rising and falling? How can equilibrium be obtained by a creature which refuses to give up the idea of hope and risk?

We fish rest quietly, on all sides supported, within an element which all the time accurately and unfailingly evens itself out. An element which may be said to have taken over our personal existence, in as much as . . . our weight and body are calculated according to the quantity of our surroundings which we displace. . . .

We run no risks. For our changing of place in existence never creates, or leaves after it, what man calls a way, upon which phenomenon—in reality no phenomenon but an illusion—he will waste inexplicable passionate deliberation.[31]

Man existing under the form of the myth moved like the fish in an element which supported him on all sides, where the past continually closed behind him and forward translation toward the future produced nothing new. Life was lived in a continuous present where individual existence was never separated from the matrix, and man, like the fish, seemed to be "accurately made in the image of the Lord—eternity. Here, man never suspected that he was *homo faber*. Divested of the myth, man walked precariously on the earth, forced to measure and plan each step lest he lose his equilibrium. The pattern of the universe was no longer clearly intelligible, but stretched out in a temporal dimension in which the outer limits were inevitably distorted whether he looked forward or back. The path he had traveled became of absorbing interest because the memory of the journey furnished the only orientation for his present predicament and the only clue to what lay ahead. Man was not at home in this state where the configuration of his environment continually shifted and where he was forced to view the tenuousness of his situation in relation to the permanence of the cosmos which surrounded him and in which his position was problematical. Yet although he was not secure on this plane, he was unable either to cast himself free from it or to anchor himself to it. By "craft," man succeeded in constructing a home in the world, but the consciousness of his own finitude and of the decay which accompanied what he had created obviated the possibility of "true welfare."

The civilizations of the ancient world were patently unique and cannot be fruitfully understood as comparable to contemporary primitive societies governed by myth and ritual, despite certain similarities such as the lack of a sense of time or self. In Egypt and Mesopotamia the myth constituted an intricate system of speculative thought which, among other things, provided a "theoretical" foundation for a complex social order. Society, as the Greeks realized and political philosophy into the modern age affirmed, is the realm of necessity, anxiety, and temporality where the awareness of finite boundaries is most acute, and only through the imposition of certain institutions and patterns of thought are the concerns of this realm ordered and contained. These archaic empires, like Kafka's conception of life behind the great wall, hovered on the brink of history, and only the condition of a static ordered space of the city presided over by the cosmological myth prevented them from toppling over the edge. The centuries from 800 to 200 B.C., which Jaspers has termed the axial period of world history,[32] marked the decline of the mythic civilizations and the emergence of existence under the form of history with conscious speculation on man's place in the world.

It is assumed here that the "Greek and Hebrew civilizations are parallel structures built upon the same Mediterranean foundation"[33] and that an understanding of both Greek political philosophy and the prophetic vision can be gained only against the background of this mythic past. In the ancient cosmological myth it was the city or what, in retrospect, may be termed "political" space that constituted the crucial point of cosmic integration and provided a home for man in the universe. For both the Greeks and the Hebrews the detachment from this space and the dissolution of the myth were decisive experiences which were retained in the collective memory and formed the limit of their past, and it was the values attached to this experience which determined the difference between the prophetic and philosophic answers to the problem of human order and the meaning of existence in time. For the Hebrews and the Greeks human time and the differentiation of man and nature destroyed the unity of existence which had characterized the mythic experience. But while the Hebrews rejected reassimilation in the objectified and spatial order of the natural world in favor of participation in the dynamic reality of God which manifested itself in the events of history, the Greeks rejected history as an ultimate order of reality and sought to regain through the idea of political order a measure of that eternal being which was most perfectly reflected in the space of the natural world and the movement of the cosmos.

From the Hebrews and Homer to Heidegger, human being has been distinguished by the condition of temporality, and it was in conjunction with the articulation of the ideas of time and history that the conscious concern with the problem of political order first emerged. Political philosophy as a symbolic form appeared in response to the problem of the existence of society in time and succeeded the myth as a means of providing a theoretical ground for human order and expressing the place of society in the cosmos. The principal focus of this study is organized around the thesis that political philosophy was at its inception, that is, with Plato, a reconstruction, on the level of conscious thought, of the vision of political order as a mediating space, a mesocosm, which would assimilate man to or integrate him with that which is most eternal and overcome historical existence, which in terms of the Greek experience meant essentially the fall from order. It is this theme which binds together Plato's speculative venture as it emerges in his political dialogues.

The discovery of the idea of the political paralleled the discovery of the reality of the psyche as the ground of social order and disorder, and political vision from its beginning has been closely bound up with the impulse to abolish or regenerate history by the construction of an ordered space, a man-made cosmos, organized in accordance with what is most permanent in man. The argument is not that the idea of the political or the symbolization of time and human being have been uniform or that the conception of man's place in the world, if his true abode was considered to be the world at all, has found "political" expression. But whenever this conception has been rendered in terms of political space there has been an irruption of the impulse toward atemporality.

Despite successive transformations, the idea of the political was never completely severed from its primeval ground; in its concern with a timeless sustaining space, political vision inevitably carried with it an element of the mythic. Political vision was never divorced from the hubristic desire to be an emulator of God which is so apparent in mythic speculation, the desire to create a virtual *kosmos*. To create the social cosmos remained the greatest art; from Plato to Rousseau there is the persistent theme that man most becomes like a god when he creates or reforms a political order.

II

TIME, MYTH, AND SOCIETY

Heaven and earth unite: the image of PEACE.
Thus the ruler
Divides and completes the course of heaven
        and earth,
And so aids the people.

                                                    I Ching

Time

TIME is a form for ordering experience.[1] More specifically, time may
be considered as "a *form* of the relation of succession," whatever the particular nature of this relation or the character of the terms.[2] The relation
between terms which follow one another leads to the other formal aspect
of time—duration. Only because of span, magnitude, or duration in succession is time different from other sequences. As sequence, time appears
as continuous and as duration it appears as discontinuous, and thus time
as duration is the form of measuring time or determining both rate of
change between successive terms or events and the length or magnitude
of the term or event itself.

Formal time is logically prior to any analysis of an empirical
instance of time since the form is the condition of any such analysis.
Experience, such as the observation of processes in the physical world,
qualifies time as such and gives it a particular structure and meaning.
Physical time, in the sense of a metric, is the most formal empirical time
and is logically prior to social, psychological, and historical time. Time as
form and measure supplies no dimensions, and it cannot "flow" because it
has no concrete reality or empirical content; "we cannot compare any
process with the 'passage of time'—there is no such thing—but only with
another process (say, with the movement of the chronometer)."[3] There *is*

time only because there is change in the world, whether this is a physical process or the movement of consciousness. But despite the logical priority of formal time, it is only at a relatively late stage that either an individual or a culture develops an abstract concept of time. For the most part individual life and social relations are not immediately perceived in terms of formal or metric time, but rather in terms of experienced content such as the intuition of flow, the sense of human finitude, and the movement and direction of historical events. Formal time is an abstraction from "lived experiences of time,"[4] and when we attempt to communicate lived or experienced time, formal or clock time seems inadequate. Bergson's notion of *durée* was an attempt to communicate this lived experience of pure flow and preserve it from formalization and spatialization, but this notion is more poetic than philosophical. In the end it may be impossible to meaningfully convey the experience of the passage of time in discursive or philosophic language; maybe only the spatially free symbols of music can accomplish this.[5]

It is this variability of content and the meaning and values assigned to it which underlie the multiplicity of time, and it is the very fact of this multiplicity which creates the difficulties which we experience when attempting to talk about time. Augustine's famous dilemma over time set forth in his *Confessions* is frequently cited as the prototypical case of such difficulties, and although it would be too narrow a view to hold that the questions he and others have raised are merely semantic, there are many aspects of these difficulties which exist "not because there is anything genuinely problematic in our experience, but because the ways in which we speak of that experience are lacking in harmony or are otherwise unsatisfactory."[6] For example, it would be quite convenient if in everyday language we could convey temporal relations in perfect analogical form, but temporal relations are necessarily expressed syntactically in most instances, and problems of syntax may lead to confusions such as those involving the distinction between spatial and temporal relations.[7] Many of the apparent problems of "time" arise from the interchangeable character of the terms and propositions expressing both temporal and spatial relations such as "place" and "distance," as well as the inherent ambiguity in what are normally considered to be purely temporal indicators such as "past," "now," "present," and "future."[8] Time and most temporal indicators appear problematical because they have many uses and contexts. We seek definitions because definitions give not only answers about the use of words but explanations: to say that something is a temporal process is not merely to describe it but to explain it. But "time" is one of those words which bear numerous significations and consequently constitute different symbols and convey different meanings.

We have different time "languages" which conform to different activities and modes of thought as diverse as science and politics, and problems arise either when we mix these languages or when we attempt to create perfect consistency between them. To ask "what *is* time" is to put a question which is ultimately unanswerable because there is no such entity. But if we conceive of time as form or as a particular mode of relation, we may see how it can be joined with diverse content or aspects of concrete experience to give rise to a multiplicity of "times" or symbolic uses of "time." It is the idea of form which enables us to abstract and talk about time in general despite differences in experience; it is succession and duration that the concept denotes although it may designate any particular "configuration of relations . . . such as the physical configuration with its 'at the same time,' the psychological configuration with its relation between past and present, the biological configuration with growth directed toward the future, etc.," as well as further qualitative specifications regarding the values attached to these relations.[9]

Since time is a form imposed on the experience of change, the difference between a consideration of time in the physical world and time in the social world should be apparent. While temporal symbols are operative in the social image, time, in the physical world as well as the meaning of change in general, is largely a function of the scientist's explanation rather than an intrinsic aspect of the universe. Whether time is somehow built into the structure of the cosmos or is a necessary attribute of nature is to some extent irrelevant, or at least it principally involves a decision on the part of the scientist. Even "the regularity of time is not an intrinsic part of nature; it is a man made notion which we have projected into an environment for our own particular purpose."[10] In nature even causes are connected with effects only because the scientist's theory makes the connection, "not because the world is held together by cosmic glue."[11] The physical scientist searches for a conceptual pattern which will explain the world—a pattern of organization or gestalt which will make the world intelligible. The investigator of social action, on the other hand, although he also searches for a pattern, confronts a world which has been preinterpreted and even preconstituted and which is held together by the "cosmic glue" of significant symbols, and the illumination of these symbols must be the central element in his explanation.

There is time in the physical world in the sense that it is a symbolic order imposed on the observation of change. But this scheme is to a large extent arbitrary or at least essentially a product of the scientist's decisions and assumptions about the world. The implication of this, in addition to demonstrating the relatively temporally amorphous character of the physical world, is that one should neither look to science to reinforce conceptions of history or social time nor project social or psychological time onto the universe at large. Physical theories such as relativity have little relevance for the subjective experience of time and have no necessary meaning for metaphysics. Einstein's theory of relativity cannot be called upon to support notions of historical relativism, and Heisenberg's uncertainty principle does not confirm ideas about the freedom of will or the openness of the future any more than the second law of thermodynamics is a justification for determinism. The clear fact, however, that symbols derived from conceptions of physical time have contributed and do contribute to notions of social and common-sense time and vice versa is significant for understanding the character of each. Physical or natural time is one symbolic order to deal with one aspect of change; it is not an essential structure, even though it is grounded in the processes of the universe. Similarly, social time is an aspect of the image and explanation of the world as defined by social actors, and it may relate in varying degrees of correspondence and differentiation to natural or clock time.

What must be continually stressed is the extent to which time is a created order, both in the social and natural world; "time presupposes a view of time."[12] Although both space and time are symbolic structures which constitute an integral part of the image of the universe and the symbolic crystal of society, there may be a real sense in which Spengler was correct when he stated that "space 'is' but 'time,' on the contrary is a *discovery*, which is only made by thinking."[13] And Mann's rendering of a common-sense dilemma finds support in contemporary psychology.

> Space we perceive with our organs, with our senses of sight and touch. Good. But which is our organ of time—tell me that if you can.
>
> Space is a collection of objects and it is these which largely determine the structure of perceived space. Time is the succession of changes, but each of these—apart from the present change—only exists for

us as a memory or an anticipation; in other words they are representations. Space is primarily presentation; it is imposed upon us.[14]

A similar notion has been advanced by B. L. Whorf, whose studies indicate that while the conception of time differs between various cultures,
"the apprehension of space *is* given in substantially the same form" although it may be viewed as either static or dynamic.[15] Space is a symbolic
order, that is, its conceptualization differs; but it is perceived in essentially the same manner by all *homo sapiens*. But "our ideas of space and
time, which according to Kant function as if they were releasers, must
instead be regarded as mental constructions which have to be learnt."[16]

By internalizing time, Kant effected a revolution; time inevitably
became a function of psyche. But for Kant time was still as absolute as
for Newton—absolute, however, in the sense of a universal apperception.
Time was not merely a property of a relation between things or an idea
formed by successive sensations as maintained by Locke, Hume, and Con-
dillac. Time was subjective, but a priori—it was a form of intuition by
which experience was ordered; knowledge was grounded in experience,
but time was not derived from experience. In this way Kant avoided the
relativism of the empiricists and made time meaningful for science while
preserving its internal base. But the internalization of time inevitably put
its "reality" in jeopardy and made it a problem for psychology. Even for
Kant, time, although meaningful for the empirical world, did not partake
of ultimate reality—it did not belong to the noumenal realm of things-in-
themselves, and thus in effect was little more than a category of perception.

The foundation for a critique of time as a necessary category for
organizing experience was anticipated in Freud's investigations of the
unconscious. Freud maintained that time is a mode of perception and
that "unconscious mental processes are in themselves 'timeless.' That is
to say . . . time alters nothing in them."[17] As with Schopenhauer's idea
of will and Kant's noumenal self, the innermost nature of man lay outside time, which was meaningful only in terms of the perceptual consciousness; but Freud went further by according time no independent
reality or universality apart from the *functioning* of this consciousness.[18]

Psychologists such as Guyau, and later Janet, began to view time as
an intellectual construction to deal with experience, and the ordering of
experience in temporal categories was closely related to cultural and

social factors. Physiological determinants and physical environment are by no means unimportant since the human organism possesses certain intrinsic natural rhythms and is influenced by natural cycles and other inputs from the physical world. In addition there are limits on the extent to which an individual can perceive an event as possessing duration and discriminate between successive events; unless an event transcends the "human instant" there can be no sense of duration, and if the interval between events is sufficiently short, succession will appear as simultaneity. Also such factors as body temperature, metabolism, and the processes of the central nervous system all affect the perception of time. Finally, there are numerous psychological factors such as attitudes and emotions that influence an individual's perception or perspective of time.[19] In fine it might be said that physiological factors determine experiential potentialities, while apperception or conceptualization is related to social and cultural communication; that is, perception is to a certain extent uniform, while the categories of conception are relative.[20]

This duality of perception and conception has been significantly developed in contemporary psychology with its emphasis on the importance of cultural determinants and the relative lack in man, as opposed to animals, of phylogenetically determined adaptations or inherited biological patterns of awareness.[21] The creation of a symbolic world is the condition of the existence of time. Although the ability to perceive change is limited, man can transcend this limitation by the symbolic representation of change. But beyond the fact that the idea of time may differ between cultures, there is considerable evidence that an intuition of time may, in some instances, be absent. Even the *perception* as well as the *conception* of time, despite its potentiality in human awareness, must be learned;[22] the temporal ordering of experience does not appear to be a necessary aspect of either individual or social existence. The lack or nascent character of temporal consciousness in the child is an obvious example, and recent studies in philosophy, and anthropology, have sharply challenged the idea of a universal intuition of time. Some of the most provocative work in this area centers around Whorf's studies of language.

The linguistic approach to the understanding of differences between cultural images of reality as embodied in Whorf's formulations was foreshadowed in the philosophy of Wilhelm von Humboldt and more recently anticipated in the work of Edward Sapir.[23] The acceptance of Whorf's conclusions not only would substantiate studies which have pointed to differences in cultural images of time but would call into question any notion of a common logical structure in the cognitive process which presupposes time as a necessary category of experience. For Whorf, a society's conception of the universe conforms to the structure of its language. Whorf has demonstrated in his studies of the Hopi not only that their language lacks any reference to time but that the grammatical structure gives no evidence of an objectification of a time-consciousness such as that present in "standard average European" forms.[24] Thus an idea of time loses its place as a necessary mode of experience, and it appears that there may be perfectly valid descriptions of the universe that lack a time dimension.[25]

Although the idea of time arises out of man's need to deal with change, time is not a necessary aspect of human awareness, for

> in relation to the psyche space and time are, so to speak, "elastic" and can apparently be reduced to the vanishing point as though they . . . did not exist in themselves but were only "postulated" by the conscious mind. In man's original view of the world, as we find it among primitives, space and time have a very precarious existence. They become "fixed" concepts only in the course of his mental development, thanks largely to the introduction of measurement. In themselves, space and time consist of nothing.[26]

By developing concepts of time and history, man gains control over the experience of change or the primitive intuition of "time" in the sense of flux—both in the social and physical world. In Western thought, the encompassing of the experience of change within the form of time has been an aspect of the propensity of the rationalistic mind to classify, abstract, and order the world, for "the mere creation of the *name* time was an unparalleled deliverance. To name anything by a name is to win power over it."[27] But the same tendency is apparent in mythic symbolization, which, instead of "temporalizing" change and giving meaning to history, denied both; like modern man, primitive man sought to dominate the unique as it continually manifested itself in the process of life.

Phenomenological and existential psychology and philosophy have stressed the identity of time and the "self": time as a function of the intentional structure of consciousness.[28] But whether or not this idea is accepted, it is clear that man begins to conceive of existence as temporal only through the process of individuation. The representation of change in terms of time, the extension of the individual's horizon beyond the spatial and static present into the past and future, is one aspect of his detachment from his environment and the differentiation of conscious-ness. The awareness of time and the emergence of conceptual thought with its distinction between subject and object are part of the same ex-perience. Also the development of the concept of time and temporal awareness in the individual and the evolution of time-consciousness in the social and cultural image present striking similarities.[29]

For archaic man, contemporary primitive societies, and children, life is lived essentially in the "present"; life is grounded in the space of their immediate gestalt or field of perception where the world is pre-sented to them. Anthropological and psychological investigations, both of individuals and cultures, give ample evidence "that a comprehension of space is developed earlier than a sense of time. It is just this supremacy of the sense of space which appears with such surprising strength in the perception of pre-historic man."[30] The child apparently perceives the world in the present until approximately age three, and although his vocabulary may be "temporal," his meaning is essentially spatial. Nearly all primitive languages lack verbs with temporal tenses and express "the reality of the objective world and not a temporal precess."[31] Only with the development of individual and collective memory and notions of mortality and history does the temporal dimension begin to take shape. An idea of the future is essential to any meaningful notion of time, but for children and primitive and archaic societies the "future" exists only as a repetition of the "past"; the uniqueness of events is not perceived, and temporal distance contracts into the present.

Human time and existence under the form of history, whatever the qualitative differences between temporal perspectives and the meaning and values attached to history, can best be understood when contrasted with the Weltanschauung of mythic societies. In mythic thought, change in the sense of becoming or the experience of unique events is sublimated in the concrete, recurrent, and spatially grounded rhythms of nature. The experiences which modern language expresses in the temporal idiom are conveyed in mythic symbolization by spatial analogies, and as long as this mode dominates, temporal categories do not appear. This lack of an intuition of time renders the present or the "now" an eternal static entity rather than a moving boundary between past and future; the present appears not as an aspect of time, "but the negation of time" where even the difference between "now" and "not-now" may not be articulated.[32] But even space is reified and nondynamic; it is not an abstract continuum, but heterogeneous, experiential, concrete, and characterized by the values attached to it. This mode of thought is well represented in mythic art in which

> all temporal dynamics is ultimately transformed into a kind of spatial statics . . . where all reality, all life, and all movement seems confined within rigid geometrical forms. The negation of mere temporality . . . is here achieved by immersion in the purely intuitive, plastic, and architectonic *form* of things. In its clarity, concreteness, and eternity this form triumphs over all mere succession, over the ceaseless flux and transience of all temporal configuration.[33]

Myth and Primordial Time

TIME in the myth is not really time at all, but the eternal present of primordial time which is, in effect, "articulated atemporality" or "intemporal time . . . a moment without duration, as certain mystics and philosophers conceive of eternity."[34] Primordial time is the time of cosmic creation, and the events narrated in the myth are continually made present and serve as archetypes which give meaning to experience. The unique event or act is meaningful only to the extent that it can be joined to an archetype. Here life moves not historically, but ritualistically between significant points in the cycle of nature and society (such as the New Year) which are in turn perceived in terms of events in a "prototypical time in which everything already happened and in which today does not begin anew but is only repeated."[35] This repetition of given paradigmatic gestures reveals an original ontology" in which profane time or historical experience is continually abolished or regenerated by participation in the sacred events of the myth.[36] To describe the "time" of the myth as cyclical is a misleading rationalization, for there is not only an absence of historical time but "no time 'as such,' no perpetual duration and no regular recurrence or succession."[37]

It may seem odd to maintain that primitive and archaic societies lack a consciousness of time when it can easily be demonstrated that such societies possess procedures which it is difficult to designate by any term other than "time-reckoning," and the high cultures of the ancient world developed complex and relatively sophisticated methods and systems for calculating "time."[38] But although ancient man engaged in what, in retrospect, may be termed "time-reckoning," there is no idea of time in the sense of an abstract concept or an order of existence or continuum. And most important, there is no distinction between the "time" of nature, the "time" of creation, and the "time" of society.

> Mythopoeic thought does not know time as a uniform duration or as a succession of qualitatively different moments. The concept of time as it is used in our mathematics and physics is as unknown to early man as that which forms the framework of our history. Early man does not abstract a concept of time from the experience of time.[39]

It would be more correct to state that early man does not abstract a concept of time from the experience of *change*. Temporal symbols are one medium for ordering the experience of change; myth is another.

In the ancient world time-calculation was not primarily a function of an interest in chronology as such, although a monopoly on this skill contributed to the power of the kings and priests; it was essentially related to the elaboration of the myth and served ultimately to bind together the rhythms of nature and society. Discrete time symbols could not appear until human existence emerged as a separate order, even in the societies of ancient Egypt and Mesopotamia which possessed the complex social structures which are normally associated with refined notions of time and multiple levels of temporal ordering. The phenomena of calendars and systems of "time-measurement" often lead investigators working from a modern perspective to overstate primitive time-consciousness, but "such an appreciation of time on the part of early man is not evident." It is clear that "the making of a calendar does not necessarily imply a time sense," for the use of calendars was ceremonial; although they may prepare "the way for what we call the measurement of time . . . its own functions are for a different purpose."[40] It may be argued that although ancient man did not possess a *concept* of time, this is merely because his thought was basically preconceptual; he *must* have experienced time despite the fact he did not call it by this name. But such a reply would be predicated on the mistaken notion that time is somehow a real "thing," and not a symbolic form of experience.[41] To a large extent this is a consequence of an identification of time with change and the propensity to forget that the encountered world is a created world. Early man did not simply see the reality of modern man from a different perspective; he saw a different reality.

This lack of temporal awareness is grounded in the participative character of the mythic vision in which the individual, society, and nature are experienced as a compact and consubstantial unity. Just as the sublimation of the unique in the archetypal contracts the dimensions of experience into the present, the interpenetration of the orders of reality prevents the distinction of human time or history as a separate realm of existence. The myth at once explains and validates nature and society and provides a prescription for action; society is perceived and patterned as a cosmic analogue and externalized in the order of nature, while the individual, the self, is externalized in the order of society. In this reciprocally sustained unity all events and activities of thought and action converge in a timeless paradigm in which collective memory as well as the awareness of individuality is absorbed in the uniform rhythm of cosmos and society which abrogates time and history.

The concern here is with myth as a symbolic form and as a total orientation, and although this concern is not entirely separable from problems of origin, function, and development, certain theories about myth which attempt to demonstrate that it is a primitive theoretical explanation of natural phenomena, an imaginative rendering of these occurrences in poetic form, or an attempt to chronicle the history of mankind[42] are rationalizations of the mythic experience which fail to reach the character of myth as a form of life. As Malinowski has noted, myth is "not merely a story told but a reality lived"; it is not primarily a description or "an explanation in satisfaction of a scientific interest"[43] but an autonomous mode of organizing experience which at once describes, explains, justifies, and prescribes. Primitive or ancient man did not make a "mistake" about the phenomena he encountered, nor was the myth an elementary instance of ideas of inductive inference and cause and effect. It is only because modern man tends to extrapolate both his phenomenal world and his mode of conceptualization in terms of a subject-object dichotomy that he fails to grasp the character of the mythic vision. The reality of the myth was simply a different reality, and, unlike that of modern man, who becomes aware of the participation of his consciousness in the symbolic world of his creation only by epistemological reflection, the experience of mythic man was that of "original participation" or the active,

immediate, and unreflective involvement of the consciousness in the phenomena.[44] It was this immediacy of participation both in the events of
primordial time and the order of the cosmos which gave to the mythic
Weltanschauung its compact character.

The mythic bond between symbol and act, the unity of myth and
ritual, has led to attempts to establish the precise connection between
the two and the derivation of one from the other,[45] but this approach
tends to ask the wrong question and obscure the complete interpenetration of thought and action in the mythic consciousness. Like other studies
centering on an explanation of myth, the ritual approach does not reach
the meaning of the myth as a mode of existence; the idea of the function
of the myth as an adjunct of *rites de passage* or a ritual libretto or a
precursor of other forms of symbolization has limited significance for
understanding the myth as an autonomous vision of reality.

The truth of the myth as myth depends on its uncritical acceptance;
the emergence of allegorization distorted that unity of symbol and reality
which characterized existence under the form of the myth. "The first
inquiry as to the literal truth of the myth marks the change from poetic
to discursive thinking."[46] The rationalization and allegorization of the
myth as well as certain functional explanations of the place of myth in
society have led to a misunderstanding of the nature of the mythic vision.
Even a contemporary scholar such as Herbert J. Muller, who accepts the
essential autonomy of the myth, finds it "necessary to emphasize the
basic irrationality of ancient mythopoeic thought."[47] However, it is
apparent that as early as Vico's "new science" the idea of myth as an
independent expression of consciousness had begun to take shape. Vico
attributed to the "Age of the Gods" a wisdom of its own with a peculiar
form of social order.[48]

The most significant attempt in recent years to understand the myth
as an autonomous vision of reality and mode of symbolization may be
found in Cassirer's *Philosophy of Symbolic Forms*. In moving away from
earlier explanations of myth and efforts to subsume it under other forms
of symbolic expression, Cassirer proceeds to justify the myth as a unique
interpretation of the universe rather than a pragmatic fiction which may
be dismissed as an illusion when measured by other standards of truth.
He maintains that all attempts to find the root or source of the myth
have been inadequate since "mythical formulations as such cannot be
understood and appreciated simply by determining the object on which

it is immediately and originally centered."[49] Cassirer views the myth both as a form of symbolization with a truth and meaning of its own for the mythic mind and as a stage in the differentiation or evolution of consciousness. In addition he emphasizes the relation of the myth to social organization.

Susanne Langer has proceeded still further in establishing the autonomy of mythic symbolization. She argues that the myth had a development of its own and must be distinguished from the creation of legends and fairy tales in primitive cultures. The myth is characterized by its serious nature, *the entrance into the public realm,* and the appearance of universal symbols.[50] The concern of the myth is not utopian or "wishful distortion of the world, but serious envisagement of its fundamental truths; moral orientation, not escape."[51] The "great step" marking the emergence of myth was the extension of thought toward an encompassing of society and nature in a cosmic unity which produced "the first universal insights ... the first embodiment of *general ideas.*"[52] Yet the myth may be distinguished from discursive thought: the symbols are simply presented, not analyzed or reflected upon.

The meaning of the myth cannot be grasped from a dissection of its logic, or lack of logic, for it is grounded in a creative and poetic activity for which the world stands open and from which nothing is barred by other forms of symbolization. Despite its nondiscursive character and lack of self-consciousness, it is a speculative venture that "attempts to *underpin* the chaos of experience so that it may reveal the features of a structure—order, coherence, and meaning."[53] Through this impulse toward order, the myth shares in the theme of political philosophy; or rather political philosophy and the myth may be understood as manifestations of man's continuous concern with ordering his existence and determining his home in the world. Although it is not possible to penetrate the interior of the mythic vision since ancient man did not personalize his speculations, it is justifiable to assume that the myth not only arose from the collective experience of society but was molded, transformed, and refined by individuals confronting a reality which they shaped and which within limits shaped them. Henri Frankfort summarizes mythic speculation as

> a form of poetry which transcends poetry in that it proclaims a truth; a form of reasoning which transcends reasoning in that it wants to bring about the truth it proclaims; a form of action . . .

which does not find its fulfillment in the act but must proclaim and
elaborate a poetic form of truth.[54]

The speculative impulse found in the myth a facile medium for free
expression since the consciousness did not confront a recalcitrant reality
such as that which drove the Hellenic mind back into the confines of contemplation. The consubstantial union of man, nature, and society provided unlimited opportunity for the speculative dialogue—a dialogue not
between subject and object, but between "I" and "Thou" in which speculation and persuasion were merged. The aesthetic experience underlies
this mode of speculation and in the form of the myth provides

> a protection which makes man secure against the pressure of his
> environment. . . . The first order attributed to the world was an
> aesthetic coherence, that . . . slipped the screen of forms between
> man and things; it was a veil thrown over what was hidden in the
> depths and over the original chaos.[55]

What distinguished this speculative venture was the concurrence of
knowing, creating, and prescribing; the myth provided norms of action
and served to establish a ground for social order as well as a "theoretical"
reason for the nature of things. One of the fundamental aspects of the
mythic experience corresponds to a central motif of political philosophy;
both are distinguished from purely theoretical explanations by their
prescriptive character. The events of primordial time related in the myth
constituted a "theoretical" foundation and justification for social order.
The function of the myth was not to explain social existence by producing
causes, either in the sense of history or science, but rather to make transparent the first cause of the world and society.

The replenishment of man and his world signified a return to origins
which "means two things in mythology. As the content of a story or
mythologem it is the 'giving of grounds' (*Begrundung*); as the content
of an act it is the 'foundation' (*Grundung*) of a city or the world."[56] The
life of society was an active participation in the poetic truth of the origin
or foundation. It is not difficult to see that forms of speculation on the
ground of human order never completely transcend one another; political
philosophy from Aristotle to the modern age never cast off the mythic
image of the sacredness of beginnings and the need for periodic immersion in the time of the founding. Myth, like political philosophy, provided

a vision of the origin or source of order and carried with it a prescription for ordering existence from the point of this ground upward. Mythic speculation in the final analysis meant

> to rebuild the world from that point about which and from which the "fundamentalist" [*Begrunder*] himself is organized, in which he by his origin is. . . . With the construction of a new world in miniature, an image of the macrocosm, mythological fundamentalism is translated into action: it becomes a founding (*Grundung*). Cities built in periods that knew a living mythology, and claiming to be images of the cosmos, are founded just as the cosmogonic mythologems give grounds for the world.[57]

The myth provided a theoretical bridge between human order and the order of nature, and this integration of society and cosmos was predicated on the lack of symbolic differentiation between the two spheres. Social existence is experienced as a cosmic analogue, and "reality is a function of the imitation of a celestial archetype."[58]

The direct participation of society in the primordial events of creation was achieved by the nullification of temporal, as well as spatial, distance. Following the retreat of the myth, the essence of the problem of social order was to be the transcendence of historical time which came between the order of society and its model, whether this model was the order of the soul or the rhythm of the cosmos. For ancient man, order on all levels was assured "through the recitation of the myth of the origin and the consequent revival of the primordial events. Myth and the sacral action connected with it guarantee the survival of the world" as well as the order of society.[59] The myth was creative since it structured the perception of reality, and it was exemplary since it prescribed the pattern of human action. When nature was in crisis or the order of society was threatened, such as during seasonal transition or upon the death of the king, ancient man restored the equilibrium of the cosmos by invoking the myth and performing the drama of the sacred events which occurred "in the holy time of beginnings (*in illo tempore*)."[60]

The natural world as well as the objects made by man held meaning only insofar as they partook of the archetype. The models or counterparts of the cities of Babylon were found in the heavens, and all which lay outside the confines of the city, which with its temple symbolized the point of creation, remained assimilated in the primeval and formless chaos which existed "when in the height heaven was not named" and "of the gods none had been called into being."[61] Society's re-enactment of the act of creation or the transition from chaos to order which took place at the navel of the earth perpetuated the city as the likeness of this sacred center and established the social order as a cosmic analogue in which social time existed only as an echo of primordial time. Although ritual participation in the decisive events of primordial time was most manifest at epochs of natural and social crisis, all human action was meaningful only as a repetition of the sacred paradigm. For life under the form of the myth was, in its entirety, "life, so to speak, in quotation, . . . a kind of celebration, in that it is a making present of the past" which results in the "abrogation of time" and in which all events "take place not for the first time, but ceremonially according to the prototype."[62]

Plato's problem was to expand the internal order of the virtuous soul into the order of society; but although exclusion from political life inevitably diminished man, the individual, faced with the inefficacy of human action, could nevertheless fashion his psyche after that timeless pattern laid up in heaven. The mythic consciousness, however, never returned to gaze upon itself or speculate in the realm of philosophical anthropology; the self took shape in terms of the objects it produced and endured only through their continuity. If the reality of society depended on a repetitive participation in primordial order and assimilation in nature, the individual's existence was assured only through externalization in the order of society. The access of the individual to the archetype was possible only by participation in that order which mediated between heaven and earth. Archaic man could not open his soul directly to a transcendent deity as did the individual of the Judaic-Christian world who aspired to see God, not as in a glass darkly, but face to face.[63]

This tendency to convert inner impulse into external objects and events is evident at that point in the creation of a work of art at which the object acquires autonomy or an existence apart from the vision of the artist and where changes are changes in the object and not modifications of the artist's conception.[64] This "externalizing tendency" may become a vehicle for social solidarity by communalizing internal experience and providing for the control of inner impulse by its absorption in an external symbolic order. In the societies of the ancient world individual identity was compressed into the form of the mythic drama through which man and society participated in the order of the cosmos. In this way "myth becomes the tutor, the shaper of identities; it is here that personality imitates the myth in as deep a sense as myth is an externalization of the vicissitudes of personality."[65] What is astonishing about the myth is not its particular prescription for social order, but its effectiveness in divesting individual action of its uniqueness and weaving it into the timeless pattern of ritual. This sublimation of individual identity and the externalization of consciousness are further illuminated by what Eliade terms the "ahistorical character of popular memory, the inability of collective memory to retain historical events and individuals except insofar as it transforms them into archetypes."[66] This could be expressed in Jungian terminology as the predominance of the "collective unconscious" where the individual consciousness is but an "excerpt" or where "the momentary conscious situation is influenced not so much from the side of the personal as from the collective."[67]

The affirmation of the unity of society and primordial order and the corresponding absence of temporal differentiation found its most characteristic expression in the ancient Near East in the observance of the New Year. The ritual performed during the New Year festival was a re-enactment of cosmogonic generation which at once identified the course of nature and society and legitimized political order by linking it to the authority of the archetype; "New Year and Creation are the reflection one of the other."[68] Yet these characteristics are more than simply a peculiarity of societies living under the form of the cosmological myth. The nullification of time is intimately connected with man's search for order, and in societies where the burden of temporality was an integral part of the individual consciousness and where time rose to the level of conceptualization, the tension between time and order became a philosophic problem. The creation of political order implies an annulment of history and a return to the principles of foundation or a regeneration of time by the imposition of structure on a chaotic condition. Speculation on human order necessarily carries with it an element of the mythic, the desire to attain to the eternal present and exist in the immediacy of being, and in the myth may be seen the same impulse which has sustained the idea of the political in much of Western thought.

> To establish a government is an essay in world creation. When man creates the cosmion of political order, he analogically repeats the divine creation of the cosmos. The analogical repetition is not an act of futile imitation, for in repeating the cosmos man participates, in

the measure allowed to his existential limitations, in the creation of cosmic order itself. . . . Hence, in his creative endeavor man is a partner in the double sense of a creature and a rival of God.[69]

Myth and Society: Egypt and Mesopotamia

AT approximately 3500 B.C. there appeared in Mesopotamia that "whole cultural syndrome that has since constituted the germinal unit of all the higher civilizations of the world."[70] Here emerged the city organized, physically and psychically, as an image of the cosmos with social life ritualistically patterned in accordance with the rhythms of nature. The city was constructed as the four quarters of a circle with its center marked by the temple or ziggurat, a tower of ascending quadrilateral structures narrowing to an apex representing the summit of the cosmic mountain, the legendary site of creation, joining heaven and earth. Revolving around the center of this configuration was the kingship, the social institution through which the symbol of the ziggurat became meaningful. Civilization found its sustenance in the authority of the king, through whom, like the constricted center or an hourglass, the divine and constant measure of the cosmos permeated society.

This was "a universe not progressing toward any end, but rendering manifest to the contemplative mind, here and now, the radiance of a divine power which, though transcendent, is immanent in all things."[71] Under the integral myth, society was experienced as a "cosmic analogue" in which "vegetative rhythms and celestial revolutions function as models for the structural and procedural order of society."[72] To argue conversely that the vision of the universe was a projection of the social order would be an equally meaningful description, but no more true in terms of mythic speculation, which was not bound by the cleavage of real and ideal. Even the claim of many states to the status of cosmic images did not shake the confidence in the belief that terrestrial order had its roots in heaven. While the high god governed in the macrocosm, his actions were mimed by the king in the mesocosm, or the polity in which the individual or microcosm participated.

Mythic speculation admitted no distinction between primordial order and the history of order just as it blurred the boundaries between the orders of existence, and man perceiving reality in terms of the myth never experienced that separation of temporal and eternal which provided an occupation for much of subsequent philosophy. In the age of the integral myth, the kingship was the medium through which the temporal gap was closed and the universe was fused. For the ancient Egyptians "the kingship was not merely part, but the kernel of the static order of the world."[73] This static quality was more than a culturally imposed illusion; it was, despite vicissitudes in the health of the polity, given reality by the persistence and relatively non-evolutionary character of the institution of divine kingship. The durable nature of the institution and its correspondence with the vision of social order in the myth is readily apparent when contrasted with the Greek experience where there was an ever-widening gap between speculations on the good order and the history of the political forms. While for the Greeks, neither a god nor a beast participated in the order of society, the Egyptians never experienced this differentiation. Since the "elements of the universe were consubstantial" the manifestation of the deity in the kingship and the perpetual coincidence of power and authority were possible; "between god and man there was no point at which one could erect a boundary and state that here substance changed from divine, superhuman, immortal to mundane, human, mortal."[74]

In ancient Egypt, the king, as the incarnation of Horus and son of Osiris, was, by a divine decision, legitimized as ruler over the kingdom and directly related to the primordial events of creation and the progeny of the creator-god.[75] An equally important and complementary aspect of the king's divinity was his status as the son of Re or Atum, the sun-god and supreme deity. Although he was not the incarnation of the sun-god, as he was of Horus, the king assumed the analogous role of creator in the order of society, and the authority of heaven flowed undiminished through him to the people. To the king were assigned the creator-god's divine qualities of "authoritative utterance" or the power of the word which brought things into being; "thou art the living image on earth of thy father, Atum of Heliopolos. Taste [authoritative utterance] is in thy mouth, intelligence in thy heart; the seat of thy tongue is the shrine of truth [justice]."[76] The king, using the material of society, continued the creative work of the primordial deity, and each of his acts and pronouncements was a reflection of that moment when order was brought from the condition of chaos.

The regulation of the sun's movements suggested (besides victory and order and immortality as rebirths without end) the thought of inflexible justice and an ubiquitous judge. Thus its behavior acquired an ethical quality. The king is judge pre-eminently as the image and representation of Re.[77]

In Egyptian mythology the goddess Maat, signifying justice, was the daughter of Re; Maat was truth or the right order of the universe to which the gods adhered and which also bound the actions of the king: "Maat, daughter of Re, presider over the palace, mistress of heaven, ruler of gods." In turn, the king, as the reflection of Re, was the dispenser of justice and order in society. Active conformance with the utterance of the pharaoh insured that "Maat will rest in her place," and the king's vizier was the "prophet of Maat."[78] From the first, Egypt, signified by the primeval hill arising from the waters of Chaos, was the province of the creator and the center of the universe, and the king was considered the son of Re to insure Re's guidance over Egypt. Through the institution of the kingship the events of creation were made present, and the orders of existence were molded into a unity.

The character of the kingship in Egypt may be likened to Plato's description in the *Statesman* of the divine shepherd who ruled in the age of Cronus. The king's concern was the sustentation of a human flock who did not share in the responsibility for the political order. The art of ruling was an attribute of gods, not men, and included not only the pronouncement of law and the function of judgment but the protection and increase of the population, the control of the Nile, and the abundance of the harvest. The king was the "good shepherd" of the society, the "herdsman of everyone"; again and again it was asserted that he was the source of "life, prosperity, health!"[79] This pervasive potency of the king was expressed in the notion of Ka, or "vital force."[80] The Ka was an impersonal force or power, originating with the creation and emanating from the creator-god, which extended to all levels of existence. Ka entered the world through the person of the king and was embodied in all his acts; for man and society "the king is a Ka" just as the Ka of the king is derived from Osiris and Re.[81] There can be little doubt "that the Egyptians apprehended the involvement of man in nature and the mediating function of their king by means of the concept of Ka."[82]

The consequence of this notion of the potency of the king was the dependence of the order of society and nature on the nonhistorical character of the kingship in which all threads of life converged. On the whole

> the Egyptians had very little sense of history or of past and future. For they conceived their world as essentially static and unchanging. It had gone forth complete from the hands of the Creator. Historical incidents were, consequently, no more than superficial disturbances of the established order, or recurring events of never-changing significance. The past and future—far from being a matter of concern—were wholly implicit in the present.[83]

The principles of order in the universe were primordially established, and legitimation of existential institutions depended on their identification with the archetype. The power of the king was symbolized by its equation with the power and sustaining qualities of the sun, and the authority of the kingship was affirmed by a "ritual perpetuation of the past."[84] The theme of the myth was the creation and restoration of order, and ritual was its symbolic accompaniment; the principles of order were continually asserted, and the utterance that commanded order repeated. The royal rituals, which were the focal point for the rejuvenation of society as a whole, centered around the passage of the king, the renewal of his authority, and the dispersion of the life-giving force or Ka throughout society and nature.

The Sed festival was a jubilee usually held in conjunction with the coronation, although its significance went far beyond a mere celebration of the king's ascendance to the throne. The ritual symbolized the revitalization of the king's Ka and could be performed during times of crisis at the discretion of the king. The date chosen for the festival, like that of the coronation, was always the New Year or another point of seasonal transition. Here "multifarious connections between gods and king, land and king, people and king, were woven into that elaborate fabric which held society as well as the unaccountable forces of nature by strands which passed through the solitary figure on the throne of Horus."[85] The drama, in which the king was the protagonist, brought together participants representing all segments of society who joined in a ritual reaffirmation of the unity of the kindom and bore witness to the vitality of the king's authority. Whatever the origins of the festival, it came to be performed, in addition to the coronation, at odd periods, and its optimistic character contrasted sharply with the mood of crisis surrounding the passing of the king.

The death of a king threatened to sunder that narrow access through which celestial order funneled into the earthly kingdom. Since it was necessary that the installation of the new pharaoh take place at a propitious time, there was often a period of suspension between the death of the incumbent and the coronation of his successor. During this interval the static nature of the kingship was maintained by a denial of the uniqueness of the crisis; the risk of chaos was encompassed by the myth.

The coronation drama, a mystery play performed at major cities throughout the country during this period of suspension, signified the new king's possession of the land and prepared the way for the coronation, the final symbol of succession, which restored the harmony of cosmos and society. There was a precise correspondence between the ritual action and the myth relating Horus' succession to the throne, the transference of the Ka of Osiris and the right of kingship, and the union of the living king with that "shadowy company of the king's predecessors and ancestors that stretched in unbroken line through the dynasties of men, demi-gods, and gods to the first king" and the creation of the universe.[86] The myth endowed the "punctual" character of the ritual with a "durative significance" which attested to the eternity of the kingship.[87] The second important ritual performed during the period of suspension was the funeral celebration of the dead king, which took place on the eve of the coronation. This was the moment of the transubstantiation of the deceased king who, on entering the world of the dead, took the form of Osiris and assumed the rule of the nether world as he had ruled in Egypt as the incarnation of Horus. Thus the static nature of the kingship was maintained by the compression of personages reaching from the first king to that nebulous group consisting of former occupants of the throne of Osiris in the underworld who sustained the current pharaoh and accompanied him as guardians in the performance of his functions.

With the arrival of the New Year, the coronation of the new king took place, and the order of the cosmos was confirmed. The purpose of the coronation was specifically the consummation of Horus' succession. The new king entered the dual shrines, the habitat of the royal ancestors, presided over by the tutelary goddesses of Upper and Lower Egypt, and received the two crowns in which the goddesses, the personification of the royal power, were immanent. At this point, the king assumed four titles:

Horus, Favorite of the Two Goddesses, Lord of the Two Lands, and Son of Re, "enduring in kingship like Re in Heaven."[88] Here, in the unity of myth and ritual, appeared "the image that resolves the riddle of time."[89]

If ancient Egypt may be equated with Plato's conception of the age of Cronus, Mesopotamia may be likened to the age in which the rule of god was no longer immanent in society. Although the existence of the city was predicated on a conformance with cosmic design, the almost complete interpenetration of the divine and earthly realms, so clearly evident in the Egyptian experience, is lacking. In addition to primordial time, another mode of temporality, although not yet articulate, had begun to insinuate itself into the order of the universe and throw a wedge between cosmic order and the order of society, and it was this temporal differentiation which would eventually dissolve the myth and create the need for a new vision of order.

Although life was still organized on the basis of the cosmological myth, conscious and continuous human effort was required to maintain the correspondence between heaven and earth. The basic civilizational framework remained essentially uniform throughout long periods in the history of Mesopotamia, despite the dominance of the Sumerians, Akkadians, Babylonians, and Assyrians at different times, but the order of society never manifested the static quality which is so apparent in much of the Egyptian experience. This may be explained, to a large extent, by differences in physical environment such as the regular and beneficial movements of the Nile as opposed to the unpredictable and often destructive forces of nature which obtained in the valley of the Tigris and Euphrates. But whatever the reason, the maintenance of cosmic order remained, in the history of Mesopotamia, extremely problematical. As in Egypt, the integrity of the cosmos was a function of the "political" and was achieved through the medium of the kingship; but whereas in Egypt a god resided in the palace, the Mesopotamian ziggurat reached toward heaven but did not join it.[90]

The Mesopotamian king remained a mortal. Although the kingship was the focal point for the ritual integration of society and nature, the king was nearly always designated by some approximation of the early Sumerian appellation *lugal*, meaning "great man."[91] In Egyptian art the king was represented as the dominating figure both in function and form; he was the symbol of the entire community towering above an enemy shown as a conglomerate of mortals. Mesopotamian sculpture, however, depicted only the gods as standing in stature above other figures while the king was rendered merely as the leader of his subjects.[92] The contrast in these symbols demonstrates not only a difference in the nature of the kingship but the emergence of a nascent acknowledgment of human time. While the pharaoh symbolized the triumph of an invincible divine order over the forces of chaos, the Mesopotamian kingship represented the struggle of a human order, subject to the anxieties and hazards of a differentiated existence, to integrate itself with the universe. Here was established that "critical dissociation between the spheres of God and man which in time was to separate decisively the religious systems of the Occident from those of the Orient"[93] and which gave rise to the basic problem of political philosophy—the creation of a home for man in the world.

Although the idea of human time could not fully arise until there was an acceptance of history, as in Israel, and "until the kingship was viewed as something less than holy,"[94] the sense of insecurity and social instability which pervaded the city-states of Mesopotamia led to a rudimentary concern with the history of social order. When a society develops the epic as a symbolic form, the capacity of the myth as a means of organizing experience has been strained to its limits. "The myth begins to decline when the distance widens between man and the world, when things begin to separate from one another and to be situated at distinct levels."[95] Unlike the omnipotent pharaoh, a deity incarnate from whom flowed the sustenance of nature and society, the hero of the epic, the prototype of the king, was cast against an alien world from which he attempted to wrest order. In Egypt the kingly rule was never separated, either in function or time, from the primordial event of creation; whereas in Mesopotamia that momentous event which took place when the kingship was lowered from heaven was, in a sense, historically situated, and the illumination of this history became an aspect of social identity. Speculation on social order took on a mythicohistorical character which served to furnish a ground for the alliance between the cosmos and society; where the Egyptians stressed identity, the Mesopotamians stressed continuity.

The redaction of the Sumerian King List, which took place at the high point of Sumerian culture and assumed that Mesopotamia had been a single and well-defined domain, consisted of a compilation and interweaving of legendary and historical reigns. This suggests not only diverse origins and the amalgamation of several different traditions but an attempt to establish continuity between mythical and historical events; it was a quasi history connecting primordial time with the contemporary state. The purpose of this "history" was not simply to describe a series of unique events but to legitimize the order of society and establish the dynasty as the descendant of that primeval reign which brought social order from chaos "when," as the opening lines of the King List states, "the kingship was lowered from heaven."[96]

According to Mesopotamian mythology, mankind was created for the benefit of the gods: "Verily, savage-man I will create. He shall be charged with the service of the gods that they might be at ease!"[97] But this herd wandered without direction until a steward with the divine symbols of authority was installed among them. It was for this purpose that the kingship was established and the arts of civilization were given to man.

The genuine kingship tradition began with the rule of the hero "Etana, a shepherd . . . who consolidated all lands,"[98] but the most famous of the hero-kings was Gilgamesh, whose epic reappears in various forms throughout the history of Mesopotamia. The original version of the epic centers around the attempt of Agga—who, according to the King List, was the last king of the first dynasty of Kish—to extend his rule over the city of Uruk.[99] Gilgamesh thwarted the siege of Agga, bringing an end to Kish's claim to dominion over the valley, and firmly established the first dynasty of Uruk.[100] These incidents probably have a historical basis since it appears that at this time occurred the transition from city-state to the earliest empire and the consolidation of Sumerian supremacy (approximately 2600–2400 B.C.).[101] The epic is concerned with the actions of men, not gods, and thus represents the crucial connection between the historical development of the kingship and its divine foundation; beginning with the first dynasty of Uruk, the king is specified by the term *lugal*.

Sumerian documents such as the King List, despite the mention of hero-kings, do not themselves elaborate a mythological theme; chronology and epic were still separate. Beginning, however, with the ascendancy of the states of Akkad over the valley, and later the rise of Babylon, the narrative developed the form of the chronicle which was in some instances a full and integrated exposition of cosmological, epical, and factual events. The uncertainties of kingship were reflected in the chronicles, which were priestly compositions in which the duration of a reign appeared directly

proportional to the king's obedience to the gods. This latter trend characterized subsequent Mesopotamian historiography such as the tablets
which constitute the Neo-Babylonian Chronicle in which, although there
is a de-emphasis of early legend in favor of more recent events, the
interpretation and theme are decidedly theocratic.[102]

It is necessary to stress that despite the growing consciousness of the
distance between god and man and the insecurity of order apparent in
these attempts to establish continuity centered in the institution of the
kingship, social life in general in Mesopotamia was experienced as a
cosmic analogue. Although the will of the gods was often incomprehensible, the function of the kingship was the maintenance of harmony
between the celestial and mundane spheres. Although social order had
become problematic in the sense of a progressive divergence of nature
and society which signaled the crisis of the myth as an adequate form of
theoretization, speculations on the foundations of human order were, as
in Egypt, essentially an adjunct of cosmology. Unlike Egypt, there was a
recognition of a temporal order of society and that "only the gods live
forever under the sun. As for mankind, numbered are their days; what-
soever they achieve is but the wind!"[103] But the "foundation of a government" was "an event in the cosmic order of the gods, of which the earthly
event is the analogous expression. What today we would call the category
of historical time is symbolized by origination in a cosmic decree."[104]

It is generally agreed that in Egypt and Mesopotamia the view of
cosmic creation reflected the historical development of political forms.
While in Egypt the first dynasty appears to have emerged suddenly with
the complete unification of the kingdom, the establishment of kingship in
Mesopotamia was a slow development from local and autonomous primitive democracies to limited and temporary forms of kingship, and finally
to a hegemony over the entire region expressed by such titles as "King
of the Land," "King of the Four Quarters," and "King of the Universe."
Similarly, creation in Egyptian mythology was instantaneous, whereas in
Mesopotamia the creation of cosmic order was an achievement arising
out of a prolonged conflict with the forces of chaos.

In the most comprehensive cosmogonic myth, the *Enuma elish*, the
"political" character of the creation epic is obvious.[105] The nature of the
cosmos elaborated in the *Enuma elish* corresponds to the developed form
of kingship existing during the periods of empire, but previous cosmol-
ogies conformed to earlier political configurations. During the era of prim-

itive democracies, the cosmos was depicted as an assembly of gods in which power was decentralized and whose decisions determined the destiny of the world and man. By the time of the early Babylonian period and the composition of the *Enuma elish,* the functions of power and authority were assigned to Marduk, king elect of the universe; empire and cosmos were reflections of each other.

In early Mesopotamia the city-states were understood as suzerainties of the gods, administrative units of the cosmos serving a particular deity. Later, when certain of these states such as Babylon attained dominion over the valley, this meant in cosmic terms, as the *Enuma elish* demonstrates, the ascendancy or election of a particular god, in this case Marduk of Babylon, to the celestial throne and accordingly that the earthly king was the choice of the gods for the rule of Mesopotamia. The Prologue to the Code of Hammurabi states:

> When lofty Anum . . . (and) Enlil . . . determined for Marduk . . . the Enlil functions over all mankind, . . . called Babylon by its exalted name, made it supreme in the world, established for him in its midst an enduring kingship, whose foundations are as firm as heaven and earth—at that time Anum and Enlil named me, Hammurabi . . . to cause justice to prevail in the land. . . . When Marduk commissioned me to guide the people aright, to direct the land, I established law and justice in the language of the land, thereby promoting the welfare of the people.[106]

The king's rule approximated on earth the rule of Marduk by waging a perpetual war against social chaos. "Cosmological symbolization is," as Voegelin maintains,

> neither a theory nor an allegory. It's the mythical expression of the participation, experienced as real, of the order of society in the divine being that also orders the cosmos . . . one stream of creative and ordering being flows through them . . . empire and cosmos are parts of one embracing order.[107]

Yet despite this manifold interpenetration of the two spheres which extended even to the construction of the city after the image of heaven, the stubborn fact remained that, unlike Egypt, this interpenetration could never be complete. The affinity of heaven and earth where the king was not god incarnate rested on the obedience of god's servant. While the coronation of the pharaoh displayed the character of an acknowledgment, the investment of a new king in Mesopotamia was the climax of a divine conflict whose outcome found earthly expression. In contrast to the static vision of the land of the Nile, not only was the divine order dynamic, and consequently the social homology, but there remained the further danger that even when the passions of heaven were still a gap might open between the ascendant god and his shepherd-executive on earth. It was essentially this latter fact that threatened to split the cosmos by the interposition of temporality. While developments in historiography did foreshadow an awareness of existence in time, they tended to represent predominantly the internal churning of a dynamic cosmos, while the possibility of disobedience on the part of the appointed king threatened society with the curse of human time: the condition of man's alienation from heaven. Whereas in Egypt the rituals focusing on the kingship tended to be a description of cosmic unity, in Mesopotamia they were an affirmation that the servant of the gods was perpetuating this unity and not straying from the divine "scheme of heaven and earth!"[108]

The king actively sought to interpret and obey the will of the gods, standing at the pinnacle of the priestly hierarchy as well as directing the administration of the realm. But to conform to the desires of the heavenly assembly was not an easy task. The burden of obedience weighed heavily on the man exercising royal rule; anxiety and pessimism surrounded his decisions, for "who can understand the counsel of the gods. . . . Where has befuddled mankind ever learned what a god's conduct is?" Or again, "The mind of a god, like the center of the heavens, is remote; his knowledge is difficult, men cannot understand it."[109] By means of oracles, the interpretation of portents and dreams, and divination, the king endeavored to conform to divine ordinance and consistently addressed written communications to the gods concerning matters of observance so that society "might remain afloat upon the waves of the unknown."[110] While in Egypt the death of a king ushered in a period of cosmic suspension during which fixed procedures governed the transition and the selection of the successor, accession to the throne in Mesopotamia, despite its symbolic significance, "was essentially an *ad hoc* solution,"[111] and the coronation, compared to that of Egypt, was a relatively simple ritual, conducted with the humility befitting the office of a mortal, in which the candidate accepted the insignia of the kingship and received the name *lugal*.

Despite the uncertainties of kingship, it was only through this institution that the hierarchical orders of the cosmos could be joined; the authority of the king was predicated on the fact that kingship and the priesthood of Marduk provided the sole medium through which society could participate in cosmic order, for his "commands, like the word of god, cannot be turned back."[112] The extensive and detailed law codes promulgated by the king included prologues and epilogues confirming their continuity with the work of creative ordering begun in heaven and justifying the divine authority of the royal person from whom they emanated. To the Mesopotamian it was evident that "if a king does not heed justice, his people will be thrown into chaos, and his land will be devastated."[113]

There was a greater tendency in Mesopotamia than in Egypt to describe the relation between the celestial and earthly societies in "political" terms such as authority and obedience. This can be explained as the beginning of the breakdown of consubstantiality, the experience which threatened the mythic vision and created that terrifying rift in the unity of existence which philosophy would eventually describe in terms of time and history. From its inception political philosophy, as well as the Judaic-Christian apocalyptic and redemptive vision, was faced with this problem of temporality, that rupture in the fabric of being which emerged with the dissolution of the myth. Although in a society still ordered in accordance with the myth, ideas of participation, authority, and obedience were not "political" ideas per se, the emergence of these notions demonstrates a need to formulate a system of relations between entities which had become distinct.

The king in Mesopotamia was a mortal among mortals whose law required justification in terms of a higher authority. The enterprise of political philosophy, which succeeded the myth as a mode of speculation regarding the foundations of social order, presupposed the differentiation of the orders of reality, and the appearance of symbols such as authority in political philosophy first expressed the proper relation between the archetype of order or the truth discovered by philosophy and the existential order of society; for Plato's philosopher-king, no less than for the king of Mesopotamia, the claim to authority depended on access to a truth that lay outside the limits of society. There was a successive contraction of the notion of authority, from its original significance as the principle of creation to the relation between deity and king to the relation between king and society; the appearance of the idea of authority in political thought as a description of the purely political relationship between ruler and ruled was the residue of mythic and philosophical speculation on the relation between social order and the truth of order. This development is similar to that of the Greek symbol *nomos* which, originally signifying the law of cosmic order, became a description of the proper relation between society and the cosmos and finally the positive law governing individuals within the existential order of the polis.

There can be little doubt that the unstable conditions of social life contributed to the pessimistic strain in Mesopotamian thought and that the continual passing of cities and kings pushed time to the threshold of consciousness. But whatever the cause, the unity of mythic symbolization was strained. Although in Egypt the death of a king resulted in a period of crisis, the ritual restoration of harmony was a positive acknowledgment of the forces of order over those of chaos. In Mesopotamia there was, in addition to these periods of accentuated crisis, the continual threat that chaos would gain the upper hand because obedience was problematical and the design of heaven was not openly transparent to man. Cosmic integration could not be complete because the king was a hero rather than a god, and the heroic drama is a tragic one.

The "compactness" of the mythic experience was possible because of the lack of differentiation between the orders of existence, but despite this compactness, which is so evident, for example, in the *Enuma elish*, there was a growing separation of the social order with a temporal dimension of its own. Although cosmic and social symbols were by no means distinct, the emphasis on the problem of authority and the difficulties in keeping society in tune with the rhythm of the universe foreshadowed the differentiation of the two realms and made consubstantiality something to be achieved rather than merely experienced. A society of mortals ruled by mortals, despite the pervasiveness of mythic symbolization, could not live completely within a womb of primordial time. Where even the most primitive awareness of human time comes between society and the archetype of order, the compactness of mythic symbolization is threatened and the experience of consubstantiality is weakened.

Nowhere is this loosening of the bonds of consubstantiality more obvious than in the later versions of the story of the demigod Gilgamesh. Here man emerges from the background as the creature who must die, for in "strong contradistinction to the Egyptians in this matter, the people of Mesopotamia viewed death with a sense of hopeless foreboding. To them no saviour god, as Osiris, offered a blissful immortality in his celestial kingdom."[114] According to the epic, Gilgamesh, after many illustrious adventures, is suddenly prostrated with grief upon the death of his companion Enkidu and begins for the first time to fear death, "the common lot of mankind."[115] Fearing the fate of Enkidu, he embarks on a perilous journey to the abode of the Mesopotamian counterpart of Noah, who was deified for saving the seed of mankind from the deluge, in order to discover the secret of immortality. Although during his journey he is warned that the gods "allotted death to mankind,"[116] he continues and manages to learn of a plant at the bottom of the sea which possesses rejuvenating powers. He secures the plant, but, while he stops to refresh himself by a pool, a serpent devours the plant and adds the final frustration to his search.

Man is distinguished from the gods by a condition of temporality which subjects him to the inexorable fate of death, and unlike other creatures he must endure the consciousness of this fate. If even a king and demigod such as Gilgamesh could not escape his end, immortality is certainly beyond the reach of the average mortal. As in another Babylonian epic, the myth of Adapa, the king of the first earthly city, which deals with a parallel theme,[117] it is obvious that the spheres of god and man are far from mutually exclusive; but in both cases, and especially in the Gilgamesh epic, it is apparent that the essential condition of man and society is temporality and death and that the compactness of the mythic vision has been challenged. In the end, Gilgamesh returns to assume the kingship of Uruk and fulfill himself by achieving a measure of immortality through the order he has created on earth.

The Mesopotamian lived a paradox: in nature, he faced a world of immanent deities which were oppressively close and undependable; yet, in regard to ordering his personal and social existence, the gods who were concerned with man appeared ever more remote. Society was suspended between heaven and earth, depending on both, but rarely at harmony with either. The lot of man in general as well as that of the king was to a large extent that of the righteous sufferer, the servant of god, but who was so far removed from Marduk that he had no way of discerning whether what he understood as just actions conformed to the will of the deity. Sometimes it appeared that "those who neglect the god go the way of prosperity" or even that there was a complete inversion and "what is proper to oneself is an offense to one's god," for "where have mortals learnt the way of a god?"[118] For all the opaqueness of divine will, man found himself disturbingly close to the gods who were continually manifest in the destructive forces of nature. Nature faced society as a "Thou," a series of immanent gods; but since the king was not a god, perfect harmony with nature was unattainable. The alienation of society from nature was a dike obstructing the goal of an integrated community of being; the time of man could not be immediately identified with the cycles of nature.

Despite the durability of the mythic vision, thought and action were no longer coincidental; the order of justice in the cosmos was not necessarily that which obtained in society although the maintenance of social stability depended on the coetaneousness of the two orders. But the myth was a prescription for action; although divine justice was clouded in obscurity, the Mesopotamian, unlike the Greek—who, perceiving the futility of human action, might find contentment in contemplative activity—could approach the truth of order only by establishing his conformity with that in which the divine was most clearly manifest: the rhythm of nature. In the Babylonian New Year festival all the threads of Mesopotamian speculation converge and "conjurest up timelessness in the mind, and invokest the myth that it may be relived in the actual present."[119]

The Babylonian New Year, or Akitu festival,[120] was the most important ritual in Mesopotamia and the prototype of numerous ancient Near Eastern Semitic rituals through which society sought to "periodically renew its vitality, and thus ensure its continuance."[121] In this ceremony may be observed "not only the effectual cessation of a certain temporal interval and the beginning of another, but also the abolition . . . of past time."[122] Through this ritual, society participated in the primordial events of creation, the transition from chaos to cosmos, and experienced, concurrently with nature, the regeneration of order. Although these symbolic gestures were community activities which drew together the society as a whole, the king was the central actor in the drama, and the ceremonies performed by the king were "transmuted, through the medium of myth, into deeds done by the god."[123] The festival also represented a repetition of the king's coronation and served, as the Egyptian Sed festival, to renew the potency of the king. The festival symbolized the renewal of fertility, the beginning of the new solar cycle, and the victory of order over chaos, and in this new beginning there was more than a hint of a release from sin and the redemption of society through its representative the king, the suffering servant. The cult was the means through which the gods made known their will so that man might avoid that fate which befell the people of Ur when the "city on its foundation verily was destroyed . . . like the sheepfold of a shepherd."[124]

The numerous connections established in this ritual between suborders of the cosmos, the interweaving of heaven, society, and nature, do not require elaboration; the abolition of past time, the rejuvenation of order through participation in the primordial time of the cosmogony, and the role of the kingship in this ritual integration are clearly evident. But despite all this, the destiny of society, unlike the optimism which prevailed concerning the persistence of Marduk's regency on high and the revitalization of nature, was not clear. The stability of social order conspicuously lacked a final determination, the assurance that it would persevere even for the duration of the succeeding cycle of the cosmos. Although the potency of society had been resuscitated by an expiation of the sins of disobedience and a reaffirmation of the conditions of its foundation, a continued conformity with the authority of the god and harmony with the movement of nature through the period of the intervening cycle was not preordained. The fate of the city was open toward an undisclosed future pregnant with the threat that society might be alienated from heavenly authority, that it would be detached from the orbit of the cosmos and plunge into the abyss of historical time. The pressure of temporal differentiation which taxed the mythic consciousness was effecting a crisis of the intellect which would cause man to begin a journey into the depth of his own being in search of a new vision of order.

What was remarkable about the mythic vision was its simplicity. It was not simple in the sense of a primitive naïveté or lack of complexity or even aesthetic elegance, but rather in regard to the encompassing boldness of its scope and the universality of its assertions which claimed a greater applicability than could possibly be sustained. This meant two things for the fate of mythic symbolization. First, disintegration would not take place through a process of gradual refinement; although man might cling tenaciously to mythopoeic images, the collapse of the integral myth as a complete orientation would take place with a devastating decisiveness, as it did with the appearance of the God of Israel and the end of the Bronze Age in the Aegean world, which would shatter the coherence of its elements. The second consequence, and the more sig-

nificant, was that subsequent speculation could never completely cast off
its mythic heritage even after experience had become intractable in terms
of the myth. Mythic symbols provided the immediate content of succeeding configurations of thought; the reordering of experience through
new symbolic forms took place on the foundation of the myth. The dissolution of the myth was effected by a differentiation of the orders of
existence and the activities of thought appropriate to each, but the internal structure of these realms was not divested of mythic symbols.
When the universe was perceived in terms of the integral myth, heaven,
society, and nature coalesced under the form of primordial time. With
the eventual failure of the myth to prevent the differentiation of these
levels, society emerged under new forms of temporality. Yet these forms,
although unarticulated, were already anticipated in the mythic vision;
the Hellenic conception of cosmic time was present in the recognition of
celestial revolutions and rhythmic cycles of nature, and the prophetic
vision of history as the progressive revelation of Yahweh's will and the
story of man's defection from His authority was adumbrated in the
Mesopotamian vision of the relation between god and man.

Whether society existed under the form of the myth or under the
form of history, there was a continuity of problems. Before the breakdown of the myth, it had been the "political" which had formed the point
of integration of cosmos and society and lifted man out of time, and after
the dissolution of the myth, the idea of the political remained a fulcrum
for establishing a purchase which would bring heaven and earth into
accord. Wherever they proved adequate, there tended to be a continuity
of mythic symbols, and this is apparent in the idea of the regeneration
of political time and the emergence of authority as a form of political
rule.

The aura of sanctity surrounding the beginning of social order has
been a persistent component of political thought, and the idea that the
act of foundation is a source of potency which must be periodically imbibed, if order is to be sustained, was elevated to a central theme as in
Machiavelli's belief that republics must frequently be brought "back to
their original principles."[125] What is involved is the perpetuation of
mythic symbolization accommodated to new experiences of order and
the problem of temporal estrangement from the archetype which political
philosophy inherited from the disintegration of the integral myth. The
mythic experience of the periodic annulment of time through participa-

tion in the primordial events of cosmic creation is transformed into a
symbolic regeneration of political time. When Aristotle said of political
order that "the man who first *constructed* such an association was . . . the
greatest of benefactors,"[126] he did not mean merely that man could only
achieve his highest end within the order of the polity, or simply that
human artifice was a necessary complement to nature, but that the act
of foundation implied the transcendence of the cycle of time which continually threatened to engulf society. Every act of foundation as well
as the perpetuation of any established order shared, to some degree, in
the truth discovered by philosophy; the "beginning" assumed the status
of an archetype, and participation in the archetype carried with it the
authority of the truth which it signified. The symbolism of the

> ritual renewal of order . . . runs through the history of mankind from
> the Babylonian New Year festival, through Josiah's renewal of the
> Berith and the sacramental renewal of the sacrifice of Christ, to
> Machiavelli's *ritornar ai principij,* because the fall from the order of
> being, and the return to it, is a fundamental problem in human ex-
> istence.[127]

The idea of authority as an aspect of political rule is tied to the
creation of social order just as in society under the form of the myth
authority was sustained by continual participation in the archetype of
the foundation, the creation of the cosmos. Authority, the principle of
creation, belongs to him who makes or sustains whether in the cosmos or
the cosmion. Maat—truth and justice—was inherent in the command
of the king and the source of his potency because his word partook of
that "authoritative utterance" which had originally brought order from
chaos; the authority proceeding from the foundation, as in the New
Testament, cannot be separated from the "word," that beginning which
not only was "with God" but "was God." But what distinguishes authority as a type of political rule is not only its de-emphasis of force in
favor of the "word" which carries a coercion of its own but its ability
to obscure the uniqueness of political action by rendering it paradigmatic,
to subsume it under the form of an archetype, whether a transcendent
truth discovered by philosophy or the exemplary deeds of gods, heroes,
or ancestors.

Cicero essentially echoed Aristotle when he stated that there is
"nothing in which human excellence can more nearly approximate the

divine than in the foundation of new states."[128] Here man mimes that
ordering of the chaos which established the authority of heaven over
earth, and, analogously, authority in social order emanates from the act
of foundation. Just as cosmological societies ritually annulled the temporal gap which threatened to alienate them from the celestial archetype,
Rome achieved a regeneration of political time and a revitalization of
the order of the city by a continual identification with its primeval
foundation; for the Romans, who lived in the glow of authority flowing
from that original divine delegation, politics was ordered according to
the mythic belief that "a magic dwells in each beginning and protecting
us tells us how to live."[129]

The Romans "were continually obsessed by the 'end of Rome' and
sought innumerable systems of *renovatio*"[130] which would release society
from the bondage of cosmic revolution. The history of Rome had been
haunted by the apocalyptic myth that the life of the city had been limited
at its origin and that time itself was about to end with the close of the
Great Year. The spectacle of the fall of Caesar, the futility of one man
as a bulwark between the empire and its dissolution, pointed to the inability of creative political action to achieve permanent order.[131] But
the advent of the *Pax Augusta* lent credence to Vergil's poetic rendering
of the eternity of Rome and to a faith in its continuing regeneration based
on a perpetual affirmation of the authority inherent in the foundation.
The ascendancy of Augustus became, in the apologetics of Livy, a second foundation, the transformation of a historical event into the image of
the archetype. It was to be the ultimate constitution which would subli-
mate imperium in the authority of institutions and law and signify not
only the restoration of the Republic but liberation from the inevitability
of the cosmic cycle. Although the differentiation of political existence from
the unity of the mythic universe necessitated new attempts at creative
ordering to meet the threat that temporality posed for social stability,
mythic symbolization persisted, wherever it was adequate, as a means
of structuring political experience. The ritual regeneration of political
time and the organization of political action in accordance with archetypal patterns remained an integral part of the tradition of political
thought. The very notion of a society under law implies existence in
conformity with the archetype.

Despite such vestiges of mythic symbolization in discrete areas of
experience, the coherent simplicity of the integral myth was demolished

with man's fall into time, and it was from this transition that the Greek, Hebrew, and early Christian answers to man's place in the world emerged. Political philosophy was an attempt to find a home for man in the world once it became apparent that his time was not primordial time and the course of society did not coincide with the course of nature. But political philosophy and its concern with transcending historical existence constitutes only one response to the collapse of the myth. In the Hebrew experience may be found an opening of the mind toward time and history and a flight from political space as the natural and distinguishing condition of human being.

III

HISTORY AND POLITICAL SPACE:
THE HEBREWS

---

*Therefore shall Zion for your sake be plowed
as a field, and Jerusalem shall become heaps,
and the mountain of the house as the high
places of the forest.*

Micah

BY accepting history as an order of reality, the Hebrews not only
opposed the vision of the integral myth but defined existence largely in
terms of a contrast with the elements of that vision. The compactness
and consubstantiality of the myth and the compression of experience
which had precluded the appearance of dimensions of time gave way to
the historical identity of Israel through a direct confrontation with and
a conscious rejection of mythic participation. The Hebrews attacked
idolatry and association with foreign cults, but the fundamental meaning
behind the rejection of idolatry was that the practice represented the
experience of participation in which the distinction between God, nature,
and man was blurred. Participation meant the objectification and spatialization of a deity whose presence was manifested historically and the
negation of the differentiation of the orders of existence which was central to the Hebrew vision of reality.

The relation between the Hebrews and their God was different from
any other relation between man and deity in the ancient world since it
was not grounded in the assimilation of society and nature, but rather
in the rejection of any such assimilation and the acceptance of the unique
events of a historical process with a definite beginning and promised end.
God was most immediately apparent in history rather than the space of
the physical world, and the relation between Yahweh and His people

was mediated by His revelation in time. It was the involvement in this historical revelation which bound the Hebrews into a community. The historical character of this community inevitably meant the depreciation of the city or the "political" order, which could not take on ultimate significance since in the myth the spatial and institutional order was the focal point for the participation of society in nature and tended to symbolize, like all idols, the estrangement of man from god.

Yahweh chose the Hebrews for His people before they evolved a political kingship, and their subsequent history, like their beginning, constituted a continuing exodus from political order. Hebrew kingship, despite its inevitable constitutional similarities to the Near Eastern model, could never approximate that of neighboring societies. The kingship was neither lowered from heaven nor the abode of a deity and thus could not ultimately serve as an instrument for mediation between God and man. Since the covenant between Yahweh and His people was consummated before a political order was established, community and kingship were not coterminous, and authority flowed directly from a transcendent God to the people and their prophets. It was the defection of the kings from this spiritual authority and the terms of the *berith* which constituted the theme of the prophetic tradition. The period of the Judges after the conquest of Canaan demonstrated the necessity of kingship; yet this meant that Israel "had reversed the Exodus and re-entered the Sheol of civilizations."[1] A fundamental tension was established between political order in space and revelation in time. History, as the scene of the progressive manifestation of the will of God, held all meaning. Despite the influence of the Canaanite cult in royal ritual, the kingship never achieved the legitimation it possessed in the cosmological empires; the movement of society in time was distinguished from political order as well as the rhythm of nature. While in Egypt and Mesopotamia the kingship was the point of cosmic integration, the journey of Israel in history destroyed the unity of society and nature which existed under the form of the myth.

Proponents of the "myth and ritual" thesis have emphasized the aspects of Hebrew kingship which correspond to the Near Eastern cosmological pattern, such as the portions of the Psalms which pertain to an annual enthronement festival, to the exclusion of the unique characteristics of the institution.[2] But Frankfort, in attempting to demonstrate the autonomy of Hebrew kingship, errs to the other extreme when he claims that there was an "almost complete separation, of the bonds which existed between Yahweh and the Hebrew people, on the one hand, and between Yahweh and the House of David, on the other."[3] This issue cannot be resolved by internal criticism of these approaches, for the source of these differing interpretations lies in the paradoxical nature of the institution itself. What is involved is the problem of the tension between the need for a stable social order and the vision of a society moving toward a future fulfillment in history. The awareness of the uniqueness of human time not only spelled the end of the myth but, in terms of the Hebrew experience, strained the belief in political order as the permanent home of man.

It was this unique quality of the time of mankind, and especially the chosen people, that characterized the Hebrew vision of reality. When they discovered that the time of man not only distinguished him from his environment but found meaning in this movement, it was inevitable that the formation of a political order and confinement in space, especially if modeled on the Near Eastern prototype which implied the assimilation of man in the time of nature, would mean the alienation of the spirit. While the Greeks experienced temporality as the decline of order, the Hebrews experienced it as the scene of the escape from the bondage of political space and the fulfillment of an unrealized promise. Although Yahweh guaranteed an eventual end to this sojourn in history, it was to be the attainment of righteousness in and through time; there was no hint of eternity in the sense of timelessness.

The Old Testament covenant tradition encompasses two conflicting themes which contributed a certain dialectic to the history of Israel. One aspect of this tradition emphasizes the direct relation between Yahweh and the people of Isreal, while the other stresses the necessity of the role of a covenant mediator. While one "is more congregational, democratic, prophetic, and ethical in tendency," the other "is more priestly, cultic, authoritarian, and dynastic in tendency."[4] This same conflict is apparent in the symbolic significance attached to the two shrines associated with the Sinai covenant. The Ark, originally understood as the throne of an invisible deity, testified to the presence of Yahweh and His immanence in the history of the wandering tribes. The Tent of meeting, however, signified the transcendence of Yahweh and the necessity for a priestly mediator. While the meaning conveyed by the Ark was that of the journey of a spiritual community in time, the Tent turned the worshipers' attention toward the sanctuary and an institutional order in space which mediated between man and God.[5]

The two distinct aspects of the covenant symbol emerged clearly after the religious controversy which resulted in the division between the tribes with the Ark going to the north with those following the charismatic tradition of Moses and the Tent going south with those continuing the dynastic priesthood associated with Aaron. After the conquest of Palestine, external pressures forced the establishment of a kingship, but there was no clear theological foundation for this institution which would eventually claim the role of covenant mediator. It was precisely the conflict between the political and sacral functions of the king which precipitated the break between Samuel and Saul.

This tension between history and the idea of political order is present in the relation between the three accounts, in the First Book of Samuel, of the establishment of kingship as a substitute for the system of judges of the prepolitical society when "there was no king in Israel" and "every man did that which was right in his own eyes."[6]

One account, which probably corresponds most closely to the factual situation, relates how Saul was proclaimed the first king of Israel after successfully leading the people in battle against the Ammonites.[7] The other two versions are concerned with the theoretical foundations of royal rule. In the second, Yahweh directed Samuel to single out Saul and "anoint him to be prince over My people."[8] Although Saul was ordained by the hand of Samuel, it is clear from Samuel's words, "the Lord hath anointed thee to be prince over His inheritance,"[9] that the king received his appointment as the "anointed one" or Messiah directly from Yahweh. The third, and probably later, version contains all the characteristic pessimism regarding the benefit an earthly monarch would hold for the people and the inference that the kingship was not chosen by God as the medium through which His will would be made known. Samuel, in his old age, had elevated his sons to succeed him as the Judges of Israel, but their weak and corrupt administration led the people to appeal to Samuel to "make us a king to judge us like all the nations."[10] In his displeasure, Samuel prayed for guidance, and Yahweh answered that the action of the people did not mean a rejection of Samuel, "but they have rejected Me, that I should be king over them."[11] Upon Yahweh's direction, Samuel set forth the nature of the kingship and the hardships that it would entail, but the people insisted on its institution, and Saul was chosen by lot. Rather than a divine institution, the kingship appears here as an apostate creation of the people, and the word of God is received and revealed only through the prophet who on the day of Saul's election, while the people cried, "Long live the king!", proclaimed that "ye have this day rejected your God."[12] The prophets, through the Servant of the Songs, understood themselves as interpreters of the covenant after the Mosaic prototype. In times of crisis, the message of the prophet was a return to the origins, to the original dispensation, and away from the heresy of cult and king.

The kingship reached its zenith in the Davidic empire. David came to power in the south where the covenant theology was most amenable to the incorporation of the institution of kingship; the Ark was placed within the Tent, and David became the mediator of the covenant and the successor of Aaron. When David was anointed king, of both Judah and Israel, and established his rule at Jerusalem, the interpretation of history as the providential course of the chosen people may have seemed fulfilled and the dimensions of empire, promised in the Lord's pact with Abram, completed.[13] The extension of the empire to neighboring lands, whose cultures were attuned to the physical environment, led to the appropriation of mythic symbolism and raised the kingdom as the center of the world and established the king as the intermediary between Yahweh and the people. David succeeded in transforming the priestly covenant tradition by attaching it to a royal dynasty, and he was hailed as the adopted son of God and ordained a "priest forever."[14] The righteousness of the people became a function of the righteousness of the king who was their shield.

The intrusion of cosmological symbolization did not mean, however, that the social order was comparable to that under the form of the myth. The essence of the Davidic reign was the establishment of a covenant between Yahweh and the king, but this was merely the last point in a history that was continually recalled, albeit a point that for a time seemed to pass beyond history by virtue of its political success. Although the kingship of Israel cannot be understood apart from similar Near Eastern institutions, the idea of the kingship took on a different significance than in cosmological civilizations when placed within the framework of the history of Israel. The enthronement ritual of the Psalms cannot be separated from the idea that "salvation has become a matter of the historical process," and not a cosmic renewal. The renewal ceremony concerned the obligations imposed at Sinai and the affirmation of the authority of Yahweh; the "primordial" events became points in the history of the chosen people. Through the royal ritual

> the worshipper's gaze is directed first, in retrospect, to the beginning of time or the creation of the natural order; in the second place, to Yahweh's control of the natural world and His active concern with the behaviour of mankind on the plane of history; and, in the third place, to the prospect of the consummation of both creation and history in a universal moral order.[15]

Yet the tension between the universalistic and historical implications of the Sinai covenant and the particular and static character of the royal covenant was never abolished; the covenant between Yahweh and His people remained unbroken during its political confinement, and it was fully reasserted after the death of Solomon and the decline of political power. The idea of David as the Lord's anointed became the central symbol of Messianic hope; the mythic notion of the integration of heaven and earth through the medium of the kingship was transformed into a vision of the future in which the Messiah was the instrument through which Yahweh would emerge as the king of mankind.

Although profoundly different in their consequences for the idea of the political, the mythic abolition of time through identification with a primordial archetype and the projection of thought into the future may in a sense be understood as partaking of the same basic intellectual operation.

> The destruction of the old world and the creation of a new one, is an event which according to the idea of the Old Testament, is often repeated in history. The passing through the Red Sea, the wandering in the desert, followed by the entrance into Canaan, as well as the Babylonian captivity and the rehabilitation of Israel, are periods of chaos and cosmos, all of which have features in common. The future destruction of the world with the subsequent resurrection of the dead, the whole of eschatology that is, is no more than the future repetition of what history has already demonstrated many times; a new chaos followed by a new cosmos. . . .
>
> Eschatology . . . is nothing but a cosmogony of the future.[16]

But despite these structural similarities in the two patterns of thought and the persistence of mythic symbols, the transformation effected by the Hebrew mind in the historization of the mythic motif produced a radically new orientation and vision of reality in terms of which the dimensions of time are joined not by identity but by their relation to the purposive activity of God in history. Although the unique events of chronological time gain significance against the background of such prototypical experiences as the exodus and covenant, the content of history is continually new and possesses ontological autonomy, and the future becomes the decisive dimension as the passage of time surpasses the past and builds toward fulfillment.[17]

The awareness of historical existence contributed continuously in Israel, and eventually in Hellas, to the depreciation of the idea of the political. Part of the result of the differentiation of the orders of existence was that participation in the ground of being was no longer necessarily predicated on participation in the order of society; the political no longer mediated between heaven and earth, and the individual could know the word of God or experience the vision of the Good directly. The decline of the polis resulting in an ethical universalism which replaced political philosophy, is analogous to the culmination of the prophetic movement which resulted in an ethical monotheism and the "Exodus of Israel from itself."[18] The God of Israel became the God of all nations. The tension, which was present from the beginning of Hebrew history, between positive law and the universalistic implications of the law discovered by individual conscience in the face of a trancendent god concerned with the righteousness of man was resolved in favor of the latter. The unity of the integral myth was shattered in both Greece and Israel with the emergence of historical existence; but whereas in Greece, philosophy, seeking the solace of eternity, retained the idea of a timeless political space as man's natural condition which was present in mythic symbolization, Israel, after the breakup of the Davidic empire, progressively rejected political answers to man's destiny. But the I–Thou relationship between man and deity which characterized the myth found new and dynamic expression in Hebrew theology as the temporal unfolding of the promise and judgment of Yahweh, who made known "His counsel unto His servants the prophets."[19] The prophetic vision was ultimately a historical vision "declaring the end from the beginning, and from ancient times the things that are not yet done."[20]

Israel was vividly depicted by the prophets as the adulterous wife of Yahweh forsaking His way and imitating the vanities of neighboring theocracies.[21] Recalling the decisive events of Hebrew history, the prophets emphasized the theme that Israel's calamities were the result of defections from the covenant and the authority of Yahweh and again projected the destiny of the chosen people toward salvation in a future time. Besides this reopening of the temporal dimension, the history of the prophetic movement is that of the transformation of political symbols into theological symbols and the failure of political solutions, the covenant between David and Yahweh, in an age of crisis. There was a progressive separation of political and religious images and a transfer of authority from the king to Yahweh's servant, the prophet. During the reign of David, Israel evolved an ideal of kingship which became the model for the early prophetic judgment of political order; the early prophetic standard was that of a sovereign mediating between God and man and ruling with righteousness "in the fear of God."[22] But what distinguishes the prophets beginning with Amos is that they not only chastise the king and the people for faithlessness but confront them with the threat of the dissolution of the covenant and the community itself.[23] Even the idea of the revitalization of political order lost its meaning with the disruption of the Davidic empire, and later prophecy turned progressively toward a vision of the future in which the earthly kingdom is displaced by the kingship of Yahweh and where the prophet himself claims the role of covenant mediator.

In the north where classical prophecy emerged, the kingship was repugnant to the covenant tradition. The establishment of the Ark in Jerusalem, originally a Canaanite place of worship, and the formation of a royal cult with Mount Zion as its center was a twofold heresy: Yahweh was understood as enclosed by the space of the city, and the political order became the symbol of covenant mediator. When Solomon began to build an oriental city and the Ark was confined within the temple, it meant to the prophets the acceptance of the idea that the God who revealed himself in history had come to rest. For the pre-exilic prophets the determinative point in Israel's history was the deliverance from Egypt and the establishment of the covenant with the people. This aspect of the tradition was primary for prophets such as Amos, Hosea, Jeremiah, and Ezekiel and in direct conflict with the tradition which developed around the House of David and Zion. The prophetic threat of the end of the covenant, the new hope for the future, and the idea of a new exodus from the fortified cities and their idols grew out of this conflict.

With the appearance of Isaiah, the reluctance of the king to heed the message of the prophet produced a decisive transfer of hope and authority from the contemporary political order to that "remnant" of Israel, the disciples of Isaiah, who, through adherence to Yahweh's word, would survive the present destruction as "signs" and at the proper moment in history reveal the secret of the future ruler that was "bound" and "sealed" within them. The prophecies of Isaiah imply that through the will of Yahweh would take place a radical transformation of the world and man in time marked by the ascendancy of an "Immanuel," a "Prince of Peace" by whom "the government may be increased" and "of peace there be no end" and who would rule in accordance with the justice of Yahweh.[24] Despite the eschatological implications of these proclamations, political symbolism is still present, for the new ruler would sit "upon the throne of David," and despite the universalistic inference of the coming of the reign of peace, it is strongly linked to the Israelite ideal of kingship, although the precise nature of the institution is never articulated.[25] But what is important here is that the future king is no longer the vehicle through which the transfiguration will be effected, but rather is a manifestation or sign; there is a definite devaluation of the political function—the "zeal" of Yahweh is the cause of the transformation and what is emphasized is the condition of *His* kingly rule. The prophecies of Isaiah mark the galvanization of the tension between the idea of the kingship of Yahweh and the hope for the restoration of a concrete political order.

It may be true that the vision of the prophets in the Old Testament, as well as the figure of the "Lord's Anointed" or Messiah who remains a this-worldly or political aspect of Yahweh's rule, is always to some extent bound to the future hope for the restoration of the institutional order of Israel in history as well as to contemporary institutions.[26] The tension between the idea of political order and the promise of the realization of the kingdom of God was never completely resolved. But as the prophetic perspective became oriented more toward the future there was less concern with the conduct of kings and the nature of a political order serving as the intermediary between man and the justice of Yahweh. The later period of early Judaism looked forward to the rule of Yahweh in history, and political kingship became an almost incidental appendage to a spiritual transformation; the idea of the Messiah began to recede into the background as in Isaiah and Ezekiel—"For the LORD is our Judge, the LORD is our Lawgiver, the LORD is our King," and although "my servant David shall be king over them . . . my sanctuary shall be in the midst of them forever."[27]

What separates the prophetic vision from political philosophy as it emerged in Greece is not simply the difference between religious and political symbols, any more than this difference is a sufficient explanation for the continuous tension between the Sinaitic covenant and Yahweh's covenant with David. Both the prophet and the political philosopher injected an idea of order into a disordered world; each understood himself as the repository and carrier of a truth of order that could not be contained within the horizon of a society to which he nevertheless belonged. Finally, the vision of each reflected the problem of historical existence. The root of the difference in their answers to the problem of order must be sought in the ontological status of time in Hebrew thought.

The Hebrew mind never pondered the "problem" of time as such; time meant essentially history as the manifestation of being. Ontological speculation was not undertaken by philosophy, but appeared in the form of successive interpretations of the past and in the prophetic promise for the future. Since Israel oriented itself in terms of a revelation in time, the order of being was never fully manifest, but emerged at the moment of the creation of the world and continuously unfolded, as the eternity of God was fused with the temporality of man, in the intercourse between Yahweh and His people which stretched from the covenants with Noah and Abraham to the universalism of the later prophets. For both the Greeks and the Hebrews being was equated with eternity, but for the latter eternity did not signify timelessness or an eternity divorced from becoming; when they spoke of God as the "Lofty One that inhabiteth eternity"[28] they meant His immanence in the course of history which was the manifestation of reality.

The common description of the notion of time in the Old Testament as a linear progression[29] is in one sense appropriate; yet in another sense it is misleading if taken as representing the meaning of the Hebrew experience. Like the frequent references to the cyclical idea of time in mythic thought, the concept of linear progression is a rationalization of the Hebrew experience of temporality and an abstraction from a pattern of meaningful symbols. The Hebrews neither conceptualized the experience of time nor formed an abstract idea of history. Chronological time was experienced qualitatively rather than as an abstract quantitative measure; it was inseparable from its content. Similarly, history was constituted by the events which occurred in it. History was the space in which the drama of individual and social life unfolded according to the purpose of Yahweh, and cosmic time simply attested to the works of Yahweh and His power over the universe.

While the image of history as a straight line implies an order of succession plotted by discrete points, one of the dominant elements in the Hebrew experience of time was the contemporaneity of past and future. This is evident in the "lack of a precise chronology" and the propensity for "making present."[30] The present was never a clearly delimited unit with precise boundaries. The present was not a segment of history; "the present moment knew no limits but was part of a continuum stretching from the beginning to the end of time"[31] and continuously informed by the past and the future. The covenants were not simply events of the past preserved in tradition, but the theme of a communal drama played out between Yahweh—He Who will be there[32]— and His people in time, for the "Lord made not this covenant with our fathers, but with us, even us, who are all of us here alive this day."[33]

The idea of time as a line is basically a spatial concept, and what distinguished Hebrew thought from both myth and Greek philosophy was the rendering of experience in distinctly temporal rather than spatial terms. For those who lived in the Greco-Roman tradition, time was "an instrument of measure rather than life's domain," and life took on meaning as it transcended temporality. The most important expression of this attitude was the value attached to the stable political space of the city. But for the Hebrews there was

> something scandalous about building in space. The Jews' vocation is to build in time; their true temples are in the human heart and consubstantial with history, never finished and indeed owing their endurance to this very incompletedness. . . . The very fact of construction, of an attempt to isolate a unit of the immense space created by God and thus to check the flow of time, was . . . shocking and almost idolatrous.[34]

The prophetic vision was that of a community existing in time under a transcendent God, and confinement in political space was the bane of the true Israel. The same attitude is evident in the lack of significant art in early Hebrew culture—the absence of a concern with imposing form on the world.

The mythic motif of a sacred space persisted to some extent in Hebrew thought and is evident, for example, in the significance attached to Sinai, and the idea of the kingdom of God was never completely divorced from spatial and political symbols. But in the content of the prophetic vision such symbols took on a new meaning which is most apparent in their subordination to a historical perspective. The significance of Sinai derived not from the place itself, but from the events which took place there, and these events gained meaning only as part of the creative activity of God in history and the course of the Hebrew community in time. The prophets continually rejected the glorification of any particular space which would signal the end of history such as when in the periods of Israel's political ascendancy the city and its institutional order began to take on meaning apart from an event in the unfolding of divine purpose. For the Greeks, being found concrete expression in the image of an ordered cosmos, both physical and social, and was properly suited for immanence in space, while the prophets viewed spatial order as a degradation and curtailment of the spirit. While for the Greeks even the gods were subordinate to a temporally and ontologically prior cosmic order, Hebrew theology understood the cosmos as a creation of God and this creation as an event in a historical order of reality. For the Greeks, history held little meaning other than the possibility of the decline of political order.

The real issue between Israel and the prophets, although couched in the language of a defection from the principles of the covenant, continued to be the desire of the people to realize the mandate of God in an external and institutional form as opposed to the prophetic conception of the kingship of Yahweh which implied an eventual spiritual transformation of the individual and the community. The mainstream of prophetic thought cannot properly be termed utopian since the nucleus of their concern was sin, suffering, and retribution in the present rather than a precise elaboration of a future order. But this present was a historical present embracing the fullness of time, and once the order of reality was understood in terms of revelation and promise, political solutions which constricted the dimensions of this present became unacceptable; the "He Who will be there" could not be transformed into the eternal present of "He Who is there."

Although the prophets never entirely freed themselves from the

symbol of a restoration under a righteous shoot of David,[35] they did
not specify the form of such an order; the divine center was no longer,
as in Mesopotamia, spatially located, but became instead a society
existing in time and eventually a community of the righteous regardless
of social affiliation. The particular character of this future hope meant
a pronounced depreciation of political action since, as was evident from
the time of Isaiah, the transformation would be effected through Yahweh's initiative rather than through an earthly mediator; the order
under God would not emerge from the order of the state. Beginning with
Jeremiah three developments are clearly evident: the passage of Yahweh's authority from the community or the chosen people and its king
to the person of the prophet, the individualization of the "remnant,"
and the universalization of the message and its transfer to the plane of
world history.

As Buber has pointed out, "Josiah's reformation meant not only
the purification of the cult . . . but also its centralization at the temple
in Jerusalem," and for Jeremiah this was evidence of "the false pride
and confidence attaching to the idea of the center of the world."[36]
Jeremiah pitted himself against the institutions of kingship and the
priesthood, and the dialogue between God and Israel became a dialogue
between Yahweh and the prophet—the representative sufferer and
vessel of divine authority who was ordained "a prophet unto the nations" and set "over the nations and over the kingdoms."[37] The problem
was no longer that of the righteousness of a particular political order,
for the scene had changed to the realm of world history whose meaning
was announced in the message of the prophet who had become the intermediary between God and men. The new covenant that Yahweh
promised through the mouth of Jeremiah was unique in its nonpolitical
character and the immediacy of the relation between deity and individual. No longer would the virtue of the individual be tied to the
virtue of society: "they shall teach no more every man his neighbor,
and every man his brother, saying, Know the Lord," and "everyone shall
die for his own iniquity." The efficacy of the new covenant, unlike that
"made with their fathers" at the time of the exodus and abrogated by
the kings, would not depend on a translation through the medium of the
political, for "I will put my law in their inward parts, and in their heart I
will write it" and "they shall all know Me, from the least of them unto
the greatest of them."[38] This emphasis is even more pronounced in

Ezekiel where Yahweh departed "from the midst of the city."[39] Ezekiel, in Buber's words, "individualizes the prophetic alternative . . . and the idea of the 'holy remnant' "; Israel ceases to be a concrete society and becomes "a multitude of individuals, each one of whom is responsible before God for himself alone."[40]

The writings of the prophet Deutero-Isaiah marked the culmination of the Messianic hope for a reconciliation of God and man by political means—the end of the prophetic involvement with the empirical order of Israel and in a sense with concrete history. Like all the prophets, Deutero-Isaiah begins with the present historical situation which is the last days of the exile. According to Deutero-Isaiah, Israel had paid many times for her transgressions[41] and Cyrus, as the conqueror of Babylon and liberator of the exiles, is to be Yahweh's instrument for the fulfillment of His promise to Israel. It was Cyrus, "His anointed," whom Yahweh "called by name" for the sake of "Israel Mine elect" and "raised up . . . and maketh him ruler over kings";[42] through His anointed, Cyrus, and His servant, Israel, the path of salvation was to be prepared.[43] There can be little doubt that in the mind of Deutero-Isaiah the restoration was near at hand and that Cyrus, through his sword, would restore right order and constitute a new exodus, a new redemptive act as a reward for suffering.[44] Yahweh was revealed as the "redeemer" of Israel, and the Persian monarch, "My shepherd, . . . shall perform at My pleasure" and "he shall build My city, and he shall let Mine exiles go free."[45] In the face of this event, the exodus from Egypt and the emergence of the Davidic empire paled in significance and were relegated to the realm of "former things" in the context of world history stretching from the creation of the world to the present moment of the new exodus and the liberation which would become the prelude to redemption.[46]

But neither did Cyrus venerate or accept Yahweh nor was Israel restored to ascendancy as a preparation for His lordship over the nations; the "servant," Israel, was "blind" and the "messenger," Cyrus, was "deaf."[47] Now, even the liberation passed into the category of "former things" and the mission of the true Servant and the advent of the "new things" was again proclaimed,[48] but the concern for the "new things" signified the final renunciation of political things. After Deutero-Isaiah, the succession of events in mundane history began to disappear as a significant realm. For Daniel and the apocalyptist who focused on the realm of last things, the meaning of God's activity was not easily discerned in the particular events of secular history.[49]

The trend of prophetic thought adumbrated in the book of Jeremiah is given full expression by the author of the Servant Songs. The Servant of the Songs is not Israel.[50] Israel as a concrete community has disappeared, or at least contracted into the person of the Servant-prophet, the vehicle of Yahweh's revelation in history.

> The LORD hath called me from the womb . . .
> And He hath made my mouth like a sharp sword . . .
> And He hath made me a polished shaft,
> In His quiver hath He hid me;
> And he said unto me: "Thou art My servant,
> Israel . . ."[51]

Neither is the Servant a Messiah; the authority once promised to the branch of David is lodged in the Servant before whom "kings shall shut their mouths."[52] Unlike Cyrus, it is not by a political act that he will "open the blind eyes" and "bring out the prisoners from the prison," but it is by his words and the spectacle of his representative suffering that "Israel be gathered unto Him." He replaces not only Israel but also the scion of David, for it is he, not a future king, that "shall be exalted and lifted up" and "startle many nations."[53] "Behold My Servant"; through his suffering he is to be Yahweh's instrument for the future establishment of His kingship.[54]

The mission of the Servant is universal and is projected forward through time until "he have set the right in the earth; and the isles shall want for his teaching."[55] The four Songs taken together are distinctly historical in scope.[56] In the First Song, Yahweh is the speaker who announces the appearance of the Servant and describes his mission, while in the Second Song, the Servant, speaking in the present, tells the nations of his appointment, characterizes the nature of his task, and relates how Yahweh informed him that it was "too light a thing that thou . . . restore the offspring of Israel; I will also give thee for a light to nations, that My salvation may be unto the end of the earth."[57] Again, speaking in the Third Song, the Servant places himself in the drama of revelation as one of the remnant, the disciples of Isaiah, who at the proper moment would reveal the message of salvation; the "former things" and the "new things" are linked together by the figure of him who speaks with "the tongue of them that are taught" and whose "seed shall possess the nations" as a redeemed Israel becomes the beacon for the world by its acceptance of Yahweh's message and His kingship.[58] Finally, at the beginning and end of the Fourth Song it is again Yahweh who speaks and proclaims the future success of the Servant's mission. The middle portion of the Song takes the form of a testimony of those who bore witness to and finally comprehended the significance of the work of him who was debased in life and suffered in righteousness and innocence for the sake of Israel. The verses are meant to represent the response of a redeemed Israel since the whole Song is clearly a prophecy related to future events.

The prophetic rejection of the myth embraced by other Near Eastern societies may be attributed to a variety of causes. No doubt such fundamental and decisive experiences as the wandering in the desert and the development of a nomadic tribal life contributed to the creation of values antagonistic to those of neighboring agricultural communities bound to the rhythms of nature. This environmental hypothesis could easily be extended to illuminate the Hebrew conception of the deity, the emergence of history as the realm of meaning and in general the importance of temporal over spatial categories, the tension between politics and religion, and finally, along with the overwhelming fact of the destruction of political society, the movement of prophetic thought away from the problem of political order. But whatever the ultimate explanation of the rejection of the myth, the principal concern here is with the nature of this intellectual transition, and it will suffice to point out that in the particular context of the Hebrew experience the break with the myth necessarily carried with it the rejection of the idea of the political as the axis for positing man's place in the universe. Despite the retention of certain mythicopolitical terminology, which is evident in such phrases as the "Kingship of Yahweh," it was adapted to a fundamentally new vision of order which was essentially antipolitical as well as antimythic. As the syncretist character of the Davidic empire demonstrates, political order in Israel was never able to transcend reassimilation into its mythic environment.

One of the characteristics which marked the Hebrew experience, as well as the dissolution of the myth in general, was the emergence of the individual as the center of the problem of order and disorder. Nowhere is "the strange poignancy of single individuals" more evident than in the Old Testament.[59] Not only was man existing under the form of the myth sustained in the universe by his absorption in the order of society and cosmos but, at the same time, his creative energy was channeled and his existence was merged with the background of a world described by two dimensions. The radical change that appears in the Old Testament is that the individual suddenly emerges in time, exposed and vulnerable; it was this differentiating experience which spelled the destruction of the myth and opened the consciousness to the experience of time. The mythic perspective begins to disintegrate when "man finds himself cut off from his environment . . . and acquires awareness of his own person. He begins to allot himself a residence in space, to measure the duration of his life."[60] Existence under the form of the myth and primordial time obscured the uniqueness of both the life of the individual and the career of the community; the release from the configuration of mythic symbols that directed and informed communal existence occurred when primordial time was transformed into a time of "beginning." Not only time itself but the time of the individual and the time of society were differentiated and circumscribed by the positing of this regressive boundary which in turn opened toward the limits of an outer horizon—the time of the end.

The breakdown of the integral myth and the differentiation of the orders of existence pushed to the threshold of consciousness the awareness of the temporal limitations of the individual and the rise and fall of political order within that stretch of time beginning at the moment of the creation of the world and climaxing with the "Day of Yahweh."[61] It is at this point

> when the myths no longer fit the internal plights of those who require them, the transition to newly created myths may take the form of a chaotic voyage into the interior, the certitudes of externalization replaced by the anguish of the internal voyage.[62]

The prophetic revelation, as well as the appearance of political philosophy, was the result of that "internal voyage" taken in search of a new idea of order and in response to the temporal differentiation that accompanied the disruption of the mythic vision of the universe. Whether it was Plato or the anonymous author of the Songs, the bearer of the new vision suffered in isolation the existential disorder of society while the constellation of symbols constituting a new truth of order took form within him and in opposition to the collective mind. He

> is as far from the men around him as he is close to their destiny. For he expresses and gives form to the future of his epoch.
>
> . . . .
>
> [Yet he is] deeply bound up with his group and its culture, more deeply than the common man who lives in the security of the cultural shell, and even more deeply than the actual representatives of this culture.[63]

The solutions to the problem of historical existence provided in the speculative ventures of Hebrew theology and Greek philosophy must be the starting point for understanding their respective answers to the problem of human order. The fall of man into time through the dissolution of the mythic vision signaled his alienation from nature and created the problematic of human existence. It may be true that "by a sort of abuse, man *creates* time . . . and whereas life or reality confines itself to proliferating within the instant, the mind has spun for itself the myth of myths which is *Time*."[64]

IV

TIME, THE SELF, AND THE PROBLEM OF SOCIAL ORDER: THE GREEKS

---

*Sharp-toothed Time grindeth all things up,
aye, even the mightiest.*

Simonides

Homer and the Emergence of Human Time

AS with the Hebrews, it was the dissolution of the integral myth and the awareness of existence in time which formed the ground of vision in the Greek world. It was through the work of Homer, Hesiod, the Greek poets and dramatists, and the philosophers that the idea of the self and its temporal limitations as well as the idea of history or the existence of social order in time emerged, and it was this orientation which gave rise to a new answer to man's place in the world and culminated in the Platonic vision of order and political philosophy as a symbolic form.

Civilization in the Aegean area, by the end of the third millennium, consisted of small but stable village-centered agricultural societies. At the beginning of the second millennium the Aegean mainland, as well as the Middle and Near East, experienced the invasion of nomadic Indo-European–speaking tribes from the north, and under the domination of the new masters the Greek language supplanted the native tongue. By 1600, there arose a new and dynamic culture which was subsequently infused with oriental elements. The Minoan civilization which flourished in Crete, like Egypt which remained essentially impervious to the foreign interruptions, was not subjected to the invasions from the north, but instead was influenced by contact with the civilizations of the east and became the intermediary between the Orient and the Aegean. Although it is still questionable to what extent society was ordered in accordance with the integral myth, it is apparent that it displayed many of the characteristics of the Near Eastern prototype, including the institution of divine kingship. Crete dominated the Aegean until the destruction of Knossos in the first half of the sixteenth century, after which it succumbed to the burgeoning pressure emanating from the developing civilizational nuclei on the mainland, such as that centered at Mycenae. By 1400, complete cultural dominance was transferred to the far-flung Mycenaean kingdoms, including such seats of power as Pylos, Knossos, and Thebes, which became the cultural leaders of the Aegean Basin.

The civilization of the Mycenaean age evolved a syncretist culture; the rulers on the mainland imposed oriental forms on indigenous social configurations and adopted many of the institutions of assimilated colonies. The fortified cities of Mycenaean kingdoms cannot properly be described as either Greek or oriental; this was an age of transition. The decipherment of the Linear B script has disclosed that the language is Greek despite the presence of etymological links with Near Eastern and early Aegean forms, and there is considerable theological continuity between the Mycenaean period and classical Greece. But in regard to political and social organization, which was at first apparently to some extent a conscious imitation of the East and Crete and later developed by the influence of trade and cultural borrowing, the Mycenaean states more closely approximated the hierarchical structures of the Near East, and in this palace-oriented culture, art, writing, and poetry were essentially court functions. The king was designated by the term *wanax,* which denoted divinity or near-divinity, and his private domain was described by the word *temenos,* land sacred to the gods. But this prospering system of palace societies survived little more than two centuries. Just when it seemed, at the height of the late Bronze Age, that the Aegean kingdoms were being drawn into a cosmopolitan oriental complex, the Mycenaean world, along with the other major civilizational centers stretching across the Fertile Crescent and Asia Minor, collapsed and fell into the barrenness of the Early Iron Age.

The cause of this collapse was both internal decline and a new series of invasions beginning about 1200. In the pottery of this period there is evidence of a loss of originality and a massive deterioration of artistic form. Although there is little direct evidence of a breakdown of political organization in the Aegean area, except what might be extrapolated from the Homeric epic, it is reasonable to assume, since art was a function of the court, that there was considerable inter- and intrastate instability. Also the sudden rise of the diverse kingdoms, and possibly the strain of such ventures as the expedition against Troy in the late thirteenth century, did not allow extensive political consolidation, and when the Aegean was again inundated by Indo-European invasions from the north, the tottering structure of Mycenaean civilization foundered and the Age of Heroes was ended. The Dorian sweep decisively shattered the political structure by 1100, and even in Athens, which was probably not sacked, the institution of divine kingship did not survive the Mycenaean age.

From the chaos of the dark period following the Mycenaean collapse, the Hellenic civilization was born. The Greek world was fragmented, but from 1100 to 800 there occurred that radical political and spiritual transformation which is comparable in magnitude only to the exodus of the Hebrews from Egypt; the remnant of the Mycenaean age emerged from the womb of cosmological existence. After the destruction of the Mycenaean palaces and shortly before 1000, there began a series of emigrations which passed through Athens on the way to Ionia, and it was in the minds of the Diaspora that the intellectual transformation took place. This movement was not one of colonization sponsored by a mother country, but a migration of diverse groups; yet it was in the process of this migration that a new mode of communal existence came into being. With the dissolution of divine kingship, the keystone of society, there was not only a collapse of social and political order but a differentiation of the spheres of god and man, a distinction which was blurred in the mythic world of Mycenae. During the settlement in Ionia, the term *wanax* lost its original meaning and was supplanted by *basileus,* which designated a limited ruler or leader of a *demos,* a people living within a defined territory.

Not only were the spheres of god and man distinguished but human existence was separated into past and present. The fall of the palaces resulted in the disappearance of written records, but the Mycenaean past and the story of the war with Troy was preserved in the oral tradition which eventually culminated in the written epic of Homer; as the Mycenaean world receded in time, the settlers became aware of a past with a different social order than their own, yet one with which they were intimately connected. As new political structures began to take shape, the contrast with the age of the gods and heroes became more pronounced, but the memory of the glories of this common past helped to unite the new communities of the Aegean which were cut off from the civilizational centers of the ancient world. The relative stability of Athens, which had apparently escaped two Dorian invasions, became a refugee center for emigrants passing into Ionia and an island of order in a disintegrating world which probably served to maintain continuity with the Mycenaean past. During this period not only did the temporal order of society emerge as an element of the Greek experience but death as an individual limitation was sharply accentuated. In contrast to the practice of inhumation which prevailed in the Mycenaean age, the congested conditions in Athens necessitated cremation, which undoubtedly contributed to the breakdown of the mythic rejection of the distinction between the living and the dead and to the acceptance of mortality as a distinguishing attribute of human being.

The two centuries from 1000 to 800 constituted a period of consolidation with a growing consciousness of a Greek world which is apparent in the creative development of a tradition of oral poetry. Although the Greeks, through the preservation of the Mycenaean past, became aware of existence in time, they first gained self-awareness in political space, and this discovery was the determinative experience of Greek culture. Interesting parallels might be drawn between the wanderers who left Egypt and those who crossed to Ionia. For both there was an exodus from a civilization, and this experience meant a break with the myth as an orientation and profoundly shaped the subsequent development of these cultures as well as the intellectual patterns of Western thought. Nevertheless, the differences are decisive. While for the Hebrews, the Egyptian civilization was not *their* past, the Greeks understood the Mycenaean world as the Greek past; the Hebrew mind was oriented toward a future and the exodus was a beginning, while the Greeks looked toward the past and viewed the experience of history as a decline. For one there was a community existing in time which was the scene of a future fulfillment, while for the other time constituted an alienation from political order; the Hebrew past was continually and completely reappropriated in the beginning of each new present, while the Greek past inexorably receded and could be regained only through the boon of Mnemosyne.

The growing political and cultural unity of the Greek world as well as the consciousness of the differentiation of the orders of existence can be inferred from archaeological evidence of the development of the potter's art. At approximately 1050 Protogeometric pottery appeared in the Aegean world, and the development of this art form presupposes an intellectual revolution which marks the beginning of classical Greek civilization. The emergence of the Protogeometric style is distinguished from the deteriorated forms of the sub-Mycenaean by a new firmness and precision, attention to proportion, and balance and unity of form in both shape and decoration. This development, which culminated in the Geometric art of the eighth century, is marked by a growing tendency toward abstraction and a recognition of an ordered universe. Society was regaining a sense of solidarity which had been lost after the Mycenaean upheavals, and this feeling was reflected in political life and in the art of Homer.[1]

The structure of the *Iliad* presents a close parallel with the Dipylon pottery of Athens. In the Ripe Geometric period, the artists gained mastery over the geometric style; order had been formed from chaos, both in the political world and the world of the mind, and innovation was widespread. A new freedom of artistic imagination as well as complexity and coherence in design began to dominate; the former rigidity of artistic forms was giving way to the characteristics which would exemplify classical art. Figures, both animal and human, appear on the pottery of this period not as mere decoration but as paradigmatic representations of action. Although the human figure was represented as a combination of parts, man clearly stood out from the background. This same innovation and release of creative energy is apparent in the Homeric epic in which inherited motifs are manipulated and transformed into a unified masterpiece representing the world of human action.[2]

Although the appearance of the epic in Mesopotamia suggested an emerging awareness of the distance between the individual and the world and consequently of human time, it was ultimately unable to break through the cultural canon established by the integral myth and create a new symbolic form. The anonymity of authorship and the evolution of content without the appearance of individual form and style point, despite the strain on mythic symbolization, to a continued dominance of the myth over the consciousness of its creator and the absorption of the psyche in the external order of society. In other words, art remained a collective phenomenon, and the artist had not gained control of his material. The experience of differentiation which may be detected in the Near Eastern epic could not be freed until the symbols were shaped and manipulated by an individual creator, aware of his opposition to the old truth, and transformed into a new reality. The epic could become a vehicle for the expression of a new symbolic form only at that point at which the consciousness of the artist transcended the consciousness of society. Although there are many parallels between the mythological themes of the Near East and those of eighth-century Greece as well as between such figures as the heroic demigods Gilgamesh and Achilles, they are, nevertheless, separated by that recasting of symbols which signified a radical break with the integral myth.

The epic was no longer a form of court poetry, but was composed for consumption by a wider audience. Although there is some continuity of themes, which suggests a renewed contact with the Orient after the isolation of the Dark Ages, the Homeric epic is distinguished by a new artistic unity, the speculation and explicit concern with human action and volition which was to become the central concern of lyric poetry. The appearance of the epic represented the "first flower . . . of a new symbolic mode, the mode of art,"[3] but in the Near East this "first flower" remained embedded in the myth, and the nascent ideas implicit in this form of expression can be extracted only in retrospect. With Homer, standing as he did at the culmination of an oral epic tradition, the ideas gained autonomy, and through the medium of his art the epic produced a new picture of man's place in the world. Through the symbolic form of art the elements of the myth were self-consciously manipulated to communicate new truths of existence, and foremost among these truths were the ideas of human finitude and the problem of social order in time. The separation of past and present and mortal and immortal was accomplished before Homer; it fell to the poet to articulate these discoveries in a new vision of the universe.

There is no need to venture into the intricacies of the "Homeric Question," for, whatever the sources of the characters and episodes of the epic, Homer's "invention was the *Iliad*";[4] the imposition of form and the interweaving of the segments of myth and legend into a unified and complicated composition signified not only a transcendence of the tradition but a new idea of man and society which, while building on the foundation of myth, artistically transformed its elements into a new vision of reality and decisively destroyed the consubstantiality of the cosmological form. Despite the numerous and diverse connections between gods and men, the gods are not primarily identified with the forces of nature, and both man and god are placed within the context of an order of being in which their field of action is more or less delimited; the gods are not

the creators of the cosmos, and their powers are essentially restricted to
the realm of human affairs. Most important, the time of the epic is neither
primordial time nor a transitional period between cosmogony and history,
but the Mycenaean present transformed into the Greek past and preserved in poetic memory.[5] Although the idea of human time could not
fully emerge until the psyche had gained complete awareness of itself as
the maker of its own decisions and until the decline of political order was
no longer understood as the ultimate consequence or echo of divine quar-
rels, the historical course of societies and the uniqueness of individual
action are the focus of the epic. Despite the ubiquity of the gods, Homer's
concern is with human action, for in a description of a world in flux and
the decline of political order, heroic deeds as well as the tragedy of Mycenae achieved a measure of permanence worthy of being remembered
in song and constituting the Hellenic past.

Not only does the complex structure of the Homeric epic imply an
individual creator, but the frequent invocations of the Muses,[6] the daughters of Memory, indicate that it was to the man Homer that the knowledge of the past was imparted. Yet, at the same time, the personality of
the poet never entirely emerges, for with Homer himself, as with the
heroes of the epic, it seems that "the intervention of the gods plays the
key role" and that the "mental and spiritual acts are due to the impact
of external factors."[7] The static unity of the myth had been broken, but
an idea of man had not yet fully emerged, and the continual oscillation
between man and god as the source of order and disorder is not easily
reconciled. As Snell maintains, there is in the epic no idea of man as such.
The word "body" (*soma*) denoted the "dead body"; the notion of an
individual body tended to be conveyed in terms of an aggregate of limbs
or external shape. The "psyche" was understood as the breath of life that
left a dying man and, as with other words pertaining to the function later
ascribed to mind or soul, was conceived as a concrete organ; a man was
apparently not understood as a unit, but as a cluster of specific parts,
and there is no clear conception of the social group as a psychic unity.[8]

This apparent lack of a clearly articulated idea of man can be supported by reference to another characteristic of Homer's work which
displays the vestiges of mythic symbolization. Although when compared
with the Mycenaean world the distance between man and god appears
striking, the two spheres are not rigidly distinguished as separate and
fixed orders of existence; not only do the epics abound with demigods

and the motivations of mortals appear to stem from the will of the deities, but the course of events on earth has profound repercussions on Olympus. But to seize upon and emphasize these aspects of Homer's work tends to obscure what is most significant in his total enterprise. Despite his rudimentary anthropology, Homer broke through to the most salient feature of the human condition, to that which made the life of the individual and society, unlike the world of the gods, susceptible to portrayal in terms of tragedy: man is a temporally limited creature, and his welfare depends on the creation of a home for himself in the world.

The Olympians and mortals are both bound by fate, destiny, or Moira, "a shadowy reality, a fixed order rather than a power,"[9] which fixes the limits of divine and human action. The Greek gods, unlike Near Eastern deities, arose from within the world rather than creating it. They are not, however, immanent natural forces, but rather symbolize nature and right order to which they are subject. Although in Homer there is, from the point of view of man,[10] often no distinction between fate and the will of the gods, especially Zeus, Moira and the Erinyes, the avengers and upholders of the moral order, constitute a higher order which encompasses them both, for even Zeus was unable to prevent the death of his son Sarpedon, "a man that is mortal, doomed long since by fate."[11] What differentiated gods and men was not that the gods were omnipotent; even if they were relatively invincible when measured against mankind, the feats of heroes like the "godlike Achilles" tended to break down this distinction. Neither is it possible to formulate the difference in terms of man and nature, for, despite the affinity between certain gods and the natural elements, which is apparent in Zeus's ability to wield the "thunder-bolt" and such epithets as "lord of the lightning" and "cloud-gatherer,"[12] the gods, by the time of Homer, had lost the immanence which characterized the integral myth and were related to nature "only as absentee proprietors";[13] since they were not the creators of the universe they were no longer coeval with nature, but were, like man, a suborder of the cosmos.

What essentially differentiated men from gods was the condition of temporality which is apparent in Homer's frequent use of "mortals" and "immortals" as terms of distinction. Homer's idea of human existence is summed up in the concept of mortality, "for not even the mighty Heracles escaped death, albeit he was most dear to Zeus . . . but fate overcame him."[14] Death was the destiny allotted to man, and only in view of this did the deeds performed before Troy become meaningful, for if "we were for ever to be ageless and immortal, neither should I fight myself amid the foremost, nor should I send thee into battle where men win glory; but now—for in any case fates of death beset us . . . which no mortal may escape or avoid—now let us go forward."[15]

It is easy to overemphasize, as Snell certainly does, the place of deities as casual factors in the Homeric epic, and even with regard to Homer himself who appears to be only the mouthpiece of the Muses, it is ambiguous whether his invocations are to be taken literally or are merely formulas and remnants of the oral tradition. Although Homer's penetration of the human soul is no doubt less sophisticated than his successors', it is a mistake to take the role of the gods as explanations of human action too literally. The gods were only related to isolated instances of human action, and, above all, even "the belief in non-human causation of human action has practically no effects on the ascription of responsibility."[16]

In the *Iliad,* the gods are by no means merely a vehicle for poetic expression, but, in Homer, art, to a large extent, triumphs over myth. If the gods are viewed as symbols from the perspective of poetic form, they take on a new significance. Although Herodotus states that Homer and Hesiod first "described the gods,"[17] Homer had a wide theological tradition stemming from the Mycenaean past from which to draw, and his characterization of the deities was inevitably shaped by the poetic context in which he inserted them. Heroic action was encased in an aura of immortality through the epiphany of the divine in human events, such as the relation between the wrath of Achilles and the plan of Zeus, and the introduction of the Olympians put into relief the temporal nature of human existence by the juxtaposition of the spheres of god and man. The condition of man was burdened with the fate of death, but through extraordinary acts he could participate, to the limited measure consistent with the dispensation granted to his existence, in that timelessness which marked the province of the divine. Only a people conscious of human time could have found meaning in the epic; acts performed in the present were transformed by song into the past of the future.

> . . . mortals, are pitiful creatures, that like unto leaves are now full of flaming life, eating the fruit of the field, and now again pine away and perish.

. . . but not without a struggle let me die, neither ingloriously, but in the working of some great deed for the hearing of men that are yet to be.[18]

It may be argued that "as men came to visualize the gods more sharply in forms like themselves so they became more aware of their own nature,"[19] but although during this period men were becoming more aware of themselves, it is doubtful that there is a direct relation between this awareness and anthropomorphism. The latter may be a better measure of the extent to which both man and god were differentiated from nature. The anthropomorphization of the gods in the Homeric epic may be explained partly as poetic symbolization, partly by the tendency toward realism and rationalization so apparent in Geometric art with its exorcism of magical and irrational forces, and finally as a presage of the propensity of Greek philosophy to explain the unknown in terms of the known. But anthropomorphism can occur only when an idea of man has not been completely symbolically differentiated, just as society appears as a cosmic analogue, or the cosmos appears as a social analogue, only when social existence has not been theoretically distinguished.

The one important attribute of man which was not transferred to the Olympian deities was mortality (or the one essential attribute of the gods which was beyond the reach of man was immortality), and it is not a coincidence that in Homer the one certain thing about man is that he must die. The problem of whether the Olympian myth is accepted as reality by Homer or merely serves a symbolic purpose in the context of the epic cannot be completely resolved because it is in fact both of these; Homer stands midway between Mycenae and fifth-century Athens. "The more the Greeks begin to understand themselves, the more they adopt of this Olympian world and, so to speak, infuse its laws into the human mind."[20]

Whatever the later Greek estimate of Homer's enterprise, whether in Xenophanes or Herodotus, the concern of the epic was human action, and it is precisely through this concern that it is possible to measure the distance of the epic from the integral myth in which human existence is but the shadow of divine movement. Homer's purpose was not to elaborate a theology. In the *Iliad* the correspondence between human and divine implies that human action takes place within the context of an ordered and meaningful universe, and in this sense the events take on a significance which transcends their historical uniqueness; what happens

on earth, especially when viewed from the perspective of the entire course
of events, finds not only its counterpart but its cause in heaven. But in
another sense the appearance of the gods in the course of human action
answers a variety of symbolic purposes. Their presence, especially in
specific instances, functions not so much as a causal explanation of a
particular act, which would have happened anyway "according to fate,"
but either as a simile which accentuates an event or enlarges it to make
it more comprehensible or as a contrast which serves to illuminate the
nature of the human condition. "The gods are, in fact, a kind of imagery,
and their uses parallel, in a way, the continuous play of figurative language on the action."[21]

Those instances where the gods enter the course of human action
are for the most part those where the life and death of individuals and
the order and disorder of society are at stake. These are matters of great
import for the world of man, bound as it is by temporal limitation, and
the presence of the gods, who are free not only from the consequences
of their action and the insecurities of creatures who exist in human society
but from the inevitability of death as well, represents unchanging principles of order and provides a dramatic contrast with human existence.
Although both man and god are subordinate to fate, the gods, unlike
mortals from whom the future and the consequence of passion is hidden,
have a timeless understanding of human events and, like the audience
of a Greek tragedy, know the end from the beginning; chance is absent
from the perspective of the omniscient deity. What makes the life of man
and political existence tragic is the temporal context. The gods experience
the same emotions and passions as men, but without the standard of
death as a measure, the passion of the gods lacks the sense of proportion
and the burden of responsibility which are integral aspects of human
action and suffering. The comedy of heaven accentuates the tragedy on
earth. Gods who perceive the limitations of time and yet are free from it,
and beasts who suffer under it yet are absolved from self-knowledge,
stand in sharp contrast to man, for, as Zeus observes, "There is naught
. . . more miserable than man among all things that breathe and move
upon the earth."[22]

Despite Homer's method of externalizing states of mind by similes
and the apparent linking of human motivation to a divine source, and
although an idea of the psyche had not risen to the level of conceptualization, it is an exaggeration to maintain unequivocally that "what was

later known as the 'life of the soul' was in Homer understood as the intervention of a god."[23] The "life of the soul" is apparent not only in the structure which the individual artist has imposed upon the variegated oral epic tradition but also in the revelation and development of individual characers in the *Iliad*. In Homer may be found the beginnings of the recognition of the "life of the soul," the discovery that would characterize the intellectual revolution of the next two centuries. Only at that point at which the individual realizes that his time is neither the time of the gods nor the time of nature and that the source of human disorder is an internal disorder of the soul could a new vision of order arise. Homer does not attempt to explore in any depth the problem of the origin of social order or to distinguish human society as a creation of man, but a theory of order is predicated on an understanding of disorder, and this understanding is adumbrated in the *Iliad*.

It is futile to engage in an extended discussion of whether the parallel between the course of events in heaven and on earth, the relationship between gods and individual men, and the use of similes to convey attitudes and emotions indicate an acceptance of the myth as reality and a lack of a conception of an internal center of will in man or whether these relations serve symbolic purposes appropriate to an essentially presentational rather than discursive medium. Both interpretations contain an element of truth. It would also be useless to attempt an allegorical interpretation of the Homeric epic or probe the poems for esoteric doctrine, but it would be shortsighted to approach the epic as simply entertaining legend interspersed with traditional gnomic epigrams. In the figure of Achilles not only are the autonomy and responsibility of the individual emphasized and the limitation of death universalized and dramatized as the boundary of the human condition, but the development of Achilles' character is a microcosmic study of the problem of human order in general.

Achilles appears like a god because in his wrath he acts with a disregard for death and the consequences of his action; he casts aside the restraint appropriate to the condition of mortals. It was this same lack of restraint and disregard of consequences and the refusal to take the step to restore order before it was too late that caused and perpetuated the Trojan war. The war was not fought for the purpose of maintaining political order or even in pursuance of such a traditional aim as power; it was the result of the internal disorder of certain individuals, such as

Paris, and the breakdown of the norms required to maintain social order, the heroic but decadent grandeur of the Mycenaean civilization. What would have been a game for immortals became a tragedy when played by mortals. Men are properly restrained by *aidos,* pity, shame, or sense of honor, but natural pride may pass over into the unnatural arrogance of *hybris* which displaces *aidos* and invites nemesis and punishment by the gods.[24] Man may be blinded by passion (*ate*), as when Agamemnon took Briseis,[25] and it was inevitable and just that such action would evoke the wrath of Achilles. But Achilles would not curb his anger or be moved by pity for the Achaeans even when Agamemnon extended apologies, compensation, and the return of Briseis and after his mentor Phoenix pointed out to him the folly of his distorted sentiments and appealed to his reason through the parable of Meleager.[26] The wrath of Achilles undergoes a qualitative change; it is no longer the momentary blindness of passion, but *hybris* which offends right order. As when he mistreats Hector's corpse, "his heart is set on cruelty . . . he has lost all pity . . . neither is shame in his heart."[27]

All men face death; the lot of Achilles was not unique. But it is ignorance of the future, the screen between choice and consequence, which normally makes life bearable. The gods know the future, but their world is timeless, and because of this, divine existence occasionally appears almost ludicrous. In the person of Achilles the problematic of human being, the dilemma of everyman, is accentuated, for he is forced to confront death as a concrete fact rather than an abstract end; like a god he knows the future, but like mortal he must suffer it. Every warrior knew upon entering battle that death might be imminent and that by retiring he might prolong his life; yet since the immortality of men lay properly in the everlasting fame of their deeds and accomplishments on earth rather than the eternal life reserved for the gods, they chose to fight despite the possibility of death.[28] But for Achilles death was more than a possibility if he fought beside the Achaeans; it was a certainty. His mother, the goddess Thetis, had revealed to him the consequences of his choices: to fight, die, and achieve imperishable reknown or to return home and enjoy a long life.

It is his obsession with this revelation and the fear of death which lead Achilles to pursue his wrath against Agamemnon and to ask Thetis to persuade Zeus to bring the Achaeans to the point of defeat so that he might intervene at the last moment and appear as their savior; he wanted

both fame and life. But his pride causes not only destruction for Agamemnon's forces but the death of his close friend Patroclus, and the shock
of this event restores his equilibrium. Faced with the ineluctable reality
of mortal life, he renounces his wrath and accepts the limitations appropriate to the sphere of men. Although from the point of view of the myth
the gods appear ultimately responsible for social disorganization, from
the standpoint of poetic symbolism they represent the inevitability of
disorder which accompanies the ailing character of men such as Achilles.
The message of the *Iliad* is tersely summarized in Zeus's speech in the
opening book of the *Odyssey*: "It vexes me to see how mean are these
creatures of a day towards us Gods, when they charge against us the evils
(far beyond our worst dooming) which their own exceeding wantonness
has heaped upon themselves."[29]

In discussing the idea of time in Homer it is necessary to distinguish
at least two levels for purposes of analysis; the sense of time and movement within the poem, and the extent to which Homer was aware of the
historical context of his composition. Some of these problems have already
been touched upon, such as Homer's consciousness of the distance between
the contemporary society and the Mycenaean past and the contrast
between timeless divine existence and the temporal world of mortals, but
several points require further elaboration.

The presentation of Achilles' character is not the revelation of a
static personality, but a progression in time; it is not simply a study
of alternate states of emotion in response to external situations, but a
continuous development, with each stage incomplete in itself and antici-
pating the next, interacting with the events of the Trojan war and constituting the time of the epic. Despite the geometric structure of the
poem the action is unintelligible apart from a temporal perspective.[30]
Given the complex structure of the *Iliad,* it would be credulous to assume
that Homer was naïve about the relation between past and present; the
apparent mingling of the dimensions is not evidence of unsophistication,
but rather a profound sense of time.

The "anachronisms" in Homer's description as well as the long
similes drawn from Ionic life serve to bring the action up to date and
to make it meaningful to the contemporary audience. But the similes
also fulfill an additional purpose: they explain an unfamiliar world in
terms of the known, and they provide a contrast between the Heroic past
and the non-Heroic present[31] which only occasionally is expressed in

more direct language: "the son of Tydeus grasped in his hands a stone—
a mighty deed—one that not two men could bear, such as mortals now
are."[32] It is significant that what superficially appear to be anachronisms
in Homer do not extend to places or characters; the Trojans and
Achaeans belong to the Mycenaean past. Homer does not create "the
illusion of an unchanging, a basically stable social order," nor can it be
asserted that "the existence of society poses no historical problem."[33]
Homer was eminently concerned with the decline of a political order
which formed the past of an emerging Hellenic civilization. A speech of
Hector encompasses the feeling of past, present, and future.

> And some one shall some day say even of men that are yet to be, as
> he saileth in his many benched ship over the wine-dark sea: "This
> is a barrow of a man that died in olden days, whom on a time in
> the midst of his prowess glorious Hector slew." So shall some man
> say, and my glory shall never die.[34]

The funeral of Hector with which the *Iliad* closes wraps the whole
epic in a decisive finality, and the inevitability of the death of Achilles
is all the more poignant in its understatement. But beyond the pathos
accompanying the passing of the heroes is that attending the destruction
of a city which had bound them together; the return of a part of order
to chaos. Homer's audience may have been the descendants of those
who stood victorious before Troy, but the tale of the leveling of the city
was calculated to evoke their empathy since the same experience belonged to the past of this audience whose ancestors had suffered the dissolution of social order after their return from Troy.

When turning from the *Iliad* to the *Odyssey* there is again no need
to broach the Homeric Question; regardless of the problem of unity of
authorship the latter work augurs the great intellectual revolution which
occurred in Hellas during the century after 750 and offers distinct contrasts with the *Iliad*. The emergence of Proto-Corinthian and Proto-
Attic pottery (720–680) testifies to a decisive break with Geometric
style and its restrained design; floral, animal, and human forms begin
to predominate, the patterns become curvilinear, the subjects become
more three-dimensional, and the sense of motion, which becomes a central
motif, is not expressed externally by sequence of scene, but is embodied
in the figures. During this period sculpture arose as an important and
independent medium, and the outlines of the human figure appear less

rigid; the eyes are open and the faces lifelike. But art was not "realistic" in an imitative sense; observation of the world resulted in a symbolic transformation in which the art form expressed the new reality. Meaning and structure were imposed on space by the mind just as the great Greek temples of this period enclosed and ordered a portion of infinite space and preserved it from chaos.[35]

Although still closer to the *Iliad* than to lyric poetry, the *Odyssey* bears the early imprint of these changes. In the *Odyssey*, the geometric design has all but disappeared, the use of simile is less frequent, divine intervention becomes rarer and less meaningful, and the individual appears more as an internally organized unity. The sense of time is more apparent both in the structure and content of the epic;[36] the successive scenes, stages in the advancement of the story, produce a linear effect, and in contrast to the sense of finality which Hector's death gave to the *Iliad*, the *Odyssey*, with Odysseus knowing Tiresias' prophecy, points to the future. This is part of the triumph of content over structure, of episode over total design, and the new concern with the immediacy of life, particular and unique events, and man's relation to the differentiated external world. Finally, while the *Iliad* might be characterized as a story of disorder, the *Odyssey* evidences growing concern with peace and the conditions of social order, community, and justice which is so apparent in Hesiod.

Hesiod and History

WHEN the mythical mode had been pressed to its limits through the art of the epic, it was followed by the autonomous enterprise of the drama; Homer stands halfway between myth and Aeschylean tragedy. But the myth formed not only the immediate material of emerging art forms but that of speculative thought as well, for "the highest development of which myth is capable is the exhibition of human life and cosmic order that epic poetry reveals" and which is "superseded by a discursive and more literal form of thought, namely philosophy."[37] The symbolic forms of art and philosophy are both built on the ground of the myth, and just as the *Iliad* is midway between myth and drama and demonstrates the conscious imposition of form on the material of the myth, the poems

of Hesiod reveal the application of rational speculation to the elements
of the myth and stand as a transitional medium bridging myth and
philosophy. The *Theogony* and the admonitory tale of the *Works and
Days* are "formed and governed by reason" and constitute an attempt
"to arrange all mythology into a comprehensive philosophical system."[38]

Like the artist who moves beyond the confines of the cultural canon,
it is in the consciousness of the individual, the theorist, that the vision of
order and disorder takes shape. It was Homer who created from the
quarry of mythic memory the past of Hellas and the story of the Mycenaean decline, and it was Thucydides, not Athens, who was conscious
of the meaning of the great *kinesis* and its origin and effect on society;
it was Hesiod who saw that order was the result of active conformance
with *dike*, and it was Plato who found in the soul a measure of the divine
cosmos. As with the Hebrew prophet, the vision of social order takes
place within the individual who suffers and gains knowledge amidst
disorder and projects the order he finds within himself onto the world.
In Hesiod the manipulation of traditional mythic elements is even more
apparent than in Homer;[39] the same process of individuation which
would mark the lyric poets is obvious. The "emergence of the subjective
is already clearly expressed."

> The myth is like an organism which undergoes incessant transforma-
> tion and renovation. The poet completes that transformation; but
> he does so not simply at his own whim. For it is he who creates a
> new life-pattern for his age, and he re-interprets the myth to harmo-
> nize with his knowledge of that pattern. . . . For in the *Theogony*
> and the *Erga* the poet's individuality appears without disguise, acts
> on his material, and uses mythology as the instrument of his own
> intellect and will.[40]

While the author of the *Iliad* is known principally through the traces
of individual artistry left on his work, Hesiod asserts his own individuality; the Muses "taught Hesiod glorious song," picked him from among
his fellow shepherds who were "mere bellies," and "breathed into him a
divine voice to celebrate things that shall be and things that were afore-
time."[41] He understands his historical position and opposes his knowledge to that of other men past and present, for the Muses "know how
to speak many false things as though they were true," but for him they
"utter true things";[42] he "is the first of the poets to regard himself as

a stranger among men . . . he looks upon himself as a special type of man, and his truth is of a special perfection," born of suffering, bestowed from on high, and inaccessible to others.[43] Like Thucydides, who sets his work off from the illusions of former times, Hesiod distinguishes his work. He is aware of the uniqueness of his existence in a present born of the past and the uncertainty of the future. In Hesiod injustice and disorder demand explanation, and his own suffering under his brother's mistreatment makes him painfully aware of his own individuality. Although Hesiod's anthropology does not penetrate the internal nature of man, who is still understood essentially in terms of his action, the consciousness of human time is articulated and creates the problem of human order and its theoretical foundation.

Hesiod's works are essentially aetiological and didactic in their concern. In the *Theogony* the Muses, the daughters of Mnemosyne, enlarge the vision of the poet and allow him to penetrate the origin of the present world order; utilizing mythic materials he develops an explanation comparable to the naturalistic speculations of the Milesians in their search for the *arche* which, with a casting off of mythic terminology, would be philosophy.[44] The kingship of Zeus is underpinned by a complex cosmogony which serves as a prelude to the consideration of the problem of human order. After the Titanomachia and the ascendancy of Zeus, the scene is set for a consideration of the determinants of social order and a moral universe; the old deities are not obliterated, but are incorporated in a new dispensation, and the "new world order gains strength by absorbing into itself such realities of a bygone era as deserve to survive because they will enrich and adorn the new civilization."[45] The chthonian order is displaced, not obliterated, but only by might could Zeus at first rule because the telluric forces continually threatened to reassert themselves against the Olympian regime.

The transition from cosmology to those deities involved with human society does not, as in Near Eastern mythology, serve to establish continuity between creation and a specific social order; the myth as an explanation and justification for human order has disappeared, and Hesiod's Zeus displaces mythic particularism and foreshadows the abstract and universal principles of order and justice of Greek philosophy. The marriages of Zeus and his offspring symbolize a progressive reduction of the world to harmony and order and the extension of this order to the earth and its inhabitants. The triumph of Zeus over deviant cosmic forces and his union with Themis (the symbol of eternal right), which produces "Eunomia (Order), Dike (Justice) and blooming Eirene (Peace), who mind the works of mortal men"[46] and mark off the spheres of the gods, set the stage for a consideration of the problem of justice. This account also provides a striking parallel with Hesiod's own sifting and rationalization of the mythic tradition which created a new vision of the nature and source of social order.

Whatever the actual chronological relationship between Hesiod's two poems, the Zeus of *Works and Days* presupposes the Zeus of the *Theogony*. If the *Theogony* constitutes rational speculation on the origin of cosmic order, the *Works and Days* is an explanation of human disorder. But what the latter poem signifies beyond this is of decisive importance. Although in the *Iliad* social disorder could be understood as deriving from the aberrant character of individuals, Homer was ambiguous on this score, especially with regard to ultimate causes. The *Odyssey* went further in absolving the gods of blame for social ills, and in Hesiod man and his world are further differentiated and assigned responsibility for their own well-being. Man has a choice between *hybris* and *dike,* and it is adherence to *dike* which enables him to partake of the transcendent order of Zeus. Injustice is not among the evils which Pandora loosed upon the world, but rather stems from human character, and the capacity for justice which distinguishes men from beasts is the source of order.[47]

Although human order and cosmic order are differentiated, what adds pathos to the picture of Hesiod's rebellion against an unjust society is that he, unlike Isaiah, cannot transcend society; it is because the individual and the social order are intimately bound and there is no solace in a life of the soul or conformance with justice beyond the political context that Hesiod wishes that he "had died before [the present generation] or been born afterwards." The interdependence of individuals is paramount since "he does mischief to himself who does mischief to another, and evil harms the plotter most." Hesiod is haunted by the fear that in the context of the unjust city he and his son will have to become unrighteous, for "it is a bad thing to be righteous—if indeed the unrighteous have the greater right."[48] And just as "a whole city suffers for a bad man," Hesiod intimates by the parable of the Hawk and the Nightingale, "a fable for princes who themselves understand," that in a society governed by the norm of "might makes right" the whole community is inevitably distorted, down to the character of the last individual.

Solon's speculations on justice and his call to action are essentially an elaboration of what is contained in Hesiod's poems except that there is a transference of the notion of justice explicitly to political life, and justice appears more often as an immanent law of society rather than an instrument of Zeus. The relation between act and consequence is more explicit, an immanent causality. But, as with Hesiod, it is the violation of justice which creates disorder, and injustice, either in the individual or in the character of the community, will contaminate the other. Disorder is the result of unrighteousness in the rulers and the ruled, *hybris*, or a lack of respect for the "awful foundations of justice, who is so well aware in her silence of what is and what hath been, and soon or late cometh alway to avenge."[49]

Ostensibly, the *Works and Days* is a speech, supported by the illustrative fables of Pandora, the Five Ages, and the Hawk and the Nightingale, in which Hesiod, in a series of exhortations, admonishes his brother Perses to refrain from greed, violence, and deceit and to pursue hard work and follow good Eris in order to conform to the ordinance of Zeus who has provided justice as the way for men. Prosperity depends on conformance with *dike,* for Zeus greets those who stray with retribution.[50] But in the course of this exhortation to Perses, the idea of the failure to follow *dike* develops into a universal theory of disorder as well as explanation of the present degraded state of society. The three fables satisfy both of these purposes; they are exemplary moral tales, such as the legend of Meleager which Phoenix related to Achilles, which constitute a prescription for action, but they also provide an explanation, couched in mythical terms, of the contemporary world. But beyond the aetiological function and the lesson that rebellion against the order of Zeus results in misery, the tales serve to illuminate the nature of the human condition, which is irrevocably severed from the world of gods and the primordial paradise, and to demonstrate an awareness of the past course of human events and the dimension of the future. In this regard, an understanding of the Myth of the Ages is indispensable.

Mythic genealogies are not historical, that is, concerned with the exploration of the past; neither are they aetiological since the events which are described do not explain the present in terms of the past, but illuminate the conditions of the timeless present by a reference to the primordial archetype. Although Hesiod utilizes the elements of the myth, his vision is not mythic; myth serves only to metaphorically elaborate the cause of the present disorder. But beyond this, he attempts a rational construction of the past by which he differentiates man historically.

It is necessary to dispose of the prevalent notion that the Myth of the Ages and the races of gold, silver, bronze, heroes, and iron constitute a cyclical theory which "reflects myths about the pattern of history already old among the Greeks" and is part of a tradition stretching from the ancient world to Hegel.[51] Even if it could be convincingly argued that his symbol of the metals is oriental in origin, it is not apparent that Hesiod's construction is inspired by the idea of a cycle, and any attempt to read a cyclical pattern into the myth remains questionable, especially with the problem of discontinuity which the "nobler and more righteous" race of heroes presents.[52] A theme of the four ages may have been present in mythology before Hesiod and accessible to him, but even if he relied on such a theme, he modified it to fit the purposes of his exposition. Hesiod deals with races of men, not ages of the world, and the purpose is not to tell about revolutions of the cosmos, but to impart a moral teaching. Yet the existence of a pattern is too obvious to be dismissed as meaningless, and it conforms to the Greek experience of decline which was already prominent in Homer.[53] Hesiod explicitly states that after the disappearance of the golden race the gods created "a second generation which was of silver and less noble by far" and of "second order" and that the third race, the men of bronze, were "in no way equal to the silver age."[54] The pitiable iron race is clearly inferior to the men of bronze, but the intrusion of the heroic race appears to mar the pattern. It could be argued that the heroes mark the point of demarcation between the realms of myth and history,[55] but although this interpretation admittedly solves the problems of discontinuity, it accepts the unnecessary assumption that there actually is such a problem to be solved. It would seem that at least part of the tale has a greater significance than a mere parable such as the Hawk and the Nightingale; the heroes and the iron race were drawn from historical memory and Hesiod's conception of the contemporary world. But it is reasonable to assume that historical memory extended beyond the late Mycenaean age; even at the time of Plato, tradition preserved knowledge of the Minoan civilization as well as the Near Eastern cultures and their relation to the Hellenic past, and during the period in which Hesiod's poems were composed there was renewed contact with the Orient. There is little basis for the hypothesis that the first two races are mythical while the latter two constitute an attempt to elucidate the historical past. Instead it would seem that the *Theogony* and *Works and Days* are parallel enterprises: one is an attempt to systematize knowledge of the gods and the cosmos, while the other is an anthropic speculation which endeavors to explore the human past.

Hesiod's statement that he will demonstrate that gods and mortals "sprang from one source"[56] means simply that both are encompassed within the cosmos and serves to establish the continuity between god and man and the dependence of the latter on the former. The vision of a golden age when men lived like gods was a persistent mythological theme before Hesiod, and its introduction into the poem not only reinforces the message of the Pandora fable and emphasizes the extent to which the passage of time has alienated man from the divine but has meaning in terms of an attempt to reconstruct the past of the Greeks. There is little reason to assume that all five ages are not part of an attempt to reconstruct this past. Since in the introduction to the tale Hesiod instructs Perses to "lay it up in his heart," the tale has the same didactic purpose as the Pandora fable. But the two stories are contradictory, and if the second reiterates a message essentially present within the first—to wit, how men once lived free from troubles—its inclusion was unnecessary unless it represented an attempt to organize knowledge of the past and render it intelligible in terms of the truth of existence discovered by the poet.

The image of history presented to Hesiod was one of degeneration and estrangement from the divine which resulted in disrespect for the gods, disobedience, and excessive violence. The introduction of the two Erides, between which one may choose, frames the history and provides a dialectic within which the course of human events moves; human time actually appears to be generated by nonconformance with cosmic order and the dictates of justice. Even if the scheme of the four metals was derived from an early mythological tradition, it was adapted by the poet's imagination to fit the purpose of the tale, and if this is true the inclusion of the race of heroes should not present a problem since the Homeric age was too well known to have been omitted.[57] The sequence as a whole depicts a process of degeneration, and there is no reason to assume that Hesiod would have been constrained to present an absolutely continuous sequence of decline.

The four metals may have served the poet simply as a device to demarcate the epochs of the past, but if this were the case, the nonmetallic race of heroes would again emerge as a problem. It has been suggested that the bronze age and the age of heroes are identical and merely signify the difference in the view of the past held by the common man and the aristocrat.[58] But archaeological evidence indicates that the "scheme takes its meaning from the use of metals and arises from tradition concerning the origins of their uses."[59] Hesiod says of the bronze age that "there was no black iron,"[60] and the iron age, which extended into the present, corresponds to the archaeological Iron Age which emerged after the collapse of the Mycenaean world; the first metallurgical advances were made in Egypt and Mesopotamia, and the races of the gold and silver may be drawn from what was known of the civilization of the Orient and Crete. The absence of a metal to designate the race of heroes may be explained by the fact that they belonged to the late Bronze Age, but those who had done such great deeds and had traveled "over the great sea gulf of Troy for rich-haired Helen's sake" demanded to be set apart from their forebears. Hesiod could scarcely have missed the manifold references to bronze in the *Iliad*. If the last three races may be understood as within the purview of historical memory, it is reasonable to assume that the races of gold and silver were an attempt to reconstruct the remote past insofar as it was accessible to the poet; if writing did not appear in Hellas until approximately the time of Homer, the world which extended in time beyond Mycenae marked the outer limits of speculation on the past and receded into fantasy.

There are also certain literary characteristics of the tale which tend to distinguish it from myth and fable and identify it with an early attempt at historiography. There is no real continuity between the races as in a mythical genealogy in which there is a "lasting efficacy of original ancestors," and time is presented as "a succession of epochs" with terminations and new beginnings. Unlike myth, the future is open and there is no real beginning or end. Such phrases as "Zeus made" or the "earth covered" may be simply metaphors announcing the beginning or end of an epoch.[61]

"For now truly is a race of iron," says Hesiod of the present. But his vision extends into the future; although the present generation "shall have some good mingled with their evils," Hesiod warns that "Zeus will destroy this race of mortal men." Like the prophets, he describes a future political order from which justice has disappeared and in which disorder reigns when "Aidos and Nemesis . . . go from the wide-pathed earth and forsake mankind." The possibility of this future reality is metaphorically presented in the "fable for princes"—the Hawk and the Nightingale. This is a fable for princes because they know that they hold the power and may use it violently, like the Hawk, if they choose, but this is the nature of bestial relations where justice is not meaningful. He warns Perses to pursue justice and spurn violence, for "Justice beats Outrage when she comes at length to the end of the race." He expands these paradigms of individual conduct into the vision of two cities: one which flourishes and enjoys peace and the other which is characterized by violence and disorder and is punished by Zeus.[62] Finally, he admonishes the princes once more, after which he launches on another extended exhortation to Perses, culminating in the charge to "work with work upon work."[63]

In Hesiod, history was not disengaged from the myth as an independent form, but the consciousness of human time had been articulated as far as was possible within the limits of mythic symbols. Beyond Hesiod the myth could no longer contain the idea of which it was the vehicle, and the vision of order and disorder and the course of society in time found new expression.

The Isolation of the Self: The Ground of Vision

As the Greeks began to discover the dimension of the self, they became more aware of existence in time, but it was within this dimension that they were to find a measure of the divine which endured beneath the flux of time and provided the foundation for a new vision of social order which would heal the gap between man and being created by the dissolution of the myth. But the discovery of the self was not a descent into subjectivity; even the lyric poets tended to view themselves *sub specie aeternitatis*. Despite the upsurgence of individual feeling in the lyric and the revelation of the individual in the artist's conscious creative mastery over his material, Greek art, like oriental art, suppresses personality, and "man, privileged as his figure may be, remains an object in Nature and a thing in the cosmos, subordinate to the perfection and divinity of the universality of Things."[64] The discovery of the self was more an awareness of separateness and differentiation from society and nature than an exploration of the depths of interiority which characterized the Hebrew experience and, later, Christianity, but as the self "realizes that it is a separate world opposed to the external law, it discovers its own inner laws."[65]

It is the experience of change and instability and the spectacle of death and despair of old age which isolate the self, accentuate the tenuousness of existence, and engender the pessimism of Mimnermus and Simonides; repeating Homer, they note that "the life of man is even as the life of a green leaf."[66] It is this sentiment which not only spurs them to assert their autonomy, expose their feelings, and render personal judgments but leads them to seek for a dimension of life beneath the flux in which "all things come at last to the same horrible charybdis" and where for each man "a death hangs over him that will not be escaped, in which good men, and bad men must share alike."[67]

It is through the process of individuation that the problem of time is encountered, for "the more freely and consciously men learn to guide their own thoughts and actions, the more inevitably they are brought face to face with the problem of destiny."[68] The response of the lyricists was the acceptance of suffering and the will to endure, confident in the belief that beyond the chaos of unique events and the inexplicable forces of fate and change life was bound by an ultimate "rhythm";[69] thought could penetrate beneath flux and appearance, which formed the superstructure of existence, to a deeper reality. Their attitude was not resignation, but a growing realism. Invocations to the Muses were a mockery of Homer and Hesiod; a new sense of individualism was challenging myth.[70] The poets of the seventh and sixth centuries were revolting, in terms of both form and content, against the past and claiming the right to advise society; just as the artists broke loose from the geometric form, the poets called into question the Homeric values and moved beyond the oral tradition by establishing new meters expressing individual style in their writings. The significance of this transition from an oral tradition to literacy must be stressed; for literacy, by making poetry the property of the poet rather than society, accentuated individuation and emphasized the break with the past. Also the medium of writing began to effect a new orientation toward time. Literacy disrupts the world of the collective mind and the sense of immediacy in other modes of communication and contributes to the temporal differentiation of the self. "The development of writing and the visual organization of life made possible the discovery of individualism, introspection and so on."[71] This manifestation of individualism in the lyric and the deepening sense of the self as an internal center of motivation did not immediately produce a theory of order, but it contributed to the understanding of disorder and the consciousness of the historical character of society and the relation beween the individual and society.

The identity of the individual and the polis was an integral part of Greek culture, and when the values of the polis were challenged by the theorist there was not a rejection of this identity, but rather a transformation of the meaning of the identity. Even with Tyrtaeus, the beginning of the differentiation of virtue is evident; it is no longer simply great deeds but specifically courage in the service of the state that wins a man immortal fame which is worthy of preservation in the polis.

In the elegiac poems of Callinus and Tyrtaeus the homology between the individual and the polis is apparent, and what is permanent in man is, as with Homer, his ability to achieve immortality through action and fame. Tyrtaeus argues that for him who dies in battle "his grave and his children are conspicuous among men . . . nor even doth his name and good fame perish, but though he be underground he liveth evermore."[72] But he is turning against the agonal culture and its emphasis on the individual alone by depreciating those virtues which were important for the Homeric hero, such as individual prowess, persuasive ability, and speed in the race by which a man could gain fame among men; *arete* is personal excellence, but only excellence demonstrated in battle in support of the state. Also, although he appears to be speaking as the voice of the people of the community, it is apparent from his appeal that the citizens are not always wont to believe that " 'tis a fair thing for a good man to fall and die fighting in the van for his native land . . . making Life his enemy and the black Spirits of Death dear as the rays of the sun"; his appeal may not have been sympathetically received.[73]

For Tyrtaeus, what creates and preserves political order is the infusion of courage in the citizens; his concern is political order and its correspondence with the immortality of the individual, although it is still through an appeal to individual striving that he hopes to instill *arete*. In one sense the promise of immortality is an incentive like the promise of fame within the city should the warrior survive.[74] Yet it is more than a patriotic speech, for what is permanent in man and what, when political action is organized in accordance with it, provides for the stability of the

city and common good are the same. Courage is the ordering virtue, and
there is a symbiotic relationship between political order and man's
search for permanence. Tyrtaeus found Achillean virtue inadequate as
an ordering principle since the fame of the individual was often at odds
with the preservation of social order. As long as personal achievement
and virtue not only remained unrelated to political order but tended to
be divisive in their effects, there was little hope of creating a home for
man in the world. By linking what was permanent in man—his ability
to achieve fame—not to the remembrance of "men" but to the memory
of the polis the maintenance of order was possible.

Solon, even more than the lyric poets in whom there is still ambiguity
between self-expression and self-awareness, engages in conscious reflection on the uniqueness of his existence and his relation to society and
reflects on the course of life, his accomplishments, his hopes and failures.
He tends to couch his observations in concrete terms related to his own
experience, rather than in gnomic fashion, and he not only views himself
as the center of moral decision but emphasizes that interdependence of
each individual and the political order as a whole which was implicit
in Hesiod.[75]

> Though the individual who detaches himself from his environment
> severs many old bonds, his discovery of the dimension of the soul
> once more joins him in company with those who have fought their
> way to the same insight. The isolation of the individual is, by the
> same token, the forging of new bonds.
> . . . .
> Cognizance of individuality and the communal establishment of the
> polis are contemporary events.[76]

It was in the capacity for justice that Solon found a link between
man's search for permanence and the hope of realizing it in political
order. Foreseeing the destructive tendency of the old morality, he sought
to substitute justice for the individualistic idea of *arete* as the ordering
virtue for the community. A culture which extols the search for individual
fame is destructive of political order and progressively leads to rule by
one man. Solon rejected the fame and power of tyranny to prove his
point; individual achievement is not his understanding of how to "surpass
the world."[77] Virtue could not be exchanged for wealth or fame. Solon

did not reject the old virtues, but saw the necessity of ordering them in accordance with a new understanding of man; *arete* was defined in terms of neither wealth nor power, but as the exercise of justice or communal virtue. The avarice of both the aristocrats and the commons, "pride and love of pelf," was the reason that "the oldest land of Ionia is being slain." It was these ills which he attempted to correct by fitting together "right and might" and making "straight justice for each man."[78]

It was the competitive spirit springing from the aristocracy and translated into the greed of the commons that Solon saw as tearing the polis apart. Order was the requirement, but while Tyrtaeus sought to construct external order on the basis of the desire for individual achievement and found permanence in the very existence of the state, Solon accepted the state as a datum, but directed his appeal internally as well as externally by calling for a new type of citizen who was motivated by a concern for the community. The norm of justice could be realized only in the space of the polis where there was a reciprocity between the individual and the city; *dike* is the permanent law of the universe of which man may partake by participation in the polis. *Arete* is meaningful only to the extent that it becomes realizable in the law and institutions of the city.

The ideas of permanence and immortality were never disjoined from the idea of the polis in the Greek vision of order, but the hope of immortalizing through the performance of great deeds was becoming an anachronism in a culture where personal achievement was no longer the prerogative of the nobility and the futility of competitive values as the guarantor of stability was becoming continually more apparent. As early as the late sixth century the aristocratic protest of Theognis that the rewards of wealth are ephemeral while "the great fame of valour will never perish, for a man-at-arms saveth both soul and city" strikes a hollow note, for it is a time when "respect for Right perished among men, whereas Shamelessness walketh to and fro upon the earth."[79] Manifold references to the prosperity of the wicked, the striving for material gain, the inscrutability of fortune, perplexity before the gods, and the pain of penury reveal an overwhelming pessimism which leads the poet to conclude the "the best lot of all for man is never to have been born."[80] Although he finds the faith to endure in the belief that suffering is the lot of man and that *hybris* which has authored social chaos will effect its own destruction, his poems attest to the failure of the agonal morality to maintain order and the inability to link *agathos* and *arete* with justice."[81]

The work of Theognis signals the passing of the old *arete* which was preserved only in Pindar, whose songs, in content and form, cling to a past in which an Olympian and earthly nobility shine with the beauty of an unproblematical excellence. Often, as with some of the lyric poets, the breakdown of the old *aretai* led to despair with regard to finding a measure of permanence in man, and consequently they embraced personal withdrawal and turned from the problem of social order toward a passionate savoring of transitory experience. But the search for a principle of order in the face of the disintegrating structure of divine and mortal society continued.

The experience of the transcendent took place not in the culture of the polis, but in the vision of the theorist who opposed his truth to that of society and set forth his discovery in the form of an appeal to the polis. For Tyrtaeus, man could capture, to some degree, the everlastingness of the universe by valorous deeds dedicated to and preserved in the man-made cosmos. But this is no longer the achievement of the Homeric hero or the aristocratic competition of the games. Man is defined or immortalized not by action which appears godlike in its disregard of death, but by deeds that contribute to the preservation of the state. With Solon there was the belief that the state could be structured to conform to a truth of order grasped by the mind, that justice could be externalized in society; conformance with justice superseded the idea of individual action as an ordering force. Finally with the Xenophanean and Heraclitean revelation of immutable wisdom as the virtue which links man with transcendent and divine order, mind itself becomes the source of the permanent.

Like Hesiod, Xenophanes opposed his truth to that of society and tradition, and even more than the lyricists, his contemporaries, he emerges from his poems as a distinct and autonomous individual. While the Ionians disengaged cosmology from the myth and substituted philosophic discourse and symbols drawn from the natural world, Xenophanes proclaimed his *sophie* as a substitute for the old values, "for my craft is better than the strength of men or of horses . . . it is not these that will give a City-State a better constitution."[82] Xenophanes appeals to society to replace the old *arete* with wisdom. The work of Xenophanes constituted an "intellectual revolution," for "he made the world of the myth a focal point for his opposition" just as the Milesians must have viewed their ideas "as patently antithetical" to the myth.[83] "Myth" was becoming a negative term almost equivalent to "untruth," and Xenophanes' attack strikes deeper than the apparent opposition of his conception of god to the Olympian dynasty. When he states that "from the beginning all have learnt in accordance with Homer" he is decrying more than the immoral content of mythical tales, that is, more than the fact that "both Homer and Hesiod have attributed to the gods all things that are shameful and a reproach among mankind."[84] He is advancing a new vision against the grotesque fictions of the past, the introduction of philosophy as a source of knowledge, and the substitution of truth for the opinion of the myth.

Just as Homer's manipulation of the myth created art as a conscious activity, the speculative advance of Xenophanes transcended the myth and created philosophy as a new symbolic form. Wisdom is no longer a gift from the Muses, and men only by "longseeking discover what is better"; Xenophanes was still wandering in search of *sophie* in his ninety-second year. The penetration of appearance and the illumination of being in the logos is precarious, for "as for certain truth, no man has seen it . . . and Opinion is fixed by fate upon all things."[85] For Xenophanes the ground of being is god or the "one" which, unlike the mythic genealogies, is not a primordial creator, but, like the monadic substance of the physicists, has neither beginning or end; like the *apeiron* of Anaximander, god is infinite and encompasses all.[86] But unlike the early pre-Socratics the "one" was divine and was no longer designated as *arche* which, like *physis,* still carried the mythic connotation of "beginning."[87]

Xenophanes' attack on the myth was more than a question of epistemology; the theorist was setting himself against the very foundation of contemporary society and its education and advocating a new idea of man and society and their relation to the cosmos. By deprecating the fact that all men had "learnt in accordance with Homer" he was indicting the social style of contemporary polis life and subverting the epic values in terms of which society organized itself; it was implicitly an order founded on appearance, opinion, and untruth. Through his new articulation of divinity—that is, that god was not created by birth and did not possess the voice and garb of men—he was not so much concerned with advancing religion as differentiating still further than his predecessors the nature of man. Here there appeared for the first time the idea that the psyche was divine and that mind was the motivating force of *kosmos*. God "sets everything in motion by the thought of his mind," and it is through wisdom and thought that man and society participate in divine cosmic order.[88] "Men gradually succeeded in depriving the gods of their power over the natural world and claiming it for themselves, for they discovered that the human mind was itself divine."[89]

The purpose here is not to explore the genesis of Plato's philosophy, but to illuminate that experience through which the individual was faced with the burden of mortality and the problem of the rise and fall of social order. Through the process of individuation, the theorist begins to seek within himself for a source of order, and the discovery that the soul belonged to, or participated in, that which was everlasting provided the prerequisite for the speculative advance whereby the order of the soul was projected into society and the universe and the order observed in society and the universe was internalized. It is this turning inward which is so evident in the thought of Heraclitus.

When Heraclitus states that "human nature has no power of understanding but the divine nature has," he means not only that mind belongs to a higher order but that he, the philosopher, is only the vehicle for the manifestation of the logos.[90] Although "the thinking faculty is common to all," others are like sleepwalkers or are unaware of what they are doing after they awake; others "believe the people's bards" and "pray to statues of the gods that do not hear them" and are deaf to the sound of the divine which he, like the Hebrew prophets, hears.[91] Since "nature likes to hide . . . men who love wisdom must be inquirers into many things," but although the senses are the threshold of knowledge, they "are bad witness to men if they have souls that understand not the language"; he ridicules Homer and Hesiod and opposes his internal vision to the "much learning" of his predecessors, for such knowledge "does not teach one to have intelligence; for it would have taught Hesiod and Pythagoras, and again, Xenophanes and Hecataeus."[92]

Here again is the image of the theorist as the carrier of a truth in opposition to society. Like Parmenides he is concerned with the Way to knowledge: "I searched into myself." Within the soul there is a measure of the divine "One" which "steers all things through all things," and although there is a limit to the depth of human understanding, since man is halfway between god and beast, the search of the soul reveals the logos which in turn reveals the meaning of the "ordered cosmos, which is the same for all, and was not created by any one of the gods or of mankind, but it was over and is and shall be everlasting Fire, kindled in measure and quenched in measure."[93] This image of the eternal cosmos evokes the idea of the circle; there "beginning and end are common."[94] Beneath the appearance of flux, the divine and measured rhythm of the logos holds the universe in tight proportion.[95]

As with the vision of the integral myth, it is impossible to penetrate to the origin of the idea of order; whether the idea is an archetype flowing from the unconscious and manifesting itself in changing symbolic forms, a projection of the order discovered in society onto the cosmos at large, an internalization of the order discovered in the physical world, or a combination of these remains a mystery. But when the idea of order and its transcendental source takes shape within the individual, it is inevitable that the existential order of society will be measured against it. The rise and fall of political order contrasts with the vision of the everlasting cosmos, and the "character" or ethos of society, as well as that of the individual, is its destiny.[96] The discovery of the truth of order becomes a prescription, and it is one step from Heraclitus to political philosophy and the Platonic response to the spectacle of the alienation of the spirit in fifth-century Athens. The regularity of the cosmic movement becomes a standard for judging the irregular course of human events; for the cosmologist, history is chaos.

Aeschylus: Art and Society

THIS new dimension of the mind and the consciousness of human time also found symbolic expression in Athenian dramatic art. In the Homeric epic, manipulation of mythic elements constituted the triumph of the creative impulse of the individual artist over the collective experience of the social myth; yet art still moved partially within the confines of mythic reality. Tragedy also had its roots in the collective experience of the group, the cultic worship of Dionysus,[97] but in the mature drama the break with the myth is complete and a new conception of reality emerges. This new reality is observable from two perspectives: it is apparent not only in the content of the drama but in the fact of its creation, for it was one of those moments when "the creative principle had its home no longer in the symbolism of a cultural canon, but in the individual."[98]

In the developed form of the drama, the ties between myth and reality are severed, since the myth which is enacted, once it is detached from the ritual situation, is no longer related to the present. But the disembodied myth does not revert to the presentation of past reality as in the epic. It becomes a medium for the creative imagination of the poet and the symbolic expression of the new reality of the universal drama of the soul. Art, as an autonomous symbolic form, is not the representation of reality, but carries a significance of its own and in this way creates its own reality; drama symbolically creates the illusion of reality, and myth itself is unimportant except as it is manipulated by the poet and transformed into a timeless expression of the life of the soul. Tragedy is literally *poiesis;* there is no pretension that it is a true story, although it gains part of its power by its reference to collective memory.

Although the lyricists had emphasized the internal side of man and his feelings and judgments as opposed to external values, they did not delve into the problem of "human action and its motivation in particular" which was the concern of the tragedian.[99] But again it is necessary to be cautious with the Greek notion of the self. Although "as man becomes increasingly conscious of his selfhood, he tends to consider his own will and reason independent of higher powers,"[100] classical tragedy was not the study of the subjectivity of the tragic hero which has characterized drama from Shakespeare to the present and which modern criticism often reads into it. "Tragedy," as Aristotle says, "is imitation not of persons but of action and life," and "character in a play is that which reveals the moral purpose of the agents."[101]

Even less than the epic was the tragedy a study of the personality of the hero; tragedy universalized the particularity of the epic tale and presented the dilemma of choice writ large in an attempt to give form and meaning to the world of action. The autonomous self emerged as the center of decision, but it was a paradigmatic self constituted by its action, not a progressive revelation of a unique personality; the audience did not identify as much with the hero as with the inner reality of the situation and the probability and necessity of the outcome, and, unlike the epic, it is the situation and not the individual which is extraordinary.

The tragic mask revealed only status and sex and served to obliterate personality and render the action archetypal;[102] this is the sense in which "poetry is something more philosophic and of graver impact than history, since its statements are of the nature rather of universals, whereas those of history are singulars."[103] With Aeschylus, the structure of the drama and problems such as the relation of *dike* to *hybris* rather than character development and personal relationships are emphasized; physical background and individual characters give way to the presentation of fundamental laws of human action and the condition of man. Tragedy was the unmasking of being, and to this end it was more "constructive" than "representational."[104]

The existence of the fragments of an Achillean trilogy attributed to Aeschylus allows a tentative comparison of his treatment of Achilles with that of Homer and a contrast between the emerging self-awareness of man in the *Iliad* and the more differentiated self of the tragedy.[105] In the *Iliad* the wrath of Achilles descends upon him and blinds him, but in the first play of the Aeschylean trilogy, the *Myrmidons*, his refusal to aid the Achaeans is truly a premeditated act based on a genuine personal decision for which he consciously takes responsibility. Not only is his action based on a reasoned decision, but when his followers rise against him in the name of legal right and threaten to stone him (the punishment for a deserter), he persists in this course of action partly from *hybris* and partly from the demand of conscience, although entirely aware of consequences. The alternatives are stressed and purposely drawn out into a paradigm of the tragic dilemma of the isolated and responsible individual severed from divine control and caught in an ambiguous world, like Antigone and Prometheus, between questionable but defensible internal and external demands. The old norm of "do good to friends and evil to enemies" no longer holds, for action, as in the case of Socrates, proceeds from internal choice rather than from the values of society and the approval and disapproval issuing from others. The law of the polity may conflict with the principle of right discovered by the individual soul; the confrontation of the noblest of the Greeks and the nobility of the law creates an impasse. And it is personal guilt and anguish, not shame, which finally cause Achilles to forsake his wrath after the death of Patroclus and choose death in battle. A decision in accordance with *dike* comes from the depths of the soul.

In *Prometheus Bound*, the "blood-red eagle" which comes daily to

devour the Titan's flesh serves the same symbolic purpose as the threat
of stoning against Achilles; it affirms the conscious and deliberate nature
of his decision not to yield to the legal but harsh demands of Zeus.[106]
Prometheus, like Achilles, has transgressed for a principle which goes
beyond the letter of the law that supports Zeus's intemperate response.
The point of departure in all of Aeschylus' tragedies is an excessive
insistence by two parties on a personal conception of right in violation
of *sophrosyne*. Only a return to moderation stabilizes *dike* and restores
equilibrium and right order to society and the universe. Both Zeus and
Prometheus stand within the cosmos, and the plight of the Titan puts
the world out of joint; the whole of nature groans from his agony.[107]
Through suffering, both Prometheus and Zeus will become temperate;
intelligence and power will eventually be reconciled, and Zeus will become
allied with fundamental right order and the powers of fate and necessity.
Through suffering, the individual gains knowledge of humility. The
reality of the soul as the ground of action and history was the discovery
of tragedy, and the evolution of tragedy was the progressive illumination
of this ground.

Tragedy grew out of the experience of human time, and in turn it
was in the drama that the Greek vision of political order began to take
shape. It is from the discovery of the autonomous psyche and the relation
between "forethought," decision, action, and consequence that the experience of history emerges. "Tragedy was the first type of poetry to
apply to the mythical tradition a regular structural principle—the conception of the inevitable rise and fall of human destiny," and the source
of this rise and fall was the degree of conformance of the soul and society
with the ordinance of *dike*. The Greek idea of history first took shape
in the art of the drama and remained bound to it.[108] There is no doubt
that the *Prometheia* and the *Oresteia*, respectively, symbolically chronicle
the appearance of a new world order and the rise of the city-state with its
immanentization of justice where "part and present are struggling toward
reconciliation."[109] These are events which belong to historical memory,
but beyond this, the drama penetrates to the problem of social order
in history.

While the gods of Homer moved in that twilight between symbol
and reality, the deities of Aeschylus are clearly subservient to the imagination of the poet. The parallel action between the gods and man, as in
the *Oresteia*, supplies tragedy with a dimension of universality which

transcends the action; the actions of mortals are not derived from the sphere of the divine. The deities symbolically frame the play as cosmic law frames all human action and provide a background which endows the unique with significance. The audience knows that the problem is not simply whether Orestes was justified in murdering his mother to avenge Agamemnon but whether the demands of political order represented by Apollo and Athena outweigh the demands of blood retribution represented by the Furies.

The tension in the *Prometheia* is between the idea of an order based on power and one based on justice, between a Zeus who rules by force and a Zeus who rules in accordance with justice. As in Hesiod, the gods are not eternal, but came into being and persist within the order of the cosmos; just as Hesiod's Zeus made numerous marriages to bind his rule to a higher conception of right order, the domain of Zeus in the *Prometheia* is unstable until his rule coincides with justice. Prometheus, when bound to the rock by Zeus, could still appeal to nature to relive his suffering.[110] The Zeus of *Prometheus Bound* is the Zeus of the *Theogony* who represents the new king of heaven who had just deposed his father and rules like a tyrant with the aid of Kratos and Bia (Might and Force who bind Prometheus to the rock). His rule is far from solidified, and he faces the vague threat, veiled in the secret concealed by the Titan, that he also will be deposed; "conquerors all are hard in the early days" and forget pity.[111]

There is no question that Prometheus is, from the first, guilty of *hybris* and undue stubbornness and that he defied the ban of Zeus, but although order and authority always possess positive value, his punishment is too severe a reward for his love of man, and Zeus is stubbornly beyond persuasion.[112] Order cannot be sustained by tyranny, lust, and retribution, which serve only to perpetuate the chain of violent insurrection and increasingly harsh regimes which hitherto had characterized the generations of the gods. Only when Zeus aligned himself with right order and took *dike* as his aide, rather than Kratos and Bia, could his rule become stable and transcend the impermanence and fear which had characterized the reigns of Uranus and Cronus, the doom to which Prometheus holds the secret. From the seed of Zeus will spring his own destruction, the retribution of the unforgetting Erinyes, in the form of his son, unless he brings his reign into accord with moderation and right order and makes justice his ally.

Prometheus' gift to man is actually a subordinate theme in the *Prometheia,* but in the *Oresteia* this gift becomes the solution to the problem of human order. The gift was not merely fire but the arts of civilization, *techne,* and above all a "living mind" and "new mastery of thought"[113]—the gift of reason. And for pitiful mortal creatures, things of "no avail" that "perish in a day,"[114] this divine gift meant the possibility of participation in the everlasting order of the cosmos; if *techne* could be harnessed to justice, through wisdom, man could, in some measure, transcend his uncertain condition. Prometheus charges that out of love and pity he had aided man and prevented him from being "cast to nothingness." Zeus, on coming to power, had treated men and gods unequally; for the Olympians he had allotted each god his place, but for man he had created no dispensation.[115] Political order was to be the dispensation of man.

The *Prometheia* symbolically recreates the evolution of the idea of justice and the conception of a moral universe with which the trilogy inevitably must end and which provides an archetype with which human society might align itself. In the *Agamemnon* the messengers of justice are the Erinyes, those daughters of night who relentlessly pursue blind retribution. Justice is not yet linked to the polis, but to that rhythm whereby *dike* eventually outruns *hybris* and society persists in that endless pattern of personal revenge which characterized the cycle of deposition and ascendancy on Olympus. In his new wisdom Zeus knows that man also must learn by suffering.

The central characters of the *Agamemnon* vainly search for the achievement of a stable order, but the goal must remain unrealized in a society where *dike* is accomplished only by revenge. This pattern engulfs each generation and, as in Hesiod, it appears that history is actually generated by injustice—in this case the endless and geometrically increasing chain of vengeance with horrors augmented by horrors. The original sin which precipitated this progression of blood feuds recedes beyond memory, but it is Paris' indiscretion which sends Agamemnon to Troy to reclaim a promiscuous wanton; even to Homer such a war was in a sense as preposterous as it was great, and Agamemnon's sacrifice of his daughter to appease the winds so that he might reach Troy, followed by the slaughter of Greeks and Trojans, already twists the relation between crime and punishment out of proportion. But just as Agamemnon was the instrument of *dike* in punishing Paris and hubristically exceeded his mandate, Clytemnestra becomes the medium of the king's downfall and ostensibly murders him in the name of their daughter. But, again, what is in one sense justice is also the operation of guilt and passion spurring the adulterous queen. Also Aegisthus, who justifies his action on the basis of what Agamemnon's father has done to his father and brothers, proceeds to add the final touch to this cumulative burden of injustice by cuckolding the king, acting as an accessory in his murder, exiling his son, and coveting his throne. Disordered souls reap only disorder, and the need for stability and release from this chaotic social structure makes the tension unbearable.

The opening of the *Choephori* hints that the chain may be broken, for Orestes and Electra are pursuing their task of revenge not with guilt or *hybris,* but from the necessity of honor. Yet there appears, even here, to be no escape from the ever-increasing enormity of the crimes as long as the family exists, for Orestes, to serve justice, must commit matricide and wait until vengeance is in turn visited against himself. But in the last play of the trilogy, the *Eumenides,* the polis emerges as the means of reconciling the necessity of justice with the demands of social stability; the polis becomes a "fortress" which for the first time provides "true judgment o'er spilt blood" and mediates between Themis and the individual and breaks the family curse and the link between revenge and guilt.[116]

Clytemnestra's fates pursue Orestes, but, guided by Apollo, he asks Athena for asylum, and the band of Furies, which "apportions well their fated burdens to mankind," agree that the guilt of Orestes shall be decided by the goddess. The value of political order upheld by Apollo, the symbol of Olympian order who supports Orestes, and the law of swift *dike* symbolized by Clytemnestra's fates, who "have their portion in the orb of Right and Eternal," are in conflict.[117] But both claims are valid. *Dike* must accommodate itself to the demands of order, but society must hitherto organize itself in accordance with justice, a reconciliation of *dike* and *nomos.* This had been the lesson of suffering, and this is in effect Athena's, divine wisdom's, answer when she defers judgment and creates the Areopagus and the jury of citizens as the "new rule" and "law for ever," for here the conflict is resolved because those who render judgments and punish are impartial with no "transgression" in their hearts. Orestes is acquitted, reason and persuasion become the instruments of justice, and the Erinyes are absorbed in the structure of the polis.[118] The past gives way to the present, and reason and political order triumph over and encompass passion and nonpolitical life, but "the displacement from individual to community is possible only as a concomitant to a reformed view of the springs of human action and human responsibility."[119]

Just as Zeus overthrew the old gods and learned the secret of order by suffering, man after following the same path also learns. He creates for himself, by artifice, a new dispensation which will insure, despite the passing of generations, a measure of that everlastingness which characterizes the cosmos and the new order under Zeus. "The well-run State is the greatest protection, and contains all in itself; when this is safe, all is safe, when this is destroyed, all is destroyed."[120]

Political Time and Space

IT is impossible to gain an adequate notion of the classical Greek understanding of history merely by a consideration of the meanings of the words for "history" and "time." Like the Hebrews, the Greeks had no word for history as an order of reality. Yet, despite the dissimilarities, existence in time was, as for the Hebrews, an integral part of the Greek experience. The idea of history, however, was, in contrast to the Hebrew experience, never divorced from, and intelligible only in terms of, political space or the concrete order of the polis.

The past was the focus of the Greek concern with history.[121] But, more specifically, the nature of this concern was aetiological, a brooding concern with the present and its relation to the "beginning." The reverence of the Romans for the foundation was paralleled by the Hellenic fascination with the decisiveness of the beginning and its superiority in relation to what issued from it. The Greek mind never succeeded, even in Plato, in extricating itself from the mythic fusion of essence and origin; the spheres of ontology and aetiology were never completely separated. The culmination of this attitude appears in Polybius' statement that "one may indeed confidently affirm that the beginning is not merely half of the whole as the ancients assumed, but reaches as far as the end."[122] This exaltation of the beginning in Greek thought can be exhaustively documented;[123] the *arche*, the primordial beginning which deserves to rule, stood beyond the flow of time which had tainted the present. The future was an abyss, and history was the scene of degeneracy and suffering.

The concern with disorder emerged in the context of the awareness of decline; historical memory was the vessel of the idea against which political philosophy set itself. The movement of society from its origins was not conceived as a steady decline, for the accomplishments of the Hellenes rose starkly above the civilizational nadir of the Dark Ages which separated the polis from the Mycenaean palace. But there was the belief that in this uneven movement as a whole there tended to be a gradual vitiation of the *arche* which culminated in the loosening of the bonds of order. The present was perceived not as an intermediate point between past and future, but the end, the disintegration of a society; the restoration of order could not be understood as anything but a break with the chaos of human time. Voegelin states the case exactly:

> The Hellenic consciousness of history is motivated by the experience of a crisis; the society itself, as well as the course of its order, is constituted in retrospect from its end. . . . The Hellenic consciousness arrives, through the understanding of disorder, at the understanding of true order—that is the process for which Aeschylus has found the formula of wisdom through suffering.[124]

Attempts to describe the Greek attitude toward history have usually been inadequate. Collingwood finds it strange that the Greeks even indulged in historical inquiry since their thought, in general, was based on an "antihistorical metaphysics";[125] but whatever the attitude of Greek thought toward the reality of change, it was far from ahistorical. Much of the confusion centers around the prevalent description of the Greek understanding of time and history in terms of a circle or cycle. This is misleading because it neglects the distinction between human time and cosmic time;[126] it is the preference for the circular, the primacy of repetition over movement in a straight line, which obscures the problematical position of temporality in Greek thought. The eternal return which characterizes cosmic movement by no means exhausts the Hellenic penetration of the problem of time.

Although when they spoke of "time" the Greeks most often meant cosmic time, they did not imply that it was applicable to the understanding of human affairs except in terms of a contrast. The course of history was played out against the background of the everlasting cosmos, and this is what lent pathos to the tenuous nature of man's existence; time (*chronos*) is simply the measure of cosmic movement, and although in the context of time man may gain knowledge through suffering, in itself time tends to signify little for the world of man except inevitable corruption and dissolution. Human time, for which the Greeks never found an adequate term, remained the disjointed realm in an otherwise harmonious universe; only to the extent that man, comprehending the harmony of the cosmos, assimiliated that harmony to his field of action and created a virtual social cosmos in political space could time penetrate and impose form on human affairs. Although it may be interesting to speculate to what degree such symbols as the conquest of one season by the next informed the Greek view of history or conversely to what extent social relations were projected on the movement of the cosmos, the fact remains that the distinction between history and nature was evident to the Greek mind.

When Herodotus, speaking through Croesus, warns "that there is a wheel on which the affairs of men revolve and that its movement forbids the same man to be always fortunate," he is not implying that history is caught in the cycle of cosmic revolution and eternal return, for he understands the course of man's life as a linear succession of days, each of which is unique, leading on to death; "man is wholly accident."[127] At best the life of man can be deemed fortunate, and he achieves happiness only in the repose of death; prosperity, like power, is "a slippery thing."[128] The rhythm of history is not that of nature, but the paradigmatic rhythm of tragedy. The work of Herodotus is more than a narrative, for like drama it is an imitation of action in which the particular events are artistically restructured and informed by Herodotus' knowledge of disorder to reveal universal significance.[129] Although the historian, unlike the tragedian, was limited by his material, and thus poetry could be more philosophical, poetry and history belonged to the same area of activity.

Herodotus' concern is with human time and particularly with "political" life which exists outside the stabilizing influence of the order of the polis. Although a single man such as Croesus may gain wisdom from his misfortunes, history continues to be propelled along its course by an ascending progression of *hybris* and retribution from which there appears to be no escape; in a sense, it is the *Agamemnon* writ large. In addition to chronicling the war of mankind, Herodotus presents a study of political disorder and specifically intends, as he states in the opening sentence, to discover the cause of the war; the rise and fall of societies is occasioned neither by the whim of heaven nor by the cycles of the cosmos, but by pride and envy which "together include all wickedness."[130] The arrogance of Apries, who believed that not even a god could cast him down, is juxtaposed to his death by strangulation; men who attempt to overstep the boundaries of moderation, which are conducive to order, by such acts as meting out excessive punishment "draw down upon themselves the anger of the gods."[131]

It was because the actions of men do not partake of the permanence of nature that Herodotus made a record of his inquiry into the war; the memory of what men have done is "blotted out by time" (*chronos*) unless these unique and unrepeatable events are transformed into the written word and preserved as knowledge; that is, the objective certainty which only attends the things of the past. For this same reason Thucydides intended his account of the Peloponnesian war to be "a possession for all time"; there was the continual threat that the past would be "obscured by time." The "exact knowledge of the past" which he professes to set forth would aid in understanding the future not because history moves in cycles but because his treatment of the war revealed the *eidos* of political disorder as surely as his analysis of the plague isolated its symptoms; the future will "resemble if it does not reflect" the past because human nature remains the same.[132] Both Herodotus and Thucydides are concerned with presenting a pathology of order; they look backward to understand the loosening of the bonds of order in the present. Human existence is always besieged by accident and chance; it proceeds in an alien world where incalculable forces such as the plague, earthquake, and eclipses render human achievements tenuous. But the real difficulty is with man himself.

The dissolution of political order would "occur as long as the nature of mankind remains the same"; it was the "fatal power of envy" and lack of moderation which produced *stasis* and led men to value private gain over public virtue and to set revenge above the law.[133] Under the strain of "imperious necessity" created by the circumstances of war the order of the polis gradually succumbed to the chaotic environment of external politics which was still governed by the prepolitical syndrome of *hybris,* fear, and revenge. Disorder was perpetuated, as in the Athenian sub-

jugation of Naxos, by needlessly applying "the screw of necessity," and
the words and actions of the Athenians at Melos were fittingly juxtaposed
to the disaster at Sicily which ultimately brought about their defeat.
Even more than Herodotus, Thucydides weaves action and speech to
produce a virtual reality which revealed the nature of social disorder.

When Thucydides challenged the authority of Homer and the poets,
it was not only because he considered his mode of inquiry superior but
because the myth and poetic utterance tended to blur the temporal perspective. His reference to the war as the "greatest *kinesis*" that had ever
stirred the Hellenes, and in relation to which the Persian war was merely
a brief antecedent, reveals his idea of history;[134] he views the war not as
a cycle of disturbances and revolutions, but as a spatial and temporal
movement from one point to another which encompasses the birth and
mortal sickness of Hellas. The focus of his concern is the present, the
"end," but it is intelligible only in terms of the "beginning"; if the true
and immediate cause of the war was the fear of growing Athenian power,
then the origin and nature of this power is decisive. In Thucydides and
Herodotus both the historical memory of the Greeks, extending backward to the civilization on Crete, and the problem of political disorder
and its anthropocentric origin find concrete expression.

For the Greeks, "this is mortality: to move along a rectilinear line
in a universe where everything, if it moves at all, moves in a cyclical
order."[135] The time of man is distinguished from everything else by its
rectilinear course, delimited by begining and end, which cuts across the
circular movement of an everlasting cosmos. This is human time in
which, as Alcmaeon says, "men perish because they cannot join the beginning to the end,"[136] and it includes the life of a political order as well
as an individual. The work of Herodotus and Thucydides was a response
evoked by a society in crisis, and at least on the level of their *logos* they
succeeded in joining the end to the beginning by imparting to the unique
and otherwise perishable actions of men a measure of permanence. It
was this concern with creating something everlasting which stands behind the idea of political order in Greek philosophy as well as the ideals
of political action.

From the events of the war, Thucydides extracted and articulated
an idea of social disorder, and although disorder was ultimately a condition of the soul, it was, as in the tragic vision and with Plato and
Aristotle, inextricably linked to political space. It may be true, as

Arendt claims, that the philosophers' discovery of the eternal and the divinity of the soul took place at the expense of the idea of immortality achieved by the performance of great deeds preserved in the memory of the polis,[137] but it did not take place at the expense of the idea of the political space of the city as the home of man. The search for the permanent which would transcend human time had continually been tied to the polis, and this did not change with the advent of philosophy. The polis, on the level of both thought and action, had traditionally meant more than a context in which the individual might "immortalize"; the conception of political order was more than "organized remembrance." It was, as is evident in the *Oresteia,* an attempt to achieve exactly what has been attributed to Plato; the desire to circumscribe the "futility, boundlessness and uncertainty of outcome" of action.[138] With the belief that philosophy could enter the world of action and order it in accordance with the truth discovered through contemplation, the creation of order in political space was understood as more than a vehicle for the performance of great deeds, for it provided a medium for integrating man with the *kosmos.*

Plato's concern with the eternal was not, as Arendt maintains, "in conflict with the striving for immortality," but he did give new meaning to the idea of the immortal.[139] He did not reject the idea of the connection between the polis and immortality, but he did reject the existential order of the polis which his vision of the eternal found deficient. The philosophers opposed the agonal culture because it was the doers of great deeds such as Pericles who had presided over the destruction of Athens; by substituting form for content, *poiesis* for *praxis,* law for individual action, Plato sought to transform the symbol of the political. But although political order was not understood as the vessel of an activity by which individuals might make themselves worthy of remembrance, the essence of the political was still that it lifted men above the futility of action performed in time. Whatever the philosopher thought of action, he retained the notion of an imperishable space as a victory over time. In the *Laws,* the creation of a political order would defy time by becoming like a drama, an imitation of action; like every work of art or piece of fabrication the beginning or act of creation would be authoritative and determinative and thus insure the nullity of history. Although a concrete polis was never created by philosophy, philosophy in creating the polis of the mind never detached itself from the idea that human order implied

the creation of harmonious works in space. Although the philosophers
may have depreciated political action, their response to the problem of
order cannot be understood as a rejection of the political as the medium
of immortalizing. The discovery of the eternal was a centrifugal force
which drew the mind upward, but the centripetal pull of the polis insured
that the vision of order remained oriented toward world immanence.

The kernel of the tragic vision, which belongs to the historians as
well as the poets, is the inability of individual action to achieve order.
Prometheus gave man intelligence and *techne*; both fire, the foundation
of the arts, and the power of the mind were divine gifts which connected
man with cosmic order and assured the perpetuation of the species, but
paradoxically they were also the source of man's alienation from heaven.
The sum of the Promethean gifts constitutes the prephilosophic idea of
the polis: the tools necessary to create a space to sustain individual action
and aspiration. Specifically, among these gifts were speech, writing, and
remembrance, or the ability to communicate and preserve in memory
man's accomplishments. And further, although seldom noted, was the gift
of action itself.

Previously men had lived in a stupor with the mind paralyzed by
the specter of death, but Prometheus endowed them with hope: "blind
hope I planted in their hearts to dwell."[140] Without the hope of immortality in the communal memory of society and obliviousness to the
immediate knowledge of their own dissolution, action would be impossible; like the heroes of Homer, man can approximate the life of the
gods only by acting as if death were not his alloted portion, but by
acting in this way he becomes guilty of *hybris* and invites nemesis or,
metaphorically, incurs the anger of the gods. Moderation and justice
and the life of action were in the end not compatible.

The ironic conclusion is inescapable; civilized society organized
around individual ambition and action is founded on a delusion. Prometheus himself, isolated and splayed on the crag, is the symbol of both the
impasse of action and speech and the failure of the knowledge of the
sophistes as a producer of social harmony. Order is realized only in terms
of an additional craft which structures action and regulates man's use
of his divinely rooted gifts; the nomothetic art sublimates individual
action, releases man from the burden of guilt, and restores him to the
life of the archetype outside human time. To act is inevitably to sin and
perpetuate disorder; the world of man achieves a measure of permanence

and immortality only when the transcendent order of *dike* is institutionalized. The futility of action performed in time was the discovery of the poets, and nowhere is this discovery expressed more poignantly than in Sophocles. But first it is necessary to distinguish once again between time perceived in relation to the experience of man and time as a component of the universe; there is nothing which can validly be termed *the* Greek conception of time, for its was conceived on many levels.

Time was understood by a significant segment of Greek thought as form; this is most evident in Plato's cosmology and its Pythagorean antecedents. When the Milesians spoke of the *arche*, they meant the source or beginning of all that is, but they also understood it in the sense of the boundless or infinite substance, as described by Anaximander's *apeiron*, from which *kosmos* was formed. This implied not only limitlessness in a spatial sense but temporality in the sense of everlastingness. A *kosmos* implies the imposition of form both spatially and temporally, and time (*chronos*), the measure of the orderly revolution of the heavens, is distinguished from mere succession or duration. Pythagorean philosophy was marked by "the exaltation of the related ideas of limit, moderation, and order"; *chronos* implied *peras*, limit, and the transformation of chaos into numerical organization. In a sense "time" existed outside the *kosmos*, but as mere succession or duration which is the "raw material" of *chronos*.[141] Here it is possible to glimpse the philosophers', and more specifically Plato's, attitude toward human time; the time of man measured against the regularity of the *kosmos* appears as mere becoming or chaos, a formless succession.[142] This view of time is characteristically spatial; time is associated with movement in space, and consequently the Greek view of eternity is not endless time, but its annihilation—the *nunc stans*—elimination of movement and the confinement of the "now" or an everlasting presence. For Parmenides, being is that which "is"; "nor was it ever, nor will it be; for now *it is* . . . immovable in the bonds of mighty chains, without beginning and without end . . . and thus it remaineth constant in its place."[143]

When time is viewed from the perspective of the individual actor, its character abruptly changes, but the idea of time as that which imposes form is not entirely lost since at least as chronometry it imparts a certain regularity to human affairs. Also there are recurring allusions in Greek literature to time as the handmaiden of *dike,* and Solon could claim that

"right good witness shall I have in the court of time," and Pindar refers
to "Time, the sole declarer of every truth."[144] Even Cornford's interpretation of Pindar as equating Cronus and *chronos* is not too fanciful;
in this sense both Zeus and his daughter, Dike, are the progeny of time
and flow (Rhea);[145] time, like the father of Zeus, devours its children
and spits them up again. The passage of the seasons and the movement
of nature are the path of right order, and again time and justice are
related in Anaximander's statement that "things perish into those things
out of which they have being, as is due; for they make just recompense
to one another for their injustice according to the ordinance (assess-
ment) of time."[146] Finally, time is understood as ameliorating pain and
suffering, and here is the continuation of the idea of rhythm and en-
durance that was so prominent in the lyricist.[147] Thus time appears metaphorically not only as justice but as both a healer and a revealer and
as that which creates and brings things to fruition as well as carrying
them away. In all these instances there is a sense of pattern or rhythm
which time introduces into the world—an idea which finds full expression
in Plato's *Timaeus*.

But time, even understood in this way, may be essentially destructive vis-à-vis man; *chronos* is the container of action, but essentially
unrelated to it except as the quantifier of change, a standard of reference which, although often personified, remains coldly impersonal and
imperious. Time often appears as a stream which sweeps men along, but
this is metaphor; time never really touches man, but alongside time or
in the course of time, change, the distinguishing characteristic of mortal
things of which time is the measure, takes place. Time is meaningful only
for men; gods and beasts are not concerned with time because they are
not concerned with change. Time measures the course of man's life in
its straight path from birth to death, and here may be seen another
sense of time which relates to man more directly.

When Heraclitus states that "time is a child playing draughts, the
kingship is in the hands of a child," time (*aion*) here obviously cannot
be comparable to *chronos,* or simply time in general, nor is it possible to
accept Snell's interpretation that this is a metaphor meaning "that time
has no proper action of its own," although this might be an apt description of *chronos*.[148] *Aion* is the nearest approximation in Greek to the
notion of human time; it may mean age or duration, but this is a later
derivation of its more basic meaning as the life of a particular person,

people, or god. Within *chronos* are contained innumerable individual lives with a beginning and end, and *aion* is often associated with Moira— fate or destiny.[149] Heraclitus' statement means that the life of the individual or human time appears incalculable and subject to chance, the difference between human and divine wisdom, the time of history and the time of the *kosmos*.

In Sophoclean drama, man is distinguished by his time-bound condition, and tragedy is largely the futility of individual action performed against the backdrop of time. Time faces the Sophoclean hero as an enemy; it is the personification of flux and flows inexorably by the individual who measures out his life in relation to it. He is caught in isolation between a past which holds no meaning for the present and a future which provides no promise. It is the permanent and regular movement of time (*chronos*) which makes individual action and the search for an island of order appear futile; the time (*aion*) of man is ruled by *tyche* which, like the mind of a child, is unintelligible and with which no prophecy can deal.[150]

In *Ajax*, Odysseus understands that measured against the cosmos men appear as shadows or dim shapes, and Athena warns Ajax that one short day may alter the balance in human affairs.[151] Ajax, in contrast to Odysseus, is the epitome of the man of action, devoid of intellectual and moral sense, and the inability of action to create order and permanence and extract meaning from the universe is symbolized by his suicide. Even when, from the standpoint of others, things appear hopeful, as when the chorus, in regard to the assuagement of Ajax's wrath, sings that "great time makes all things dim," the ironic conclusion is that even as time ameliorates it destroys. Previously Ajax has expressed the same sentiment, but, unknown to the others, he has already decided on suicide rather than relent before fortune and social pressure.[152] This is the lonely and stubborn self besieged by the spectacle of change, yet assuming the heroic posture in the face of the onslaught of time before which his fellows tend to bend and which they rationalize by false hope. By suicide he puts himself beyond the reach of time, yet is vanquished by it. This may be the first manifestation of Durkheim's egoistic suicide in Western literature.

Ajax, the man of action, is continually out of place; the age of heroes is irrevocably past, and the demands of social order are paramount.[153] The old *arete* no longer fits, and although in death he in a

sense finds salvation and a measure of the immortality and permanence
he sought, his demise is by no means the triumph of Homer's Achilles.
There is no doubt that Ajax is criminally guilty and consumed by passion and that he remains so until the end; he cuts himself off from society,
renounces communal virtues, and sets himself against the gods who are
the symbols of an ordered universe. The only hope lies in a psychic re-
orientation, but he lacks the ability to introspect. Athena sides with
Odysseus and wisdom against the blindness of Ajax; like Aeschylus'
Orestes, Odysseus is the hero dedicated no longer to great individual
deeds, but to communal values. It is he who understands the human condition and the demands of social life and demonstrates moderation even
in the case of his enemy, for he knows that "I too shall come to that
necessity."[154] He prevails on the others to extend to Ajax a suitable
burial not because he is a hero but because, as in the conflict between
Creon and Antigone, the demands of humanity take precedence over the
letter of the law as expressed by Agamemnon and Menelaus; if there
is order to be found, it must first find its expression in the well-ordered
soul. The final line of the chorus is truly a summation, not only of the
drama but of the attitude of the poet toward human time and the human
condition.

> What men have seen they know;
> But what shall come hereafter
> No man before the event can see,
> Nor what end waits for him.[155]

Sophocles' disenchantment with the possibilities of heroic action
reveals more than the "tragic sense" of life; his work is imbued with a
consistent pessimism.[156] The "tragic" equally characterizes the three
great Greek dramatists, but an enormous gulf separates the social vision
and the optimistic tone of Aeschylus' trilogies from the work of Euripides, which reflects the decline of the polis and public life and the
disintegration of the Athenian ethos which leaves the self homeless in
the world and alienated and oppressed by its burden of responsibility.
Sophocles dwells in this gulf.

In the work of Aeschylus, "the confident progress which speaks in
the trilogies is the progress that shone in Athens."[157] The struggles of
the past lead to the attainment of order in the historical space of the
polis and to a harmonization of the orders of existence. But in Sophoclean

tragedy, the trilogic form gives way to the single play just as the scene contracts from political order in history to the present and gives way to the moral dilemma of the individual in society. For Aeschylus, suffering is the result of sin and guilt, but suffering in time brings wisdom which purges guilt; while for Sophocles there is little correspondence between guilt and suffering, and suffering by no means ends in wisdom. Oedipus can legitimately ask, "How was I evil in myself?", or state that "I suffered the deeds more than I acted them."[158] For Sophocles, suffering is the lot of man with his limited vision cast against an ordered and immortal cosmos; it is not necessarily punishment for *hybris* nor the consequence of a family curse as in the *Oresteia*. The focus is on the differentiated self and its fragile and time-bound condition; there tends to be neither individual development nor the ultimate reconciliations that mark Aeschylean drama. There is no connection between goodness and good fortune, and only the dead no longer suffer; the chorus continually reiterates in one form or another that hope should prevail even in the face of immediate pain, for "grief and joy come circling to all, like the turning paths of the Bear among the stars." But this is the attitude of the onlooker, not of the actor, for, as Deianira answers, "May you never learn by your own suffering how my heart is torn. You do not know now."[159] Oedipus sums up the view of time from the perspective of the individual who searches for permanence.

> The immortal Gods alone have neither age nor death!
> All other things almighty time disquites.
> Earth wastes away; the body wastes away;
> Faith dies; distrust is born.
> And imperceptibly the spirit changes
> Between a man and his friend, or between two cities.
> . . . . but time goes on,
> Unmeasured Time, fathering numberless
> Nights, unnumbered days . . .[160]

The references to *chronos* in Sophocles are not meant to convey the idea that the rhythm of the cosmos extends to human affairs;[161] what is important is the contrast between the two. The external repetition of cosmic time becomes a measure of the rectilinear movement of human life, and from the perspective of the tragic hero it is personified as a destructive force which oppresses and annihilates him. Clytemnestra laments that "time, supervisor, conducted me to inevitable death."[162] In the "course of time" both good and bad are evident, and *dike* may appear to outrun injustice, but although it is not justice in a moral or political sense, neither is it a cosmic pattern; the rhythm or pattern in human affairs is of human origin. Injustice occasions retribution, and this may be metaphorically expressed by an analogy with nature when viewed from afar; but to the actor his alienation from nature is all too clear.

In the course of exploring the problem of human action, Sophocles challenged the competitive standard of excellence which persistently reasserted itself in various forms and never disappeared from the culture of the polis. Only in those periods in which religion was meaningful was this spirit successfully contained and subordinated to the demands of social order.[163] For Sophocles, wisdom and moderation, rather than the idea of *arete* typified by Ajax's egotistical striving, were the preconditions of social order and individual well-being. As with all conceptions of *arete,* Sophocles' formulation was tied to political order. The search for *arete* was the search for permanence, in regard to both the individual and society, and the heroic standard was found wanting.

From Homer to Plato, the basic problem in Greek values was the reconciliation of the "competitive" idea of excellence which informed the ideal of individual action and the "co-operative" or "quiet" virtues which maintained the community of the polis.[164] The heritage of the Homeric system of values continued to come into conflict with new conceptions of excellence which appealed for the authority to order social life and claimed priority in terms of both individual fulfillment and political order. For Homer the essential content of *arete* was proficiency in the skills which contributed to success in battle, wealth, and social status, and in the context of Homeric society these values were honored because they contributed to the preservation of that society. But with the emergence of the polis, it was necessary either to contain the agonal spirit and channel it in a manner compatible with social stability or to transform the meaning of individual excellence and link it to the values of justice, moderation, and wisdom. The latter was not an easy task, however, since the idea of individual excellence was never disengaged from the Homeric legacy in terms of which excellence was judged by the external criterion of success; it was necessary to demonstrate that the just or wise man was also the successful man or happy man or that in the exercise of justice and wisdom could be found a measure of individual immortality as well as social order.

On the level of the existential order of the polis the need for a bond between individual action and political order found its most concrete realization in the ideal of the polis as the vehicle for individual immortality through the preservation of the fame of great deeds. The classic expression of this ideal is contained in Thucydides' account of Pericles' funeral oration, but the ideal finds its full articulation at the moment when it becomes no longer meaningful or viable. Pericles was not a theorist challenging the order of society with a new idea of virtue, but a man of action attempting to draw upon and voice an idea of excellence which was becoming obsolete and harness it to the preservation of an empire. The aristocratic spirit of *agon* translated into the democracy of Athens was subverting the meaning of polis life, and individual striving and the permanence of the state were becoming incompatible as political man gave way to economic man.[165]

Pericles' offer of "the renown that never grows old" and the fame which is "eternally remembered" and becomes a "sepulchre" for the individual meant little to a society in which unrestrained self-interest had broken down communal values and where loyalties were shifting from the city to the empire and its economic rewards. When Athens fell victim to the plague and Attica was invaded for the second time, the people turned against Pericles as the author of the war. This time he could only appeal realistically to their material self-interest and warn that they could not, under the burden of necessity, give up the imperialistic venture once it had been begun; they could not "decline the burdens of empire and still expect to share in its honors."[166] Despite Thucydides' admiration of Pericles, only an insensitive reading of his work could fail to sense the blame attaching to Pericles, as well as the statesmen who followed him, for the decline of Athens. Sophocles also found in the spirit typified by Pericles the cause of the breakdown of the community; "Sophocles stood for the old polis, and with Pericles began its dissolution."[167]

The opposition to the competitive conception of excellence which shaped the culture of the polis and yet destroyed its own creation took form in the mind of the visionary who, on the basis of a new idea of man, and consequently of *arete*, set forth a new idea of order. But this idea, despite its transcendent source, was never divorced from the polis; a change of style and content, but not an elimination of the vessel. Just as the original conception of the polis was based on that which in man most resembled the immortal—that is, the possibility of performing great deeds—the disenchantment with the possibilities of individual action as a source of social order resulted in the demand for recognition of a new idea of man and virtue with which the order of society might be infused; the audience of Sophocles as well as Xenophanes and Plato was the polis, not mankind. Man's permanence must be found in political order, and political order must be based on what is permanent in man.

The defeat of Athens indelibly impressed on the Greek mind the meaning of history and human time and the estrangement of man from the cosmos. The teachings of the sophists were an attempt to educate man to find his way along in an alien world where neither nature nor the polis provided compatibility. Man fell back upon himself and abandoned the problem of order. But it may have been as much a sense of desperation as a fierce pride in humanity which prompted Protagoras to proclaim that "man is the measure of all things."

V

THE IDEA OF THE POLITICAL: PLATO

*His wish always was to leave a memorial
of himself behind.*

Diogenes Laertius

The Language of the Theorist
and the Conflict of Symbols

IT is easy to lose sight of the fact that while Socrates was challenging the sophists' conception of *paideia* it was Homer who remained the "educator of Hellas."[1] While Plato openly attacked the idea of a culture nurtured on sophistic rhetoric, he more subtly but just as consistently attempted to undermine a society of sleepwalkers who in public and private life moved numbly in a poetic dream;[2] these are the inhabitants of the cave who are bound to the past and immersed in the darkness of the Hellenic myth which held them "fettered from childhood" and allowed them to see themselves and others as well as their world only as shadows.[3] Although less consciously oppressive than sophistic oratory which won its point by overwhelming the listener, the spell of poetry had become a soporific that equally resisted the dialectic of Socrates and the philosophy of Plato.

For Plato, knowledge could be conveyed neither by the minstrels of the poetic tradition nor by the precepts of the sophists; knowledge was the result of an experience of the autonomous psyche. When Plato claimed for himself the authority of Athenian statesmanship, he did so because he rejected not only the "flattering rhetoric" of the politician[4] but the sensually evocative rhythms of the poet which aimed at pleasure and the perpetuation of a cultural trance rather than fulfilling the criterion of the *Phaedrus* that good discourse presupposes a knowledge in the mind of the speaker of the truth of his subject.[5] If the source of order was to be the just soul which conformed to the vision of the Good, the values conveyed by poetry and its *mythos* as well as its mode of expression would have to be replaced by philosophy. Plato called for a society ordered in accordance with a new symbolic form; he opposed philosophy to the poetic state of mind of the culture of the polis.

In Plato's work as a whole the sophists, as in the *Protagoras*, are more explicitly the focus of his attack, but this is because they were his rivals as successors to the exhausted vitality of the old *paideia*; both injected a prosaic and rationalistic note into a decaying poetic tradition. Yet there was an inescapable affinity between Plato and the poets. Although he relegated both poetry and the doctrines of the sophists as well as political rhetoric to the realm of *doxa*, the polemic against the poets was partly a manifestation of an internal battle within the Platonic soul just as his withdrawal from the political life of Athens was effected reluctantly and at the expense of the whole man. But while embarking on his new career in which "politics" meant the right management of the soul in accordance with philosophy, Plato reputedly "consigned his poems to the flames."[6]

The philosophic dialogue was in one sense a work of art in competition with the drama of Athens, and although it may be an exaggeration to understand the *Republic* as "the true tragedy" and as "a play of the blessedness of the just and the misery of the unrighteous,"[7] Plato, like his predecessors, opposed his art to the tradition on the claim that it was informed by a superior knowledge; his dialogues are incontrovertibly a contrived and artistic construction, a transformation of the Socratic conversation, and an image of the experience of the dialectical ascension to the truth.[8]

Plato, however, recognized the inherent weakness of the written word which when questioned, like a painting, maintains "a most majestic silence" unlike "living speech, the original of which the written discourse may fairly be called a kind of image," and he believed that writing was potentially dangerous and subject to misuse. For the possessor of *episteme*, communication through writing must remain within the domain of play, a form of recreation for the serious but isolated individual which imitates the serious dialogues of personal confrontation and oral *logos*;[9] his writing is the play that is akin to seriousness just as the polity ordered in accordance with the written laws is a serious play that mimes the true model. The dialogue was serious play; that is, for adults who could not deal seriously with the nonserious play of poetry.[10] In one sense writing or imaginative play becomes the only recourse left to the philosopher who is a stranger in the polity and unable to communicate directly with those around him, and unlike Socrates, in whom the creative impulse was not so strong and who apparently never felt the need to create tangible form, Plato found in the dialogue a medium for giving issue to his architectonic vision.

But there was yet another and more important reason why Plato felt constrained to express himself in writing: philosophic writing and prose were an integral aspect of the overthrow of the oral poetic tradition and a society molded by the speeches of politicians. There is a timeless quality to the written form that provided an educational vehicle which transcended the cumulative transformation of oral poetry and the repertoire of speeches which served the needs of the moment. Oral poetry like all poetry depended not on concepts, but on the formulas and combinations of words which evoked visual images, while discourse, especially written, made the words significant and autonomous objects with a fixed association. By writing, Plato was going one step further than Socrates in defeating the *poietes*.

In the *Menexenus* Plato engages the ideals of the society by presenting a parody of Pericles' funeral oration; the dialogue "is a document testifying to the tense relationship between himself and his native city."[11] Such speeches are, like poetry, a type of enchantment that distorts the truth (for example, in the parody he speaks as if Sparta had not won the war) and obscures knowledge of the self. Socrates says that as he listens he becomes "enchanted by them, and all in a moment I imagine myself to have become a greater and nobler man than I was before"; sometimes it is days before one comes to one's senses." Knowledge becomes impossible because these speeches "steal away our souls with their embellished words"; this is exactly Plato's complaint: society is ordered by values embedded in a mesmeric folk memory and perpetuated not only by the poets but by the statesmen. He suggests that the woman who was the author of the speech he recites was also Pericles' speech writer and that the two orations differ only by virtue of minor improvisations; this was precisely the means of "political socialization" —the unexamined untruth of Athenian society.[12]

The same contentions are the substance of his attack on the poets and the rhapsodes who set the style of society, and in the *Ion* he ridicules

a man whose occupation is giving recitals of Homer. In the *Ion* it becomes
clear that the poet and the philosopher are "expressing different modes
of existence."[13] For Plato, art like discourse presupposes a knowledge of
its subject, and on this basis he facetiously states that certainly one could
not be a rhapsode unless he understood the poet's thought, for otherwise
how would it be possible for him to render an interpretation to the audience?[14] But this is exactly the point, for "speaking well of Homer is not
an art." The entire process of poetic acculturation from the Muse which
bereaves the poet of his senses through the poets and rhapsodes to the
individuals in society is, according to Plato's analogy, like a magnet
which does not simply attract but imparts to the objects it attracts a
similar power until an indissoluble chain is formed. It is not only the
poets whose "mind is not within them" but a whole culture that has
fallen under the spell and is "possessed by Homer, and so, knowing
nothing" appear to know everything. Ion, who memorized the military
strategy of the *Iliad,* fancies himself the best general because he is the
best rhapsode.[15] If the Homeric epic is, as Plato maintains in the *Republic,* thrice removed from reality, the rhapsode and his audience are
four times removed—"interpreters of interpreters" in a tradition which
as in two mirrors face to face appears as an infinite repetition of reflected
images whether one looks forward or backward. A society thus constituted becomes, to parody Plato's remark about the sophists,[16] the greatest of all poets. Sophistic arguments and poetry are similar since what
poetry amounts to when stripped of such accouterments as meter and
rhyme is a "rhetorical public address"; it is a "kind of flattery" offered
to the polis in order to gratify rather than prescribe what is best.[17] As
Protagoras avers regarding his predecessors, the "sophists' art is an
ancient one," but in order to escape "odium" it has been disguised as
poetry.[18]

　　Philosophy becomes for Plato a purification of the soul, or release
from the spell of society and, inevitably, the enemy of the existential
order of the polis; the idea of philosophy as a communal as well as individual way of life becomes a rival for the organization of action within
the state. At the center of the concern of political philosophy, from its
beginnings, is the problem of undercutting the social style of a community. The competition between Plato and the poets was a competition
for the soul which in Athens remained bound to a debilitated myth which
had been reified and assimilated into the cultural canon where it was no

longer, as in Homer, a symbolic production of the creative mind with its openness toward the world. The vitality of the Homeric symbolism had been played out, and its ties with the transcendent had been replaced by its adaptation as a tool of political education;[19] Homer not only was a source of educational material but had become virtually institutionalized in Greek society. The symbolic content of Homer had been lost while the tradition formed an oppressive environment which was intolerable to the differentiated psyche of the philosopher. With Plato the mythic language of the poets is no longer adequate to express the new reality of the mind, and this is not only because new symbols have been created but because the old ones have lost their meaning through their appropriation by society. Political philosophy like art found its genesis in the resistance of the creative self to absorption in society.

When Plato argued that he was the only true statesman, he was proclaiming, like Isaiah, that he was the "remnant" or carrier of a truth of order which could not find expression in a world where reality was understood in terms of the poetic and sophistic *doxa*. But the paradigm of order demanded projection into space, and this presupposed the destruction and reconstruction of *paideia* since order in society as in the cosmos was a function of the psyche. Attempts to exonerate Plato of the charge of antipathy toward poesy or to produce ameliorative interpretations of his treatment of poetic art must necessarily fail since his attack struck to the very heart of the poetic experience.

As Plato concludes his final animadversions on poesy, he remarks that "there is from old a quarrel between philosophy and poetry."[20] This does not mean simply that philosophy and poetry were antithetical modes of discourse and symbolic expression or even that the relationship was like that between science and religion in the modern age. Plato means, first, the difference between truth and falsehood, the opposition between the search for knowledge (*episteme*) of being and the world of opinion (*doxa*) which is the province of society. Second, he refers to the historical struggle of the psyche to extricate itself from the myth and the articulation of the idea of the soul by such predecessors as Xenophanes and Heraclitus which had at last found consumation in the "divine sign" which Socrates had received and which had "happened to few or none" before.[21] Finally he alludes to the demand of wisdom and philosophy for status as ordering virtues in the polis, the progressive differentiation and reorganization of *arete*. The *Republic* "questions the Greek tradition as such and the foundations on which it has been built. Crucial to this tradition is the condition and quality of Greek education . . . and at the heart of this process in turn somehow lies the presence of the poets."[22]

It is Homer, as "the first teacher and beginner" of mimetic art, who is the focus of Plato's attack; he is the "most poetic of poets and the first of tragedians."[23] It is incomprehensible that Plato was attacking the motivation of the tragedian or the meaning of the drama; what he wished to discredit was the "poetised statement" and the "poetic experience" as a mode of social communication. The Homeric epic, with its repeated oral presentation, was the most obvious target, for all Hellenic poetry was to some extent a derivative of this prototypical work. Much of the pre-Socratic literature was explicitly, as with Xenophanes, or implicitly, as with the pre-Socratics, an attack on this type of statement; yet none completely escaped it. It is Plato's complaint that all those before him who have endeavored to elucidate the truth have done so in an offhand manner and "treat us as children to whom they are telling a story."[24] The Greek culture was probably maintained entirely by an oral tradition until after the beginning of the seventh century, and although the early philosophers applied rational speculation to the sources of knowledge, the exigencies of communication perpetuated the oracular and gnomic style. Probably full literacy did not come about until late in the fifth century. The pre-Socratics were "essentially oral thinkers" who tried to "devise a vocabulary and syntax for a new future, when thought should be expressed in categories organized in a syntax suitable to abstract statement."[25]

Plato's attack on art was part and parcel of the need to raze the foundations of Hellenic culture established by traditional education and was only the last word in the "old quarrel" first entered into by Hesiod when he opposed his truth to that of Homer. Through the progressive differentiation of the psyche the old formulations receded into the realm of untruth until with tragedy the myth itself as reality was transcended; yet communication remained impossible except through the presentational medium of poetry organized around the mythic tale. It fell to Plato to abolish, at least on the level of the creative mind, this last residue and to articulate the truth of existence in discursive form as far as was possible.

Not only do the stories themselves become inane and even harmful when devoid of symbolic content but poetic thinking paralyzes reason;

art based on *mimesis* is "a corruption of the mind of all the listeners who do not possess as an antidote a knowledge of its real nature."[26] After attacking, in the Second and Third Books of the *Republic,* the effect of uncensored tales and the nature of poetic thinking, Plato's polemic culminates in the Tenth Book with the substitution of philosophy for poetry as the educational principle of the polis. This meant the rejection of paradigmatic action as an ordering force;[27] to be a speaker of words and a doer of deeds—that is, the Homeric *arete*—was no longer the mark of excellence and nobility. The poetry of action was to be replaced by the poetry of the mind; the dialogue was the imitation of the activity of thought.

As Havelock states, "It is fair to conclude that the cultural situation described by Plato is one in which oral communication still dominates all the important relationships and valid transactions of life."[28] In such a situation, poetry as "preserved communication" constituted a "massive repository of useful knowledge, a sort of encyclopedia of ethics, politics, history and technology."[29] Poetry in this circumstance became the carrier of group consciousness just as the historical memory of the Greeks first found expression in the Homeric epic and gave substance to the communities of immigrants from the Mycenaean world. Poetry, in both form and content, presided over the foundation of the polis and remained authoritative. Plato's aim was to re-establish society on a new foundation, and the *Republic* was as much a work of destruction as the revelation of a new symbol of order. One cannot stress too strongly that "social order is not independent of the possibilities which language provides. As civilization imposes itself on primitive living nothing can be brought into being that has not previously been thought out—and this means formulated in speech."[30]

The preservation of culture in an oral tradition depended on its osmotic absorption by each individual through the use of standardized epic formulas and techniques of rhythm and meter which facilitated, along with exposure to manifold and regular repetitions of the epics, the maintenance of a living memory. This created not only what might be called a poetic state of mind but virtually a poetic way of life where patterns of speech came to control patterns of thought and where the individual, almost as in the integral myth, found his life organized and played out in an archetypal fashion in which the epic paradigm became the norm of action. An identification was achieved between the hearer and what was heard; the epic became a didactic instrument, and nowhere was this more true than in regard to ethics and the organization of political action. To undermine the old *arete* meant necessarily the displacement of oral poetry and the Homeric education, which essentially was a process of making the past present.

The psychology of the oral culture preserved many of the features of existence under the integral myth; there was an absorption of the individual psyche in the rhythmic movement of society and an externalization of the self which may be likened to the continual participation of an audience in a drama.

> The learning process . . . was not learning in our sense but a continual act of memorization, repetition and recall. This was made effective by practising a drastic economy enforced by rhythmic patterns both verbal and musical. In performance the co-operation of a whole series of motor reflexes throughout the entire body was enlisted to make memorization and future recall and repetition more effective. These reflexes in turn provided an emotional release for the unconscious layers of personality which could then take over and supply to the conscious mind a great deal of relief from tension and anxiety, fear and the like. This last constituted the hypnotic pleasure of the performance, which placed the audience under the minstrel's control, but was itself the ready servant of the paideutic process. Pleasure in the final analysis was exploited as the instrument of cultural continuity.[31]

This is not unlike Plato's solution to the problem of political order in the *Laws,* except that there the poetic experience was utilized to inculcate a new conception of *arete.* Arendt's contention that the pre-Socratic polis was a community organized for individual action is correct; but the action remained archetypal, and this explains the effectiveness of Pericles' oratory which depended on a complete emotional involvement on the part of the audience with the traditional images evoked by the speech. For Plato it was not easy to distinguish between Pericles and Ion, between the statesman and the rhapsode, for each played upon the mimetic experience where there was a complete identification of poet, image, performer, and audience, and each represented the age of the decline of the polis.

It is possible to understand Plato's apparent antipathy toward action only by the fact that in the poetic education what were imitated were actions of epic heroes and deities. Whatever the symbolic meaning of the epic, the significance of the concrete events described in poesy were lost when translated into the public realm as paradigms of action. The inability of the pre-Socratics to move completely beyond presentational communication and the limitative requirements of the oral form, such as the necessity of retention in the communal memory which probably largely determined the episodic character of the epic, required that ideas be couched in terms of discrete and concrete actions. The essence of poetic experience is communication by imagery, and although it cannot be replaced by philosophy, it can, in the form of a dominant cultural style, prevent the break-through of discursive thought. It was precisely this sensual and emotive appeal achieved through oral presentation that confronted Plato as an enemy.[32]

Hesiod went as far as possible within a mythic mode toward conceptual thought, and the history of the Greek mind from Xenophanes may be viewed as a movement toward conceptual discourse and away from the particular and time-bound yet paradigmatic actions of epic poetry. The poetic culture was a "concrete" culture, and Plato was attempting to develop the power of abstract and conceptual thought, to separate the idea of justice from particular instances of just action. The theory of forms emerges in direct conflict not only with the content but with the form of Greek culture. Although poetry from the time of Homer was reduced to writing, it was often only to facilitate oral presentation. Poetry, even when written, could not serve as the vehicle for philosophy, for its aim was to evoke feeling and concrete images which, for Plato, fell into the category of opinion. The written word was only a tool for memorization so that school children reading of the deeds of epic heroes "may be inspired to imitate them and be like them," and lyric poetry and the music of the lyre added to the enchantment. The point of the *Protagoras* is to demonstrate that virtue is the result of knowledge rather than imitation.[33] The poetic experience and action were indissolubly linked, and to destroy the first meant to destroy the pre-eminence of the other.

It is necessary to emphasize again that the discovery of the psyche was the discovery of isolated and creative individuals, not a common possession of the polis, and was only fully articulated in Socrates' teaching. As long as the psyche remained a possession of the poetic culture a reconstruction of political order along the educational lines conceived by Plato was impossible. With the discovery of the soul as a motivational center and the differentiation of thought and action, the very nature of the mimetic experience was called into question as an alienation of the self; "the doctrine of the autonomous psyche is the counterpart of the rejection of the oral culture."[34] Socrates' charge against the poets as well as the politicians was that they had no knowledge of themselves or their work and its content, but, like prophets, "deliver all their sublime messages without knowing in the least what they mean."[35] And the rhapsode or the actor and the audience participate in this mimetic chain which subverts the admonition of the Delphi oracle. It was Socrates' task to question the poet and sophist about the meaning of what they had written and the citizen about what he had heard, and this in effect broke the chain and required the separation of the self from the word-image. The advance of literacy and the decline of oral communication had somewhat the same effect since learning became, rather than active participation in a group situation of self-identification with particular actions performed in the past time, an individual reflection on an object of present knowledge.

This separation was the prerequisite for conceptual knowledge and the whole system of education envisaged in the *Republic*. Everything said by the poets was "a narration of past, present, or future things,"[36] and education consisted of repetitive exposure to the identification with the paradigmatic actions related in the poem. For Plato self and nonself were clearly distinguished; justice and virtue were objects to be contemplated. Through the ear that hears the divine measure and the "eye of the soul"[37] virtue becomes known and manifest in the well-ordered soul rather than a feeling gained by a recollection or an immersion in the events before Troy. The dialogue in competition with poetry was the substitution of a discourse on being for one on becoming, the substitution of the timelessness of *episteme* for the narrative of action in time.

In the *Symposium*, Diotima, in defining love, makes an analogy with poetry. There is more than one kind of poetry, for, beyond what is usually called poetry, poetry in general is "calling something into existence that was not there before, so that every kind of artistic creation is poetry."[38] It is the same with love; there are many objects of love, and those who pursue their good in any field are lovers. In pursuing one's good one wishes it should be everlasting, and the activity of loving is "to bring forth upon the beautiful, both in body and soul"; love is a longing, not for the beautiful, but for that creation which contact with the beautiful inspires.[39] The analogy with poetry was not random, because to love means to create; love is the principle of creation, the intermediary between the temporal and the eternal which binds heaven and earth together.[40] It is *eros* that inspires men to seek for immortality whether through progeny or fame; a mortal approaches the divine and eternal by his impulse to create which derives from *eros*. Through creation the "temporal partakes of the eternal."[41] Likewise *eros* is the principle of creation in the spiritual realm, and "those whose procreancy is of the spirit rather than of the flesh . . . conceive and bear the things of the spirit. . . . Wisdom and all her sister virtues" are the work of the poet and the creative artist.[42] The wisdom which "governs the ordering of society" is the most important; he who has great *eros* looks for an object on which to bestow it and finds this object in the soul and the state—in political education which results in "something lovelier and less mortal than human seed"[43]—for here in the founding or educating of a state is a type of immortality that surpasses even the fame of great deeds.

In these passages Plato discloses more clearly than anywhere else, except for perhaps the *Seventh Letter,* the nature of political vision. This is the type of immortality that belongs to "Homer, and Hesiod, and all the greatest of our poets" as well as lawgivers such as Lycurgus and Solon. The "immortal progeny" of the poets is not simply their works but the notions of *arete* which they have transferred to society.[44] It is immediately clear that Plato is as much a "poet" as his predecessors when he sets forth the nature of the virtuous soul and creates in discourse the well-ordered state and plays the founder of a cosmic polity; it is the urge to create in the face of the beautiful or the good. It is the vision of the divine reached by philosophy, the supreme *eros,* which leads Plato to challenge the authority of the poets. Only through the ascent to the Idea, to beauty itself, does the soul, the eternal in man, become free, and only in the face of the most beautiful does it achieve perfect virtue.[45] The poetry of Homer and the "poetry" of Plato are rivals as educators of the soul and the state, for the mimetic character of the poetic education holds the soul and the state in the bondage of semblance.

Plato begins his destruction of poetic education and the values of Hellenic culture in the *Republic* at the point in the hypothetical founding where the interlocutors proceed from the "luxurious city" or "fevered state," which can be none other than contemporary Athens, to the good or "purged city" achieved through a process of "purification" beginning with a program of censorship.[46] Plato is concerned here with the content of poetry or with poetry as a body of ethical and social values. He emphasizes at the outset that the participants are speaking as "founders of a state" and, "at present," not as "poets"[47] and as such are not required to compose pedagogical tales, but rather to regulate and set the patterns of composition. Later Socrates will be a "poet"—that is, an educator— when describing the curriculum for the philosophers. Here he is concerned not with abolishing poetry, but with a system that will create virtue in the guardians by means of right opinion, the aim of all musical education, and this entails an elimination of tales that are unseemly, inappropriate, and "untrue" in view of the symbolic advance of Plato who has arrived at such concepts as the "good" and "justice."

He complains that the poets such as Homer and Hesiod "composed false stories which they told and *still* tell to mankind."[48] The purified state can be attained only by a purification of a living tradition which undermines such virtues as self-control and courage. Falsehood is not inadmissible if used constructively, for the world of man is not perfect; but here Plato also hints for the first time that poetry becomes subversive in its very "poeticness" by numbing the mind with pleasure.[49] But at this point his complaint for the most part approximates that of Xenophanes; these stories distort the idea of god and, consequently, of man and his relation to the transcendent, and even if they are grounded in truth, their effect in the public realm is to induce wrong action.[50] The unseemly stories about the gods are undesirable mainly because they confound the spheres of god and man—that is, present gods acting like men—and show gods as the authors of men's trouble.[51] Plato is not so concerned with demonstrating the true nature of gods as with elucidating the autonomous condition of man; only by destroying the old education and its teaching about man and his place in the world would it be possible to relate human being to the cosmos in new terms.[52]

In Book III Plato suddenly shifts from the content of poetry to an attack on the very nature of poetic speech and the poetic experience; the problem now is not the "matter" of speech, but the "manner."[53] Plato's concern becomes principally the form rather than the content of communication. This is a recognition that "the medium is the message" and that it is "the medium that shapes and controls the scale and form of human association and action."[54] Here attention is directed to the oral recitation of poetry. In these passages there is some ambiguity between the poet as the artist and the poet in the sense of a rhapsode, but his main concern is with the "middle ring" in the chain despite his implication that the artist himself is also a mimic. In an oral culture the work of an artist had no independent existence apart from its performance and the speech of the rhapsode was determined by the form set by the artist. For Plato the self can become autonomous only by extricating itself from the mimetic experience which underlies Athenian culture.

When the poet or rhapsode delivers speeches "as if he were someone else" it is not "pure narration "effected through imitation."[55] He assimilates his own diction to that of his subject, which constitutes an imitation of the subject. Drama, which is made up entirely of speeches, is the most extreme form of this type of narration, while lyric poetry, which involves a simple narrative recitation by the poet himself, would be the least offensive; epic poetry would contain both speeches and pure narration.[56] Plato is concerned with the "how" of speech because imitative poetry results in a discourse in which there is a failure to show oneself, an activity based on "seeming" which does not stop at the level of the rhapsode, but proceeds in the direction of that process of identification elaborated in the *Ion* in which a whole society is captured in an orgy of imitation. Plato charges Ion that when he recites Homer he is "carried out" of himself and that the result is to "produce the same effects in most of the spectators, too."[57] Is the answer to exclude tragedy and comedy, which are entirely imitative narration, from the city? Plato hints that "perhaps even more than that."[58] At this point Plato offers no alternatives, but goes on to describe the right kind of imitation for the guardians.

Mimesis—that is, the poetic experience—is education, the transformation of the soul; imitations "settle down into habits and second nature in the [action], the speech, and the thought."[59] The guardians' education should include only imitations of worthy characters and their discourse. They must maintain a constant rhythm of all their faculties and not spread themselves thin; one must be a "good mimic" and not imitate everything. The figure of Ion was a parody of traditional education which resulted in the "fractioning of human faculty" and a discordant soul[60] which had no true knowledge although it professed to know all things. The style of the well-regulated character is pure narrative, and this will be the only type of poetry allowed in the state where every man performs one function; those poets who depend in their nar-

ration on much "imitation in voice and gesture" will be excluded from the
state in favor of the "more austere and less delightful poet and taleteller,
who would imitate the diction of the good man and would tell his tale in
the patterns which we prescribed in the beginning."[61] There is a necessary
relation between speech and action, and a confusion of forms of diction
results in a disordered soul.

Since the education of the guardians is a matter of instilling right
opinion, education remains a mimetic experience, and the founders could
order the state by establishing patterns of discourse and applying the
"noble lie" to a purified Athens. But in the production of philosopher-
kings Plato finds it necessary to assume the role of true poet-educator,
forsake constitutional arrangements, and place himself in opposition to
education by music and gymnastics,—education by *mimesis* and habit—
by creating a philosophic curriculum based on "number and calculation"
which transcends opinion.[62] In Book X, Plato confronts the poetic mind
of society and rejects it.

Once the parts of the soul have been distinguished it becomes even
more imperative to dismiss imitative poetry which appeals to the passionate elements. After presenting the theory of forms, Plato embarks on
a broader definition of *mimesis* which goes beyond mere dramatic imitation to include, quite specifically, the creative act of the poet and his product.[63] He finds it hard to speak because he has loved and revered Homer,
and this is so not only because of the pleasure which Homer induces but
because, like Homer, Plato himself felt the need to give issue in creative
form, both in the written work and the shaping of virtue. Yet "we must
not honor a man above the truth,"[64] and here Plato makes his famous
comparison between the painter, cabinetmaker, and God as creators.
He establishes the painter as the creator whose product is, like that of
the tragedian, "three removes from nature," "an imitation of a phantasm
[*eidola*]" of reality;[65] imitation, then, is opinion, the absence of knowledge (*episteme*). Yet his polemic is not directly to the point; it is inconceivable that Plato saw in tragedy no more than a representation of
actions and objects produced by others.[66] What Plato was attacking was
the poetic experience itself as a mode of communication and education
and as a catharsis of passion and a transmitter of an obsolescent *arete*.
Homer, not Aeschylus or Sophocles, is the direct object of his attack;
Homer was the father of a social style which Plato sought to subvert by
the substitution of philosophy. His aim was to create a different form of
life.

The problem is that the public believes, like Ion, that the poets "know all the arts and all things human pertaining to virtue and vice, and all things divine";[67] these are precisely the province of Plato's philosophy. Here at the end of the *Republic*, philosophy and poetry stand face to face in an either/or situation; Plato must discredit the authority of the poets by demonstrating that their work is but a poor imitation not informed by knowledge. Plato's argument is that if they knew virtue and the arts they would "do" them, rather than talk about them; he will not bother to consider Homer in regard to such things as his imitation of physicians, but will proceed to those arts "concerning the greatest and finest things of which Homer undertakes to speak, wars and generalship and the administration of cities and the education of men." Here he addresses the poet directly and challenges:

> Friend Homer, if you are not in the third remove from truth and reality in human excellence, being merely that creator of phantoms whom we defined as the imitator, but if you are even in the second place and were capable of knowing what pursuits make men better or worse in private or public life, tells us what city was better governed owing to you, even as Lacedaemon was because of Lycurgus . . . and we of Solon. But who says it of you?[68]

In this passage is contained the crux of Plato's grievance with the poets. The irony could not be more plain: Plato is attacking Homer as a political scientist and as a founder, and what he accuses Homer of having failed to do is exactly what he knows Homer had done: Homer in a very large sense had been the lawgiver, not only of Athens but of Hellas; no one "says it" because the Homeric education goes below the level of consciousness to the very perception of the world and style of existence.

Plato continues to challenge Homer on the ground that he did not develop a school of followers "who transmitted to posterity a certain Homeric way of life just as Pythagoras";[69] but in fact the disciples of Pythagoras were infinitesimal compared to those of Homer, whose school had been the entire Greek world. Plato points out that no one asked for the advice of Homer or Hesiod about governing a city or "constrained them to dwell with them in their homes" or followed them "wheresoever they went until they should have sufficiently imbibed their culture";[70] but Homer more than anyone else was the creator of the tradition and the taproot of the culture. Those who formed schools were, like Plato, the strangers in the Homeric dwelling, and Plato knew this all too well.

In the totality of the Homeric universe it was difficult to see his handi-work. Plato, after constructing a scheme for the education of the philoso-pher-king, ends by banishing the poets and claims the place of Homer for himself just as he claimed the role of true statesman.

In Book X, Plato proceeds to the pathology of the mimetic ex-perience and its perversion of the soul. The "poetic tribe," again "begin-ning with Homer," are like painters who can fashion anything and know how to imitate and embellish their product with "rhythm, meter, and harmony." When presented to the uninformed, "who see things only through words" or with the ears and other senses rather than with the eye of the soul, "mighty is the spell that these adornments naturally exercise, though when they are stripped bare of their musical coloring and taken by themselves" they are nothing but appearance.[71] Plato is no longer calling merely for restrictions on certain types of poetry but for the substitution of philosophic prose, and probably writing, which convinces and teaches the listener rather than inducing a spell. Poetry communicates by repetition and feeling while discursive prose stands apart as an object to be considered and breaks the mimetic chain. There are three arts: the user's, the maker's, and the imitator's. Excellence, beauty, and truth refer to use, and the user possesses knowledge; the maker operates by right belief derived from the user; and the imitator has neither. Yet, to "the ignorant multitude," what is imitated appears beautiful. Poets of all kinds "are altogether imitators," and "imitation is a form of play, not to be taken seriously," unlike the serious play of the Platonic dialogue.[72]

It is the multitude who have "farmed out their ears to listen to every chorus in the land." These are the "lovers of spectacles and the arts, and men of action" who are "lovers of sounds and rhythm and de-light in beautiful tones and colors and shapes and in everything that art fashions out of these, but their thought is incapable of apprehending and taking delight in the nature of the beautiful itself." This is the distinction between opinion and knowledge or science.[73]

Imitation appeals to the "inferior elements of the soul," while "measuring and numbering and weighing" are the functions of "the part of the soul that reasons and calculates."[74] This is true of imitation that appeals both to the eye and to the ear, that is, painting and poetry; the perception of the senses is subject to distortion, while measurement corrects distortion. Plato rejects poetic communication as necessarily inferior and the poetic experience as psychic dissipation. The question most important to Plato is, in fact, not how many times removed from reality oral or written discourse is, but the form of its presentation and whether or not knowledge informs its composition. Poetry thrives on dramatic action and displays to the public the fretful and passionate soul which characterized the "reality" of Greek culture; it was precisely the passionate and poetic, the Dionysiac, which Plato sought to destroy.[75] Emotion should be purged by the triumph of reason, not by a cathartic through which the self is surrendered. Thus philosophy and poetry as ordering principles and Plato and Homer as founders confront each other.

> You meet encomiasts of Homer who tell us that this poet has been the educator of Hellas, and that for the conduct and refinement of human life he is worthy of our study and devotion, and that we should *order our entire lives by the guidance of this poet.* . . . We must know the truth, that we can admit no poetry into our city save only hymns to the gods and the praises of good men. For if you grant admission to the honeyed Muse in lyric or epic, pleasure and pain will be the lord of your city instead of law.[76]

The hint of Book III has been fulfilled; not only comedy and tragedy which were overtly mimetic but the whole of poetry partakes of imitation and must be expurgated. But Plato, "constrained by reason," dismisses poetry from the city reluctantly just as he reluctantly suppresses it in the inner *politeia* of his own soul. He would admit poetry if she could justify herself for "we ourselves are very conscious of her spell" and "feel her magic," but, like men who have fallen in love ill-advisedly, it is necessary to stand firm against enchantment. It is "owing to the love of this kind of poetry inbred in us by our education in these fine polities of ours" that men find it so difficult to break the attraction for Homer and his apostles, and only constant attention to the "counter-charm" and "fearing for the polity in his soul" will prevent that slipping away of the self into the mimetic pattern.[77]

Arendt contends that Plato wished to substitute the certainty of making for the uncertainty of action performed in the public realm and that the Platonic scheme destroyed action by the separation of ruler and ruled, or knowing and doing, and that this "substitution of rulership for action" was reinforced by the analogy of making or fabrication.[78] But Plato's rejection of action goes beyond the problem of its uncertainty. Although Plato often evokes the image of the craftsman in discussing the political art, the only instance where he appears to confront fabrication and action directly is in his discussion of *mimesis*. From Plato's perspective, the relation between thought and action in the polis was such that the self could not emerge; knowing was submerged in doing. The act of making was, like philosophy, a purification which dissolved the mimetic chain and raised the individual to self-awareness. If, for Plato, the political realm was such that action constituted little more than conditioned response, his final goal was not so much to destroy action as to substitute a new paradigm. If society still moved to a large extent within the reality of the myth, the "inner affinity" of *theoria* and *poiesis* signified more than "the philospher's love for the eternal and the craftsman's desire for permanence and immortality."[79] The connection between political philosophy and fabrication is evident; it is the desire to create something that would transcend the instability of action performed in time. But, on another level, fabrication, like philosophy, in separating knowing from doing and subject from object, freed the individual for self-consciousness and meaningful action.

The conflict between the poetic and the philosophic *paideia* which is so apparent in the *Republic* is paralleled but presented from the opposite perspective in Aristophanes' *Frogs*. This play is concerned with the transition between poetry and philosophy as social styles and the relegation of drama to the realm of "art" which, although fully accomplished in the work of Menander and Callimachus, was already apparent in Euripides. This comedy marks the point where the traditional culture is threatened and becomes acutely self-conscious of its role, where poetry defends its right to perform the task of political education. Aristophanes, throughout his work, asserts his right to advise the city, for "it is fitting that the sacred chorus should jointly recommend and teach what is useful for the state."[80] He is consciously attempting to prevent drama from becoming "art," and this could happen only when the sophists and others had made the separation between art and education and politics.

Aristophanes characterizes the poets as "teachers" and as "diligent servants of the Muses,"[81] and although this means teachers of the chorus, he in turn sees the chorus as the teachers of the audience and thus is articulating the mimetic chain described by Plato in the *Ion*. The poets are extolled as providing a veritable catalogue of useful knowledge, including medicine, agriculture, and war, and are described as the schoolmasters of adults.[82] In the contest between Aeschylus and Euripides, the latter represents not only the sophistic and Socratic influence which had intruded into the old *paideia* but the transition from public to private life and from the moral and political solidarity of the past to the contemporary divisiveness.[83] The poets are summoned to save the city, and both protagonists agree that the role of the poet is to "make the people in the cities better."[84] But while Euripides claims he has introduced "calculation and consideration" to produce prudence which would enable men to better handle their affairs, Aeschylus dwells on the paradigms of action which he has presented for emulation. The contest symbolizes not only the tension between two ideas of education but the conflict between two conceptions of public life. Euripides had pushed tragedy to the point where its message could only be taken up by philosophy. The great actions were disappearing from the stage and giving way to a variety of characters caught in the throes of personal decision; the heroes were disappearing further into the background, and the scenes which had produced the vigor and splendor of tragedy were giving way to the realistic and mundane dilemma of everyman. What was becoming important was that with which Plato was concerned: the drama of the self and its criterion for action.

Although Jaeger overstates the case when he argues that in the *Republic* "everything Plato says about the state and its structure . . . is introduced merely to give an 'enlarged image' of the soul and its structure,"[85] the dialogue does constitute an attempt to illuminate the nature of the self. It is not by chance that the myth of Er directly follows Plato's final critique of poetry which emphasizes the autonomy of the self and the necessity for an education which creates an awareness of this autonomy and prepares one for self-government. In this tale of a Pamphylian, a universal man who must be the "messenger to mankind" and is no other than Plato himself, it is revealed that the individual is burdened with the responsibility of choice; no longer is decision a matter of the gods nor is consequence governed by unintelligible necessity. Virtue, which "has no master over her," is not a problem of external conformance nor is justice, as with Homer and Hesiod, proven best by objective rewards, but grounded in interiority; necessity is the function of the constitution of the soul for "the blame is his who chooses. God is blameless."[86] Man must choose the pattern of his life and therewith his character and fate, and the fate of the social order rests on the nature of these choices as much as it contributes to shaping them. In Homer there was a budding awareness of the differentiated psyche and the seeds of the problem of order in history, and in the *Republic* that awareness finds full articulation. The myth has been transcended, and the relation between man and the cosmos must be restated on a level consonant with this new self-consciousness. At this point political philosophy emerges.

The appearance of the Pamphylian tale at the end of a work that is essentially narrative raises the problem of the status of the myth in Plato's thought. If Plato rejected the reality of the myth, the significance of the particular myths contained in the dialogues must be clarified.

The tale is both allegory and myth. As an allegory, it sums up the central idea of the *Republic* regarding the necessity of justice in both society and the individual, but as a myth it is an attempt to penetrate to that which lies beyond the grasp of conceptual discourse. The myth is the path to those things of "inconceivable magnitude" such as those dimensions of time which the mind vaguely comprehends as extending beyond the perceptible life of any concrete individual,[87] and it is the medium for communicating the periphery of the province of the ineffable for which as a whole "there is no way of putting it in words like other studies."[88] On this level the myth becomes the instrument of the creative mind. An essential part of Plato's whole enterprise was to oppose *logos* and *mythos*, to move beyond the "fancies of mankind" and restate the truth of existence in terms of philosophy. But although the myth as a vision of the world was false (*pseudos*) and Socrates could not accept the old tales of the gods, the myth, at its origin, springs from that same openness of the mind toward the cosmos which was characteristic of Plato's own thought. And the myth not only contained an element of truth but served as an adjunct to conceptual discourse.[89] At first the myth is rejected vis-à-vis conceptual thought and only appears as a metaphor or in those instances where *logos* seems to be incapable of encompassing what the mind perceives. It is in the attempt to illuminate the nature of the soul and immortality that the myth becomes an indispensable component of the dialogue; that is, as the discourse moves toward the limits of being and attempts to express the movement as well as the essence of mind. In the later dialogues, as Plato approaches the idea of *kosmos* and being-in-the-world, the myth becomes an integral part of the dialectical path.

When the sophist Protagoras is given the choice of using a "story" or "reasoned argument" to convince the audience that virtue can be taught, he selects the former since it would be "pleasanter."[90] This indicates not only "the arbitrariness of the procedure"[91] but the tendency of the sophists to revert to the poetic tradition and pleasure as a means of persuasion. This is a sharp contrast with Socrates' use of the myth as a handmaiden of the dialectic where the "blend" of discourse and myth hopefully produces a "degree of truth" and "plausibility."[92] Sometimes, as in the case of the myth in the *Statesman*, the myth serves several symbolic purposes. There it not only provides a medium for penetrating those areas which are not amenable to conceptual analysis but serves, on another level, as an allegory and tool of persuasion within the structure of the argument. After the conceptual argument the Stranger proceeds to "begin all over again from another starting point and travel another road," and this road is the myth abstracted by the philosopher from a mass of legend "for our purposes" and after which, he announces, he will return to discourse and logic. The myth becomes a pleasant story to help "relieve the strain of the argument" as well as illuminate it and further persuade the audience.[93] At the end of this gap in the discursive argument, the Stranger states that the work of "storytelling" was injected to "discern the extent of the mistake in our earlier argument in our delineation of the king or statesman"; the myth serves as an extension and mediator of the dialectical argument.[94]

The eschatological myths are not merely an alternate mode of expression nor do they supersede reasoned discourse in the sense that they constitute a substitution of faith for reason; they are attempts to extend an argument already made within the limits of available symbols.

> The great myths of the soul, at the conclusion of a work, evoke the unknowable beyond, after the theoretical and practical order has been first established with a view toward eternal being. They are variations on the same theme, each variation fitting into the particular dialogue where it occurs. . . . They presuppose conceptual analysis and carry it beyond the limits set for human existence and human knowledge; . . . mythology makes sense only if it can be shown that the myth carries forward the lines or argument set by the *logos*.[95]

The nature of immortality can only be expressed in a tentative way.[96] Plato makes it clear that the stories need not be accepted literally and may even appear absurd but that "they reveal what I want to put to you" and will be used to express a truth otherwise uncommunicable; the tale "will save us if we believe it."[97] Plato's use of the myth in these instances presents a contrast with the vague traditional stories of the "beyond" invoked by Cephalus and unsupported by conceptual discourse;[98] the myth is no longer the myth of society, but the vehicle of the speculative mind. But unlike the tragic poets the myth is more than a medium for artistic expression; it would not be too much to say that in Plato the essence of the mythic experience has been recaptured, but now on the level of the differentiated consciousness.

Plato well understood that attempts, such as that of the sophists, to allegorize and rationalize myth missed the point just as modern attempts to present a sociology of myth approach the problem on only one level. When questioned by Phaedrus about the truth of the tale of Boreas and Orithyia, Socrates declines to attempt a casual explanation of such stories in favor of accepting the "current beliefs about them" and directing his inquiry, instead, toward his own nature.[99] Phaedrus rebukes Socrates for resorting to an Egyptian tale to support his argument, but Socrates responds that there is a wisdom to be regained from these tales and that the ancients were "content in their simplicity to listen to the trees or rocks, provided these told the truth."[100] They were better men who lived nearer to the gods.[101] But at that point at which the myth becomes folklore and of interest only as a social artifact and an object for the critical mind, it is devoid of symbolic content. For the exhausted myths Plato substitutes the myths of the soul, culminating in the grand structure of the *Phaedrus* where the myth serves to illuminate the nature and movement of the soul and its cosmic setting;[102] like the myth on the most archaic level the unity of psyche and cosmos is regained.

For Plato, the nature of the soul and its place in the cosmos could be perceived by the intellect, but, like the forms,[103] lay beyond the limits of discursive speech. In the later dialogues the myth moves into the center of his work and finally, in the *Timaeus*, occupies the entire stage. Dialectical inquiry is adequate to prove that "justice in itself is the best thing for the soul itself, and that the soul ought to do justice whether it possess the ring of Gyges or not,"[104] but for the articulation of the consubstantial unity of psyche, state, and cosmos, the myth remains the irreducible medium of symbolic expression.

Plato's use of myth in his cosmology is not predicated on a dichotomy between conceptual knowledge and myth as modes suitable to the illumination of being and becoming, respectively, for the cosmos is being-in-becoming.[105] The return to the myth was the return to the threshold of creativity. The Platonic myth in its most extended form is not so much an extension of conceptual thought as the displacement of it, not the manipulation and refinement of symbols, but the creation and transformation of symbols. The "consciousness can develop only where it preserves a living bond with the creative powers of the unconscious,"[106] and the development of consciousness cannot be equated completely with the differentiation and advancement of rationalistic thought which necessarily involves an impoverishment of man's openness toward the world.

The old myths of society became untrue when viewed from the perspective of the differentiated self, and in this fact inheres the seeming paradox of Plato's attitude toward the myth: simultaneous rejection and acceptance. What separates Plato from the myth of the Near East is that the myth is understood no longer as reality, but as a virtual representation of the ineffable perceived by the eye of the soul, and what precipitates his rejection of the Hellenic myth is its detachment from its ground and its absorption in the cultural canon.

In Plato "the myth retains the seriousness of its 'truth' but is at the same time consciously an imaginative play."[107] As the creative mind gains mastery over the symbols of the myth, as with the tragic poets, the myth becomes the medium for expressing the new freedom of the psyche. Or, as Huizinga points out, "to the degree that belief in the literal truth of the myth diminishes, the play-element, which had been proper to it from the beginning, will re-assert itself with increasing force."[108] The rejection of the old myth at the level of the conscious self does not mean a rejection of myth as such for

> the philosopher discovers that the myth is the ineluctable instrument for communicating the experience of the soul; for he must himself develop mythical symbols in order to express his discovery both as a process and as a result. And through that opposition of his conscious myth to the less conscious forms he becomes aware that the old myth also expresses the truth of the soul, merely on a less differentiated level of consciousness.[109]

It is not difficult to understand that the creative man often appears as a child at play because childhood is the point of openness toward the world which is only recaptured by the individual who breaks through the communal mind. What to the adult appears to be play is seriousness from the perspective of the child. The difference between the creative man and the child or those living in the cultural myth is the consciousness, not the seriousness, of the play. "Man's maturity: to have regained the seriousness that he had as a child at play."[110] From Plato to Heidegger the myth stands at the portal of being.

It was the deprivation of political life which turned Plato toward philosophy, and his discovery of the Idea can in no way be dissociated from his desire to change the character of society and regain the transcendent foundations of political order. As soon as the *Republic* is understood as simply politics viewed through the filter of philosophy, the meaning is lost. His decision to enter Athenian politics was frustrated at once by his disillusionment with the reign of the Thirty and the attempt to implicate Socrates in the unjust actions of the government. He was forced to withdraw "in disgust from the abuses of those days," and when, after the collapse of the government of the Thirty he was again, although less quickly, "moved by the desire to take part in public life," the new regime charged Socrates, "the justest man of his time," with impiety "which he least of all men deserved." The subsequent condemnation and execution of Socrates by the people meant nothing less for Plato than the vitiation of the substance of the Hellenic spirit, and his eagerness "for a public career" was weakened. Although as he dizzily "gazed upon the whirlpool of public life" he continued to wait for a propitious moment to act, it was at last apparent that the conditions of political life were beyond restoration short of a miracle.[111] Since, from his perspective, society was completely unregenerate, he drew the stark alternatives. Political order could no longer be a function of creative statesmanship.

This exclusion from the life of the community was a deprivation in the most fundamental sense—a loss for which the contemplation of the eternal and the management of the inner *politeia* could not compensate. For Plato, unlike the Hebrew prophet and the primitive Christian, the renunciation of political action could not mean a rejection of a spatially immanent order in favor of redemption in time. *Eudaimonia* was intimately bound to political space and its *paideia* which as in the integral myth remained the point of cosmic mediation even for the philosopher who had viewed the *agathon;* the makeshift community of the academy could enjoy only a tenuous existence in a decaying political order.

To argue that Plato's reconstructoin of the polis was based on a radically "nonpolitical" model is in one sense true, but his reconstruction was not a fantasy or a vision drawn down from heaven. Nor was it simply a recommendation for the imposition of a rigid order on a self-conscious and creative society; such a society was in fact impossible from Plato's perspective and the cause of Plato's estrangement from the polis. Only if it is understood that the Platonic symbolization of order took form in direct opposition to and at the same time in terms of a profound emotional involvement in the concrete political life of Athens, and that the shape of what he opposed determined to a large extent the shape of what he created, does his vision become intelligible; it is impossible to separate the Platonic vision of order from the existential problem of disorder. What Plato opposed was not action but actions, not the possibility of individual self-assertion but the sublimation of consciousness in the poetic spell, not political man but men who had lost touch with their world and for whom the problem of order was no longer a subject of discourse. These were the experiences which constituted the anguish from which Plato's speculative venture was born and from which a new configuration of ordering symbols arose. Drawing once more upon Neumann's analysis of the creative man:

> The individual history of every creative man is always close to the abyss of sickness; he does not, like other men, tend to heal personal wounds involved in all development by an increased adaptation to the collectivity. His wounds remain open, but his suffering from them is situated in depths from which another curative power arises, and this curative power is the creative process. . . . Only a wounded man can be a healer, a physician. Because in his own suffering the creative man experiences the profound wounds of his collectivity and his time, he carries deep within him a regenerative force capable of bringing forth a cure not only for himself but also for the community.[112]

For Plato the problem of politics was essentially a problem of restoration—a restoration which would have to take account of the dimensions of the universe discovered by Greek philosophy. But Plato's theoretical reintegration of man and the cosmos was formulated in view of the ineluctable reality of history or human time which had emerged with the last stages of the disintegration of the Hellenic myth. By destroying the myth Plato also destroyed the Olympian religion, but, unlike the sophists whose treatment of the traditional religion as a socially invented bogeyman[113] constituted a cosmic rupture that obviated discussion of the transcendent foundations of political order, he retained its symbolic meaning. The sophistic disruption of the correspondence between *physis* and *nomos,* or, more precisely, the symbolic contraction of *nomos* to the sphere of conventional law, meant a radical descent into human time. *Physis* was in no way a substitute for the *nomos* of Heraclitus or Pindar;[114] it was simply another datum of experience of which the self had to take account to insure its preservation in an alien world. Man belonged to neither nature nor society. From the perspective of the Platonic opposition both the sophists and the decline of the polis were manifestations of the same phenomenon: the exhaustion of the substance of the Greek spirit which found its final diminution in the execution of Socrates whose attempt to regain the meaning of *dike* went unrecognized by the city. For Plato the revitalization of the spirit meant the regeneration of time and the abolition of the past by a reconstitution of the primordial unity of man, state, and cosmos. Plato's aim was to situate the state outside of history.

If Plato understood his problem as one of restoration, it was evident that such a restoration could not take place on the level of contemporary politics. Since the conditions of public life were such that he was denied access to the realm of action, he could enter "politics" only as a founder. If creative statesmanship is impossible, one might act as an adviser to his city, but when the city at the crisis of its illness refuses to heed the advice of the physician and reorder its constitution, only a charlatan would continue to give piecemeal advice that would merely sustain the city in its sickness. Nor should the sage attempt to take charge of the patient by force or risk his life by criticizing an order that is beyond redemption.[115] Plato eventually renounced the role of Socrates as well as the role he had tried to play in Sicily; only as a participant in a new foundation could he ultimately find a place to act. When he wrote the *Laws,* his involvement with Athens had run out. It is hardly a coincidence that as Plato set down these autobiographical passages in the *Seventh Letter* he was in the process of composing his final work. When justice and the truth of order exist nowhere but in the souls of the "uncorrupted remnant of philosophers," earth and heaven must bide their time.[116] This is reminiscent of the prophets, except that restoration and the regeneration of the spirit are tied to political space and in no way depend on anything like the zeal of Yahweh; restoration is the problem of man.

History and Order: the Republic *and the Problem of Actualization*

BY the end of the fifth century, the time-bound character of society had become painfully evident, and in the *Republic* the problem of actualizing and perpetuating the philosopher's vision of political order hangs like a shadow over the entire inquiry into the nature of justice. The dialogue is attended by the constant paradox that while it is illuminating the truth of human existence it is, at the same time, demonstrating that man and society on the existential level are radically deficient. But before considering Plato's treatment of the problem of actualization in the *Republic,* it is necessary to emphasize once more the character of the dialogue as a mode of communication.

It is a mistake to analyze the dialogues with the purpose of extracting either exoteric or esoteric philosophical systems or clearly defined doctrines. Probably no greater or more prevalent misinterpretation of Plato has occurred than that which has resulted from attempts to discover within the totality of the dialogues a consistent and tightly constructed theory of forms. Such attempts have necessarily been unsatisfactory because the premises are improperly posed. The Platonic dialogues do not represent definitive statements of sets of philosophical principles, but rather a series of intellectual probes or explorations of emerging and not fully articulated problems within a limited range of available symbols. Plato was in the process of specifying as well as investigating areas which contemporary philosophy might describe in terms of the ground of being, the relation between universals and particulars, or the connection between concepts and objects. Similarly, with regard to his consideration of the possibility of actualizing a just political order, it would be futile to seek a final and systematic answer, although it is possible to discern a certain coherency in the development of his formulation and investigation of this problem. For Plato the dialogue is a reflection of the probing which characterizes philosophical activity; the dialogue is a dramatic expression of the "conflict of ideas" transformed into a "clash of characters."[117]

Plato was serious about the question of actualization; he was not merely engaged in exploring human nature and constructing a large simile by projecting the well-ordered soul on the fabric of society.[118]

Jaeger argues that "we started out with Plato to find a state. Instead we found a man" and the "perfect state is only the proper space which he needs as a frame and background for his portrait."[119] But the problem of Plato's symbolism does not reduce itself to a question of alternatives; state and psyche are homologous, and there is a constant interplay between the two. He is articulating what had long been implicit in Greek thought: order and disorder in society are ultimately functions of the soul.[120] The *Republic* constitutes a theory of social order and a prescription for action as well as a paradigm of the just man and the good polis; these are different levels of symbolism which are not mutually exclusive, but necessarily interdependent. If any weight is to be given to his statements in the *Seventh Letter,* the problem of actualization posed in the dialogue must be taken seriously and is not resolved by the observations at the end of Book IX. The fact that justice is a pattern which may be realized in the soul, and must be realized there first, does not eliminate the problem of actualization. "I feared to see myself at last altogether nothing but words, so to speak—a man who would never willingly lay hand to any concrete task." Plato was continually plagued by the need for concrete action, and although it is impossible to completely understand this motivation, his whole enterprise would be unintelligible apart from it.[121] But Jaeger's thesis serves to illuminate an important point. Whatever the influence of the *Republic* on the tradition in regard to theories of political institutions, it is meaningless to view it as a specific plan for an external political order; on the level of the *Republic* the problem of the particular organization of political space is not seriously encountered.

Socrates proposes, "Let us create a city from the beginning, in our theory,"[122] and the understanding is not simply that the purpose is illustrative but that the problem of justice is necessarily the same in the soul and the city. The inquiry will be cast in terms of a founding, and this is significant in several respects. First, the road traveled is the dialectical path which must be followed to achieve a well-ordered soul, and it is obvious that Plato is to a large extent recapitulating his own experience. Second, the creation of the pattern in thought, in the soul of at least one man, is the prerequisite to any future question of realization. Third, on another symbolic level, this is a foundation play which transcends the tales of the myth. It is a theory of the origin of the state which replaces myth, and although it is not a history of a particular state, it takes account of the historical conditions of the formation of the polis and the "origin of justice and injustice"; it is more than a logical construction. The state is neither descended from heaven nor a conspiracy of the weak; it finds its origin in man's needs, and the rise and fall of social order is a problem of human time or history. Finally there is a correspondence between the "founders" and the stages of growth, with the psychic constitution of Socrates requiring the good polis; state and soul are inseparable. Again this has historical relevance, for in its parts the constitution of the state recapitulates the spiritual evolution of Hellas and the content of *arete.*

After Socrates and his companions turn from a description of the luxurious city, which approximates contemporary Athens,[123] they begin a consideration of the purified polis and its system of education. For the first time they consider a city which resembles nothing visible to the eye and which stands beyond historical existence; this city appears only in "discourse."[124] This is not only a symbolic contrast but the historical moment of the challenge of the paradigm, which exists in the soul of Socrates, to concrete society. At this moment the question of actualization, although not specifically mentioned, becomes a problem and is implicit in the program for the transformation of the old *paideia;* the contrast between the good and unhealthy state has been achieved. The context has shifted from the fable designed to elucidate justice and the correspondence between justice in the city and the individual to the question of "feasibility," and the question appears almost as an alien intrusion in this discussion of justice and injustice.[125] The symbol of the foundation emerges on a new level, for with the poles of "good and right" and "bad and mistaken" clearly drawn, the problem of relevance cannot be escaped.[126]

The question of the possibility of actualization is first explicitly encountered in the context of the discussion of the community of women and children. This discussion is meaningful only when viewed from the perspective of the problem of the realization of the purified polis—a problem which cannot be avoided now that the character of the just city has been presented. Socrates is challenged by his companions to take up the subject of the communism of women and children which had been alluded to earlier,[127] and although their specific request is for an explanation of the character of this institution, he shifts the ground to a consideration of its possibility. Thus Socrates is the first to raise the question of "whether what is proposed is possible" as well as "the provisions that precede it," and in doing so he implicitly raises the problem of whether the just city as a whole is possible or only a "wish-thought."[128] But the institution of communism is found to involve and presuppose the equality of men and women, and this is the first of the three "waves" of paradox, or conflict with custom and tradition, and it presents grave questions regarding the possibility of actualization.[129] Socrates concludes that it would be possible as well as beneficial for men and women to engage in common pursuits,[130] but in reaching this conclusion, and theoretically surmounting this wave of paradox, he not only contradicts custom but passes lightly over the "natural" obstacles to such innovation. As with each aspect of the consideration of actualization in the *Republic,* this proposed equality is predicated on an abstraction from material conditions; it takes little account of the physical differences between the sexes and the resistance of such natural associations as the family.[131] The argument proceeds on the assumption of the complete malleability of the bodily aspects of existence and their suppression by art. This is an assumption which is revised in the *Statesman* and *Laws.*

In returning to the institution of communism, Socrates observes that this would be "a far bigger paradox" than equality and presents even graver questions "as to its possibility and its utility." The purpose of communism is to insure the "unity" of the city, but this again contravenes the natural order of life and procreation and demands the sublimation of bodily and natural existence in the conventional and artificial order of the city. Socrates wishes to discuss only the question of possibility, but since the others force him to consider the utility and benefits of such an enterprise, he delays a consideration of feasibility.[132] When it is finally agreed that communism would be beneficial, Socrates again turns to the question of the possibility of such a community and to how it might be created, but he immediately digresses without answering his own question.[133] Since communism must be incorporated in the plan for the good city, the problem of actualizing the city as a whole is raised again and becomes more vital than ever. The question of the possibility of communism is subtly transformed into the more comprehensive problem of the actualization of the just city as a total entity.

Glaucon finally presses Socrates directly with the demand that he speak of two things: the "possibility of such a polity coming into existence and the way in which it could be brought to pass."[134] This implies a "great third wave of paradox," but his companions insist that he go on. But Socrates hesitates to grapple with this paradox and reminds the others that from the beginning the "purpose was not to demonstrate the possibility of the realization of these ideals,"[135] but to inquire into the nature of justice and injustice in man and the state and to discover a "pattern" or "model." The pattern which has been created in words, like the work of a painter who portrays an "ideally beautiful man," is not a reflection of a physically visible object, but an idea. For both the individual and the state the pattern is a standard which exists as a reality in the psyche of Socrates and in his *logos* and the truth of which is not impaired by nonrealization. The pattern is no less valuable if a state cannot be formed exactly in accordance with the description, for it is not "possible for anything to be realized in deed as it is spoken in words," since action necessarily partakes less of truth than speech and thought.[136] Yet it is worth while to attempt "to show how most probably and in what respect these things would be most nearly realized."[137] Thus the good polis may be possible in a limited sense, but even then only under conditions which must be described by words such as "luck" and "miraculous" or "dispensation of providence."[138] But although it can never be realized precisely, it will suffice to demonstrate how it "might be constituted most nearly answering to our description," and the conversation shifts to a consideration of the smallest change required in existing states for them to be governed justly. The answer is that for such a constitution to come into existence "within the limits of possibility" would require that the third and greatest wave of paradox be overcome and that "either philosophers become kings in our states or those whom we now call our kings and rulers take to the pursuit of philosophy seriously and adequately, and there is a conjunction of these two things, political power and philosophical intelligence."[139]

Although limited actualization has been established as a theoretical possibility, it is highly unlikely that the necessary condition will be fulfilled, given the character of contemporary society, the "great beast" which not only is ignorant of how to make use of the philosopher but tends to corrupt the philosophic nature.[140] The "small remnant" such as Plato find themselves alienated from society and deprived of the possibility of acting and are forced to turn their attention inward to withstand the onslaught of the multitude. But this is a great deprivation because the philosopher will "not have accomplished any very great thing" if he has been denied the opportunity to "attain his full stature" and "pre-serve the commonweal."[141] No existing polity is worthy of the philoso-pher, and the philosophic nature cannot endure in the contemporary environment. Thus there is little chance that the condition of the philos-opher-king will be fulfilled.

If, however, the philosophic nature should find a polity truly worthy of it, such a state would be "in truth divine." It would be a form of government which would transcend not only present forms but the pattern of the merely just or purified polis; it would include "an element having the same conception of its constitution . . . that the lawgiver had in framing its laws." A polis fit for a philosopher must be one in which the philosophic nature can be perpetuated. But this raises the further problem of how "a state that occupies itself with philosophy can escape destruction. For all great things are precarious and, as the proverb truly says, 'fine things are hard.' "[142] In this leap from the purified polis to the philosopher's polis, Plato alludes to the final question of how to maintain philosophic rule once it is achieved or the status of the "divine" once it enters history. The paradox is that the attainment of a just city requires philosophical rule, but such rule may be beyond the scope of earthly existence.

Socrates, however, sets aside for the moment the question of the preservation of the philosophic state and returns to the problem of at-taining the coincidence of philosophy and power. He affirms that it would be "unreasonable" to assume that such a situation "cannot possibly come to pass" or that it is in the realm of "daydreams" that "some chance compels the uncorrupted remnant of philosophers" now held in low esteem to rule or that those in power will embrace philosophy. It is not inconceivable that in the course of time or in a foreign region the "philo-sophic Muse" has been, is, or will be in control of a state, for "it is not a thing impossible to happen, nor are we speaking of impossibilities."[143]

In order to constrain or compel the philosophers to take control of the state, it is necessary to convince the multitude of the merits of philo-sophical rule; they must be persuaded of the benefits of seeking out the person who has assimilated himself to the divine "in the measure per-mitted to man" and who can project "on the plastic matter of human nature in public and private the patterns he visions there." But such a transformation would extend beyond the purified polis or the reorganiza-tion of any existing polity because this "political artist" will insist, unlike other reformers, on a "clean slate" from which to begin; both the city and human nature must be wiped clean in order to create a city suitable for the philosopher. Even the appearance and acceptance of the philosopher-king is not sufficient unless he finds or creates a condition which offers his art no resistance, and this is not an "easy task." All this presupposes a radical transformation of human nature and social life; it assumes that the individual and society can be made infinitely malleable and that art can overcome all resistance and create a human character which would be virtually the "image and likeness of God."[144]

Socrates appears to take an optimistic attitude toward the possibility of persuading the many to accept philosophic rule. But such an attitude strikes an unreal note after the previous discussion of the nature of the multitude, and how to "compel" the philosophers to rule is a question which is never explicitly answered.[145] Socrates devotes more attention to the problem of persuading the many because it is easier, given the proper conditions, to induce the philosopher to rule. The philosopher is compelled from "within" to give concrete expression to his vision and knows that only in the polis can he find solace and the opportunity to perpetuate his character. But to convince the many requires the mediation of rhetoric; just as Moses needed the mouthpiece of Aaron, the philosopher must employ the art of persuasion.

One cannot say "that there is no chance that the offspring of kings and rulers should be born with the philosophic nature" and remain uncorrupted, and the appearance and acceptance of only one such person would be necessary for the realization of the polity which has been constructed in discourse. Although the problems encountered in effecting the conjunction of power and philosophy seem overwhelming, Socrates maintains that the actualization of such a state is "not impossible."[146]

Granted the possibility of the ascendancy of the philosopher-king, Socrates turns his attention toward the problem of the institution of a philosophical education and the maintenance of a philosophic class— the "preservers of the constitution."[147] To establish the proposed system of education and thus preserve the philosophic polis and provide the most expeditious way to "reorganize and administer the city" would again require a clean slate or the banishment of all persons over the age of ten.[148] Plato still clings to the answer that such a "polity is not altogether a daydream," and although "it is difficult, it is in a way possible."[149] But although it may be "possible" to actualize the philosophic

polis in the sense of bringing it into existence, the question of whether
it can be maintained remains to be answered.

The philosophic nature required a state which was constitutionally
one step beyond the purified polis, but this one step brought it to the
threshold of the divine. By adding an element which would have the
same conception of the constitution as the lawgiver, the philosophic
polis is created and the question of how to preserve the rule of philosophy, and consequently the pattern of justice, is encountered. It is not
only the just character of the state but its immortality which enables it
to approach divinity, but both factors depend, in the end, on the maintenance of the philosophical class—the essence and saviors of the constitution. At the center of the question of the perpetuation of philosophical
rule, once the obstacles to creation have been overcome, lies the problem
of the perpetuation of the philosophical class.

Plato's famous statement at the end of Book IX does not pertain
to the problem of the possibility of actualization; it is a return to the
situation of the philosopher in a corrupt society which was encountered
in Book VI. Since injustice is not profitable and is bad for the soul itself,
the just man must pay attention to his body only for the "sake of the
concord in his soul" and must shun all activities which would tend to
overthrow "the established habit of his soul." This can be accomplished
by keeping "his eyes fixed on the constitution in his soul" and not taking
part in politics except in a city that conforms to his nature, and although
such a city may exist "nowhere on earth," it "makes no difference" if the
pattern has been constituted in his soul.[150] These remarks should not be
understood as a sudden revelation of the answer to the question of
immanentization, for they are no more than a reiteration of the solution,
already given, to the maintenance of the truth of order in the context of
disorder. There has been no flight from the concern with immanent order
or a resolution of the problem that this preservation of the spirit in a
few men is not in itself "any very great thing."

Plato has made it clear that even on the level of the just polis
actualization can be achieved only in a limited sense, and although the
creation of the philosopher's state is a "theoretical" possibility there is
still a fourth paradox which exceeds all the others and which Plato does
not attempt to resolve within the context of the *Republic*: the paradox
of being in becoming. What Plato has constructed in this founding fable
is a psychic approximation of the Egyptian cosmological state. Through

the medium of the ruler who participates in the divine, the pattern of heaven is impressed on the subjects in such a way that man, society, and being become more than contiguous entities; they are completely assimilated. But at the level of the philosophic consciousness, the levels of existence have been differentiated and such a construction becomes, in a sense, a contradiction. Plato well clarifies the extent to which form could be incorporated in matter. The moment that the philosopher's polis is realized will be, paradoxically, the moment that it begins to decline; this is the penalty of actualization. The *Republic* does not solve the problem of a political order which can overcome the limitation of human time, because it makes no compromise with bodily existence or with the material which confronts the political artist.

The continuing debate over Plato's intention in Books VIII and IX is another manifestation of the reluctance to admit the presence of manifold levels of symbolization in a work such as the *Republic*.[151] Once he has concluded the "digression" on the problem of actualization, Socrates states that he will return to the systematic analysis of the correspondence between the character of the individual and the constitution of the city, this time in terms of the defective types.[152] On one level, then, it is a continuation of the "inquiry as to the relation of pure justice and pure injustice" with which the dialogue had begun, and the progression constitutes a logical sequence which symmetrically balances the early books. Yet this is also an explanation of social disorder which, although it does not represent a specific "history," is grounded in the historical experience of decline and fixes the soul as the source of disorder and differentiates the time of man.[153]

The fact that "not even such a fabric as this will abide for all Time [*Chronos*]"[154] is bound up with the unfathomable mystery of becoming, that man insofar as he is corporeal is a limitation on the embodiment of the Idea. This ultimate mystery of cultural deterioration is not completely accessible to reason, and Plato "playfully" expresses the notion in a "scientific" myth. Here he pretends like Homer to invoke the Muses who "playing with us and teasing us as if we were children address us in a lofty, mock-serious tragic style."[155] The immediate reason for the failure to preserve the best state once it is actualized is the inability of art to overcome nature or the inability of man to escape his involvement in matter; this ultimately causes a eugenic miscalculation and consequently makes the rulers unfit as a receptacle of the Idea. A state based on an abstraction from its material base cannot last; the neglect of the physical aspects of human being now takes its toll. This does not mean that the time of society is bound to a cosmic cycle (*chronos*), but quite the contrary. Political time or history is twice removed from eternity while the cosmos, which is everlasting, is only once removed, and political change can be explained in no other way than as a function of the psyche of those who determine the constitution of society. Beyond the point of original sin, the movement of history ceases to be a mystery. Just as in the *Timaeus* the demiurge could not create eternal being in the cosmos, man cannot found a perfect polity. The philosophic state and the transhistorical state cannot be identical; one must be sacrificed to the other.

The Statesman: *Cosmos and History*

IN the *Statesman*, the philosophic stranger from Elea, who is Plato or the true philosopher described in the *Theaetetus* who moves like a stranger in Athens, begins and ends by confronting a hopelessly recalcitrant Athens with the authority of the true statesman which he had claimed for himself in the *Gorgias*. But on the way the state, like the psyche in the *Republic*, finds its place in the cosmos.

The situation is not unlike that of the *Republic* where the philosopher-king is faced with the problem of stamping righteousness on society, but here the statesman who carries the paradigm in his soul comes up abruptly against the unformed matter of the city and the rivals for his authority as well as the limitations on perfect embodiment. While the fabled discourse of the *Republic* affirmed the reality and truth of the paradigm in the soul, the *Statesman* explores the existential problem of the statesman-philosopher vis-à-vis the imitative statesman-sophist[156] in a society where true authority and power are not coincidental. While wisdom and power attract each other, it is only in rare circumstances that they are conjoined and the Idea attains a noteworthy measure of immanence.[157] When Plato wrote the *Statesman* he had no hope for Athens and little for Syracuse; the dialogue was written after Plato's second visit to Sicily and the failure to convert Dionysius II to philosophy.

Ostensibly the myth in the *Statesman*[158] is an illustrative fable that will aid in demonstrating the nature of the true statesman, but in the course of the tale the question which the *Republic* left open receives at least a partial answer. The myth moves on several levels; the Stranger announces that "there is a mass of ancient legend a part of which we must use for our purposes."[159] This does not imply a rationalization of the myth, but the manipulation of its symbols to convey a truth inaccessible on the levels of both ancient legend and discursive thought. He appeals to the young Socrates to listen "as a child would";[160] that is, to free his mind for the speculative journey. All of these old tales "originate from the same event in cosmic history,"[161] and that event was the emergence of the political life and the beginning of human time, the beginning of the tension between order and history.

There was a time when god (demiurge) propelled and guided the revolutions of the universe and imparted immortality to it, but when the revolutions "completed the due limit of the time thereto appointed," there came a moment when he released his control and the universe began to revolve in the opposite direction under its "own impulse," or "innate force" and under its own guidance.[162] This was possible because it was endowed with an intelligent soul by the creator-demiurge. Reverse motion was the least variation possible from its original condition since it was burdened with bodily form and could not partake of complete constancy, which is an attribute only of the most divine. During such cosmic crises which take place from time to time, the entire universe is affected, including mankind, of which only a small remnant survive. When god undertook to rewind the universe, as at the beginning of the cosmic period prior to the contemporary age, human creatures grew young and finally disappeared. But a new race grew out of the earth whose children were the ancestors of the Greeks, and this race lived in the reign of Cronus. God was, as before, the governor of the universe, and man did not labor; in fact there was no autonomous human action or family and political life, for all provinces of the universe, including the human flock, were superintended and cared for by deities. But at the end of this era, god again released the helm and the cosmos began, from "fate" and "inborn urge," to revolve in reverse. This was the beginning of the present world period, and after the initial shocks of the cosmic crisis, the universe, remembering the instructions of its creator, settled on its present course. In the present world order, that of

Zeus, man as well as the universe took sole responsibility for its course. But in time cosmic recollection faded because its bodily elements, which belonged to it before it was ordered and brought from chaos by the creator, began to reassert themselves. As forgetfulness sets in, the ancient chaotic condition begins to appear, and as the crisis mounts, god again takes the helm, "bringing back the elements which had fallen into dissolution and disorder to the motion which had prevailed under his dispensation" and restoring the cosmos to immortality.[163]

An interpretation of this myth must proceed on several levels. Man and society, as both psyche and body, participate in the cosmos, and, as with the cosmos, it is the bodily element which prevents them from being ever "steadfast and abiding" which is the prerogative of the "divinest of things only."[164] Here, again, is the ultimate failure of actualization as in the *Republic*; whether it is the eternal forms perceived by the demiurge or the pattern of the best state in the mind of the philosopher-king, there is a limit to which the bodily vessel can serve as a receptacle. But this does not only constitute an original limitation on immanentization, for there is a continual threat of the reassertion of the primeval chaotic condition, which now becomes co-eternal with the Idea. This is the impenetrable mystery of cosmic movement which in the *Republic* accounts for the eugenic miscalculation. "The fact that the revolution of the heaven is sometimes in its present sense sometimes in the reverse sense" is beyond the ken of man.[165]

Through the medium of the myth, Plato is elevating human history, or more precisely the history of Hellas, to the level of the cosmos. This history was not completely inaccessible; the course of events from the time of Homer and before could, within limits, be comprehended and set forth, and he places them in the context of the cosmic myth only to illuminate what was impenetrable in strictly discursive terms. That human time is a differentiated realm and that the rise and fall of social order is primarily a problem of the psyche is clear. But beyond this remains the inexplicable fact of social growth and deterioration, the recovery and loss of the substance of the Idea in historical space. What Plato is attempting to convey is that man, state, and cosmos partake of both intelligence and matter and move between the poles of order and disorder, and although philosophy has moved beyond the relatively un-differentiated world of the ancients, something akin to Moira remains inaccessible to the human *logos*. God remains in control for the time "appointed" or "ordained" when fate or errant cause, culminating in the reassertion of chaos, moves the universe. Even god cannot reverse the motions of the cosmos at will.[166] It is evident from the *Timaeus* that the scheme of cosmic reversals in the *Statesman* cannot be taken literally; yet the mythical symbols serve to render the truth of existence.[167]

Symbolically woven into the cosmic myth are the concrete experiences of historical existence on the level of social order. In the age of Cronus political life did not exist; this was existence under the form of the integral myth where the king was a deity. Whether this refers specifically to Egypt, Crete, or early Hellenic kingship makes little difference, but the provinces of the universe were distributed among an assembly of gods. The picture Plato draws is that of a static civilization where social conflict as well as each phase of political, social, and natural phenomena extending from procreation to cultivation were sublimated in primordial archetypes. This was an atemporal existence where "all men rose up anew into life out of the earth, having no memory of the former things."[168] Plato specifically rejects this age of the undifferentiated consciousness, where man and nature lived in a compact unity, in favor of the present age of Zeus.[169] Neither the individual adult nor mankind could or should return to the condition of the child and myth.

The cosmic reversal which ended the age of Cronus is the point of the distingeration of the integral myth and the birth of the Hellenic world and human time; the precise explanation was as opaque to Plato as in a sense it is to the modern age except that it was accompanied by vast natural and social upheavals. From the chaotic conditions of the transition emerged both political life and the Olympian theology; this is the new world order of Hesiod and of Aeschylus' *Prometheia* and *Oresteia* where Zeus reigns according to *dike* and where the lesser deities "relinquished the oversight of their regions."[170] The allusion here to the differentiation of the orders of existence and the retirement of the deities once immanent in nature to the transcendent Olympian order is too obvious to be ignored. After the collapse of the integral myth and the intellectual and political chaos of the Dark Ages, "the interval needed for recovery," the world, "attaining quiet after great upheaval returned to its ordered course and continued in it, having control and government of itself and of all within it and remembering, so far as it was able, the instruction it has received from God, its maker and its father."[171] This was the emergence of a new vision of order and the beginning of the age of the polis.

At the beginning of "the cosmic order now existing" mankind found itself, like the world as a whole, burdened with the "sole responsibility and control of its course," with all things human moving in a line from birth to death, for "a new law governing conception, birth, and nurture was made binding on the whole universe." Each order of existence, the "constituent elements" of the universe, became autonomous, and men, "bereft of the guardian care of the daemon," were helpless and alone until they received the gifts of Prometheus and Hephaestus and were able to "manage their lives and fend for themselves in the same way as the whole universe was forced to do."[172]

Plato had no illusions about the truth of the Promethean tale;[173] what he is describing is the appearance of a conscious political life and the awareness of human time where the ruler must be a mortal among mortals. At the end of the tale, Plato states that it has served the purpose of delineating the nature of the statesman and pointing up the mistake of the results of the first attempt at a definition; that is, that the royal ruler is a shepherd or sustainer of a human flock. This figure "is a god, not a mortal"; life can no longer be lived in terms of the mythic city.[174] In a very real sense the first definition not only was a mistake within the context of the present dialogue but extends to the conception of the best polis in the *Republic*. It is in the *Statesman* that Plato concedes the ineluctable fact of change and the limiting matter with which the ruler must deal. An attempt to return to the age of Cronus can only be defined in terms of tyranny, which is a gross imitation of true statesmanship, yet sometimes the most difficult to detect because of their formal similarity.[175]

For Plato both the age of Cronus and the age of Zeus represent instances of the embodiment of the Idea in history, the *kairos* where eternity enters time. But the relationship between the two eras cannot be described in terms of progress or decline. The philosophic consciousness which emerged in the age of Zeus could not be renounced, yet it constituted an estrangement from that experience of cosmic unity that existed on the unconsious level of the myth; the Olympian theology was, so to speak, only a memory of that unity.[176] The Platonic vision of a cosmos permeated by *nous* and psyche was a restoration of that unity, but a restoration that could not obliterate the fact of differentiation that accompanied the appearance of philosophy. Philosophy was, from the beginning, a paradox, an endeavor torn between its speculative and critical functions; while the latter disintegrated the world, the former leaped toward a stable ground.

Within the age of Cronus there was no internal decline, but, as with the integral myth, the collapse was sudden and decisive. The confusion that ensued was ameliorated by the memory of the heroic past, transmitted by the oral tradition, which provided a cultural foundation for the new society. Hellas had moved from the myth to the plane of historical existence. At first, the "instructions" were remembered clearly, but in time the "recollection grew dim" and the bodily element, the vessel of the Idea, began to return to

> its most primeval condition, for before it came into its present order as a universe it was an utter chaos of disorder. It is from God's act when he set it in its order that it has received all the virtues it possesses, while it is from its primal chaotic condition that all the wrongs and evils arise in it—evils which it engenders in turn in the living creatures within it.[177]

Plato at this point has proceeded beyond the part of the tale necessary for "the delineation of the king"; yet he continues to describe the end of the contemporary age.[178]

> At last, as this cosmic period draws to its close, this disorder comes to a head. The few good things it produces it corrupts with so gross a taint of evil that it hovers on the very brink of destruction, both of itself and of the creatures in it.[179]

This is his indictment of Athens in the present where "the title of Sophist goes to those who most deserve it, to the men who get themselves called political leaders."[180] The issue is drawn between the sophist-statesman who stands at the end of this historical era and manifests the exhaustion of the substance of the Idea and the philosopher-statesman through whom the *eidos* will again enter human time. For Plato as for Heidegger history itself as well as "Die Geschichte des Seins beginnt und zwar notwendig *mit der Vergessenheit des Seins.*"[181]

For Plato there are no illusions about a return to the golden age of Cronus nor is such a return desirable. To understand the myth as a cyclical theory of historical recurrence is to miss the point. Man is not bound to a cosmic cycle; the "reversal" must be attributed to man himself and his alienation from the divine, although the precise reason for this forgetfulness is beyond the reach of reason; it is part of the mystery of maturation that extends from individuals to civilizations. It is "fate" or "inborn urge" which causes the bodily elements to crowd out the divine and causes the rise and fall of social order and history.[182] This last moment in the tale, when god, fearing that the cosmos will "be dissolved again into the chaos of unlikeness," restores order in the universe, is the promise of the regeneration of time through the incarnation of the truth of order existing in the psyche of the philosopher. In this last reversal, god, by taking hold of the cosmos, "achieves for it its agelessness" (as it is found in the *Timaeus*), and this remains Plato's problem with regard to the order to be imposed on political space. Plato, himself, is the true "statesman," for the "possessor of this science then, whether he is in fact in power or has only the status of a private citizen, will properly be called a 'statesman' since his knowledge of the art qualifies him for the title whatever his circumstances."[183] But in Athens the circumstances are impossible; only through Plato and the Academy and their influence on someone like Dion does it appear possible that the Idea will again enter political space.

The problem of actualization demanded a shift from the emphasis on the imperfection of the existential world in relation to the forms and the neglect of the problem of change that characterized the *Republic*. The status of reality not ordered by the Idea is the problem of the *Theaetetus* and *Parmenides* where being and becoming, the one and many, body and soul, the philosophic advocates of reality as flux and immutability, are juxtaposed.[184] In the *Statesman* it was necessary to recognize the existence of both poles and to discuss the relation between them. This reconciliation had been effected in the *Sophist* where it was announced that being on the whole must somehow encompass change and the many; the philosopher, it seems, must reject both extremes and "like a child begging for 'both,' he must declare that reality or the sum of things is both at once—all that is unchangeable and all that is change."[185] Also in the *Statesman* it becomes necessary, in the course of distinguishing the statesman from his rivals, to admit the existence of forms of rule which do not conform to the standard and to illuminate the relation between them just as in the *Sophist* it was necessary to admit the sophist and false judgment into the scheme of reality.

In the *Sophist*, the art of image (*eidolon*) making or imitation (*mimesis*) consists of two parts; likeness (*eikon*) making and semblance (*phantasma*) making. Also imitation, art, or production is further distinguished as divine or human.[186] The products of the divine art consist of originals such as living creatures and the elements of the universe and their corresponding images such as dreams and shadows. The products of human art consist of originals or actual objects such as a house and images of these objects such as a painting which is "a manmade dream for waking eyes." Semblances, although false, "have a place among existing things," and the general category of producing semblances or mimicry is subdivided into that which uses tools and that in which the person by either opinion or knowledge produces the semblance by his own action. Those who act from opinion about virtue often "succeed perfectly" in appearing to be virtuous. Finally this mimicry by opinion is divided into those who imagine that what they believe is knowledge and are sincere and those who are insincere. The purpose of this division is to define the sophist's art as belonging to the lowest form of semblance making, but the same scheme is also applied in the *Statesman* to judge the imitations of true rule.[187]

Only the rule of the statesman is a true rule or an actual likeness, while the others are merely semblances which, although false, must be awarded a place in existence. Plato distinguishes the art of statesmanship from the contributory arts existing in a community and the auxiliary arts such as persuasion, generalship, and administration of justice by an analogy with weaving, which is differentiated from related arts by its concern with direction and measurement, not in a relative sense but with regard to a "fixed norm," "due measure," or "due time."[188] Mimics "acting their part in public life" are "hard to distinguish from the real statesmen and kings," but the criterion for judging them "must be the presence or absence of an art directing the ruling."[189] Those forms of rule which provide for government by law, although imitations, are sincere copies that follow the ideal "fairly closely," while those forms without law are "more or less shocking caricatures."[190]

Since the criterion reduces itself to the possession of knowledge, the old classification of governments according to rule of the "many" or "few" is irrelevant as well as the problem of whether the subjects are "willing or unwilling"; statesmen may "purge the city for its better health" as long as they follow "essential justice and act to preserve and improve the life of the state."[191] Since a state governed by law is the "justest and most desirable course as a second best," the criterion of law is not irrelevant, but it remains that the "political ideal is not full authority for the laws but rather full authority for a man who understands the art of kingship and has kingly ability." Law operates externally and hampers flexibility, precision, and the acknowledgment of new truths, and although it may preserve the lives of the subjects, it permits only a minimal reformation of their character.[192] But the most damning indictment of the laws is the fact that they, in the end, could make possible the death of a man like Socrates. Laws are only the reflection of the condition of the soul of the men who frame them, and as in Athens, over time, the content of "these more perfect copies" is corrupted until the state finally passes over into the lawless forms which are "grosser and less adequate imitation."[193] The classification of modes of rule is grounded in the historical experience of decline.

Although the element of force necessarily enters into the process of ordering chaotic matter, it is the statesman's direction of persuasion which is essential for molding the mass of the population and instilling right opinion.[194] The statesman's art "weaves all into a unified fabric with perfect skill" by its control over all arts which enter into the guidance of action, and the kingly art exemplifies this control by virtue of its ability to "perceive the right occasions for undertaking and setting in motion the great enterprises of the state."[195] The royal weaver must combine opposed characters in which courage and moderation predominate into a unified whole, and to this end he must oversee the education and preparation of the strands to insure that, although they may be dissimilar, only the sound are introduced into the warp and woof of the fabric.[196] The combination is to be effected first by instilling right opinion about justice which, since it is a conviction based on an absolute, provides a divine bond. Second, the divine bond is supplemented by eugenics, through which an adequate material basis is provided for its sustenance by the regulation of intermarriages between the strands.[197] This is the science of statesmanship which Plato will build into the structure of the *Laws* and which finds its model in the *Republic*.

Through the philosopher-statesman the Idea could conceivably find a rebirth in political space, but the problem of historical decline is in no way solved. The essence of the royal weaving is that it is a constant process carried on by a man who is a mortal; he is the mediator between the divine and the human through whom social order is sustained. Unlike the physical cosmos, the social cosmos has no self-sustaining mechanism since its soul and body are vitalized by the statesman in a process of continuous creation. Men despair of finding anyone with the capability of performing this function, and it would be doubtful, even if he were present in a city, that he would be recognized and distinguished from a tyrant. Although if a ruler did appear in whom power and intelligence were perfectly combined he would be acclaimed, it remains that cities do not spontaneously spawn and voluntarily accept such individuals in the way that a royal bee arises in the hive. Instead, cities continually go chasing after a "fading vision of the true constitution," and despite the inherent strength, that inborn inertia, that political communities possess, cities fall and will continue to fall in the future.[198] But beyond the fact that few such men are likely to arise in any city and the probability that only one or two may exist in the entire world, even though such a savior should exist and, what is even less likely, come to power, his appearance would be but a fleeting moment in time and his creation but the beginning of an inevitable deterioration of the soul and the city.[199] The problem of political order and history has not been solved.

The Descent into the Past: The Prelude to Order

WHETHER Plato, in the later dialogues, modified the substance of his metaphysics and the theory of knowledge or whether the discrepancies between the earlier and later works are to be explained in terms of a shift of emphasis need not be explored here.[200] What must be insisted on, however, is that just as Plato originally discovered philosophy after a paralysis of creative action, the content and tone of the later dialogues are set by the problem of incarnation. The complete failure of the Sicilian ventures, the failure of Dionysius to become a philosopher and of Dion to consummate his rule, ended the hope of finding that "one man" who might create a political order which would halt the "unending succession of governments."[201]

The problem of actualization is immediately apparent at the beginning of the *Timaeus*. At the commencement of the dialogue Socrates recapitulates a discussion held the previous day on "the best form of society and the sort of men who would compose it."[202] This summary clearly represents the *Republic* which will now, by an act of memory and imagination, be transferred from the realm of psychic reality to historical space and from a fabled discourse to a true event.[203] Plato is now prepared to answer more conclusively the question of the relation between the paradigm and existential politics.

After Socrates completes his synopsis [204] of the best state, the other participants, Timaeus, Critias, and Hermocrates, agree that all the main points have been included, *but* it is all too obvious what has been omitted. The account extends only to the discussion of eugenics and the community of women and children in Book V of the *Republic* and includes only the external structure and institutions of the purified polis; the summary breaks off before the appearance of the philosopher-king, and the implications cannot be ignored. Beyond the fact that this description of the best society is to be transposed into a prephilosophic incarnation of Athens and the emphasis on external organization is necessary to give it an image of tangible substance in space, the omission of the philosopher-king constitutes an acceptance of the limitations on the embodiment of the Idea which forms a central theme of the cosmology to be elaborated by Timaeus. The psychic and "divine" order of the *Republic* cannot be completely actualized.

Socrates' lament, that he feels "like a man who has been looking at some noble creatures in a painting, or perhaps at real animals, alive but motionless, and conceives a desire to watch them in motion,"[205] cannot be understood as anything other than Plato's concern with the intractable relation between the truth of order and contemporary Athens. Socrates feels unequal to the task of effecting this transition; Plato speaking through Socrates is the Plato who, alienated from the city, turns inward in search of himself and upward in search of the Good through philosophy. Yet he can rely neither on the poets and their mimetic art anchored in the spell of opinion nor on the spurious knowledge of the sophists divorced from political order to grasp the meaning of the Idea and celebrate its immanence in history. Only Plato speaking through Critias—the Plato who has never severed his involvement with Athens and is intimately a part of the life of the city both past and present—is suited to perform this role.[206]

The tale related by Critias, which is summarized at the beginning of the *Timaeus* and further elaborated in the incomplete dialogue bearing his name, is a consciously constructed myth, but it is a myth whose content is related to historical memory. On one level it is an illumination of the relation between order and history, just as the central myth of the *Timaeus* moves beyond what is accessible to discursive language to render the meaning of cosmic order and describe how things in the world move toward the Good. But on another level it is a *recherche du temps perdu*, an attempt to move beyond the concrete memory of the polis to the youth of the civilization by a penetration and reorganization of the Hellenic myths.

What separates this enterprise from that of Hesiod is that this descent into the past and its symbolic reconstruction is now governed and supplemented by the philosophic consciousness. The fact that the cosmological myth is introduced by a summary of the exploits of an archaic Athens and is followed by an enlarged version of this tale serves, as the myth in the *Statesman*, to project the mystery of order and disorder on the canvas of the cosmos. But here the strands have been disentangled; the juxtaposition no longer simply serves to throw into relief the problem of political order and its rise and fall, for human time is disengaged from and contrasted with the everlasting cosmos. The species and the individual soul are immortal because they belong to the cosmos, but what man creates by action and artifice belongs to the realm of the perishable, or history, and persists only to the extent to which it can be infused with the order of the eternal. But the history of political order is one of decline, a temporal estrangement from the foundation, which has its source not in the inexorable revolutions of the universe, which are just the measure of history, but in the fate-bound deterioration of the spirit which, similarly, can be overcome only by chance—by the appearance of a man like Plato.

That the intent of the dialogues is "political" is apparent from the beginning where the purpose of celebrating the best society in action is announced and those present are held by Socrates, in contrast to poets and sophists, to be qualified for the undertaking since they are "equipped by temperament and education for both philosophy and statesmanship."[207] But before entering into what, in terms of the Hellenic world, amounted to an ancient history, it is decided, or rather taken for granted, that the time of man must be prefaced by a cosmology presented by Plato through the mouth of the fictitious astronomer-statesman Timaeus who "will begin with the birth of the world and end with the nature of man."[208] Plato has substituted his figurative discourse for the "barbaric slough of the Orphic myth"; for the philosopher who through the "eye of the soul" and the medium of the dialectic has viewed the "good in itself," the old cosmogonies and mythic genealogies no longer suffice.[209] Man and nature separate into distinct entities occupying their respective temporal dimensions. But the exploration of the creation of order in the cosmos becomes more than simply a prelude to this history of man which stretches from the nebulous and ancient past of the *Critias* to the post-Homeric world explored in the *Laws*; the ordering power of *nous* in the *Timaeus*, and in fact the entire structure of the dialogue, becomes the indispensable prologue to an understanding of the problem of creating the social cosmos of the *Laws*.

Critias' journey back into the collective memory of the Greeks is above all to give virtual reality to the idea of the best society and to demonstrate the frailty of historical embodiment. The past of a dying Athens is regained, and on the level of the myth the substance of the Attic spirit is self-consciously revitalized and the temporal gap eliminated as in the choral lyric; this is a paean in memory of a city and its citizens once ripe with the fruit of the Idea. There is a sharp contrast with the irony of the *Menexenus* and its satirical hymn celebrating the Athens in which the Idea has been exhausted. Here, then, at the moment when time has run out, when, in terms of the symbolism of the *Statesman*, the innate vitality has been expended and the eternal ceases to animate the temporal, the mythic motif of a return to the primordial time of the beginning asserts itself in the *Timaeus-Critias* nexus.

The dialogue constitutes a necessary introduction which adumbrates and informs Plato's attempt to resolve the dilemma of political time in the *Laws*. The tale related by Critias, which he heard from his grandfather, who had received the story from Solon, his father's friend and relative, is continually affirmed as true.[210] That the circumstances of the dialogues themselves are a Platonic fiction cannot be doubted, but the "truth" of the tale emerges on at least two levels. First, it is an attempt to render a truth about the problem of political order; and second, the tale of Atlantis and Athens is permeated with historical meaning.

The origin of the story in Egypt points to Plato's continuing concern, which extends through the *Laws*, with this static culture which, as modern scholarship has affirmed, remained relatively unaffected by the upheavals that were so determinative for the Hellenic world. Egypt becomes Plato's symbol for a political order that, unlike the Attic states, stood beyond the reach of historical decline, and he turns to Egypt to posit the source of this account of the Hellenic past which the Greeks had "forgotten through lapse of time and the destruction of human life."[211] Solon brought the tale from the priests of Saïs, a city presided over by the oriental counterpart of Athena.[212] This allusion to the oriental origin of Greek theology and the "kinship" with the Near East cannot be passed off as an unconscious intrusion in the dialogues;[213] apart from the symbolic purposes of the story, Plato is seriously concerned with the past of Hellas.

It is these old men who have within their lifetime witnessed the rise and fall of Athens and who now descend through *mnemosyne* and *mythos* to the beginning of the *aion* of the Attic civiliation. The priests charge that the Greeks have no knowledge of antiquity and are "always children" because they, unlike the people of the Nile, have at various times suffered destruction "by fire and water." [214] Without straining the symbolism, it should be apparent that these passages are pregnant with historical meaning. The culture and environment of Egypt was preserved from the afflictions which lent instability to much of Asia Minor;[215] here the art of writing and the tradition were not destroyed as in Attica with the collapse of the Bronze Age. The Greeks were relatively "only lately enriched with letters and all the other necessities of civilization" and had to "start again like children, knowing nothing of what existed in ancient times here in your own country." Their knowledge of the past amounted to little more than "nursery tales"; they remember only "one deluge" and are ignorant of their illustrious ancestors "because the survivors for many generations died leaving no word in writing."[216] The similarity of this account to the Mycenaean world and its collapse, the Dark Ages and the partial preservation of the past in oral poetry, and the beginning of classical culture is apparent.

The tale of the contest between Atlantis and Athens contains such a rich symbolic content that it would be shortsighted to attempt to narrowly confine its meaning. No doubt the story is in part shaped by the memory of the Persian war[217] and the traditional conflict between West and East represented in the *Iliad*. Again, there can be little doubt that through the symbol of the war there is a transference to a historical plane of the conflict between wisdom and necessity which dominates the *Timaeus*.[218] Also Athens and Atlantis represent the tension between mythic culture and the vision of a society ordered by philosophy. But granting the manifold strata of symbolization embedded in the account, it would seem that the material on which the symbols are imposed is no mere fiction; the content of the *Critias* is grounded in a past which, however vague, was partially accessible to the philosopher. Although the thesis has rarely been expounded,[219] the conflict between Athens and Atlantis bears a remarkable resemblance to the decline of the Minoan thalassocracy in the middle of the sixteenth century B.C. and the transfer of power to the developing Mycenaean empire on the mainland. The natural disasters which were said to have washed Athens away and submerged Atlantis may well refer either to the earthquakes which apparently struck Crete and other areas of the Aegean during this period or to Mycenaean or Dorian invasions.

What separates the expression of history in the *Timaeus, Critias,* and *Laws* from the *Republic* and earlier dialogues, and even the *Statesman,* is not only an increasing prominence but a new concreteness; human time is explicitly differentiated from the cosmic context, and the problem of history is no longer merely abstractly and symbolically expressed. Although historical accounts always remain subservient to the philosophic purpose and although Plato never becomes a "historian," there is an increasing concern with unique events, and the past becomes significant in itself as the problem of actualization begins to weigh more heavily on his thought. There is an increased emphasis on the "truth" of the accounts, as far as any discourse dealing with becoming can be true and serious.

The concern with the reconstruction of the past and the difficulties of such a project discussed at the beginning of the *Critias* were meaningful. Only in the developed city-state does such an investigation become possible "for legendary lore and inquiry into ancient things both visit cities in the train of leisure, when they see men already provided with the necessaries of life, and not before."[220] Historical as well as philosophic discourse is a form of play or amusement that emerges only in the context of polis life. But this penetration of antiquity is not an easy task, and, even more than a tale describing the physical or supernatural world, it must be accepted as only "an affair of imagery and picturing."[221] Just as an artist's representation of nature is accepted even if there is only a "faint degree of resemblance," so it is with a discourse on nature, while a portrait of a human form or a discourse on human history is expected to be exact. But Critias pleads that much indulgence is required in a reconstruction of the historical past which must rely on the tenuous resources of social memory.[222]

What Plato has constructed in his portrait of Atlantis is an "ideated Orient."[223] Exactly what information Plato might have possessed about Minoan or other ancient Aegean civilizations is impossible to know, but such information may have been preserved in Egyptian records, and there can be little doubt that he was aware of the close connection between Crete and the East. In addition to the island's physical similarity to Crete and various rituals including the religious symbol of the bull and the practice of divination and other numerous affinities with the luxurious Minoan kingdom, the city Plato has described is a paradigm of the oriental state in both structure and cultural content with the institution of divine or semidivine kingship, the sacred mountain and palace at the center of the city, and the tight geometric design.[224] But whether the image of Atlantis is grounded in the history of Crete or a similar civilization, the city represents the realm of the integral myth or at least that form of it which penetrated the Aegean world. Atlantis, which fell to Poseidon when the parts of the earth were apportioned among the gods according to justice, is ruled by a semidivine dynasty along with a set of sacred laws bestowed by Poseidon and established by the earliest kings whose primogenitors were the offspring of the sea-god's union with a mortal and the founders of the monarchy.

Although both cities were infused with the divine, the presentation of Athens provides a sharp contrast. First, there is, as compared with Atlantis, almost a complete lack of physical description; the intricate spatial structure of Atlantis is absent in the city which finds its substantive order in its psychic rather than external form. Just as Atlantis is an "ideated Orient," this is an ideated Athens which is probably constructed from the memory of the Mycenaean age. Atlantis was not ruled directly by a deity who was the shepherd of his flock as in Egypt, for at this historical stage the gods "set the course of the living creature from that part about which it turns most readily, its prow, controlling its soul after their own mind by persuasion as by a rudder, and so moving and steering the whole mortal fabric."[225] But while the kings of Atlantis are demigods and there is no clear separation of the divine and human, Athens, although under the tutelage of Hephaestus and Athena, who provided through their "love of wisdom and artistry . . . a home meet for prowess and understanding" and "produced from the soul a race of good men and taught them the order of their polity," is clearly ruled by mortals despite the immanence of divine elements in the rulers and citizens.[226]

Plato is presenting two contemporaneous societies. Neither belongs strictly to what in the *Statesman* was understood as the age of Cronus, but they conform closely to the historical situation of the Minoan and Mycenaean civilizations. The conflict between the two states gains its symbolic import and historical meaning from that transition which marked the decline of oriental form and the rise of the Hellenic world, the collapse of the integral myth and the beginnings of the Olympian theology, the passing of the age of Cronus and the emergence of the order of Zeus and his daughter Dike. In Greek mythology it was Poseidon who challenged the new dispensation of Zeus and sided with the chthonic deities and their old tyrannical regimes based on power and passion.[227]

Plato says of this race of men of Bronze Age Athens that

> their names have been preserved, but their deeds forgotten by reason of the destruction of their successors and the lapse of time. For the remnant of survivors . . . was ever left unlettered among its mountains, and heard no more than the names of the country's rulers and a few of their deeds. So they were well pleased to give the names of their sons, but as for the virtues and laws of older generations, they know nothing of them beyond dim reports, but were, for many generations, themselves and their children, in want of bare necessaries.[228]

The similarity of this description of the collapse of the Mycenaean kingdoms, the end of Hesiod's bronze race, and the ensuing Dark Ages cannot be ignored; as for gold and silver, "they made no use of these metals for any purpose." These were the forebears of Homer's heroic Achaeans who were "at once guardians of their fellow citizens and freely followed leaders of the Hellenes at large . . . and had the greatest name of their time."[229]

Although at the end of the *Critias* it is Zeus, "the God of gods, who governs his kingdom by law," who prepares to render judgment on Atlantis, this may be no more than a symbolic expression of the fate of a city suffering from internal deterioration.[230] The meaning of Plato's explanation of disorder must be found not in divine decision, but in that impenetrable movement whereby the bodily and chaotic element in society begins to reassert itself; this is the problem of human time and the dilemma of imperfect embodiment. The divine element which presided over the creation of the city becomes attenuated as the prosperity and wealth, which the citizens and rulers at first counted as "a little thing" and carried as "a light load" in their devotion to the divine, begins to corrupt them and "when the God's part in them began to wax faint by constant crossing with much mortality, and the human temper to predominate."[231] But beyond this mythical symbolization of the mystery of decline, the account finds its truth in the history of the internal deterioration of the opulent Minoan empire and the breakdown of the integral myth and the institution of divine kingship.

It would be a tour de force to extract from the *Critias* and Book III of the *Laws* an integrated and chronologically consistent reconstruction of the past of Hellas, but in both cases Plato is moving within the realm of the historical. Yet, despite the historical ground of the *Critias,* the history in the *Laws* must be further distinguished. The time of Book III is not the abstract and fabled time of the imaginative discourse in the *Republic,* but neither is it the prehistoric twilight of the *Timaeus* and *Critias* which was created by a combination of collective memory and an act of will as a canvas on which to paint the character and fate of the incarnation of the Idea. Although the history in the *Laws* is still shaped by the notion of embodiment and disembodiment, it is distinguished by an even greater concreteness, which may be explained by two factors.

First, the scene is now, for the most part, the relatively accessible past of classical Greece: not the prehistorical age of Cronus but the age of Zeus. Plato asserts that he is dealing with true events of the past and not "mere abstraction."[232] Second, Plato's concern is now with the decline of Greek culture and the reintroduction of the Idea, preserved in the psyche of the philosophic "remnant," into the political realm. The causes of the decline become the indispensable prologue. Although, as in the early books of *Republic,* Book III of the *Laws* remains an integral part of the artistic design of the dialogue with the account balanced and interwoven with the participants and the constitutions which they symbolize, it nevertheless approaches the substance of a historical account.[233]

For Plato the political cycle is a function not of cosmic revolution but of the internal balance between form and matter.[234] Although natural events have meaning for human time since man remains a part of nature, cosmic time and political time are distinguished; no form of political rule (*arche*) is destroyed "except by itself."[235] Book III is a historical inquiry into the causes of political order and disorder from the perspective of that "interminable length of time" within which innumerable cities have appeared and perished and every form of *politeia* has been manifest and during which some have grown larger or smaller and better or worse.[236] Against the background of the essentially neutral and constant movement of *chronos*, Plato casts the instability of human affairs. History is the visible symptom of the disease of political disorder for which he is prescribing the antidote. During the age of Zeus, order had appeared only sporadically like the instant of rest between the rise and fall of an object thrown into the air.

At the beginning, Plato poses the question of the truth of the old legends concerning the catastrophic destructions of mankind, and Clinias asserts that such tales "must be perfectly credible."[237] At the moment when the Hellenic world seems to be on the brink of such a destruction, Plato returns to its beginnings in order to extract the principles which must inform a new beginning. His serious attempt at a reconstruction of Greek civilization in one sense parallels the early portion of the *Republic* except that what is now presented is more than a paradigmatic representation of the evolution of the polis; far more than Aristotle, he is moving in the realm of history to the extent that it is intelligible from the sources, such as Homer, that were available.[238] The story is no longer touched by myth, and culture is no longer the gift of the gods or a cultural hero; the rediscovery of the civilizational arts belongs to man himself, and this includes the political art.

Men were at first not only politically naïve but, as in Rousseau's state of nature, free from conflict and the problem of good and evil, which arose only as consequences of society, and they lived in the simplicity of the myth where "what they were told about God or man they believed to be true."[239] Yet, Plato avers, even here in the preliterate society, there was a form of *politeia* based on patriarchal rule and tribal custom. The unification of tribes led to larger units with early forms of representative government and legislation, and from the plurality of leaders was established an aristocracy or possibly a monarchy (*basileia*). The third type of *politeia* to arise was a blend of all varieties of states and constitutions; this was the city of the plain and the point of the foundation of Ilium and of the Achaean states which besieged Troy.[240] Relying on a story that the Dorians were Achaeans who, after being driven off by the younger generation upon their return from Troy, conquered and resettled the Peloponnesos and established a federation between Lacedaemon, Argos, and Messene, Plato proceeds, having reached the point of the foundation of a city (Sparta) which still exists, to give a history of the establishment and failure of the Doric federation. In this manner it is possible to discern "what has been commendable in such foundations, or the reverse, what types of laws lead to their preservation, where it is achieved, and what in the opposite case, to their dissolution, and what kind of changes will contribute to the happiness of a community."[241] After the discussion, in the first two books, of the correct psychic balance that must be established within a state by legislation, Plato now takes another road and turns to the problem of embodying this balance in the institutional structure of the city. When one is seriously concerned with the problem of actualization, the body of the state like the body of the individual must be formed as a suitable receptacle for the spirit.

The cause of the breakdown of the confederacy, which was expected to endure indefinitely and was designed to protect not only the Peloponnesos but the whole of Hellas, was not a tactical failure, but an internal flaw; that is, a constitutional defect in both the rulers and the institutions. The degeneration of the laws and constitutions of Argos and Messene was caused by the dissonance between reasoned judgment and passionate desire in the soul of the rulers, which is the worst folly (worse than miscalculation). In both an individual and a state the imbalance between the ruling part and the ruled is the worst form of ignorance while the existence of the right relation is the greatest wisdom. The difficulty was forestalled only in Sparta and even there only by fortuitous circumstances rather than the wisdom of the rulers or quality of the legislators. It was an institutional balance which provided the required "due limitation" and eventually enabled the Lacedaemonians to gain ascendancy in the Peloponnesos and aid Athens in saving Hellas during the Persian war.[242] From his analysis of Peloponnesian history, Plato concludes that the correct institutional structure, which will aid in securing the proper balance in a state between the elements of wisdom, liberty, and amity and which the legislator must have in view in his enactments, is a combination of the two prototypical forms of constitution: monarchy and democracy which are best exemplified in Persia and Athens, respectively.[243] For a society to survive it is necessary that the laws provide for the awarding of honor and dishonor according to a hierarchy in which the qualities of the soul take first place and the goods of the body and material wealth assume second and third places; both Persia and Athens degenerated from the failure to adhere to this principle. In the case of Persia the principle was violated by an excess of "servitude aristocracy" and in Athens by the encouragement of "the multitude toward unqualified liberty."[244] The "due proportionality" of autocracy and democracy is the prerequisite for minimum well-being in a society.

At the beginning of the dialogue, the Athenian and his companions are engaged in a journey from Knossos to the Cave of Zeus, and this ascent symbolizes the recovery of the Greek past as a prelude to a new foundation. The historical survey and the principles elucidated in the first two books come at a propitious moment, for Megillus is a member of a commission charged with framing the legislation for a new Cretan colony, and the participants in the dialogue will now combine their search for the means by which both a state and an individual life are best managed with an imaginary founding. The return to Crete is a return to the beginning of Hellenic civilization, and the participants represent the successive phases of Greek history. But the symbols of historical decline and a new beginning reach far beyond the literary structure of the dialogue. The history of Greece had heretofore been the failure of its lawgivers to secure the proper beginning, and this is the indictment which Plato brings "against the so-called statesmen and legislators of both past and present."[245] History is the scene of "iniquity," and the source of this "iniquity" and disorder is not attributable to the gods or the cosmos, but to the failure of man to achieve the right measure,[246] and the achievement of this measure, now perceived for the first time in its fullness by Plato, means, potentially, not only the abolition of the past and the regeneration of time by the reintroduction of the Idea into the world, but the negation of history. And from the study of the iniquity of the past "God has shown us by the event how a government should have been constituted then and must be constituted now, if it is to have good prospects of permanence."[247]

VI

THE PLATONIC RESTORATION: THE *LAWS*

*The due measure of servitude is to serve
God. The extreme of servitude is to serve
man.*

Plato

The Principles of Order

FOR Plato the beginning or foundation in any enterprise is determinative, for "the beginning is more than half the work, and a fair beginning has never yet been commended to its full merits."[1] To overcome the cycle of political time requires a secure foundation, and this is possible only when the original laws create the type of rule and institutions which will preserve harmony and unity. As long as the foundation remains authoritative, the state will endure in perpetuity, and the founder, like the god in the myth in the *Statesman,* may withdraw, "for in the affairs of man's life the first step holds the place of God himself and makes all the rest right, if approached with proper reverence by all concerned."[2] Unlike the state overseen by the royal ruler who continually weaves the strands into a harmonious fabric, the "tuneless dissonance" of political time is to be overcome in the *Laws* by structuring the city and its soul according to the founder's "insight into due proportion" so that it will participate in the divine measure.[3] In creating such a beginning man himself comes as near as possible to divinity and immortality, for "in very truth to make a legislation or found a society is the perfect consummation of manly excellence."[4] In Plato one hears the echo of the ancient myth, and in Aristotle, Cicero, and Machiavelli may be heard the echo of Plato.

Plato's notion of "due proportion" is central to the *Laws* and cannot be understood without reference to the ontology of the *Philebus* and the

cosmology of the *Timaeus*. Any dichotomy between being (*ousia*) and
becoming (*genesis*), between the forms and the world, including human
affairs, is no longer maintained.[5] Even in the *Sophist*, existence (*einai*)
does not necessarily imply changelessness as differentiated from becoming (*gignesthai*). Being no longer means the negation of activity. The
earlier dialogues often appear to make a sharp contrast between things
in the physical world (and human events) which are *gignomena* and the
ideas which are *onta;* the things in the world seem to hover between that
which is and that which is not. According to this view it would seem that
the forms are intelligible (through *noesis*) and result in *episteme* or
gnosis or, broadly, *sophia* (wisdom), while the material world is apprehended by sense perception (*aisthesis*) and results in opinion or belief
(*doxa*) which is halfway between *episteme* and *agnoia* (ignorance). But
it is questionable that Plato ever meant to deny existence or reality to
the physical world or that the traditional interpretation of the theory of
forms with its sharp distinctions derived from the earlier dialogues including the *Republic* can be accepted on its face.[6] If the *Sophist* and
later dialogues are not a radical departure from the earlier work, it must
be assumed that Plato did not deny reality to the world. It appears that
when Plato opposes "to be" and "to become" he is not maintaining that
they are mutually exclusive, but is rather positing extremes within the
realm of existence which is bounded on one side by the Good or that
which is beyond being and on the other by nonbeing—of neither of
which is it possible to give an exact account. Things are infused with
being to a greater or lesser degree; the transcendent forms are pure being which eternally persists in perfect sameness, and the remainder of
existence is understood as becoming or less than ultimate being.[7]

In the *Sophist*, Plato attempts to clarify the issue by confronting
those who assert that existence belongs exclusively to matter and understand being (*ousia*) as the same as body and those who hold that existence means only bodiless forms and maintain that all else is not real
being but becoming (*genesis*).[8] Plato rejects these alternatives and concludes that reality cannot be identified with either motion or rest or both
of these at once; it is a third thing since reality cannot be an attribute
of any other property. Both activity and inactivity are real and can be
said to be, while reality is by its very nature neither rest nor movement.
This is not a paradox because activity and inactivity are predicates of
being, not identifications, and can combine with being. There is no need

to proceed step by step through Plato's argument regarding predication and participation since this is sufficient to illustrate that he intended to destroy any notion of perceiving the world in terms of an absolute dichotomy between " 'becoming [*genesis*]' and 'real being [*ousia*].' "[9] Both rest (*stasis*) and motion (*kinesis*) can be combined with being or be said to be. However, certain aspects of the argument must be further explicated.

One side argues that existence, or that which is, belongs to matter and can be grasped only by the senses; they define being as the same as body (*soma*), refusing to admit that anything without body is real. The advocates of the forms (*eidos*) argue, conversely, that true reality consists of intelligible and bodiless entities and that what the others understand as true is devoid of being (*ousia*) and only a moving process of becoming (*genesis*). Plato's main concern is with the partisans of the forms, and against the materialists he simply urges the existence of the soul (*psyche*). In opposition to the other position, Plato argues that since it is the soul that knows, and real being is capable of being known, and to be known is to be acted upon, real being must in some sense be changeable. He also asserts that change (*kinesis*), life, soul, and understanding (*phronesis*) must belong to reality, and since the real does not exclude life and intelligence and the soul in which they reside, it is necessary to conclude that that which changes and change itself belong to reality. Yet it cannot be denied that all real things, all things which partake of ultimate being, must in some way be unchangeable, or otherwise intelligence and its objects would not exist and knowledge would be impossible.

It must be understood that Plato is not only attempting to discredit the advocates of flux and the partisans of forms but trying to rescue both the forms and change, especially change. After mentioning those who oppose *ousia* and *genesis*, Plato does not again speak of activity and change in terms of *genesis*. His point is that there is change which is not pure *genesis* or that there is becoming which is not devoid of being and that even *genesis* must be accepted as part of existence. Plato usually refers to the things of becoming in the physical world as *gignomena*, and this is the decisive point: the choice is not between *ousia* and *genesis* for there is becoming which is infused with being. For Plato, as for the partisans of the forms, there is a split between being and becoming, but the split is not irredeemable and the poles cannot be defined in terms of change and changelessness; only that which is actually beyond being is changeless in every respect, and only in a condition, such as that described in the *Statesman*, where the world is on the brink of dissolving into dissimilarity does change threaten to gain complete ascendancy, when matter is no longer ordered by mind and when the parts lose their place in the whole.

It cannot be expected that the distinctions above may be consistently and unequivocally apparent in all the dialogues; Plato by no means always uses the same words in the same way nor can it be expected that he would have had adequate symbols at hand to make his distinctions entirely precise. Again, it must be stressed that the Platonic dialogue is an exploratory venture, and its meaning is obscured if one attempts to seek doctrines or systems. Plato was in the process of forming as well as manipulating symbols, and before charging him with confusing the relation between categories, one must realize that he was engaged in this process of creating "logical shape."[10] Nevertheless, it seems on the whole that Plato recognized a certain ontological schema which approximates that outlined above.

One of the continual difficulties in interpreting Plato is to disentangle the ontological argument from his epistemology; the difficulty and probably the impossibility of unraveling these threads has created a residue of ambiguity. Nowhere is this more apparent than in regard to the problem of *genesis*. In the discussion of the "line,"[11] Plato sets forth four divisions: science (*episteme*), understanding (*dianoia*), belief (*pistis*), and conjecture (*eikasia*). The first two divisions are encompassed under intellection (*noesis*) which deals with essence (*ousia*), and the second two divisions under opinion (*doxa*) which deals with generation (*genesis*). Although Plato does not make clear the implications of the use of these inclusive terms, it is obvious that for *noesis* and *ousia*, and *doxa* and *genesis*, there is more than one level. These distinctions are important for understanding the epistemological sections of the *Timaeus*, but in that dialogue, as well as the *Philebus*, *genesis* is also used to denote a type of change or becoming not previously elucidated: the motions of chaos and the process of coming into being. The categories used in the epistemological sections are not entirely comparable with their use when discussing cosmology and ontology.

The ubiquity of disorder forced Plato to admit its reality, and in these later dialogues the idea of being or reality as a continuum becomes increasingly apparent. He never fails to make it clear that ultimate being is perceived by intellection; only through the art of dialectic is there access to "that which is, that which exists in reality, ever unchanged"— only to this study whose object is true being do the terms *nous, episteme, phronesis,* and *aletheia* purely apply. The transcendent forms apprehended by intelligence remain the scene of ultimate being and are sharply distinguished from the things of becoming in the *kosmos* and the degree of truth which attaches to them.[12] Nevertheless the physical world and the world of human artifice contain many manifestations of being.

Plato remarks that the men of old who lived nearer to the gods have passed to us the knowledge that all things consist of a one and a many and have "in their nature a conjunction of limit [*peras*] and unlimitedness [*apeiron*]."[13] Not only do all things which now exist in the universe show these same characteristics—limit and unlimited—but there is a third characteristic arising out of the mixture of these two.[14] The relation of this to the task of the royal weaver in the *Statesman,* who orders his materials according to due proportion, is obvious. Plato argues that the creation of this mixture is the source of all conditions such as beauty, health, and order in the world; the mixture of limited and unlimited creates a unity, for the introduction of limit means a coming-into-being (*genesis eis ousian*).[15] But all this presupposes a cause or making which Plato introduces as the fourth element in the scheme, and this cause is present in all things in the universe which exhibit order and harmony, both human and divine products which have come to be through this mixing of limited and unlimited.[16] The "king of heaven and earth" is intelligence, and this accounts for the ordered movement of the cosmos whose constitution, like that of the human body, exhibits wisdom; the cause of all order is the result of the presence of *nous* in *psyche.*[17]

The good life, which is an example of being-in-the-world, consists of a mixture of wisdom (limit) and pleasure (unlimited), either of which by itself is insufficient. To obtain a good mixture it is necessary that only the best pleasures be admitted, but the case is different with knowledge. There are varying degrees of knowledge, and the arts that correspond to them have varying degrees of exactness such as the difference between carpentry which relies on precise measurement and the playing of music which includes practice, guesswork, and repetition. Here Plato admits that knowledge of the physical world is possible and can be properly classed as knowledge even though it is less true than knowledge of everlasting being. Knowledge of the physical world is not simply *doxa,* because the cosmos partakes of true being. A man is not adequately possessed of knowledge if he can give an account only of the divine circles and justice and remains blind to justice and the circles in the human and physical world.[18] The point is that all levels of knowledge must be admitted into the wisdom which gives meaning to the good life, although only the best pleasures such as those which are compatible with health, temperance, and virtue in general can be admitted. The ontological correlate of this argument is that perfect embodiment is not a prerequisite for applying the term *ousia* to order in the world.

For a thing to come into being and persist in being it is necessary that truth (*aletheia*) enter into the mixture, and at last Plato asserts, "We have created what might be called an incorporeal ordered system for the rightful control of a corporeal subject in which dwells a soul," and this constitutes the appearance of good in the world.[19] Next in value to the good must be placed intelligence which, being nearest to truth, is the cause of the good and creates measure and proportion which are the source of all beauty and excellence; the good cannot be comprehended under a single form (*idea*), but exists wherever *peras* has been imposed on *apeiron* in such a way as to produce a conjunction of beauty, proportion, and truth.[20]

The *Philebus* provides the metaphysical foundation for the cosmology of the *Timaeus* and the system of political order in the *Laws,* both of which exhibit instances of the *peras–apeiron* relationship. The existence of recalcitrant matter has been fully admitted as coeval with the forms, and incarnation is no longer a question of perfect embodiment and the displacement of chaos by ultimate reality, but rather the imposition of measure and law on the world by a creative and mediating intelligence whose vision encompasses both eternal being and the becoming of unordered existence. The *Timaeus* is impenetrable apart from the *Philebus,* and the threads which bind the *Timaeus* and *Laws* together are so numerous that it would require a separate study to trace them completely through the entire fabric of the dialogues. What Plato sets forth in the *Philebus* is a key for the reintegration of the universe; the unity of the integral myth and its vision of an ordering force emanating from creative intelligence which binds together heaven and earth is consciously recaptured. The edifice can be understood in no other way than as a restoration, and in this restoration, as in the myth, it is political order which ties man to the cosmos.

Cosmos and Polis

In a sense, the *Laws* like the *Timaeus* is a myth, but they are myths consciously calculated to render a truth of order; and this truth, which was also accessible in the old myths, is that order is the product of creative intelligence. But in these last dialogues the symbols are completely subservient to the play of the speculative mind and its idea of the unity of man, state, and cosmos.

Plato approaches the main theme of the *Timaeus* through a consideration of the continuing problem of being and becoming.[21] He makes a distinction between that which always is (*to on aei*) and has no becoming (*genesis*) and is apprehended by *noesis* and accessible to *logos* and that which is always becoming (*gignomenon*), never has true being (*ontos on*), and is the object of *doxa*. The separation of existence into two realms is the broad division utilized in the simile of the "line" in the *Republic*, and Plato is not concerned, at this point, with refining the distinction since his purpose is merely to demonstrate that the model (*paradeigma*) which the demiurge used in fashioning the cosmos was the forms and not a generated entity. He next argues that the physical world belongs to things that become and must have had a beginning (*arche*) or cause, but he is quick to add that the world is "good" and the "best of things that have become," and thus its maker must have been good and fashioned it after the eternal.[22] The cosmos, then, is an image (*eikon*) of an eternal model, and of a likeness only a likely story (*eikos mythos*) can be given as opposed to the rational account of the unchanging, for as *ousia* is to *genesis* so is *aletheia* to *pistis*. But it does not suffice to interpret this passage, as Cornford does, as simply a reiteration of the earlier passage describing the two types of models; in regard to the physical world it is not enough to say that "it is a realm, not of being, but of becoming," for it is in fact being-in-becoming. The world is not itself an object of ultimate knowledge, but even in terms of the epistemological question there is not the sharp dichotomy that such traditional interpretations as that of Cornford maintain.[23]

The "likeness"–"likely" relation must be understood as essentially a play on words and cannot be taken too seriously; it is a symbol without an exact and literal meaning. It is probably true that Plato intends to point to the necessarily tenuous and probable nature of cosmology and physical theory vis-à-vis the dialectic. Since the world constitutes being-in-becoming, it is not the ultimate reality, and the types of knowledge and accounts belonging to it are also not ultimate; the forms are apprehended by intellection while of the world there is only true belief or trust.[24] But the meaning of "likely" goes beyond this, for the dialogue attempts not only to give an account of the constitution of the universe but to tell about "the gods and the generation of the universe" and to render the truth of creation and describe how things in the world strive toward the good and have come to possess rational order. This is possible *only through myth which is neither intellection nor opinion.*

Plato, as the founder in the *Laws*, is the demiurge who, at least in discourse, creates a social cosmos. The *Laws* is a fable, but just as the *Timaeus* symbolizes the truth of cosmic order, it is meant to convey the truth of establishing a stable political order. But to argue that Plato understands himself as a human demiurge, although figuratively impelling, is in a sense misleading because the demiurge is a mythical symbol; one is forced back into the paradox of the origin of symbols. Does the notion of the demiurge inform Plato's conception of the founder, or does the experience of the craftsman-maker and the political founder inform the symbol of the demiurge, or are both informed by the general idea of the autonomy of creative intelligence as the source of order in the world? In any event, the demiurge and the political founder are parallel symbols.[25]

Plato explains that the cosmos was framed because its maker was good and wished to create the universe in his own image. Faced with the overwhelming beauty of the eternal, the demiurge longs to create. In seeking the good which is the object of love one seeks to possess it everlastingly, and this is the source of procreation for love is a "longing not for the beautiful itself, but for the conception and generation that the beautiful effects."[26] The Idea is mirrored in the demiurge or pure intelligence who "desired that all things should come as near as possible to being like himself" and conceived and gave birth to the *kosmos* by imposing order (*taxis*) upon the disorder of all that was visible with its "discordant and unordered motion."[27] And because he deemed order to be best, he formed the universe by fashioning *nous* in *psyche* and *psyche* in *soma* and made his creation immortal and as perfect as possible. It is the *eros* of mediating intelligence that unites being and becoming by constructing a unique world in the likeness of the unique living being which is the system of forms.

This intelligence which is capable of apprehending the forms is shared "only by the gods and a small number of men" such as Plato who desires to give issue to an immortal offspring in the social world which will reflect the goodness and excellence of his well-ordered soul.[28] It is the disordered motion of social activity that he wishes to infuse with order and relieve himself of the fetal burden conceived by the contemplation of eternal beauty. The polity like the cosmos must be fashioned as a living being with soul in body and with intelligence immanent in the laws which govern its motion. In the *Symposium* and in the description of the motive of the demiurge in the *Timaeus*, the source of political vision is revealed; in the most complete sense Plato understands his life as the imitation of god.

Like the *Timaeus*, the *Laws* is a fable whose truth resides not in its correspondence to any actual event of creation, but in the illumination of what must be the case if a creation is to be everlasting. The purpose of the two dialogues is to convey in approximate terms what must have been the case in regard to the cosmos coming into being and what will have to be the case in the formation of any future stable political order. It is the correspondence between cosmic and political creation which gives meaning to Plato's statement that "a society is likely to enjoy but a second-best constitution."[29]

He states that there are many who are unfamiliar with lawgivers who are not despots and might disagree, but it is not the absence of the autocrat and an initial purgation or "carding" or even the fact that it is a law-state that makes only a secondary excellence possible. In the *Laws* the problem of purgation has already been obviated by the circumstances of the foundation which permit a process of selection which allows only proper types of individuals to be admitted. Also the laws of this polity are not the "second-best" laws discussed in the *Statesman* for here the art of the royal weaver is built into the laws themselves.[30] What determines the secondary quality of the state is the inherent limitation in the nature of the human material.[31] Mankind in general cannot stand the full impact of being, and as Moses was the mediator of the covenant before Sinai, so is Plato the mediator of the divine measure. Just as with the creation of the cosmos, perfect embodiment is unattainable because of the inability of the receptacle to accept the

full measure of being—"human kind cannot bear very much reality."[32]
What Plato describes as the best society is obviously the *Republic,* but
it is a society fit only for gods or the sons of gods while the state being
founded in the dialogue is intended neither for gods nor for a race of
heroes; it is founded by mortals for their progeny.[33]

There are, for example, two kinds of equality. A state that gives
equality to all regardless of merit produces a discord for "equal treatment of the unequal ends in inequality when not guided by due proportion." Perfect equality is that exemplified in the *Republic* which proceeds precisely according to merit giving "more to the greater and less
to the lesser," but although this true geometric proportion is "sheer
justice" and must be the ultimate aim and model of the statesman, it
has a limited scope in human affairs, and the legislator must "apply
these standards with some qualification, if it is to escape dissensions
somewhere among its constituent parts." In all respects the polity must
be a mixture of monarchy and democracy and thus there must be a
distribution according to lot as well as merit.[34] In this sense the Mag-
nesian state will be second-best for "the state builder will intend the
possible; the impossible he will neither make the object of a futile intention nor attempt it."[35]

The best state should be the model for creation in political space
although its reality finds expression nowhere but in the soul of the
creator. The society that is "utterly one" cannot be made immanent and
endure, but the Cretan polity will approximate oneness. Although it is
beyond the capacity of men to till the soil in common, the citizens will
each count their lot as part of the common property of the society.[36]
Just as the abstract unity of the forms was expressed in the order of the
Republic, the institutions of the *Laws* become approximations of the
purity of the *Republic.* The difference is well expressed by Plato's comparison between carpentry and music in the *Philebus* where it is argued
that the nature of the material determines the degree of exactness of an
art. In carpentry, where the material is fixed and static, there is a maxi-
mum of measurement while the playing of music depends on guesswork
and deals with movement.[37] Human matter like music requires legislation based on approximation, and its ordering is a problem of rhythm
and the proper mixing of elements rather than the severe and static
divisions in the *Republic.* Yet both music and legislation must be performed according to a precise and measured score. The human good is

to be found in the mixed life which is not devoid of motion and change, but is a mixture in which movement is attuned to the divine measure.[38]

The *Laws* is itself a paradigm and, like the *Republic*, a verbal rather than an actual founding;[39] it is explicitly a model for a future ruler or lawgiver who would wish to found or reform a state. It is, so to speak, a prolegomenon to any future foundation, and it is not meant to serve as a blueprint, but as a standard or set of principles which may be adapted, more or less, to any particular set of circumstances.[40] Although it is not entirely beyond comprehension that the fortunate conjunction of wisdom and power which would produce the best constitution might come into existence, the divine measure cannot be expected to enter society through the philosopher-king or true statesman, who will be rare specimens, and even when they exist are, like Plato, likely to be denied their proper field of action. The alternative is that the true statesman become the lawgiver and founder of an actual state or the creator of a model in which the art of the statesman, based on due measure and proportion, is built into the institutional and legal order.

Although the polity in the *Laws* is a paradigm, its actualization is understood as possible; it would be, like the universe, the best of all possible orders. But the concurrence of circumstances that would enable such a founding would be exceedingly rare, and Plato is willing to speak in terms of third-best constitutions.[41] Human affairs are largely a matter of chance (*tyche*) and accident because man and his creations are affected by the aberrations of nature; legislation cannot be conducted without recognition of the fact that man and the state are rooted in the physical world. But although it may sometimes appear that the course of human events, such as that coming together of circumstances which would add up to the condition appropriate for a stable founding, is determined purely by chance and that god, in co-operation with *tyche* and *kairos*, is the shaper of human destiny, *techne* is the important variable in every situation. Every propitious founding presupposes the appearance of a true legislator.[42] But if the legislator hopes to make the utmost use of his skill, he must pray that fortune will provide that the society be ruled by a young and moderate autocrat (*tyrannos*) so that the best and most rapid settlement can be achieved. An autocrat can most easily change the constitution of a society, and what is difficult is not producing the change but finding that happy circumstance where there is a concurrence of power, wisdom, and temperance which is the

precondition of the good polity. Only at such a moment does the Idea
enter the course of history.[43]

From the *Republic* to the *Laws* the prerequisite for a good founding
has not changed; what has changed is the degree to which the Idea can
be made immanent. Even the second-best constitution presupposes the
coincidence of wisdom and power which in the tale of the *Laws* is satisfied by the fortunate circumstances assumed to surround the foundation.
Plato has obviously not discounted the feasibility of a relationship such
as that which he hoped for between Dionysius and himself. But the possibility is remote, and if the Idea is to enter human time it is likely to be
through a legislator or ruler using as a guide the paradigm which em-
bodies the art of the true statesman. The existence of the paradigm will
eliminate the element of chance connected with the appearance of the
true legislator, and Plato, even if denied the possibility of participating
in an actual foundation, can leave behind an imperishable monument to
his goodness in the image of a political science. But beyond this, the
polity outlined in the *Laws*, and to a lesser extent any constitution
modeled after it, is calculated to solve the problem which plagued the
Republic and the *Statesman*: the perpetuation of the foundation. And
in light of this it is necessary to re-evaluate to what extent the *Laws*
may properly be termed "second-best."

It is sometimes forgotten that despite a deep concern with the
quality of social existence, Plato and the majority of subsequent political philosophers were addressing themselves primarily to a crisis in
social order. Their ultimate concern—that which in the last analysis is
common to them all—is the establishment and maintenance of order
itself. In the context of Greek culture the preservation of the polis was
always the fundamental value, and the problem of the theorist was to
identify the idea of excellence with those qualities which contributed
to this end.[44] Plato's task was to demonstrate that justice and moderation, as he defined these terms, were necessary for the perpetuation of
social stability even if, as in the *Laws*, individual choice, including that
of the rulers, was absorbed in the institutional order of the state. To
join the end to the beginning: this is the problem.

The *Republic* could not be realized because the weight of being was
too heavy for the vessel to bear. Even should circumstances prove
favorable for the appearance of a royal ruler as presented in the *Statesman*—a ruler who takes account of the quality of the human material

and only attempts to weave it into due proportion rather than radically transform it—there would be only a regeneration of time followed by an inevitable decline. As the *Republic* demonstrated, there can be no hope for the perpetuation of a dynasty of such men. The alternative to the royal rule was the rule of law which Plato found to be, at best, second-best, but *nomos*, in this instance, was used in its limited sense which does not conform to the use in the *Laws*. The appearance of the paradigm of the *Laws* in history is tantamount to the appearance of the true legislator, and the polity of the *Laws* is designed to solve the problem of perpetuity, to make the foundation everlastingly authoritative and abolish history or political time. The failure to accomplish this was the ultimate defect of both the *Republic* and *Statesman*, and in this sense the *Laws* is either not second-best or second-best in the same way as the *kosmos*: the least possible deviation from the eternal, not only in the degree of reality but in the degree of immortality.

The forms are apprehended by pure intellection or the dialectical ascension beginning with the perception of their visible images, but the forms themselves cannot be discursively articulated.[45] Every expression of the forms or pure being must be in terms of some manifestation, and the institution of the best polis in the *Republic* would be a *virtual* representation molded after the idea of justice; but, as in sand sculpture, there is the continual incapacity of the matter to sustain the form. The cosmos is the manifestation of the forms and exemplifies the limitation created by the resistance of the medium on which the forms are impressed; cosmic order is achieved through the mediation of intelligence; that is, the imposition of *peras* on *apeiron*. Thus although Plato states that the polity of the *Laws* is modeled after the constitution of the best state when it is also obviously patterned as a cosmion, this creates no conflict since both the pattern of justice in the *Republic* and cosmic order are reflections of the forms. The order described in the *Republic* and *Statesman* is useless to the ruler who cannot attain to the forms, but the visible cosmos exists as a concrete image that not only provides a paradigm for the foundation of a polity but serves as a visible pattern which may be constantly apprehended by rulers who are not philosophers. By building the order of the cosmos into the order of the state, political time and political space are assimilated to cosmic time and space. The actualization of the second-best state would constitute the abolition of history and the integration of man, state, and cosmos, and this means an approximation of existence under the form of the integral myth—but now it is a myth which serves reason.[46]

Although the idea of justice in the *Republic* is the ultimate model, the type of constitution that will be "theoretically" imposed on the polis will be that which will most nearly "imitate the life of the age of Cronus" and which if actualized will "be in its fashion the nearest to immortality."[47] This is the essence of the Platonic restoration. In the age of the differentiated consciousness a return to the integral myth is neither possible nor desirable. On the level of the philosophic conciousness a complete oneness with the divine would be the institution of the *Republic*, but since this is not feasible, the creation of a neomythic state will achieve something of the best of both worlds; that is, the "reasonableness" of the *Republic* and the "timelessness" of the myth. "Real constitutions" are those which cannot properly be described by the terms autocracy, democracy, or monarchy,[48] and this lack of differentiation is true historically of the integral myth and theoretically of the *Republic*. Only historically with the breakdown of the myth and theoretically with the disintegration of the best state do the particular forms of political rule corresponding to the dominant element in a society begin to emerge. In this sense the mixed constitution of the *Laws* is symbolic of the best state: the new beginning, the return to the earliest cities of the plain, and the assimilation of the past in the present.[49]

This society, like those of the age of Cronus, will take its name not from a class of men but from a god, "the god who is the master of rational men"; that is, the law.[50] The path to stability and due proportion in human affairs is to follow the divine measure or god which is manifest in the cosmos; the integral myth contained a truth which is now rediscovered and consciously applied. Government by men must be rejected in favor of the rule of god and his law which in this case is not a "religious" symbol, but stands for the *kosmos* and its measured rhythm in which reason is immanent.[51] This form of rule, Plato argues, belonged to earlier forms of government and is still "reflected in the best of our present-day communities," and the conclusion is almost inescapable that his reference is to Egypt which throughout the *Laws* he holds up as an example. His hope is that the new polity "will be one of the few well-governed states and countries that enjoy the beams of the sun and his fellow gods."[52]

According to the myth of Cronus, god set over man a race of

daemons who established complete justice and order, and the truth of the myth is that god and not man must be the ruler (*arche*) of a state; the polity will be an imitation of the myth and in turn an imitation of god or the cosmos.[53] The injunction is to "order both our homes and our states in obedience to the immortal element within us, giving to reason's [*nous*] ordering [*dianomas*] the name of law."[54] The daemon or divine dispensation of the myth which also implies permanence now appears in man as reason or the divine element which links him to the *kosmos*, and in *nomos* is found *nous*.[55] As in the *Philebus*, it is sovereign intelligence, in the cosmos, state, and individual, which imposes limit, proportion, and measure on pleasure and passion and creates order. And as long as god or the cosmos (manifest intelligence) remains the measure, political time is overcome, because as the adage states god who "holdeth the beginning, the end, and the center of all things that exist, completeth his circuit by nature's ordinance in straight, unswerving course."[56]

The Platonic idea of order is inextricably linked to the creation of a definite political space and implies a radical transformation of political time, but as with the ordering of the cosmos, the resistance of material, that which is real but lacks being, becomes an irreducible datum and a limitation on creative intelligence. Both the state and the cosmos are the product of the triumph of intelligence (*nous*) over necessity (*ananke*);[57] here there is a recapture of the mythic motif reaching from the Near East through the symbolism of the *Oresteia*. But creation both in the physical and human spheres is not a radical transformation of chaotic matter. An analogy between the *Republic* and the Egyptian myth on the one hand and the later dialogues and the Mesopotamian myth on the other, although possibly strained, is illuminating. In the former case there is an authoritative imposition of static form, while in the latter instance order is the result of an encompassing and organization of chaotic motion.[58] In the *Timaeus* and *Laws* chaos and disorder are recognized as forces which are coeval with the forms and never completely annihilated, and beyond this, disorder and history are synonymous.

The dynamism of existence or the source of becoming (*genesis*) belongs to the original chaos; primeval becoming, social disorder, and passion constitute the chaotic motion of the physical, political, and individual realms, respectively. Order in all three cases is the application of limit by intelligence. Besides the motive of the founder, there is another principle or cause in every foundation or beginning "for the generation of this universe was a mixed result of the combination of Necessity and Reason."[59] The relation between order and disorder exemplified in the duality of god and fate or inborn urge in the myth of the *Statesman* now appears as the everlasting tension between intelligence and the "errant cause" or necessity. The time of creation cannot be understood as a point in historical time; the overcoming of chaos in the cosmos has no chronological significance. Chaos emerges as an ever-present force which in the cosmos is contained, but in human affairs continually threatens to burst forth. As law decreases in human affairs chance increases until order disintegrates into randomness or mere historical succession. The circumstances of cosmic origin can be articulated only through myth, and the end of the cosmos is inconceivable; but in the course of human events "beginning" and "end" with intervening growth and decline are historically visible.

The cosmos is established by the creation of order within space. Space (*chora*) is the canvas or material on which the image of being is imprinted; it is the "receptacle" which furnishes the ground for the actualization of the paradigm. The intelligible and immutable being of the model, mediating intelligence, the visible and becoming copy, and the sustaining medium or "nurse" of becoming are the elements entering into the creation of order.[60] The receptacle, as that in which the images appear, is as permanent as the forms, but it possesses no qualities of its own and is not even apprehended by *doxa*, but only by a "bastard reasoning"; it is "invisible and characterless, all-receiving, partaking in some very puzzling way of the intelligible and very hard to apprehend."[61] It is real, but untouched by being. Being and space are primordial entities existing before the creation of the cosmos.

The contents of space were in a chaotic condition, and although the qualities of fire, water, earth, and air were vaguely reflected in the receptacle, they lacked "proportion and measure" and possessed only "vestiges" of their true nature. The situation was one of discordant motion produced by the unbalanced state of the qualities, and the receptacle was "shaken by these things, and by its motion shook them in turn." This was the condition of necessity which confronted the demiurge, who began by persuading necessity and imposing on chaos "a distinct configuration by means of shapes and numbers."[62] Precosmic motion or chaotic becoming which moves by necessity is designated as *genesis*,[63] and by stating that the receptacle or space is the nurse of becoming, Plato means that it is the container of this chaotic motion which is ordered by the demiurge. But it is also the container of ordered motion. The role of space is essentially passive and is likened to a mother in whose womb "that which becomes (*gignomenon*) is born" while the forms or paradigm are compared to a father;[64] it is the *eros* supplied by divine intelligence which, as in the *Symposium*, moved by the vision of beauty longs for conception and procreation and overcomes necessity and brings cosmic becoming and *chronos* out of *genesis*.

While in the *Republic* there is little consideration of the "receptacle" or the problem of political space, the *Laws*, like the *Timaeus*, emphasizes this dimension and its unformed contents; space and the necessitous conditions it contains become a concomitant of the Idea. For Plato human time is not differentiated beyond the life of the individual and the life of the state, which are encompassed in the idea of political time or history, which is in turn anchored to the discordant movements of political space; in the symbols of fate, chance, and inborn urge in tragic drama and in the *Statesman* may be found the counterpart of *ananke* and *genesis*.[65] The founding of the state is the creation of a virtual space, the structuring of its contents, and the imposition of an ordered pattern on their motion, and since history is defined by the disintegration of political order which is in turn the result of the disordered soul, the foundation and organization of the state means the arrestment or regeneration of human time.

From the movements of the unstructured souls and their capricious tendencies which only faintly reflect true virtue, the founder-statesman creates order through laws introduced by persuasion just as the demiurge overcame Necessity; the subjects must "give a ready audience to persuasions to virtue, and plainly this is the effect at which our legislator will aim throughout his legislation."[66] The measure and proportion of law is to be introduced into the necessitous realm of society; this is to be accomplished through the use of persuasive prefatory statements preceding the whole body of the laws and each individual law, that will render men, who do not naturally move toward the good, susceptible to guidance. Given the limited educational potential of the mass, who are only capable of true belief induced by persuasion rather than the knowledge that proceeds from instruction,[67] law, which imposes *peras* on *apeiron*, and the force that implements it, supplemented by persuasion, become the instruments of the legislator-physician, who, as the vehicle of mediating intelligence, administers to society and brings it to a condition of stability and health. The authority of the law involves both force and persuasion and is thus itself a mixture—a combination of autocracy and democracy.[68]

It is through persuasion that eternity enters history and chaos submits to form and gives birth to its likeness.[69] What is continually overlooked in commentaries on Plato's last work is that the laws and their preambles, whether written down or not, are disseminated to the public in oral form and instilled by repetitive recitation.[70] Plato, who began by a vitriolic attack on a mesmerized oral culture, now, in the grand edifice of his magnum opus, becomes the poet-founder of a cosmic mythocracy. It is the spell of rhetoric which soothes the audience and serves "to prepare the auditor of the legislator's enactments to receive his prescription . . . in a spirit of friendliness and docility."[71] The figure of Socrates, who faded into the background in the later dialogues, has finally disappeared; the critical mind recedes as the anonymous Athenian invokes the myth and finally vanishes altogether in the face of apodictical law and the orthodoxy of creation. A society ruled by rhetoric can be accepted because now the rhetoric proceeds from and serves wisdom by acting as a palliative for the "dictatorial prescription" of the law. Like the "high-wrought and elaborate preludes" prefixed to "nomes" or odes and other musical compositions, the preambles aid in imposing the measured rhythm of the laws, or the real nomes, on the discordant movements of society.[72] The laws, then, although prosaic, are to serve the same purpose as oral poetry set to music and preceded by prologues that evoke the proper mood, but these nomes are literally the laws of reason.[73] However, it is not just the preambles to the laws that perform the function of persuasion; the whole system of the polity constitutes a grand persuasive and educational structure.

When viewed from the perspective of the *Philebus* the symbols of creation and foundation in the *Timaeus* and *Laws* emerge clearly. To create being in cosmic or political space means to bring harmony and unity out of discord through the mixture of limit and unlimited. What characterizes the *Laws* is the themes of moderation and proportion, and just as the Athenian, at the beginning of the dialogue, brings the participants into accord, a true theory of legislation must aim at organizing and balancing the hostile forces within the state.[74]

From the *Republic* to the *Laws*, the correspondence between city and psyche is maintained, but now the analogy extends to the cosmos. In the Platonic vision of the autonomous and differentiated psyche, the self is the ground of history and the ultimate battleground of the forces of order and disorder, and order must follow from "the primal and subtlest victory, victory over *self*,"[75] or the limitation of passion by reason. The same holds true of social entities where order proceeds from the adjudication of rival claims, and at this point Plato renounces the applicability of the *Republic* and the vertical integration of the good as a theory of legislation. For the multitude, at least, the victory over self is not to be obtained by a complete expurgation of the unrighteous elements, and in a social unit there is an alternative both to the extermination of the worst and to a system where the governance is in the hands of the good who bring the worst into voluntary submission. The Athenian suggests that an adjudicator might "take in hand a family at variance with itself, reconcile its members for the future by his regulations, without the loss of a single life, and keep them on permanent amicable terms."[76] So it is with the constitution of a polity.

When the demiurge had created the primary bodies of earth, air, fire, and water and given them the "most exact perfection permitted by necessity willingly complying with persuasion,"[77] he took care to combine the four elements into a unity and to blend them according to geometrical proportion which creates the most perfect of all bonds. It was in this manner that "the body of the universe was brought into being, coming into concord by means of proportion, and from these it acquired amity [*philia*], so that coming into unity with itself it became indissoluble."[78] The goal of the legislator must be to create a similar bond within the body of the state and reduce the relations wherever possible to a numerical order.[79] And after establishing the physical and spatial configuration of the city, first attention must be given to eugenics, the regulation of sexual behavior, and the laws concerning marriage so that the primary matter of the state, although not attaining to the unity and perfection of the *Republic,* will be as suitable as possible.[80] Next, the supreme aim must be to bring the citizens into a condition of mutual attachment and happiness which will mold all the parts into an indestructible whole.[81] The old *arete* or valor in war is rejected as the organizing principle of the state which should aim toward the autonomy and internal peace that result from friendship and the elimination of faction.

In each phase of polis life the principles of moderation and proportion must be observed to avoid the extremes of despotism and excessive liberty which, in the case of Persia and Athens, respectively, broke the bond of amity. The appropriate mixture of monarchy and democracy is woven into all the institutions of the polity.[82] When the state is not organized according to partial virtue, but after the principle of "complete righteousness," which means awarding each virtue its due and achieving the proper mixture of pleasure and wisdom and the right proportion of goods, both divine and human and of body and soul, it cannot be unbalanced either by internal forces or by an assault from the outside.[83] What must be emphasized is that Plato intends that the state, like the cosmic body, will be self-sufficient and *complete and free from age and sickness.*"[84]

Although it sometimes appears that the state is man writ large, or at other times the cosmos writ small, attempts to narrow the symbolism are misleading for the state stands halfway between man and the whole of cosmic order.[85] Human being is a part of cosmic creation, and although the species and the individual immortal soul are coeternal with the universe, the problem of the perpetuation of society constitutes a gap in existence which can be bridged only by human artifice. Man stands halfway between the heavenly gods or celestial bodies with their nonswerving rationality and the lower species or animals which lack an immortal soul. The creation of men and animals, who unlike the celestial mechanism are subject to birth and death, was delegated by the demiurge to the created and immortal gods. But the demiurge supplied the immortal or rational portion of the soul which was made from surplus portions of the mixture constituting the world soul and, being less pure than the world soul, was *subject to disorder.* After a journey in the chariots of stars during which they were instructed in the laws of destiny, the immortal souls were sown in the divine planets, the "instruments of time," where they were received by the gods and incarnated in dissoluble bodies along with the mortal portions of the soul; the immortal portion of the soul was lodged in the head, and lower portions were embedded in the trunk.

As in the *Republic,* the well-being of the individual on earth and the fate of the soul after death depends on the choice of a good life,[86] but when the soul is first incarnated (the condition of the *child*) it is subjected to the violent necessitous motions of the corporeal vessel, and its revolutions become disordered and irrational. As the individual grows older the rational tends to bring the organism under control, but this can be completely achieved only through education and participation in a well-ordered state where the soul imitates the motions of the divine to which it belongs.[87] The creation of an imperishable political space assimilated to cosmic order becomes the *sine qua non* of the good for man in both the here and the hereafter.

> When men of so bad a composition dwell in cities with evil forms of government, where no less evil discourse is held both in public and private, and where moreover, no course of study that might counteract this poison is pursued from youth upward, that is how all of us who are bad become so. . . .
> . . . .
> . . . By turning his thoughts toward the divine, man possesses immortality in the fullest measure that human nature admits. . . . The motions akin to the divine part in us are the thoughts and revolutions of the universe; these, therefore, every man should follow, and correcting those circuits in the head that were deranged at birth, by learning to know the harmonies and revolutions of the world, he should bring the intelligent part . . . into the likeness of that which intelligence discerns, and thereby win the fulfillment of the best life set by the gods before mankind both for this present time and for the time to come.[88]

The immortality appropriate to the species is guaranteed by its perpetuation as part of the cosmos, and the immortality of the individual is assured through the divine element in his soul, and for certain outstanding men there is also a measure of immortality secured by great deeds retained in memory and the objects of artifice they leave behind. But the immortality of the state which is necessary for the welfare of the individual can no longer be, as in Pericles' funeral oration, the memory of its greatness. The immortality of the state must be an immortality that approximates the everlastingness of the cosmos; when the state crumbles there is a rupture in cosmic unity as the temporal abyss that separates man from the source of order opens and engulfs human existence.

The demiurge fashioned the world body in the shape of a sphere since this figure "comprehends in itself all the figures there are" and best fits the nature of the living creature which is itself all-inclusive. Similarly, the polity in the *Laws* is constructed on a circular pattern with the capital city located at the center and around which the markets and temples and the frontier garrisons form concentric circles. District boundaries extend from the center to the perimeter with radial highways running through each district.[89] The world body was assigned "the motion proper to its bodily form," the circular movement revolving about a fixed center and manifesting the wisdom and intelligence of the rational soul,[90] and when this motion is imposed on the body politic, it means the negation of that forward translation which constitutes history. The world soul, being in all respects prior to the body and guiding its motion, was set "center to center" with the cosmic body and permeated and enveloped the whole structure in order to create "a divine beginning of ceaseless and intelligent life for all time."[91] In the same way the founder sets over the system of the polity "a body of guardians endowed some with wisdom, some with true beliefs, to the end that intelligence may knit the whole into one, and keep it in subjection to sobriety and justice," and it is through this soul of the state that the foundation is perpetuated and a provision is made for "a means of salvation, endless and complete for our creation."[92]

From indivisible existence and divisible existence and from sameness and difference, the demiurge constructed an intermediate mixture constituting the world soul.[93] The soul has being or existence which is intermediate between ultimate being and that which becomes. The soul, as the repository of intelligence, provides the link between the eternal and immutable forms and the body of the cosmos; it is immortal and in this sense partakes of the forms, but it is alive and intelligent and in this sense is akin to change.[94] The soul, in both the world and the individual, forms a realm of everlastingness that is halfway between the eternity of the forms and, for example, the everlastingness of a species or the constituents of the cosmos which persist through all time but lack individual immortality.

The mixture constituting the soul was marked off by geometrical proportions which were mixed and bound together by harmonic and arithmetical means and resulted in a geometrical progression or diatonic scale.[95] The demiurge then split the strip and formed it into two revolving circles, inclined with respect to each other, with one (the Different) moving counterclockwise within the other (the Same) which revolved clockwise. The Same, being supreme and uniform, was left intact while the Different was split into seven unequal circles revolving, according to the progressions of the scale, about the common center. Three of the circles moved at a similar speed, and the others each moved at varying speeds different from the first three. The circle of the Same, symbolizing the dominance of reason and rational discourse resulting in knowledge and understanding, corresponds to the uniform movement of the sphere of the universe as a whole including the fixed stars, while the seven circles of the Different, symbolizing true belief and discourse about the sensible world, represent the subordinate but independent motions of the planets.[96]

When the demiurge had created the cosmos as a self-moved creature after the likeness of the intelligible creature—"a shrine brought into being for the everlasting gods"—he undertook to make it even more like the paradigm.[97] The model was eternal (*aionios*) without duration in time or movement of any kind, but it was impossible to impart this character completely to the cosmos. Thus he created "of eternity that abides in unity, an everlasting likeness moving according to number—that to which we have given the name Time [*chronos*]" and which constituted the smallest possible deviation from the eternal; the forms are beyond time and have "being for all eternity, whereas the Heaven has been and is and shall be perpetuated throughout all time."[98] Months, days, and years came into being with the cosmos as part of time, and terms such as "was" and "shall be" should be ascribed only to things that exist in time while eternal being can be spoken of properly only as "is"; that is, the eternal present without temporal duration. Time, as the imposition of number and form and as opposed to space which exists from necessity, is the creation of intelligence and the manifestation of rationality in the cosmos. The becoming of time and the cosmos is neither *genesis* (the movement of chaos) nor eternal duration, but a becoming that partakes of being. *Genesis* can be understood as the raw material of time or as pure succession, and in fact it is time which provides the link between the intelligible and sensible realms.[99]

The motions of the world soul are invisible except as they are manifest in the paths of the heavenly bodies or celestial gods consisting of the stars, planets, and earth which are placed in the shrine of the heavenly sphere with its revolving rings. The rational order and inner harmony of the world soul is apparent in the movements of the heavens and the world body as a whole. It was the creation of the planets set in the seven circuits of the Different that brought time into existence and established the cosmic clock. Primary among the planets is the sun which through the alternation of day and night enabled man to observe the uniform revolutions of the entire heaven or the Same and to "possess number" and, along with the movement of the moon, made possible the calculation of the month and year.[100] The everlasting recurrence of these motions brought the cosmos as near as possible to eternal being.

Just as the demiurge created the world soul and fitted it to and extended it through the cosmic body to insure its perpetual and harmonious revolution, the founder fits the soul of the state to the body politic for the same purpose. But, as with the individual, the body and soul of the state must be constructed so as to *accommodate its existence on earth,* and thus by necessity the immortal soul, which makes possible the rule of righteousness over passion, is compounded with a body and the mortal soul.[101] Plato finds that the projected state can best be understood by an analogy with human being.

In the individual, the rational soul, which, although provided by the demiurge, is corruptible, is composed, like the world soul, of the mixture of Same and Different and possesses similar harmonic divisions and revolutions.[102] In the individual the two revolutions (Same and Different or understanding and true belief) which constitute the immortal portion of the soul are housed in the head which is copied by the creator gods from the spherical shape of the universe; the head is the seat of both vision and hearing as well as intelligence.[103] It is sight which makes possible the observations of divine celestial movement, and hearing makes possible the perception of musical sounds which give pleasure to the unintelligent and delight to the wise "by the representation of the divine harmony in mortal movements."[104] Although the divine part has its central seat in the head, it is extended throughout the human frame in the "marrow," for "the bonds of life, so long as the soul is bound up with the body, were made fast in it as the roots of the mortal creature." The head, spine, and certain other bones contain the marrow which includes the brain as its central portion and is the seat of the immortal soul and to which the mortal portions of the soul and the body are bound.[105] The mortal soul, consisting of the spirited and appetitive elements, is contained in the chest and lower trunk.[106] It is always the intrusion of the necessary motions of the bodily elements which deranges the revolutions of the immortal soul and must be controlled.[107]

Plato understands the body of the state as culminating in the Nocturnal Council or the "soul and head" of the polity which, as in the individual, stands above the trunk of the body and contains intelligence and the endowments of vision and hearing. The eyes and ears of the state are the commissioners sent abroad to observe other states and report to the Council, and "without observation and inquiry of this kind . . . no scheme of polity is perfectly stable."[108] The two classes of councilors, the senior and junior, correspond to the revolutions of the Same and Different, together forming the bond between the divine and the state through the combination of wisdom and true belief, respectively.[109] But the rational portion of the soul of the polity is by no means restricted to its "head" for as in the cosmos and the individual it extends throughout the entire structure; the guardians as a whole constitute the immortal soul of the state.[110] The manifold references to the thirty-seven-member body of senior citizens designated as *nomophylakes* attest to their decisive importance along with the Nocturnal Council.[111] They are clearly understood as crucial in effecting the proper beginning of this enterprise, which has "neither father nor mother, other than the society which is founding it," and its continued preservation by keeping it from coming into variance with the foundation. The duties of the guardians of the laws are joined to every piece of legislation and touch every phase of the life of the individual and every institution, official, and activity within the city.[112]

Like the soul of the cosmos and the "marrow" in the individual, the body of guardians with its apex in the Nocturnal Council maintains the entire organism and its harmony while the institutional framework—auditors, magistrates, and lesser officials of the state—interconnects and forms a network of bone, sinew, and tendon that binds the flesh of the body politic together, prevents its dissolution, and ties the mortal soul of the state to its divine and intelligent part.[113] The citizens constitute the higher portion of the mortal soul, the heart of the state, which, since it is placed "within hearing of the discourse of reason and join with it in restraining by force the desires, whenever these should not willingly consent to obey the word of command from the citadel," enables the "noblest part to be leader among them all."[114] It is the artisans and slaves who, corresponding to the appetitive elements in the human soul, form the lower part of the soul of the state and are denied participation because they cannot "understand the discourse of reason" and thus must remain tethered "like a beast untamed but necessary to be maintained along with the rest if a mortal race were ever to exist."[115] The psychic unity of man and state in the *Republic* has now extended to the entire body of the individual, and while in the *Republic* only the soul of the individual was united with the cosmos (myth of Er), now the soul and body of the individual and state as well emerge as cosmions.

The guardians of the laws, the "marrow" of the state culminating in the Nocturnal Council, provide the final touch to this imaginative founding.[116] Like an artist who has accomplished a work of great beauty, the founder wishes that his creation should be immortal and "never grow worse, but always better, as time went on." But neither the painter nor the founder is immortal, and thus some agency must be provided to insure that the creation does not "degenerate through time," and like the demiurge, the founder utilizes particular agencies in his creation to remedy its deficiencies and perpetuate the entire structure; that is, the celestial gods and the guardians of the laws are parallel symbols which characterize the everlastingness of the system. In order that the society may not deteriorate and that the laws originally framed with the "closest approach to absolute perfection" remain adequate, the guardians must also become legislators.[117] Here is the solution to the problem of inflexibility in a state ruled by law that haunted the *Statesman.* The Nocturnal Council (consisting of the ten senior guardians, the distinguished priests, the incumbent and retired ministers of education, and the younger protégés that each of the members selects) is charged with the ultimate "supervision of the laws,"[118] and along with the other guardians it provides the vital substance of the state, which like the soul of the cosmos, preserves and gives autonomous life to what the founder has created. In the skull of the state or the Nocturnal Council the vision of the younger guardians, who keep watch over the polity and are chosen "for the quickness of all their faculties," supplements the wisdom of the elders and altogether constitutes a self-perpetuating institution that provides for "the real salvation of the whole state."[119]

The mere founding of the state, the imposition of limit and proportion through the basic laws provided by the legislator and provisions for bodily health and salvation, is not sufficient. The best society of the *Republic* would degenerate precisely because in the last analysis it was not suited for existence in a cosmic context. Like the demiurge—who, after establishing the body and soul of the universe, decided that something further was required to make his work everlasting and as far as possible a likeness of the eternal paradigm—the Athenian, stepping back and surveying his creation, finds that it still lacks provision for the "salvation (*soteria*) of the laws."

In the *Republic* only the individual soul was integrated with the cosmos, but now it is a question of the state as a whole. In the myth of Er after the individual soul had chosen his life or destiny he was committed to the Fates; Lachesis assigned to each the guiding daemon that accorded with his choice, Clotho spun the thread of doom and ratified the destiny, and it was Atropos, the "savior-third," who made the web of destiny irreversible. The daemon which the founder has chosen for the state is reason or the cosmos itself, that "perfect god," which like the polity was brought out of necessity and created in the likeness of the eternal forms; and to insure the proper destiny of the state, the founder must now provide for the laws "a right mode of naturally implanting in them this irreversible quality" and supply a safeguard that will instill in the souls of the citizens true law and prevent the state from imbibing the waters of the River of Forgetfulness.[120]

The Nocturnal Council is the "savior-third" just as in the individual organism or a ship it is the intelligence and the quickness of sense in the soul and head or the captain that is the salvation of the creature or the vessel.[121] The polity, like the cosmos, is created with *nous* in *psyche* and *psyche* in *soma* and stands as an image of the forms and as a testament to the goodness of its founder; yet it remains, like the product of the artifice of the demiurge, a shrine that must be filled by guides who manifest as well as understand the nature of the product and the revolutions imparted to it. In the cosmos it was the celestial gods who filled the gap in creation and imparted irreversibility and salvation to the universe; they were created by the demiurge to exemplify and perpetuate his handiwork and to make it resemble as much as possible the intelligible model. In a similar manner Plato crowns his work with the Nocturnal Council which is placed in the shrine of the state to guide its movements and supervise the laws. To serve its aim, the foundation must provide

> some element which knows, in the first place, what that political aim . . . really is, and, secondly, in what manner it may attain this aim. . . . But if any State is destitute of such an element, it will not be surprising if, being thus void of reason and void of sense, it acts at haphazard always in all its actions.[122]

The aim of the state, which the councilors must always have before them, is the attainment of the whole of virtue presided over by understanding; for while the mass follows the lead of true belief in "conformity to the tradition embodied in the laws," the men who are the "real guardians of the laws must readily know the true nature of them," and this entails a proper education which will enable them to proceed from a perception of the "many" to a knowledge of the divine that encompasses and gives life to all and to understand the unity of virtue and be equipped with all virtue. The wisdom that is pre-eminent and produces such understanding is that concerning the existence of the gods and their power, and what Plato means by "the gods" is nothing but the heavenly bodies, for faith in the gods comes only through acceptance of the dogmas in the *Timaeus* and Book X of the *Laws:* that the soul is divine and prior to all else and is the source of all being (*ousia*) developed from becoming (*genesis*) and that the order of the cosmos and the motion of the stars and planets is the work of intelligence.

It is necessary for the guardians to study astronomy to achieve these truths for through observation of the cosmos one is led to an understanding of the work of divine reason.[123] Wisdom is now held by Plato to be possible by ascending inductively through observation of the order in the universe; from the observation of the sun as it illuminates the heavens the individual glimpses the reflection of the good and how it illuminates the forms.

> Sight, then, in my judgment is the cause of the highest benefits to us in that no word of our present discourse about the universe could ever have been spoken, had we never seen stars, Sun, and sky. But as it is, the sight of day and night, of months and the revolving years, of equinox and solstice, has caused the invention of number and bestowed on us the notion of time and the study of the nature of the world; whence we have derived all philosophy. . . . The god invented and gave us vision in order that we might observe the circuits of intelligence in the heaven and profit by them for the revolutions of our own thought, which are akin to them, though ours be troubled and they are unperturbed; and that, by learning to know them and acquiring the power to compute them rightly according to nature, we might reproduce the perfectly unerring revolutions of the god and reduce to settled order the wandering motions in ourselves.[124]

The guardians must acquire this knowledge and understand the "connection therewith of musical theory, and apply it harmoniously to the institutions and rules of ethics . . . and shall participate in all the education . . . to keep ward over the State, and to secure its salvation."[125]

The guardians, who thus hold the closest possible intercourse with the celestial gods, are themselves spoken of as divine, and as with existence under the form of the integral myth and the institution of divine kingship, it is through them that the order of the cosmos flows into the structure of the state. An important aspect of the scheme is the self-perpetuating nature of the body of guardians which through elections and the system of protégés overcomes the problem of succession.

The function of the Council is resolved, to a large extent, into a "giving of time" to the polity. Unlike the cosmos whose creation is coeval with time, political order is a creation in history and, like every creation, has a temporal dimension of its own. The establishment of the state momentarily overcomes the *genesis* of human affairs, but political time or history is a movement that inevitably degenerates into the original "dissimilarity" of chaos. The salvation of the state is possible only if, like the cosmos, it is endowed at its foundation with an element which can impart to it the quality of everlastingness by assimilating it to the time of the universe at large. *Chronos* is an image of eternity proceeding according to number, and the celestial bodies "define and preserve the numbers of time";[126] the polity of the *Laws* is constructed according to number, and through the mediation of the Council the numerical order of the state and its harmonic structure are preserved and brought into accord with the heavenly measure. In this manner "we shall have as an accomplished fact and waking reality that result which we treated but a short while ago in our discourse as a mere dream."[127] The organization of the state according to the rhythm of *chronos* exemplifies the application of *peras* to *apeiron*, and the cord of *nous* in *psyche* running through the cosmos, state, and individual provides the bond which unifies the three dimensions of existence. However, the guardians' contemplation of the order of the heavens and the transfer of this order to the polity is not merely a symbolic expression of a mystical connection between conventional and divine law; the connection between the two orders is concrete and objective. In the *Republic* the introduction of justice into the state proceeds from the decisions and laws of the philosopher-king who has seen the ineffable good and who from the wisdom derived from this experience can best bring order into human affairs. But the order which the Council mediates is the order of the forms only as they are objectified in the cosmos.

It is a mistake, and a crucial one, to read into the Council the image

of the philosopher-king, for the philosopher-king is the Athenian who
enters the state only through the foundation and the laws. The guardians
supervise and supplement the laws, but like the celestial gods created by
the demiurge, they cannot exceed the bounds of the structure into which
they are built, and altogether they do not equal one royal ruler. They are
neither kings nor philosophers, but pious men who by association with
the divine motions of the cosmos through the study of astronomy come,
like skilled theologians, to "know" through the "proofs" of the priority
of the soul and the order of the celestial sphere that the gods exist rather
than merely accepting the dogmas on faith as the public must.

The problem of the *Republic* and the *Statesman* was the scarcity of
philosopher-kings and the need for providing an adequate and uncon-
taminated supply, but this problem is not touched upon in the *Laws*
because the system does not require philosopher-kings. The guardians
are never spoken of as "philosophers," and they are not kings; if judged
by the standard of the "line" their province is cosmology and mathematical understanding (*dianoia*) which, although belonging broadly to
intellection and wisdom and concerned with dialectic, stands between
belief and philosophy or *episteme*. Such understanding is by no means
accessible to the average citizen, but neither is it restricted to the very
few capable of becoming philosophers. The polity is predicated on the
existence of a continual supply of men qualified for such studies without
the institution of the strict system of eugenics and education that would
produce the philosopher-kings of the *Republic*. Although the necessary
understanding is not open to all, it can nevertheless be taught to many.

Whether the elaboration of theology and the education of the guardians in the *Epinomis* is the work of Plato or Philippus of Opus it adds
nothing new to the principles in the *Laws* and simply reinforces the
"nonphilosophic" nature of the Council. Disorder is the status of that
which has not been structured according to number, and astronomy produces that knowledge of number on which the order of both the universe
and the state is based; the science of number, the basis of all true art
including statecraft, is the gift of the god called *Kosmos*. When the
Athenian states that for the salvation of the polity there must be some
body within the state that understands the principles of the laws, he
means that the guardians must understand that "there is every necessity
for number as a foundation"[128] if political order is to be imperishable.
Man, endowed with intelligence, can grasp the meaning of the cosmic

clock, and "to the man who pursues his studies in the proper way, all geometric constructions, all systems of numbers, all duly constituted melodic progressions, the single ordered scheme of all celestial revolutions, should disclose themselves."[129] There is no indication that the guardians must have access to the forms themselves, but only their mathematical images; mathematics and harmonics (the study of the concordance of numbers) leads to the perimeter of ultimate being, but does not penetrate its center. In the order of the cosmos, justice, beauty, and temperance are immanent and can be concretely perceived. Beneath the appearance of the physical world lies the truth of being, and beneath the appearance of human activity in the polis lies the pattern of justice embodied in the principles of the constitutional order.

Brumbaugh's study of Plato's "mathematical" passages has done much to clarify Plato's intentions by recognizing that these sections are neither meaningless obscurities nor a trove of esoteric doctrine, but metaphorical illustrations which supplement and illuminate the discussions in the text.[130] Behind the use of such metaphor was the assumption that there was a correspondence between pure mathematics and the social and physical world; that is, "that the genera and differentiae into and by which numbers were classified were not regarded as peculiar to numbers, but were classifications derived from and shared by non-mathematical subject matters."[131] Plato utilizes many other forms of metaphor and allegory, but the use of mathematical imagery is restricted, for the most part, to discussions of the nature of order and disorder, such as in the *Republic* where justice is described in terms of joining and harmonizing the three "notes" or "principles" in the soul or state by "temperance" or in the discussion of the nuptial number and the decline of the best state.[132] The idea of order is symbolized as mathematical harmony which is the embodiment of the forms, and the extended use of mathematical metaphor is symptomatic of Plato's belief in the ineffability of the forms themselves. The use of such metaphor constitutes an explicit rejection of mythic symbolism and poetic formulas although these new formulas and similes fulfill an aesthetic purpose; mathematical symbolism severs thought from the traditional categories just as prose breaks the poetic spell.

There are definite limits to any critical analysis of these symbols. When Plato uses the metaphors of the physician, the military commander, or the ship's captain to illustrate the function of the Nocturnal

Council he means that the councilors must understand the ultimate purpose of the state, and it is meaningless to argue that these are not strict or logically compatible analogies. They are presentational symbols which supplement the discursive argument. But they are more than mere imagery, since there is, or should be, an underlying affinity between the various manifestations of *techne*. In the same way the figurative language describing the construction of the world soul, for example, is a metaphor which illustrates and makes intelligible to the reader the proposition that the universe is ordered by mathematical proportion. The description of the harmonic progressions of the world soul is presented as part of the myth of incarnation and neither primarily as a symbolization of the music of the spheres nor as a descriptive astronomical theory. It is a metaphorical elaboration of how dissimilar entities are blended in an ordered structure. Yet, the metaphor is not arbitrary because Plato assumes that mathematical proportion is the foundation of the study of music, astronomy, and cosmology as well as the key to political order.

In the *Laws,* it is apparent that the state constitutes a paragon of mathematical planning. Not only is there an attempt to apply the principles of mathematical proportion to the harmony of classes and institutions and to criminal law, but every phase of social organization and administration is meticulously reduced to a mathematical scheme. One of the pivotal numbers in this construction is 5040, the number of household or family property divisions, which Plato states is a "convenient" and "useful" number because it has "the most numerous and most consecutive subdivisions" (it has 60 divisions including the integers from 1 to 12 with the exception of 11) and is most suitable for administrative purposes both in peace and war.[133] But although it is particularly suited for successive hierarchical divisions, the choice of this number is not dictated merely by the requirements of an "administrative logistic";[134] 5040 is a "cosmic" number par excellence and relates to 12 which is the dominant number in the organization of the state.

Plato's mathematical plan is a wondrous combination of Pythagorean and oriental number symbolism blending octaval, decimal, and sexagesimal numerical systems. The number 5040 is divisible by 12, and 12 is the symbol of the circle and corresponds to the months of the year, the zodiac, and the sun which is the measure of *chronos* and illuminates the motion of the Same and provides knowledge of number. Also 5040 is the product of the integers 1 through 7 and symbolizes the seven planets (the instruments of time), the seven intervals in the world soul, and the days of the week; the number 7 is also the Pythagorean symbol for the union of the human and divine. Further, the state is composed of three general classes (guardians, citizens, artisans and slaves), and the citizens are in turn divided into four property classes which together add up to 7; the prominence of the number 4 is related to the Pythagorean tetractys in which the sum of the four digits equals 10 or the perfect number. The capital city with the central sanctuary is located in the center of the territory, and both are circular and divided into twelve sections, each with its village, temple, and shrine located in the center; the 5040 households are divided into twelve tribes, corresponding to the twelve territorial divisions, which are assigned to and named after "the twelve gods" (presumably the Olympian deities). In addition the produce of the soil is distributed in twelve parts and the workmen are divided into thirteen sections, one for each territorial division and one apportioned among the twelve divisions of the capital city. The representative council contains 360 members (the degrees of the circle) with thirty from each of the twelve tribes (corresponding to months and days), and it is in turn divided into four groups (seasons) of ninety from each of the four classes; groups of thirty members, or one-twelfth of the body, serve actively for one month of the year. There are monthly festivals honoring the twelve gods of the tribes, and sacrifices are conducted on each of the 365 days of the year to insure that they are performed "by at least one magistracy to some god or daemon on behalf of the state, its members, and their chattels without any interruption." All this is only part of the intricate interweaving of cosmic numbers and solar symbolism, and there is no end to the speculations possible concerning the connections between the numerical symbols. For example, the auditors are elected in conjunction with the occurrence of the summer solstice in a place dedicated to the sun, and after the election they are in turn dedicated to the sun and reside in the place of their election.[135]

It would be a mistake to interpret all this as the amusement of an old man who, having failed to change the world, decides to play imaginative games with it to satiate his manipulative urges, but neither is it correct to assume that this complexity of numbers and calculation is simply a "realistic" attention to detail. Finally, and most important, there is no need to delve behind the symbols for esoteric meaning. It is very clear that Plato has constructed the state as a cosmic analogy or a

mathematical simile; in a very real sense the life of the state is a metaphor, a life in quotation marks like existence under the form of the myth.
But now the myth is the conscious creation of reason, and the state becomes a work of art.

Although the heavens provide a visible model for the order of the
state, it is inconceivable that Plato believed that by using "cosmic"
numbers in the construction of the polis a union between the two orders
would automatically be effected. He does not make use of the Pythagorean idea of mystical mathematical unity of soul and cosmos except as
a metaphor. Men can learn number from the celestial order and can observe there with the mortal eye the manifestations of justice, beauty, and
moderation and gain a notion of them, while the forms can be seen in
themselves only with the eye of the soul. If one attempts to perceive the
forms through sight, it is like gazing into the sun and creates a "darkness
at noon."[136]

For Plato the compact unity of state and cosmos which characterized the integral myth was broken, and his problem was one of restoration, although the restoration could not be an actual return to the age of
Cronus. The physical and institutional order of the state could be constructed by the founder so that it would best overcome the problem of
decline, but above all the psychic order must also be such that a sense
of "timelessness" is created in the mind of the people. The temporal
order of the state and the life of the individual are assimilated to the
cyclical celestial archetype, and the style of social life becomes that of a
cosmic and mathematical ritual.

Both the physical and mental pattern of the polity are the intelligent order of *chronos*, and in *chronos* is heard Cronus. Plato says of the
twelve sections of the polis that "each division must be *thought of* as a
sacred thing, a gift of God corresponding with the months of the year and
the revolution of the universe,"[137] and festivals must be planned according to the "grouping of days into monthly periods, and months into the
year in such fashion that the seasons with their sacrifices fit into the
natural order."[138] But as in Egypt the idea of circular continuity is to
be imposed on the life of the individual as well as the career of the state;
Pluto, the god of the underworld, is not to be feared, but raised to the
status of the Olympians and honored on the twelfth month "as the constant benefactor of mankind, for union of soul with body . . . is in no way
better than dissolution."[139] In the end, political time and history are

abolished by the ritualistic organization of the polity and the cosmic spell of the law.

Plato does not deny the traditional gods of Greek religion, but the primary deities which guide the life of the polity are the heavenly bodies whose divinity must be affirmed by law.[140] He takes lightly the theology of Homer and Hesiod and the mythic cosmogonies and theogonies, but although such stories as the irreverence of Zeus toward his father are not conducive to morality and obedience, they may be permitted in the state because of their "antiquity." The old myth retains its element of truth, and the real enemies of piety are the "modern scientists," the materialists who deny the gods altogether along with the divinity of the "sun, moon, stars, and earth."[141] The complex base of traditional religion is retained although it is fused with and subordinated to the heavenly shrine. Since the average citizen can never attain to complete understanding, the power of the cult must supplement the command of reason. In religion, as in other institutions of the polity, Greek history and the political cycle of growth and decline are contracted and assimilated in the new beginning; the Greek religion was born from the worship of the heavens, and in the celestial religion of the *Laws*, combined with the chthonic and Olympian deities, the spiritual past of Hellas completes a full circle and merges in the present.

The *Laws* is the reinstitution of divine rule, but now the god is *nous*, and *kosmos* enters society through the mediation of the institutionalized sovereign or the Nocturnal Council which remains as deathless and impersonal as the pharoah. The argument for intelligent order is substituted for the old myths of creation, and in fact the theology of Book X, the preamble to the law against impiety, is nothing more than a paraphrase of the cosmology of the *Timaeus* designed for popular consumption; the spell of poetry gives way to the spell of discourse. The polity can become an imitation of god only when, through the gentle persuasion of the *logos*, the citizens believe that *nous* in psyche is in every way prior and the author of harmonic celestial motion: "that it is the existence of the soul which is most eminently *natural*."[142] The legislator must instill the belief that the gods have imparted right order to the universe down to the smallest detail and that human life is a part of this intelligent creation and should be brought into accord with it.

In Book X, Plato attempts to bridge the gap between *nomos* and *physis* by the demonstration that law is the result of *techne* and that art

proceeds from creative intelligence in soul which, since it is prior
to everything else, most deserves the name of natural. There is thus
a correspondence between *nous* and *physis* and their product which is
nomos. For Plato it is crucial that art and nature are identified and that
law is understood as a product of art and not convention. Chance, necessity, decay, and iniquity or historical time are mysteries which can be
explained only as the reassertion of the motion of the chaotic bodily
elements and the destruction of intelligent art and the limits it has imposed on disorder. The state, then, partakes of both art and nature and
exhibits, like the product of all true art, order and orderliness; statesmanship like all art aims at order and regularity which when present in
the soul are called "law and lawfulness" and result in "justice and
temperance."[143] The just soul is that which has been ordered by the
political art of the true statesman or his law, and it is this law and the
state which relate the individual to the intelligent order of the universe,
for "heavens and earth, gods and men, are bound together by fellowship
and friendship, and order and temperance and justice."[144]

The dogma of the *Laws* is that man and "all living creatures, like
the world as a whole, are the chattels of the gods" whose superintendence
extends throughout the cosmos. The individual must be persuaded that
he is a part of the great fabric and was created for it, rather than it for
him, and that he is created to serve the "general good" of the whole.[145]
Yet in this grand design something is missing, for the god who is pic-
tured as the "mover of the pieces" is not an omnipotent deity, but the
cosmic order itself that merely affirms the fate (*moira*) of the immortal
soul which is determined by its "own action or that of some other
soul."[146] Human action forms an autonomous realm because choice belongs to men and "the cause of change lies within themselves"; the gods
are exonerated from responsibility for the destiny of the individual.[147]
The struggle, then, is between "wrong, arrogance, and folly" and "righteousness, temperance, and wisdom," between "undoing" and "salvation." Salvation for the individual depends on the cord of law that binds
together the order of the universe or *nous* with that element in man that
most resembles it;[148] that is, salvation depends on the mediation of the
state.

The psyche is a field of forces, both good and evil, and it is the law
which must maintain the proper balance and insure the victory over

self by manipulation of the flow of pain and pleasure, for "whoso draws from the right fount, at due times, and in due measure, be it city, or person, or any living creature, is happy, but he that draws without science, and out of due season, has the completely contrary lot."[149] The rebellion against the spell of the oral tradition and its mimetic chain which characterized the *Republic* and the earlier dialogues has been modified because the class of men capable of true selfhood is not sufficiently large to inform the order of the state. The chain now becomes the cord of reason that emanates from the philosophic muse, and *pistis* is substituted for *doxa*.

In the *Republic* the order of the state and the pattern of justice were a projection of the true self of the philosopher in whose soul the divine order was reflected and the paradigm maintained. But this was essentially a psychic order which could not persist in space since the ruling class could not be sustained, and no provision or allowance was made for existence on earth and in the cosmos at large. The *Laws* is also a projection of the true self, but it is expressed in the law and the external order of the polity which is as "good" as necessity will allow. There is no class within the state in which the paradigm is reflected. The state is the soul and body of everyman writ large—an everyman in whom orderliness has been established by the divine founder. And just as the true statesman founds the polity and provides for its salvation through the Council, or its rational soul which links it to the cosmos, the individual, or microcosm, is bound to the state, or mesocosm, through the law which guides the rational element of his soul and secures his salvation. But just as the guardians do not possess the complete understanding of the philosopher and only apprehend being as it is manifest in the visible cosmos, the citizens follow the law only from true belief induced by persuasion.

Pleasure and pain once more become, as in the oral tradition, the instruments of cultural continuity. They are "the very wires or strings on which any mortal nature is inevitably and absolutely dependent."[150] Man is cast in the image of a puppet created by the gods, "possibly as a plaything, or possibly with some more serious purpose," and pulled to and fro by the strings or internal tensions and expectations between the poles of vice and virtue, and he must be made to yield to the pull of the pliable golden cord or "judgment which goes by the name of the public

law of the city" and resist the hard cords of iron and other substances
that draw in the opposite direction. But if the golden or reasonable
element in the soul is to prevail and co-operate with the law and achieve
the victory over self, its persuasive force must be supported and channeled by the manipulation of the forces of pleasure and pain.[151] This is
the spell of the laws which like the performance of a rhapsode draws the
body and psyche into an archetypal pattern.

Existence in terms of life lived as a ritual play is the principle of
the educational system of the *Laws*—the correspondence between *paidia*
and *paideia*; it is the symbol of play which marks the return to the myth
and the unconscious. Education is the molding of "the soul of the child
at play" so that in adulthood he will be capable of "knowing both how
to wield and how to submit to righteous rule"; that is, perform his role in
the civic drama.[152] Maturity is not essentially a growth in consciousness,
but a facility for participation in the organization of the state, and this
facility is perpetuated by insuring that the adult remains as receptive and
susceptible to impression as the child. The puppets, as they grow old
and become inflexible, are plied with wine and "brought back to the
mental condition of remote infancy" so that they remain malleable and
susceptible to the pull of the law;[153] in the ritual play devoted to Dionysus the sense of time falls away as it did in childhood.

Plato devotes the whole of Book II to the theory underlying the
laws regulating choric art; it is the program of music on which the educational pattern of the state is based and which, in the final analysis,
gives to the life of the state its timeless quality. Education, the "rightly
disciplined state of pleasure and pain," is achieved in young and old
alike through the choric art consisting of song and dance (*mousike*);
music provides the "fixative" which holds both the order of the individual soul and the order of the polity static. The constant and irrational
motions of youth, like the precosmic chaos, are brought into harmony
and rhythm; it is through the god-given gift of sound that the citizens
are strung "together on a thread of song and dance."[154]

> All that part of music that is serviceable with respect to the hear-
> ing of sound is given for the sake of harmony; and harmony, whose
> motions are akin to the revolutions of the soul within us, has been
> given by the Muses to him whose commerce with them is guided by
> intelligence, not for the sake of irrational pleasure (which is now
> thought to be its utility), but as an ally against the inward discord

that has come into the revolution of the soul, to bring it into order and consonance with itself. Rhythm also was a succour bestowed upon us by the same hands to the same intent, because in the most part of us our condition is lacking in measure and poor in grace.[155]

What must be guarded against above all is innovation in the pattern of musical education, for it is to this lack of attention to the enforcement of traditional musical forms that Plato attributes the decline of Athenian culture. The musical forms, once strictly differentiated, were confused, and the performances which formerly had been regulated by the elders were judged by the uneducated multitude who had only "contempt for musical law." The disintegration of musical discipline led to the disorder of soul and state and historical decline.[156] For Plato rhythm is "order in movement"; it does not denote linear flow, but *pause, the steady limitation of movement*" like the rhythm of a statue in which motion is caught and suspended and time is negated.[157] An alteration of rhythm means the intrusion of chaotic motion, and Plato finds his social ideal in the static culture of Egypt where historical time was abolished by the absence of innovation in music and art. Plato saw clearly what modern archaeology has affirmed: the persistence of artistic form through vast periods of time.[158]

Existence under the form of the myth included the experience of temporal nullity, and it is this experience which Plato attempts to re-create in the *Laws*; this is the end toward which the regulation of poetry and music aims. Enchantment that prevents deviation from the laws "proves to be the real purpose of what we call our 'songs.' They are really spells for souls directed in all earnest to the production of the concord of which we have spoken, but as the souls of young folk cannot bear earnestness, they are spoken of as 'play' and 'song' and practiced as such."[159] But it is not only children who cannot bear earnestness. Men in general suffer from distortions of judgment caused by a temporal perspective; the distance between act and consequence often makes injustice appear pleasant and justice seem painful.[160] The legislator must use "institutions, eulogies, and arguments" to instill in the citizens the conviction that what is just coincides with pleasure and "ensure that the whole of such a community shall treat the topic in one single and selfsame lifelong tone, alike in song, in story, and in discourse."[161] The conviction that the best life is the most pleasant is reinforced by making it a doctrine of the cults of the Muses, Apollo, and Dionysus to which the choruses of children, adults, and old men are respectively dedicated. The effectiveness of the chants or spells and dances depends on a constant repetition which creates a pattern of conditioned response. The songs "must be recited without intermission by everyone, adult and child, free man or slave, man or woman; in fact the whole city must repeat it incessantly to itself."[162] Through the repetition of the spells a perfect concurrence of thought and speech and action is produced. Like the bead game, education is reduced to a ritual which is "primarily a making of music," and in music is found a "powerful and proven method of bringing a number of men into the same mood—unifying their breathing, their heart beats and their state of courage."[163]

The key to the choric performance is the correspondence between speech and movement, myth and ritual, symbol and act; "it is from this representation of things spoken by means of posture and gesture that the whole art of the dance has been elaborated."[164] Just as the demiurge directed the harmonic movement of the heavens where sameness and diversity are brought together in the rhythmic dance of the planets, the motions of intelligent order are introduced into the polity by the legislator through the choric art. The dance symbolizes everlastingness and uniformity in movement which is the appearance of eternity in time.

> At the still point of the turning world. Neither flesh nor fleshless; Neither from nor towards; at the still point, there the dance is, But neither arrest nor movement.[165]

The hallmark of existence under the form of the integral myth was the sublimation of all action in archetypal patterns and the externalization of the self in the order of society; that is, the obliteration of unique experience that produces the sense of time. It is such an aim that informs Plato's strictures against innovation in music and the insistence on uniformity in children's games; life must be ordered so that "no one remembers or has ever heard of a time when things were otherwise" if time is not to enter the threshold of consciousness. Reverence for the system must be inculcated in the minds of the citizens, and as in everything else, the beginning is determinate; if legislation is to be permanent, the play of children must be continually conducted in the same manner with the same toys in order to prepare the young for the more serious activity of political life with its own fixed pattern. The great "paradox" is that the play of children becomes the most serious play of all.[166] But it is not only written legislation that must remain unchanged but custom and tradition, the "law of our forefathers," which provide "the mortises of a constitution," bind the structure together, and provide a foundation for the entire edifice. The primordial time of the ancestors must be made continually present; the dimensions of past and future cannot be allowed to intrude.[167] Again, Plato finds Egypt a useful model for selecting devices for preventing musical innovation. In the polity there can be no frustration of expectations; dances and melodies must be consecrated to the appropriate deities and daemons, and festivals and feasts are to be regularly celebrated on fixed dates. In other words there is a canonization and harmonization of music and ritual, and types of dance, such as those suitable for expressing attitudes of war and peace, are strictly differentiated by individual nomes to prevent the confusion of forms that results eventually in a disordered society.[168]

Plato has returned to the position of the purified polis in the *Republic*; the quality of citizenry is such that the mimetic experience must form the basis of education. The choric performance is a mimetic presentation in which the actors assimilate themselves through voice and movement to the pattern of action which is reproduced and in which the audience is vicariously drawn into the characterization through the pleasure that the exhibition evokes. Since men tend to become like that which they enjoy, no music or poetry can be allowed except that which produces the best pleasures and consequently the best action; the judges of the music admitted in the state must be the old men, the guardians of the law, who are educated and have listened to the law and by long habitation can best judge what characters may be properly imitated. Comedy and burlesque which displayed nonserious action and defective characters must be excluded. The censorship of poetry and music is supplemented by a plan for retaining traditional literature, but rewriting the objectionable portions.[169]

The standard by which the guardians and the minister of education are to judge literature will be the *Laws* itself; the discourse which has unfolded like a divinely inspired poem becomes an authoritative manual of education and guide to virtue.[170] Plato intends to replace the poets such as Homer as the educator and legislator of Hellas, and in this lies his memorial; the cultural encyclopedia of the Homeric epic, which provided concrete standards for politics, religion, education, and family life, is superseded by the equally extensive provisions of the *Laws*. But the dialogue is not only a cultural paradigm that provides a new social content; his rivalry with Homer extends to a revision of social style. Despite the emphasis on poetry and music as devices for ordering society, it is the preambles to the laws and the entire dialogue itself which define the new social style: mathematics and discursive prose. Music and poetry render men receptive and fix their convictions, but the patterns of thought provided by the spell of the law are ultimately prosaic and mathematical. Again, there is a symbolic contraction of past and present in this fusion of oral poetry and literal education. The formal education of the citizen provides him with an ability to function correctly within the system: in a mathematically ordered state which is governed by laws prefaced by persuasive rhetoric, mathematics and literate studies become prerequisites for participation. Life is conducted, so to speak, "by the numbers," and although only the guardians pursue mathematical studies in detail, the rudiments of number and astronomy are indispensable for the duties of citizenship and the practice of religion. Since the order of both the state and the cosmos is one of mathematical "necessity," education must be appropriate to accommodating existence in these orders, and like all education, including reading and writing, the study of numbers is first introduced on the level of children's play.[171]

The legislator's systematization of music serves, like the shipwright who begins by constructing the keel and skeleton of a vessel, to give form and to produce a fitting receptacle for the noble characters which the law will provide and to sustain and give rigidity to the product once it is complete so that it will endure the *"voyage over the sea of time to best purpose."*[172] Yet for all this attention to the production of good characters, the Athenian states that "man's life is a business which does not deserve to be taken too seriously" and that lawgiving cannot be a serious man's most earnest concern; it is only the game of sober old men.[173] However, this cannot be taken, in any sense, as a rejection of the positive value of human affairs or as a turning away from political space in favor of the contemplation of the eternal. It is only with Aristotle that there is a decisive split between *theoria* and *praxis*; Plato's vision is a mediating one in which the eternal and the temporal have meaning only in terms of each other.

What is understood as serious is a relative matter. From the perspective of god or cosmic order, human affairs appear as a nonserious realm, like children's activity seen through the eyes of an adult, in which men "play their play, win heaven's favor for it, and so live out their lives as what they really are—puppets in the main, though with some touch of reality about them, too."[174] But just as children's play has serious consequences for their adult life and the order of the polity, political order determines the destiny of the soul, which belongs to the everlasting cosmos, and guides its choices; thus "we cannot help being in earnest with it, and there's the pity."[175]

In the general category of human affairs as play, Plato clearly distinguishes between serious and nonserious play; serious play, the play of both the lawgiver and the polity, is that which is conducted for the sake of order and not pleasure. It is the inversion of precedence in Athens which is condemned; that is, the belief that war is a more serious activity than peace and is waged to secure a life of pleasurable play or leisure for the individual. In war there is no play or education of importance conducted for everlasting ends; war must be the diversion and not the serious concern of a community. Human affairs must be treated earnestly precisely because men tend to lose sight of what is serious; order is the serious goal which separates the *poiesis* of Homer from that of Plato. It is in the creation of political order that the exceptional man imitates god, and it is through participation in this order that men in some measure overcome the limitation of human time. Man is indeed constructed as a "toy for God," but this does not mean that he is an object tossed about by an inscrutable will; he is a toy for god because there is an element in him that makes him suitable to play a part in the order of the universe, and thus men should spend their life in making their "*play* as perfect as possible."[176]

The symbolic configuration of the *Laws* is summarized in the image of political life as a drama which is set forth in the Athenian's mock address to the tragic poets who would visit the city and offer their entertainment.

> Respected visitors, we are ourselves authors of a tragedy, and that the finest and best we know how to make. In fact, our whole polity has been constructed as a dramatization of a noble and perfect life; that is what *we* hold in truth the most real of tragedies. Thus you are poets, and we also are poets in the same style, rival artists and rival actors, and that in the finest of all dramas, one which indeed can be produced only by a code of true law.[177]

The dialogue itself is an artistic work with a dramatic situation and a structure possessing form and meaning. But it is a play within a play, for the polity which is described by the Athenian is to be conducted like a drama, and the intention is that, like the tragic epics of Homer, the imaginative work will become a paradigm for future legislators. The poets such as Tyrtaeus and the tragedians are challenged by the true statesman as legislators for Greece; it is Plato who asserts his right to become the author of the social drama and the teacher of its chorus. Like a tragedy, the polis is an imitation of action where the personalities of the performers do not emerge, but are hidden beneath the mask of the archetypal self; like all Greek tragedy the reality that is created and the action that is imitated is the movement of the soul, and in the recitation of the formulas of the laws and their spells and in the motions of the dance, the heroes cast off their humanity in their imitation of god. In the play there is an externalization and distention of the psyche in the time of the drama, the time of a virtual reality, which, although grounded in historical experience, exists outside history. Alternately as performers and audience the citizens are drawn into the mimetic play of the drama where the end is contained in the beginning.

VII

CONCLUSION

... this entity is not "temporal" because
it "stands in history," but that, on the
contrary, it exists historically and can so
exist only because it is temporal in the very
basis of its being.

Heidegger

Time and Order: Aristotle

PLATO created political philosophy as a symbolic form, and his vision
of a political order which would lead to the abolition of history informed
much of the Western tradition of political thought. Although the answer
to the problems of human existence would not always be rendered in
terms of political space, the tension between time and the idea of the
political remained, and this tension became progressively more sharply
defined as historical existence became a more distinguishing characteristic of the human condition. But it was with Aristotle that the poles
of time and political order were most clearly and explicitly articulated,
and it has been between these poles that much of political philosophy has
been forced to move. Plato's belief in the regenerative power of philosophy could not survive; like the integral myth, the Platonic vision of an
integrated order of being claimed more than could possibly be sustained.
But the threat came not only from history, where the existential situation
of the polis began to negate any hope that it could serve as a mesocosm
binding the world together, but from within the realm of thought as well,
where the aesthetic will came up abruptly against the differentiating
mind of Aristotle.

To attempt to explain retrospectively the theory of forms from the
perspective of contemporary logic by arguing that Plato, awed by the

discovery of conceptual thought, confused a logical order with real existence is to miss the point. To maintain that Plato made a "mistake" is not very illuminating, and as with the mythic vision, no such analysis can encompass the meaning of his speculative venture. However, the difficulties raised by this argument reach to the heart of the problem of symbolic transformation. Plato postulated a transcendent order of being and in doing so moved beyond the limits of contemporary Greek thought, but in expressing his vision he was simultaneously bound by the symbols available to him. Although in certain areas myth was the irreducible speculative tool, to revert to the Olympian myth to express the experience of transcendence would have constituted a theoretical regression. Just as the pre-Socratics had at first applied the symbols of Greek theology to their explanation of the natural world, Plato creatively transformed the symbols developed by Greek philosophy into a new vision of the universe, and the symbol for expressing the metaphysical dimension of the forms was the perceptible world itself; the forms were symbolized in terms of a cosmic analogy.

The history of Greek thought which culminated with the sophists was marked by a progressive contraction of reality into an immanent natural order and within this order by a differentiation of nature and society. It was in response to this narrowing and differentiating vision and the loss of the transcendent foundations of both the natural and the social orders that Plato sought to restore the realm of being to its ancient fullness and coherence and to place the order of society within the order of the cosmos. Plato's symbolization of ultimate being in terms of the forms, a dimension of metaphysical universals, laid the foundation for the problem of dualism, but in terms of Plato's vision "dualism" is a misnomer. Despite the disparity between ultimate being and being-in-the-world, the latter possessed identity and reality only through participation in the former. This was essentially the solution embodied in the integral myth, but now it was discursively articulated and took into account the differentiation of the orders of existence. The compactness of the myth could not be regained, but the gap between being and beings, eternity and time, could be bridged. Man as contemplator saw the unity of being and how the cosmos participated in the transcendent order, and man as maker—that is, mediator or *demiourgos*—could extend this order to the realm of human action and eliminate the discordant notes struck by the instability of political order,

Aristotle set out to explore a universe created by Plato, and his exploration was restricted by the limits of Platonic symbolization. But in the course of this exploration that universe was radically transformed and the fulness of the Platonic vision was lost. The realm of being again contracted into an immanent reality, and the orders of existence which Plato had attempted to bind together began to fall apart. For Aristotle, Plato's symbolization of transcendent being appeared as an unnecessary duplication of an immanent order and as a confusion of logic and reality.[1] With one stroke he abolished the notion of transcendent forms along with the myth of creation and embodiment. The Platonic idea of eternity did not disappear, but it lost its substantive content. The problem created by Aristotle's rejection of the transcendent forms was that the eternal or what Plato understood as the eternal was retained, but it was emptied of reality. For Aristotle reality is completely immanent and inheres in the concrete particular; the essence or universal, the secondary *ousia,* has no real existence apart from the individual substance or primary *ousia.* Ultimate being belongs to the "this," not the "such"; to the particular, not the species.

By applying symbols which Plato had developed to articulate the relationship between being-in-the-world and its transcendent ground to immanent reality, Aristotle created a problem of dualism which has been coeval with the history of Western thought. Although it might be argued that Aristotle "reversed" Plato by making the essence or the universal an attribute of the particular, such a description is misleading, for neither in Plato nor in Aristotle are such problems as realism or nominalism encountered. But with Aristotle's formulation the roots of these problems were established. By contracting the realm of being, a tension between the universal and particular, the essence and the existent, and the eternal and the finite was established which has been the burden of much of subsequent philosophy. Between an individual thing and its form or definition—for instance, Socrates and man—there is a logical difference; the mind grasps reality by means of the definition, but it can never reach the particular itself. Aristotle attempted to overcome this problem by locating the essence in the particular substance as form (*eidos*) or formal cause, which, along with the material substratum (*hyle*) or material cause, constituted the principle of individuation. But the problem was actually insolvable. By emptying Plato's Idea of reality he never overcame the difficulty which he attributed to Plato's system, but rather created it; making the essence an attribute of the concrete and individual substance did not alter the fact that the matter-form duality was the difference between empirical and logical and that science and knowledge were, at best, knowledge of a virtual reality or secondary order of being.

For Plato the universal or ultimate being was real and knowable in itself, while the particular was knowable and real only to the extent that it partook of ultimate being. For Aristotle, also, the particular is knowable only in terms of *eidos* or form, but the form only distinguishes a species and has no independent reality. From one perspective it is form which individuates, and from another perspective it is the material substratum which gives identity, but the individual, the repository of being, as a whole is ultimately unknowable; what is knowable is the form or essence which in itself is not primary being.[2] What has happened, as Heidegger has correctly pointed out, is that truth and knowledge now adhere to *logos* as discourse rather than to being itself,[3] but although this could not have happened until the Platonic symbols had become a datum of thought, it was with Aristotle, not Plato, that the transformation took place. For Plato truth did not belong to the idea as an abstraction, as a definition or concept. The result of Aristotle's philosophy was a pervasive dualism; there was a split between truth and being, epistemology and ontology, being and value, abstract and empirical, and timeless and temporal.

By the transformation of the forms into timeless objects of thought devoid of independent ontological content, eternity no longer supported the temporal world in its reality, and the timeless and temporal came into collision. In terms of Aristotle's formulation the problem could not be resolved in favor of either pole. The achievement of truth through contemplation was the highest activity, but, however abstract, it was a truth which referred to an immanent reality. The individual fulfilled his nature and immortalized by an activity that lay essentially outside the realm of human affairs, but unlike Christianity where the soul was transformed through grace, the molding of a nature capable of contemplation could be achieved only in the time-bound world of the polis. The philosopher grasps the nature of the best man and the best polis just as he grasps the *telos* of the things in the natural world and gains a standard for judging all deficient actualizations, but he cannot condemn these deficiencies as lacking reality. Although the realms of the timeless and temporal are not unrelated, they are thoroughly differentiated, and through this differentiation both gain an independent validity and autonomy which was impossible in terms of the Platonic ontology.

Just as the early physicists rationalized the myth, Aristotle rationalized and conceptualized Plato's cosmological myth. Aristotle is the discursive thinker par excellence with whom all elements of myth disappear and for whom nothing knowable is ineffable. God is no longer a demiurge who creates the cosmos and endows it with a world soul; god becomes the psychic principle itself which no longer inheres in a world soul and the lesser gods that permeate the universe, but encompasses its perimeter as merely the irreducible boundary of a system of causes which together constitute nature as a principle of motion. This timeless pure thinking-on-thinking, which is itself marked by an absence of *kinesis*, imparts, by attracting, an everlasting circular motion to the heavens, and this everlasting motion becomes eternity; eternity is the life (*aion*) of the cosmos which has neither beginning nor end—eternity has contracted into that which Plato had designated as time (*chronos*). The eternal motion of the heavens imparts motion to the things in the sublunar world which is the realm of constant change and which now becomes the realm of time. And in the center of this space of generation and decay, of imperfect rectilinear motion and finite time, stand the world of human affairs and the careers of the individual and society. Not only have the eternal forms, the idea as reality, disappeared but also the realm of nonbeing or chaos. Aristotle's contraction of the realm of being and his rationalization of the myth of creation left an immanent reality irrevocably split between the eternal or that which lasts forever and the temporal where everything that comes to be eventually perishes. The split between the timeless idea and reality, theory and practice, is accompanied by the dichotomy within the cosmos between eternity and time.

Aristotle's formulation did not significantly alter the cosmology of the *Timaeus* except for a certain amount of demythologizing and change of terminology. There is a timeless realm occupied by god who is a final cause in somewhat the same sense that Plato's eternal forms constituted the ultimate *arche*; there is an everlasting heavenly motion which is the measure of time, as well as time being the measure of it, and which in its infinity approximates the timeless (not unlike Plato's notion of time

as the image of eternity); and there is the world of finite change and
human affairs which is in time and measured by it. But what, in terms
of the magnificent imperiousness of the Platonic vision, had been potentially harmonized broke apart before the critical intellect of Aristotle.
Not only the timelessness of the divine but the eternity of the heavens
is beyond the reach of man and the objects he creates; reality splits
into the eternal and temporal. Social order can no longer be integrated
into the order of the cosmos. Nature and man coexist in the sublunar
region as makers, but nothing that either man or nature makes resists
change and time.

The things that belong to nature are assured immortality through
eternal recurrence; what nature creates is specifically, although not
numerically, identical since there is no generation or decay of a species,
and the individual as a member of the human species belongs to nature
and achieves a measure of immortality. Also, insofar as his soul is active
intellect—that is, partakes of divine *nous*—the individual may achieve
a certain immortality. But immortality in terms of nature or *nous* does
not reach the self; the eschatological myth has disappeared in Aristotle,
for unlike Plato he sees no transcendent immortality of the individual
soul. Immortalizing for the individual is the contemplative life, the life
in accordance with the highest virtue; but the paradox of Aristotle's
dualism is that immortalizing becomes an otherworldly activity that
must nevertheless be performed in time, and this activity can be achieved
only within the polis which, although natural and necessary to human
perfection, is itself a product of human action (*techne onta*) and belongs
to that most tenuous of all domains where chance abounds. This is the
world of human time and unique events, of politics and history, which
is unamenable to strict theorization and control. Through *nous* man is
related to the divine or timeless, and as an organic being he is grounded
in eternal nature; but as an individual who strives for fulfillment and
integration of both his divine and natural elements he belongs to a
separate order of existence in which he must construct a home for himself.

The remarkably persistent notion that Plato and Aristotle understood history as part of the cyclical course of nature continues to obscure
the degree to which human time had been differentiated in classical
philosophy. For Plato and Aristotle the idea of history was tied to the
rise and fall of political order, and "the *polis* is the historical place, the

there *in* which, *out* of which, and *for* which history happens."[4] Although history was not understood as the career of humanity under the form of universal time, the history of political order was not sublimated in the circular rhythm of nature. Political order was the product of human action, and its stability and instability were ultimately dependent on the success and failure of action. It is patently incorrect to sum up the Greek view of time in terms of Plato's metaphor in the *Timaeus*. When Plato spoke of time as the moving likeness of eternity he was specifically referring to the time of the cosmos, to time as a principle of order in the universe, which, although it contained, and was the measure of, all other time, was differentiated from all other temporal orders such as the finite career of an individual or state. However, Plato neither systematically treated these dimensions nor undertook a discussion of the "problem" of time, and he never explicitly applied time as a category of description to things and events in the sublunar world. This task fell to Aristotle.

When Aristotle contracted Plato's cosmic myth into a rational description of a self-sufficient and self-contained universe without beginning or end, the eternal circular motions of the heavens which encompassed this universe became eternity, or the measure and fullness of time. Although in a sense time remained the image of eternity, it was now the difference between an infinite time and a finite time, the heavenly and sublunar world, time as such and the careers of perishable things contained in time and measured by it. The movement of the heavens provides the measure of years, months, and days and is time as such or eternity and chronometry, and since this movement is circular and continuous, time can be spoken of as circular and continuous. Time is the measure of motion, any motion; but primarily it is the measure of perfect rotary motion or locomotion which belongs to the heavens and which is the measure of all other motion and change, such as rectilinear locomotion and generation and decay.

> This is why time is thought to be the movement of the sphere, viz. because the other movements are measured by this, and time by this movement.
> This also explains the common saying that human affairs form a circle, and that there is a circle in all other things that have a natural movement and coming into being and passing away. This is because all other things are discriminated by time, and end and

begin as though conforming to a circle; for even time itself is thought to be a circle. And this opinion again is held because time is the measure of this kind of locomotion and is itself measured by such. So that to say that the things that come into being form a circle is to say that *there is a circle of time; and this is to say that it is measured by the circular movement.*[5]

God and the heavens which are coeval with time cannot be said to be *in* time for "plainly, things which are always are not, as such, in time, for they are not contained by time, nor is their being measured by time. A proof of this is that none of them is affected by time, which indicates that they are not in time."[6] In the same way, nature, although a realm of constant change, to an extent overcomes time and reflects eternity by the recurrent generation of the same species. It is the things contained and measured by time, the career of the individual and the history of the objects which man creates, that constitute the realm of temporality—the realm where time is a meaningful category.

For Aristotle history and nature are not identical, and historical time is not a function of cosmic revolution. Plato viewed cosmic order and political order as differentiated entities, but he could still visualize a microcosmic-macroanthropic state which would bind the universe together and lift the individual and political order out of history. For Aristotle this was impossible. The goal was still to create a political order that was self-sufficient and would endure through time, but the cosmic symbolism was gone; the idea of the state was no longer that of a cosmion, a *perpetuum mobile*. Within time as a whole, within the circular motions of the cosmos and the infinite generation of the species in nature, there remain the finite careers of the individual and the polis. The famous comment attributed to Aristotle that the men who lived at the time of Troy were not "prior" is misleading when offered as evidence of a belief in the identity of history and nature—that historical time constitutes a cycle. "If then human life is a circle, and a circle has neither beginning or end, we should not be 'prior' to those who lived in the time of Troy nor they 'prior' to us by being nearer the beginning."[7] Here the subject is not individuals or events, but man as a species which is immortal and to which the terms *before* and *after* cannot be meaningfully applied. When Aristotle speaks of the Trojan war, a unique event created by individual men, he finds it meaningful to speak of it as "prior in time."

Some things are prior in time; some by being farther from the present, *i.e.*, in the case of past events (for the Trojan war is prior to the Persian, because it is farther from the present), others by being nearer the present, *i.e.*, in the case of future events (for the Nemean games are prior to the Pythian, if we treat the present as beginning and first point, because they are nearer the present).[8]

Human time or history is conceived in terms of a rectilinear path constituted by events and measured backward and forward from the point of the present. When Aristotle refers, as he repeatedly does, to the recurrence of ideas, opinions, inventions, arts, and so on, he is not alluding to a cosmic repetition of the same, but to the inevitable loss and recovery of knowledge which accompanies the vicissitudes of political order in the course of history.[9] It is necessity that causes men to invent, and the freedom gained by men enjoying a civilized life makes philosophy and the pursuit of knowledge for its own sake possible; but these possessions are lost when, as in the case of the Mycenaean world, the social order collapses. The cycle of history, if it may properly be termed a cycle at all, is the rise and fall of political order, and the cause of this rise and fall is located, as with Plato, in the nature of political life itself and the psychic order of the rulers and the ruled. Although Aristotle's thought moves essentially within the confines of the civilizational unit of the polis and its history, he recognizes, like Plato, a historical past that extends beyond Hellenic kingship and culminates in the contemporary world of the polis. In the course of this history he recognizes the progression in levels of knowledge and speculative activity that culminated in the Academy, but, like Plato, he recognizes that the ancient myths preserved in tradition contain elements of truth, for "even the lover of myth is in a sense a lover of wisdom, for the myth is composed of wonders."[10]

Although time as a measure is primarily the measure of perfect or rotary locomotion—that is, the movement of the heavens—motion that is absolutely continuous actually negates time because time is the "number of motion in respect of 'before' and 'after' "[11] and "before" and "after" are meaningful only in terms of a linear conception of time and in terms of a human perception of past, present, and future. Time, then, attaches to motion—any motion; yet it is neither the same as movement nor independent of movement. As Aristotle attempts to define time it begins to assume a very tenuous existence, for it seems to exist only insofar as there is a conception of a before or after in motion; that is, when there is a soul present to number motion or when there is movement in the mind as in darkness where there is an awareness of an elapse of time. Here Aristotle seems to imply that time is a component of the universe only insofar as man is present in that universe. To state the nature of time seems impossible for Aristotle, since it seems to exist only in an obscure way; in this sense he appears to award it somewhat the same measure of reality as Plato gave to the receptacle and *genesis*. It has existence of a sort, but it is devoid of any real being or substance. And although he can state that time is "present and equally everywhere and with all things," he cannot escape the fact that it appears that "one part of it has been and is not, while the other part is going to be and is not yet."[12] The past and future fade into the realm of nonbeing, and only that which is immediately present really "is."

For Aristotle movement is in itself ultimately unknowable; what is knowable is that which moves. The same holds true for time. He finds that the nature of time is best understood in terms of the "now," which is both the category through which time is perceived and the indivisible unit of time. In the passage of time, the "nows" are different; yet they are the same in the sense that they are the substratum of time, just as an object moving through space retains its identity while passing through different locations. Time and "now" are the same just as motion and the moving body; the "now" is the number of the moving body, and time is the number of motion. Time and motion are continuous; yet the mind may perceive the moving body in a "now," and it is the "now" which can be numbered and gives to motion its numberable aspect. But Aristotle clearly points out that although "nows" are irreducible perceptual units of time by which motion is numbered and that the past consists of "nows" that are no longer and the future of "nows" that are not yet, they are not like points on a line; time is no more a string of "nows" than a motion from place to place is a string of points in space. A "now" does not stop the flow of time, which is an infinitely divisible continuum—it is not a motionless instant, although there can be no motion within a "now" because it is indivisible; the "now" as the present both separates and joins a before and after: it is simultaneously the end of a past and the beginning of a future, and only the present can really be said to "be." Since Aristotle's whole consideration of time was "from the standpoint of the 'now,' the actual moment . . . Being in the sense of already-thereness (presence) became the perspective for the determination of time."[13] The more closely Aristotle attempted to grasp the idea of time the more its reality seemed to elude him, because time for Aristotle, as with Greek thought in general, tended to remain tied to space. Aristotle could not grasp reality as time and change. What was real was the thing which at any "now" was in a particular state with a particular *eidos*. For example, Aristotle well recognized the polis as an entity with a historical existence—for example, Athens existing in past, present, and future; yet only insofar as the form, *eidos,* or constitution remained the same was Athens the same polis. In terms of Aristotle's ontology this problem was unavoidable. He knew that there was change through time, such as the history of Athens; but he could only precisely articulate changes *in* time—that is, a series of discrete constitutions or forms.

However, the whole analysis of time as the number of motion—time as a category for the description of the physical world—does not encompass his understanding of temporality. In his discussion of time, Aristotle does not distinguish between movement and change; change is the more inclusive category, but he uses change and motion interchangeably as that of which time is the number. Yet the analysis of the "now" and the idea of time as a number apply primarily to the type of change which Aristotle in other instances restrictively defines as locomotion: that is, movement from place to place as distinguished from absolute change, which involves creation and loss of substance and changes of quality and quantity. He holds that time is the number of all change, but these latter forms of change, as well as things at rest, are measured by time only indirectly; that is, to the extent that the change is "timed" by reference to time as such or the rotary locomotion of the heavenly chronometer. These changes, then, are understood as "in time" and things at rest as persisting through time because they are measured by it, but in the end it seems equally true that things change because they are in time.

In Aristotle all the elements of Greek thought about time coalesce. Time as such or time as a measure, especially of heavenly movement, is that which gives form to the universe. But time as experienced is the time of Greek poetry—the dimension of existence which is marked by chance and decay and which is meaningful only in terms of mortals—this is time as the essence of change—*chronos* as a living force. Time is not only a measure of specific changes; it becomes for Aristotle a dimension of existence. Although the idea of time as number and "now" is developed specifically in terms of locomotion and applies only incidentally to a course of events, generation and destruction, maturation, and the like, it provides a conceptual framework for grasping and exploring time as the dimension of change; time as past, present, and future and as a rectilinear path juxtaposed to the circle of the cosmos, which had been implicit in Greek thought, is now discursively articulated. Beyond any particular change conceived in terms of "before" and "after" is the greater time of history which stretches backward and forward into the past and future. "Of things which do not exist but are contained by time some were, e.g., Homer once was, some will be, e.g., a future event."[14] The more that Aristotle attempts to convey the nature of time and the meaning of existence in time the more he is forced back to examples and analogies from human experience. "Before" and "after" may be demonstrable in terms of physical motion, but it is only in terms of human affairs that they have ultimate significance.

Finally, even beyond the notion of time as the dimension of change, Aristotle comes to regard time as a destructive force; things made by man and nature remain stable or persist only to the extent to which they overcome time which eventually carries all things away.

> A thing, then, will be affected by time, just as we are accustomed to say that time wastes things away, and that all things grow old through time, and that there is oblivion owing to the lapse of time, but we do not say the same of getting to know or of becoming young or fair. For time is by its nature the cause rather of decay, since it is the number of change, and change removes what is.
>
> . . . .
>
> In time all things come into being and pass away; for that reason some called it the wisest of things, but the Pythagorean Paron called it the most stupid, because in it we also forget; and his was the truer view. It is clear then that it must be in itself, as we said before, the condition of destruction rather than of coming into being (for change, in itself, makes things depart from their former condition), and only incidentally of coming into being, and of being. A sufficient evidence of this is that nothing comes into being without itself moving somehow and acting, but a thing can be destroyed even if it does not move at all. And this is what, as a rule, we chiefly mean by a thing's being destroyed by time. Still, time does not work even this change; even this sort of change takes place *incidentally* in time.[15]

At last, after this almost poetic lapse in which he submits to the traditional image of time as the great destroyer, Aristotle returns, almost as an afterthought, to the fact that change is the basic datum, and time, since it is only the measure of change, is incidental. Yet this is true only in terms of natural philosophy; the course of human events constitutes a temporal dimension that cannot be dismissed as incidental. In history there is no substratum of motion from place to place, and it is only by placing events in terms of "before" and "after" on a temporal continuum that coherence between them is etablished. And even in regard to the life of an individual or a state, where maturation and death constitute a type of change that is measured by time simply because it is in time as such, Aristotle cannot escape the fact that although the change only incidentally takes place in time—that is, its duration is measured in temporal units—a life constitutes a unique and finite temporal career that cuts across and gains pathos in contrast to the infinite circular movement of eternal time.

In terms of Aristotle's immanent metaphysics, time becomes an acute problem. For Plato chaos was coeval with the Idea, and from this tension between being and nonbeing emerged immanent being. In Aristotle's contracted universe in which being itself is the immanent union of form and matter, existence is suspended in a tension between substance and time. Actualized forms both in the natural and social world must be wrested from time; Plato's implicit equation of chaos and temporality is now explicit. The problem is not only that, unlike Plato, there is no compensatory realm of being—that is, that being-in-the-world is ultimate being or reality and that everything permanent had to be won in the face of time—but that in regard to human affairs there is no hope of abolishing historical existence. The foundation of a new polis or the preservation or stabilization of an old one might arrest time, but man could not ultimately escape history. Not only was there an unbridgeable gulf between human affairs and timelessness but there was an equally great distance between the uniqueness of human affairs and the specifically recurring phenomena in the natural world. Aristotle could not visualize a social order in which the particular or unique was eliminated.

In his view of the social universe, the same discriminatory vision is evident. Activities within the polis and types of individuals and their interests, such as the philosopher and statesman and the rich and the many, differentiate and gain autonomy and validity just as the mind categorizes the elements of the world in general and distinguishes the sciences

appropriate to its spheres. Aristotle's classificatory procedure is symptomatic of his differentiating approach, and in society, where the ordering
of the parts presents a problem for action, political sicence, although it is
an integrating science, is limited by its inability to overcome the autonomy
of that which has become differentiated. The ontological foundation of
Aristotle's political vision lies precisely in his "politicization" or democ-
ratization of reality. The pregiven nature of the best polis and the best
man can be grasped by the philosophic mind and serve as archetypes for
judging existential men and states, but the acceptance of the ultimate
reality of nonarchetypal existence limits the mandate of a practical science
of politics. When the truth of order becomes a value rather than an aspect
of existence, it no longer carries with it such a decisive prescription for
action. The lawgiver is still a mediator, but not in the sense of Plato's
statesman or founder; the idea of a demiurge is foreign to Aristotle's
vision because god is no longer a creator. The lawgiver acts in society as
nature acts in the physical world; he is a mediator between thought and
political reality just as nature is the mediator between god and physical
reality. An ultimate correspondence between contemplation and making
persists, but the gap has widened; contemplation and making are differentiated activities just as the psychic principle in the universe has
withdrawn to the perimeter of the natural world. Man and nature are
both makers, and in fact Aristotle's whole ontology and view of *physis* is
constructed around the notion of *techne,* but nature as well as man fails
to construct perfect actualizations in each instance; even in nature there
is often a gap between essence and the concrete particular with its form
and matter—for example, between the "nature" of man and "this" man.
Neither nature nor the statesman can overcome the fact that they must
operate within the temporal sphere.

For Aristotle history was to man what change was to nature, and
both could be encompassed in the idea of time; the meaning of time was
decay and dissolution. Every actualized substance, created by man or
nature, denies time as long as it persists, but eventually it is dissolved in
time. Even more than Plato, Aristotle was conscious of the age in which
he lived and of the decline of the polis, and although as for Plato the
polis remained the terminal civilizational unit, its regeneration became
increasingly problematical. The polis was "natural" in the sense that it
was necessary for the actualization of human potential, but the foundation and preservation of a polis was a problem of action, and action

belonged to the realm of history. The creation of the best polis was a theoretical possibility, and the Platonic ideal of a "divine" rule by one man remained within the purview of Aristotle's thought; yet there was no hope that such a state, even if realized, would persist in time. Unlike Plato, Aristotle did not entertain an idea of a polis constructed in terms of an institutionalized statesmanship, a self-perpetuating social cosmos or cosmic analogue that would fit into the order of the universe as a whole. The state existed in an alien world, the world of time, and the Platonic vision of a unity of man, state, and cosmos survived only in the weakened and demythologized idea of self-sufficiency or autarchy as a goal. The role of the lawgiver was to inject as much order as possible into the polis. In a sense Aristotle's polity—the state constructed in accordance with the mean—may be understood as a recognition of the claims of the many for participation and the realization that unity cannot be the overriding concern of political life. But in another sense, the polity was the residue of the Platonic vision of due measure surviving in a universe whose parts had differentiated and gained autonomy to an extent that the mind was humbled in the face of the plethora of reality.

Aristotle's problem was not the abolition of time, but the creation of an order that would persist through time and the conception of political science that emerges in the *Politics* is a science of order. Just as he was forced to admit the vagaries of reality and many interests within the polis, he was forced to give positive value to many types of states which were found wanting if judged by the standard of that which was best by nature.[16] Political science became a tool for the preservation of constitutions that were even inferior, a task which Plato explicitly rejected. Part of the problem was philosophical: truth and reality had parted company, and Aristotle was forced to derive values elsewhere than from the now substantiveless region of essences; namely, from the demands of political life itself. But part of the problem was simply that time was running out for the polis. With Aristotle, immortality was no longer a matter of great deeds preserved in memory nor, as with Plato, in the otherwordly survival of the soul, but the polis nevertheless remained the vehicle for individual immortality, since an order of the polis type was the prerequisite both for forming a character capable of contemplation and for supporting this activity. Although immortalizing was an activity of thought, a space within which to immortalize was as much a necessity as ever. There might be little possibility of creating a state in which every individual could be simultaneously a good man and a good citizen, but an ordered space was the *sine qua non* for the possibility of ultimate happiness. Even more than for Plato stability and order as ends in themselves were beginning to take on value as bulwarks against time.

Time and the Tradition

PART of the legacy which Greek philosophy left to the tradition was the tension between political order and history. To create political order was to establish a home for man in the world, a social cosmos that would withstand or annul the destructive force of time. But in later Greek thought the immediate fate of both the idea of the political and the discovery of historical existence was their sublimation in nature. With the collapse of the world of the polis, man lost not only a home in the world which would sustain the individual in fulfilling his potential whether this potential lay in action or thought, but the uniqueness of human existence itself. The polis was carried away in the flux of history, but history, which had been tied to the order of the polis in space, was lost in the stream of cosmic revolution. Political order and human time were swallowed up in cosmic time with its perpetual cycles of creation and decay. The orders of existence which had been so magnificently differentiated by Greek philosophy were compressed into a sphere where eternity, time, history, and the life of the individual merged; the tension between time and political order was obviated. With the decline of political particularism, the idea of a universal mankind that was detached from political space and was more than a species of nature began to emerge in Stoicism and later Hellenic thought, but the career of man remained bound by cosmic symbolism.

The uniqueness of the experience of Rome and its empire produced the most profound sense of history that appeared in the classical world. Although the idea of history was still tied to political order and permeated with the symbols of the cosmic myth and the idea of cyclical movement, history for Polybius was understood as an autonomous order of development culminating in the grandeur of Rome and guided by fortune to that end, and in Vergil's *Aeneid* the sense of the depth of historical time embracing the past of man was significantly expressed. However, despite the universalistic trend, the work of the Roman historians and the consciousness of the tradition to which they gave expression moved to a large extent within the confines of mythic symbolization. The political vitality of the empire made possible, despite the temporal perspective, the persistence of the myth of the foundation and the belief in the continual rejuvenation of a spatial order where mortals and immortals were joined in a compact unity. In fact, Rome persisted, especially in the later years, as an anomaly in a world where the myth had been decisively broken by Greek philosophy and the Hebrew and Christian theology.

For Plato and Aristotle history had meaning only insofar as it was the realm of disorder and decay. For the Romans, history was far from irrelevant because it was a storehouse of examples and the scene of the fulfillment of Rome's greatness, but it was the history of Rome that was meaningful; the idea of history was still bound to political space. But with primitive Christianity, history and temporality, as with the Hebrews, took on ontological significance and were divorced from the political foundation. History emerged as the temporal career of mankind. Although the advent of Christ was understood as the only truly unique event, all incidents on both sides of the epiphany gained a measure of meaning as part of the movement toward the establishment of the kingdom of God. As with the Hebrews, eternity did not mean timelessness, but the infinite time of God's reign where the world would be transformed. Time was the home of man and the scene of salvation. Yet although the Christian community was essentially a community in time, it also possessed a strong proselytizing impulse which inevitably pulled it toward space; and, just as the Hebrews had periodically placed hope in the empire of David, the Christians, especially after the ascendancy of Constantine, began to attach faith to the apparently perpetual empire as the portal to, and the place of preparation for, the final judgment. But with the sack of Rome, Christianity fled from the world and from history.

Although recent scholarship has overemphasized Augustine's Hellenization of Christianity and the neo-Platonic aspects of his thought, his solution to the problem of the *parousia* was a significant departure from early Christianity and was decisive for the meaning of time in Western thought. The incipient dualism of the Pauline teaching provided Augustine with the theological foundation for a system which expanded the more compact vision of primitive Christianity into a hierarchy of orders. Neither the Jews nor the early Christians had anticipated any significant break between their journey on earth and the kingdom of God; history was the unfolding of His promise. But the possibility of the resurrection of the individual through grace and faith and the emphasis on inherent sin and predestination led to a devaluation of history and made the expectation of the second coming less meaningful. The kingdom of God became the kingdom of heaven; time and eternity parted company.

Augustine did not so much reject the mundane world as make what happened in it theoretically unimportant; it became a realm of disorder, although its reality was accepted. The course of events held little meaning because man's home was in eternity. History was in a sense still a progression toward redemption, but it was not for man to know when the event would take place. The emphasis was centered on the salvation of the individual rather than of the world and on a flight from time to an eternity which was timeless and spatially distinct. Augustine rejected the Hellenic notion of historical cycles, but history and the rise and fall of political order possessed little more meaning than in Hellenic thought where they were absorbed in nature. The history which he commissioned Orosius to write was not worth his theoretical attention; apart from the one unique event it had no meaning except as a catalogue of human fallibility. As with Aristotle, timelessness and time were differentiated, but now eternity had substantive content and meaning for the individual, and what man did on earth, especially in view of the doctrine of predestination, had little relevance in regard to individual immortality. Yet political order did not lose all significance because although the *Civitas Dei* and the *Civitas Terrena* were symbols of the difference between eternity and time, the political realm contained members of both cities. It was from this notion that the idea of the church as the spatial representative or mediator between the two cities would emerge, the recurring symbol of the earthly remnant. The church began to appropriate the mythical motif of the intermediary between eternity and the individual in time, and its organization made it appear as a timeless impersonal order that bound the orders of existence together and annulled the passage of secular time. As in Hebrew thought, this tension between time and order in space could never be completely resolved.

Once the life of the spirit and the life of the body or secular existence, eternity and time, were thoroughly differentiated, Augustine could not escape the question of the exact nature of time which now presented itself as a problematical realm.[17] He could not deny the reality of time since it belonged to the universe created by God; yet although time seemed to exist, it always tended toward nothingness. Time belonged to the universe because the nature of the universe and corporeal things was change. There was no "time" before God created the universe; the eternity of God stood apart from time, which existed only because of the nature of the material world. Even more than for Aristotle, time insofar as it had any reality outside the soul was equated with change and disorder. For Augustine it was the soul that measured time, and time was essentially a function of the soul, a making present of things and events which were "no longer" and "not yet" by means of memory and anticipation. The past and future belonged to nonbeing, and even the present was completely divisible, for otherwise it would have been eternity. The "now" was merely the point of the soul's immediate attention. Augustine anticipated the modern understanding of time as centered in the psyche, but for Augustine the soul itself was not in time. The life of the individual as a corporeal being was in time, and the mind encompassed the dimensions of time, but the soul or the essence of the self was not constituted by these dimensions. The soul occupied a midpoint in the realm of being and could contemplate the eternity of God or timelessness as well as the flux of the universe or temporality.

Thus time was relegated to a continually changing material world that constituted a sharp contrast with eternity; time lost its importance as the scene of fulfillment and was meaningful only as an apperception of an inferior order of being which included human events. However, this formulation was not a radical neo-Platonic rejection of the reality of time and the material and historical world. There was a decisive differentiation, but the ultimate result was not that the temporal lost reality, but that both time and eternity began to take on an independent validity. Eternity was a self-sufficient substantive realm on the one hand, and history could not be denied or overcome by the action of men on the other. The inevitable result was that the foundation was prepared for secular history as an autonomous realm.

Within Augustine's scheme there was an irresolvable tension between eternity and time and faith and reason. Man belonged to both worlds; yet both worlds were distinct. With the Scholastic introduction of Aristotelian philosophy and the idea of the infinity of time and the universe, the tension was openly manifest. The growth of the institutional structure of the church, the demands of the secular and political world, and the events of mundane history inevitably created the need for a reconciliation of the orders of existence which had been so starkly differentiated by Augustine. Aquinas' synthesis of philosophy and revelation and reason and faith served to allay the inevitable clash and bind the orders of existence into a coherent whole which rivaled the Platonic vision, but in a sense the goal was achieved at the expense of faith and eternity. The solution claimed too much and could withstand neither the internal challenge of a burgeoning nominalism nor the external challenge of historical events. In the end, the solution served to reinforce the validity of the material world and secular history, and his analysis of time, which was a mixture of Aristotelian and Augustinian elements, only added to the growing importance and autonomy of nontheological time. But, unlike the fate of the Platonic vision, the realm of being did not contract into an immanent reality; the strength of the Christian message was too firmly grounded. Rather, faith and reason, transcendence and immanence, and eternity and time split apart and existed side by side.

The tension could not be resolved. While some such as Joachim clung to or reformulated Christian eschatology and others embraced a neo-Platonic perspective, the Renaissance, in general, learned to live with both worlds, and like Nicolaus Cusanus, accepted eternity and time and faith and reason as differentiated yet complementary areas of experience with neither imposing limits on the other in their respective spheres. God or the absolute sustained the universe, but the human mind "knew" the universe and ordered it. Time stretching into infinity on both sides of the present was conceived as the realm of man's activity, and history was the product of his creativity, not a meaningless swirl of events, but the product of man's making. But man had to continually give meaning and order to the universe and human affairs or else both would be swallowed up in the infinity of time. Both the sensible world and society became the medium for the creative activity of the mind, but, even more than for Plato, to know without giving issue in the world was no very great thing. Theory and action again merged, but both now concerned an immanent historical reality. Man was the god who acted in the world; he was enclosed by temporality and forced to create order in the face of fortune and history which were coeval with the mind. Man in his freedom was again the imitator of God in the most literal sense, for the universe belonged to him, and in it he realized and manifested himself. Order and permanence once more became secular and world-immanent problems, and to achieve order meant that it had to be wrested from time.

The immortality of the individual soul now had little significance for the secular realm, but the idea of an earthly immortality of the species again became meaningful; mankind was coeternal with time, and it was incumbent on man to create a home in the world. The need of an ordered space within which to act, create, and give play to the power of the mind and the potential of action became important, and as with the Greeks, the very creation of such a space, a cosmion that would emulate the constancy and stability of nature, became a problem of human action. The idea of the political was again that of a mesocosm, although not in the sense of an order that would bind man to nature or a transcendent realm. But the political order existed alongside the natural order, and the founder of a state was nevertheless a completer of the universe. Both physical and political nature opened their secrets to the mind, and the idea of secular immortality and the hope of creating and maintaining a lasting political order once more became a matter of concern.

All the threads of the new age converged in Machiavelli, who not only accepted the differentiated and autonomous character of human affairs but situated himself firmly in the world of action and history and devised symbols to explore it. This was his "new route."[18] He was by no means an atheist, and when he left the world he sought the solace of the church. But for the duration of his sojourn on earth he concerned himself with earthly things and insisted on Christ's admission that His kingdom was not of this world. For Machiavelli, man, like the realm of being, was a differentiated entity torn between faith, reason, and passion, and a knowledge of the nature of this creature, which he continually insisted remained uniform and constant,[19] made possible its control and the construction of a political order that would remain equally constant. Human passions could be directed, manipulated, and organized either by the instrumental skill of a prince possessing the necessary knowledge or by the structure of a republic in which this knowledge and skill were institutionalized. The transition from the *Prince* to the *Discourses* is not unlike the path followed by Plato in moving from the *Republic* to the *Laws*. The dependence on a single and ultimately vulnerable individual gives way to the idea of the objectification of wisdom in an institutional order, an idea which has informed constitutional theory from Machiavelli through the

founders of the American republic. In a sense the state was still understood as man writ large. Although it was not a projection of the psyche,
it was constructed to contain it. The knowledge of human nature provided
the basis for a political science which was purely a science of order
directed toward bringing an enduring political structure out of the chaos
of individuals moving in the flux of society through history just as in the
physical world the manifold particulars remained constant in their movements through infinite time.

In one sense history as a whole or as a total progression in time was
irrelevant to Machiavelli since he believed in the possibility of creating
by artifice a political order that could, to a large extent, withstand the
decay of time. "There is nothing more true than that all the things of
this world have a limit to their existence; but those only run the entire
course ordained for them by Heaven that do not allow their body to
become disorganized."[20] His concern with history and change was not so
much to find meaning in the course of events or to explicate a theory of
change as to determine how to create a permanent order. The conditions
necessary for political order had been neglected, and he set out to fill the
vacuum. History was essentially the scene of decay, for just "as all human
things are kept in a perpetual state of movement, and can never remain
stable, states either naturally rise or decline."[21] But although in the
course of historical time cycles of political order were discernible, they
were not part of a cosmic movement. The cycles of governments were
grounded in immanent causes such as the success and failure of action,[22]
and the idea of history as a process of decline overrode any notion of a cyclical return of the same. Yet, since the springs of human action remained
uniform it was possible to find in "long experience of modern events and
a constant study of the past" a recurrence of similar patterns and a set
of examples from which principles of political order could be extracted
and through which fortune could be overcome by art based on knowledge.[23] The period from Rome to the present was one of political decline,
but by a return to the principles which had vitalized the ancient republic,
a founder could create a state which would persist.

For Machiavelli the state could best endure if it were the creation
of one man, a sculptor who molded order from the clay of society.[24] By
this act of foundation man becomes most like a god, not the imitator of a
a hero, but a maker or creator, and the man who created order was most
worthy of praise while the worst of men were those who destroyed it.[25]

For Machiavelli the foundation was the determinative act, and the sustenance of political order depended on a periodic reaffirmation of the foundation for a renewal of its vitality.[26] The regeneration of the authority inherent in the act of creation and belonging to the maker could overcome the cycle of decline and annul the temporal distance which intruded itself between the foundation and the present. There was the continual threat that society would pass away into its original disordered condition and that the chaotic tendency inherent both in the prepolitical autonomy of the individuals who composed society and in the passions of these individuals would reassert itself. The perpetuation of order was grounded in the abolition of history and the sublimation of the unique. As man began to concern himself again with the problem of creating a permanent political space, the mythic symbols began to flood in, and history appeared more and more as a process without meaning.

The devitalization of the Christian community and its representative in the church, as well as the chaotic effect of religion on public life, created the demand for a secular theory of politics and threw into relief the role of man as a creator in the realm of political nature and the problem of developing a science of order that would bring meaning and stability out of the flux of history. With Hobbes not only did history as a whole lack coherence and meaning but even attention to the past as a quarry of knowledge and experience was called into question. For Hobbes, knowledge of past and future was inferior and grounded merely in conjecture since it was based "only on experience which produced no universal knowledge or 'immutable truth' "; prudence was only the "memory of succession of events in times past" and defective in comparison with reason and artifice based on reason.[27] History for Hobbes was simply the symbol of disorder, the scene of the unique and perishable, and to attempt to build on the past and experience was to build on sand.[28] Time was a process that carried order away; the future and past were unreal—only phantoms and decaying images in the mind which existed in fiction and memory. In Hobbes's geometric world, reality meant the denial of time, for "the present only has a being in nature."[29]

Hobbes's act of creative imagination which annihilated the world in order to build it anew meant an abolition of the past and a control of the future, the simultaneous destruction, creation, and fixation of meaning. The idea, arising in the Renaissance, that man had the task of conceptualizing and thereby in a sense creating the universe found full expression in Hobbes's philosophy. To know the future was to create it, "for the foresight of things to come, which is providence, belongs only to him by whose will they are to come."[30] With the explicit extension of this assumption to social phenomena, it appeared that it could be even more effective since social reality consisted only of individuals as concrete entities, and the relationships between them were open to manipulation. Philosophy and reason could enter the social world, and although an eternal commonwealth might be beyond possibility, since all earth-bound creations were subject to decay, it might approach immortality if properly constituted. Even more than with Machiavelli man through reason could become a god in the world and find salvation for society. "Though nothing can be immortal, which mortals make; yet, if men had the use of reason they pretend to, then commonwealths might be secured, at least from perishing by internal diseases. . . . Therefore, when they come to be dissolved, not by external violence, but by intestine disorder, the fault is not in men, as they are the *matter;* but as they are the *makers,* and orderers of them."[31]

The temporal present, upon which Hobbes gazed and dreamed of destroying and re-creating in terms of a social cosmos of controlled motions, was the state of nature. The condition postulated by Hobbes stands as a classic description of the despair of man marooned in the flux of time and overwhelmed by the instability of human affairs; it is equaled only by the sense of personal perplexity in the face of time so apparent in Augustine's *Confessions* or Pascal's *Pensées*. The idea of a state of nature was meaningful only in terms of existence in time where memory and Promethean foresight created anxiety and perpetual fear.[32] The state of nature symbolized not only an existential crisis in society but a condition which, like Plato's chaos, could never be completely abolished since its roots could not be entirely eradicated. And again it approximated Plato's chaos in the sense that it was like the fate of dissimilarity which entered the world when history reached the point where order ceased to inform its motions and all continuity and tradition were broken. Yet for Hobbes, as for Plato, there was a belief in the possibility that theory could be put into practice and that, through the science of politics linked with power, time could be regenerated and by an act of will a founder or "very able architect" properly situated could abolish the anxieties of historical existence and create a permanent home for man in space.[33] By fixing symbols and meanings, thought and action could be equally stable and channeled, and as the dispenser of meanings, the sovereign, like God, could become the continuous creator of a social universe.

For much of political philosophy from Plato to Rousseau society or the subpolitical realm appeared as the great beast to be tamed by the imposition of political order. Society was the realm of anxiety, instability, uniqueness, and temporality; it was the scene of necessity, the arena of the passions, and the root of human disorder. Despite the intellectual gulf which separates Plato and Rousseau, both ultimately understood the political as a means of containing society and abolishing history. For political philosophy the idea of order proceeded from a philosophical anthropology, and although political thought after Machiavelli began to lose concern with the function of the state as a vehicle for an internal transformation of the individual, the idea of order was nevertheless grounded in the belief in certain immutable characteristics of human being which rendered society susceptible to the imposition of form. The loss of an idea of the political which could defend its claim against society took place only when society had appropriated the self, and this in turn was only possible with the historization of human being. The decline of the idea of the political and the rise of society and history as the home of man were complementary developments.

Numerous intellectual threads were woven into the fabric of the Enlightenment. The scientific rationalism of Bacon and Descartes, Montesquieu's dismissal of fortune and providence and uniqueness in history in favor of the pervasive notion of "cause," the belief in an infinite universe and an infinite time, and the heritage of the idea of universal history including the thought of Bodin and Vico, all contributed to the idea of a secular career of mankind reaching infinitely into the past and future and to the idea of the infinite perfectibility of man and society through the development and exercise of reason. Although there was still an idea of man, the wielder of reason, the individual was in general understood as malleable and susceptible to his external environment; man's home was no longer political space, but society's temporal career, a history which as Vico had argued was the product of man's making and consequently intelligible and which in the vision of thinkers such as the Abbé de Saint-Pierre, and later Kant, could be directed toward an earthly and universal peace. The God of Descartes, who had insured the existence of the universe and was contemporaneous with it, had withdrawn to the position of the great watchmaker and like Aristotle's god was nearly

irrelevant since secondary causes ruled the world. The transcendent realm
was contracting into the infinity of the cosmos itself, and the individual
and society were becoming oriented toward an immanent salvation in
time. The extent to which the symbols of political order were being transformed and applied to other areas of experience or discarded altogether
is evident in the loneliness of Rousseau, who, standing on the threshold
of the historical consciousness of the nineteenth century, vainly attempted
to recapture the myth of political order and an idea of man which transcended society and time.

Rousseau's state of nature was the condition of man prior to the
anxiety produced by the awareness of temporality, after which memory
and anticipation pulled him to and fro between past and future; it was
the condition existing "when the race was already old, and man remained
a child,"[34] the form of existence under the myth, where human being was
devoid of the faculties acquired through the expansion of consciousness.
In the compactness of this existence, life was lived in the eternity of
primordial time where the individual soul was "wholly wrapped up in
the feeling of its present existence, without any idea of the future."[35]
Here man lived in the passivity of the unmediated experience of being
without reflection on himself or the world. The exit from the state of
nature was the entrance into social and economic life where the Promethean gifts, despite their power to mold the external world, threw men
into the realm of necessity, dependence, social intercourse, and vice and
virtue—into the world of memory and imagination, the world of history
and time.[36]

In society and time man first became aware of himself, but at the
same time his being was taken over by the world in which he had come
to move, so that it was impossible to "distinguish what is fundamental
in his nature from the changes and additions which his circumstances
and the advances he has made have introduced to modify his primitive
condition."[37] Not only the individual in the temporal unfolding of his
life but mankind in the course of history as well were disfigured by time
and society and estranged from the unity of their original existence. The
present was no longer the eternal present of the natural man, but an
instant in the flux of time. The process of history created the temporal
distance which separated man from the condition of his natural freedom
and created the inequalities of social existence. The progress of man in
society was the progressive alienation of the self. "In reality, the source

of all these differences is, that the savage lives within himself, while social man lives constantly outside himself, and only knows how to live in the opinion of others, so that he seems to receive the consciousness of his own existence merely from the judgment of others concerning him."[38]

Like Plato, Rousseau neither visualized nor recommended a return to the condition of the myth, but unlike Plato, he could not conceive of a political order that would have restored coherence among the individual, the state, and the cosmos. The orders of existence had been differentiated, and the past could not be recovered. At best man could regenerate time and halt the forward movement of history by the establishment of an archetypal community within a political order created by artifice; this would be a society which would allow the individual a measure of the equality and freedom which belonged to him before his perfect orientation in the world had been destroyed by the accretions of history.

Rousseau found in the idea of the political an answer to the problem of social existence,[39] but the social contract was but a vestige of the vision of a science of order which could create a home for man in the world.

> Everything upon the earth is in continual flux. Nothing in it retains a form that is constant and fixed, and our affections, attached to external things, necessarily pass and change like the things themselves. Always, ahead of or behind us, they recall the past which no longer exists, or they anticipate a future which often will never come to pass: there is nothing there solid enough for the heart to attach itself to.[40]

The hope for the establishment of a political order based on the principles which governed man's original condition and which would sustain the self and assure its autonomy was only the dream of a man who himself felt ravaged by society and hungered to escape the world and history, yet was unable to attain either the certainty of his own selfhood or find anything more substantive in man than an original condition of existence. Rousseau was seeking a communal security for the individual which paradoxically was possible only in a mode of life which was prior to self-awareness. Like Plato, he found that a return to society for a man such as himself was in the end impossible;[41] he was eventually constrained to visualize his participation in society only as a lawgiver or founder of a new order, and ultimately his architectonic vision found expression only in the literary work of the artist. Finally, the social contract, even

if realized, could only arrest the inevitable decay which he understood as
the fate of the individual and all that he created, even a political body
that was best constituted.[42]

The complete historization of existence accomplished in the nineteenth century was adumbrated in the previous century when history
rather than nature became the home of man, and society the immediate
reference for the individual within the stream of history. The ground of
this development was the dissolution of the self. With Locke, society
rather than political order was already the more basic concept, and this
was so because the individual was fast becoming a product of his social
environment, and political order essentially a guarantor of social and
economic activity. The idea of the political had hitherto been fundamentally grounded in the assumption that a political space could be
erected within the world which would conform to the nature of man, but
with Locke man was known in terms of a self which was becoming little
more than a floating consciousness; personal identity was simply a state
of mind or a changing configuration of ideas preserved in memory. Con-
dillac and the French Ideologues and Utilitarians such as Destutt de
Tracy and Helvétius radicalized this trend by making all ideas, and even
reflection, not something innate, but only the product of sensation; both
the content and faculties of the mind were merely built up from impres-
sions of the external world, and man, created by sensation, was merely
the receptacle which in the course of time became the sum total of its
experience bound together by a memory which provided a sense of duration. Hume, who more than anyone else hastened the demise of the
substantial self, defined the self as the feeling derived from reflection on
a series of perceptions; again, only memory provided continuity. With
the English Utilitarians the concept of the self contracted into a sensa-
tional core and gave way to the idea of the individual as a mirror of
society. Rousseau's fear was becoming a reality.

Kant, who in one sense put all reality into question except the self,
actually succeeded in nearly obscuring the self altogether by dismissing it
as an object of experience and placing it in the noumenal world. The
attempt to save the self from being engulfed by the flux of time was
achieved at the cost of its intelligibility. When seeking his nature, man
could only point to his phenomenal self or personality existing in and
subject to the form of time and causality—the social self of Hume

and Adam Smith. The problem of securing the self in the face of the increasing ontological significance of time was accentuated by the Kantian dichotomy; subjectivity demanded a ground, but Kant's self was little more than a functional concept, the self of pure apperception which was ultimately unknowable. Schopenhauer believed that he had found the self in the will which lay beyond the knowing consciousness that was temporally situated, but individual identity grew more nebulous. For Kant even memory had served no place as a means for preserving identity, and in the end only Proust was able to turn memory into an instrument for recovering a self that bridged the void between past and future and escaped change in the chronological order of time. But the tendency toward the dispersion of the self was only part of a more comprehensive transformation of reality.

The growing historical consciousness of the age culminated in Hegel, who gathered the orders of existence, including the individual, man, society, nature, and God, into a movement of the spirit in history. Reality contracted completely into history, and truth and being became manifest in time. The orders of existence which had been progressively differentiated were reintegrated, and the break between the particular and universal, theory and action, mind and matter, faith and reason, was repaired. Yet Hegel, and Marx after him, sought to harmonize the permanent and temporal in a process which constituted a dialectical timelessness, an eternal returning-upon-itself where the past was continually appropriated in the present and history was drawn into the infinite time of a final fulfillment which annulled temporal succession. Being in the end stood beyond and encompassed history, and although order and meaning were situated in the historical process, history had its end, and the vision of society was that of a society beyond time. The eschatological myth of Hegel and Marx, like the integral myth and the systems of Plato and Aquinas, claimed too much, but it served to ground ultimate reality in the very process of time and becoming. By his inversion of the traditional relationship between political order and society, Marx completed the foundation for the modern conceptualization of human affairs in terms of history and society. But just as Aristotle retained Plato's symbols to describe a world no longer ordered by Plato's vision, Marx's successors rejected the laws of the dialectic and the myth of secular historical meaning, but retained the categories of history and society for describing man's place in the world. History was transformed into formless succession and society became a process, but reality as a process seemed as unamenable to discursive articulation as Plato's chaos.

With the collapse of a substantive historical vision—that is, meaning in history—the very coherence of human affairs was threatened. Reality had been transformed into temporal process, and the process had been emptied of meaning. The loss of permanence was not easily accepted, and much of the historical speculation of the nineteenth century was devoted to an attempt to give some measure of form to historical time. This tension is apparent in Nietzsche's vision of eternal recurrence, the epochal cycles of Troeltsch and Spengler, and eventually the conceptual typologies of historical sociology. No one felt the problem of "historicism" and historical relativism more strongly than Wilhelm Dilthey. Dilthey insisted on the historical nature of man and argued that the appearance of the modern historical consciousness was the momentous event which not only freed human existence from the bondage of nature but made possible an autonomous science of man. Yet, For Dilthey, man was, as a temporal creature, distraught by the problem of the insecurity of his existence and throughout history had attempted to lift his creations as well as himself out of the flux of time; Dilthey sensed the problem, and his work symbolizes the transformation which was taking place. But he believed that what he termed the eternal contradiction between the creative and historical consciousness could be overcome in his era since at last the creative mind was contemporary with the full development of the historical consciousness and could see that its work was part of a historical continuum and not a final truth. In the end, however, Dilthey was able neither to find an ontology of historical existence nor to accept the historicity of human being and the formlessness of history; he attempted to find permanent empirical structures in the human consciousness and postulated a series of recurring historical Weltanschauungen.

Bergson signaled the acceptance of time as constitutive for human being and open-ended process as the ground of reality; the tension between form and time, between man's creative impulse and history, was theoretically resolved. For Bergson the self could not be conceptualized; it could be understood only as it lived, created, and changed itself in time. Memory bound the instant and the past in an intuitive whole which moved forward by creative activity. The attempt to wrest reality and the idea of man from the flux of time gave way to the attempt to perceive reality and human being in the undetermined flow of time itself; being was time and history, and form in history, even cause and effect, gave way to process. What separated Bergson's notion of memory from that of Proust was that for Bergson memory never recovered a self that persisted through time, but a self that was constituted by time. The end of the nineteenth century brought with it the apotheosis of history. With Croce historical knowledge was understood as complete knowledge, and history and philosophy were confounded. In the idea of history, man found a substitute not only for nature but for the idea of the political; the continuity of history appropriated the symbols of permanence. Humanity and the self were now known through and defined by history and time; man was what he had done and what had happened to him. Action became of decisive importance, for it no longer merely determined the circumstances of existence but the very being of man; to make bold claims against time was impossible, for it meant the annulment of the ground of existence. Ortega summed up the vision of an age by the observations that the "essence of human being is change" and that "man has no 'nature'; he has a history."[43] The relationship between history as *res gestae* and man was the same as that which obtained between nature and "things." Man was neither a divine nor a rational animal nor a political animal, and only incidentally was he a social animal; he was in the last analysis a historical animal.

Historicism has resulted in a narrowing of consciousness as severe as that which faced Plato. The result of this contraction of vision has been a phenomenon which can best be described as the contextualization of human being. Whether one turns to contemporary philosophy or sociology and psychology, the most salient characteristic of the idea of man in the modern age is the contextual and fractured character of his existence. The idea of self, man, or human being has lost its substantive content, and with this transformation has come the loss of the idea of the political as a means of sustaining the individual against the time-ridden and necessitous realm of society. The atrophy of political philosophy cannot be attributed to the decline of utopian faith or the rise of fatalistic attitudes in modern thought, nor is the answer to be found in contemporary explanations of the "end of ideology." These are only the symptoms of an age in which man has lost a meaningful idea of himself and his home in the world. The loss of the idea of the political was grounded in the absence of an ontology that could give support to a vision of political order.

Yet faced with a vision of reality from which the permanent has been
excluded, modern man nevertheless finds himself in need of permanence;
man in society still faces the problem of order. The contemporary age
with its proliferation of techniques and modes of organization possesses
manifold and unparalleled potential for ordering society and directing
the process of social activity along constant vectors, but paradoxically
these techniques exist in a world where the problem of the theoretical
foundations of political order has been forgotten.

The solution to the decline of political philosophy, if a solution is
at all required, cannot be found in attempts to reverse the course of the
tradition and reappropriate old political symbols; Plato well understood
the impossibility of reordering the world in terms of past truths. The
contemporary symbolic crisis has been especially acute since the very
continuity of the tradition had assumed the burden of permanence; but
if it is true that the principal concern of political philosophy has been
the question of man's home in the world, it is also true that political
philosophy has no ultimate claim to providing an orientation, and in
the modern age, despite the irreducible problem of order in society, it
may not be meaningful to expect "political" answers to be fundamental
or that the meaning of the "political" will not undergo a radical transformation. Speculative thought cannot simply renounce the extent to
which temporality has informed the contemporary vision of man and the
world and seek the meaning of existence in symbols which lack relevance
in terms of the modern understanding of the human condition. Advances
in thought must be made in terms of a creative transformation of the
symbolization of man as a historical animal. But the same intellectual
developments which have led to the idea of contextual man have also
provided the basis for such a transformation. The answer, however, is
not one that is likely to be meaningful in terms of providing a new
theoretical foundation for politics; philosophical anthropology has ceased
to speak to political philosophy.

The attempt to preserve identity from annihilation by time and society found artistic expression in Baudelaire's characterization of the
drunk and the dandy, in Proust's involuntary memory which inexplic-
ably saved the self, in Valéry's regeneration of self and time through the
creative act, and in the Nietzschean man who refused to be entranced
by the mesmeric performance of history and with heroic honesty declined

to become the plaything of time, even in the face of the fact "that all foundations are breaking up in mad unconscious ruin and resolving themselves into the ever-flowing stream of becoming; that all creation is being tirelessly spun into webs of history by modern man, the great spider in the mesh of the world-net."[44] Unlike Kafka's flight to the sanctuary of the moss between the burrow and the world or Mann's mountain where time was negated, time, although it was still the great destroyer, began, nevertheless, to become the indispensable medium for existence. The self which with Kant had begun to fade away into nothing more than a hidden impetus now found expression in action in time; the self found that it could continuously create and preserve itself, and time became the dimension of its existence and realization. As with Bergson, creative rather than contemplative activity revealed and insured the existence of the individual. Only through the creative and artistic act was the self prevented from falling into nothingness and maintained above the facticity of the objects of the world and space which for man meant objectification and absorption in the realm of nonbeing. Despite the profound sense of temporal limits, human being was grounded in time where man became the creator of himself.

The new vision began to find philosophic expression in Dilthey, but although Dilthey, and Croce, overcame the trend toward the sublimation of history in scientism they were unable to deal effectively with the problem of historical relativism, and one result of their work was the emergence of perspectivism, historicism, or contextualism not only as an approach to historical knowledge but as a vision of the world. These same trends have at least partially informed much of contemporary philosophy and social science which founders in its attempt to formulate any substantive idea of human existence. Although existentialism in general has attempted to understand man as a temporal creature, only Heidegger, and to a certain extent Jaspers, have succeeded in developing a significant ontology of historical existence, a philosophy appropriate for a vision of man *en situation*.

Heidegger's project for the destruction or overcoming of Western metaphysics, the avowed return to the pre-Socratic understanding of being, is actually neither a "destruction" nor a "return" in any usual sense of the word any more than Plato undertook to destroy the philosophy of his predecessors and to return to the myth.

> This path to the answer to our question is not a break with his-
> tory, no repudiation of history, but is an adoption and transforma-
> tion of what has been handed down to us. Such an adoption of
> history is what is mean by the term "destruction." . . . Destruction
> means—to open our ears, to make ourselves free for what speaks
> to us in the tradition as the Being of being.[45]

Heidegger's project is an attempt to recapture, as Plato did, the ground
of being and transcend modern subjectivism. But, as with Plato, he
cannot reject the extent to which human existence has become differentiated. His return is the return of the mind to participation in the
world; it is not a return to a past philosophy or symbolic configuration.
His destruction of metaphysics is not a renunciation of philosophy, but
the rejection of the old truth, the old symbols, that no longer conform
to experience or provide a medium for the movement of the creative
mind. His recovery of the past is an attempt to recover a meaning for
historical existence that has been lost through the derailment of the
historical consciousness into the vision of contextual man.

It is out of the very ruins of the contextualist vision that he attempts to articulate a new idea of man and his world. Heidegger's use
of language is grounded in the creative process of symbolic transformation, and in the end Heidegger, like Plato, finds himself forced to aban-
don discursive speech and seek expression in art and the presentational
language of poetry and myth where the symbols flood in from the unconscious. For Heidegger the pre-Socratics and the posttraditional poetry
of Holderlin signify the pretheoretical and creative encounter with existence, the primordial experience of being, where the subject-object
bifurcation and the dualism in general, including the poles of time and
eternity, ontological and ontic, and language and object, that stem from
the persistence of Aristotelian symbols, can be overcome.

Heidegger breaks through the confines of the contextualist reduction and historical relativism by providing an ontological foundation
for the historicity of human being. For Heidegger man and the self are
grounded in time in their very being, and an ontological illumination
of mankind and the individual must be conducted in terms of history
and temporality. But human being is neither merely a subject of history
nor determined by history, but rather the very reason that there is
historicity in the world is because man, through whom being becomes
manifest, is historical in the depth of his existence. Man is not a func-

tion of history; history is a function of man. Man, for Heidegger, is in a sense a condition—the human condition signified by *Dasein*. But this condition is neither a historical situation nor a natural fact nor something discovered by sociological investigation. Building on the symbols of historicism, he attempts to elucidate a condition that is known by philosophical understanding and that is universally human; it stands outside time and history in the sense that it is the condition of all thought and action.

Man is a temporal being because of the intentional structure of consciousness and the universal structures of the human condition such as guilt, nothingness, death. In this situation, which, once understood, gives meaning to existence, the self continually realizes and creates itself by its choices, but faces alienation and a fall into the object world of nonbeing if its choices cease to be authentic or made in accordance with the nature of the condition which situates man humanly. In the term *Dasein*, or being-there, "there" has the meaning of "forward"—the future or realm of choice; man is continually "there" not "here"—in time not space. The self exists simultaneously in the past, present, and future; man exists in these ecstasies of time and continually confirms and creates his being by running ahead of himself while choosing his possibilities.

In Heidegger's symbolization of man as the creature who virtually is the human condition, the symbols of social, political, and historical existence have been creatively transformed into an analogical representation of a new vision of human being. Terms such as anxiety, freedom, choice, which were meaningful as descriptions of man in society, have been transformed into ontological symbols in a way similar to Plato's representation of the soul as a political order. Now it is history and society writ small that symbolize *Dasein*. When man becomes temporal in his being there is little choice other than to articulate the vision, the new reality of the soul, in terms of symbols that analogically express the experience of temporality; that is, the condition of man in society and history. Plato, faced with the crisis of man in a decaying political order, turned inward and sought in the soul the ground of order and disorder; Heidegger, faced with the crisis of man in historical existence, has also turned inward and sought for the meaning of historicity in man himself.

NOTES

I. INTRODUCTION

1. Ernst Cassirer, *Essay on Man* (New Haven: Yale University Press, 1944), p. 26.
2. Ludwig von Bertalanffy, "On the Definition of the Symbol," in Joseph R. Royce, *Psychology and the Symbol* (New York: Random House, 1965), pp. 55, 68.
3. Susanne Langer, *Philosophy in a New Key* (New York: New American Library, 1948), p. 61.
4. Kenneth Boulding, *The Image* (Ann Arbor: University of Michigan Press, 1961), p. 44.
5. Langer, *op. cit.*, pp. 91, 45.
6. *Ibid.*, pp. 77–89.
7. Alfred Schütz, *Collected Papers I: The Problems of Social Reality* (The Hague: Martinus Nijhoff, 1962), p. 293.
8. Cassirer, *The Logic of the Humanities* (New Haven: Yale University Press, 1961), p. 74.
9. Karl Jaspers, *Reason and Existence,* trans. William Earle (New York: Noonday Press, 1957), p. 52. Also *Truth and Symbol,* trans. Jean T. Wilde, William Kluback, and William Kimmel (New York: Twayne, 1959).
10. Martin Heidegger, "A Letter on Humanism," in W. Barrett and H. Aiken (eds.), *Philosophy in the 20th Century* (New York: Random House, 1962), Vol. 3, p. 288.
11. Jaspers, *Reason and Existence,* p. 52; Cassirer, *Language and Myth,* trans. Susanne K. Langer (New York: Harper, 1946), p. 11; Schütz, *op. cit.,* p. 341.
12. Cassirer, *The Logic of the Humanities,* p. 22.
13. Stuart Hampshire, *Thought and Action* (New York: Viking, 1960), p. 21.
14. Eric Voegelin, *The New Science of Politics* (Chicago: University of Chicago Press, 1952), p. 27.
15. Ludwig Wittgenstein, *Philosophical Investigations,* trans. G. E. M. Anscombe (New York: Macmillan, 1953), p. 226e.
16. Wilbur Marshall Urban, *Language and Reality* (New York: Macmillan, 1939), p. 454.
17. See Owen Barfield, *Worlds Apart* (Middletown: Wesleyan University Press, 1963).
18. See Barfield, *Saving the Appearances* (New York: Harbinger, 1965).

19. Thomas Kuhn, *The Structure of Scientific Revolutions* (Chicago: University of Chicago Press, 1962).

20. Sheldon S. Wolin, *Politics and Vision* (Boston: Little, Brown, 1960), p. 5.

21. Peter Winch, *The Idea of a Social Science* (New York: Humanities Press, 1958), pp. 23, 61–62.

22. See Marshall McLuhan, *The Gutenberg Galaxy* (Toronto: University of Toronto Press, 1962); *Understanding Media* (New York: McGraw-Hill, 1964).

23. Heidegger, *Existence and Being* (Chicago: Henry Regnery, 1949), p. 276; *An Introduction to Metaphysics*, trans. Ralph Manheim (New York: Doubleday, 1961), pp. 11, 144.

24. Jaspers, *Reason and Existence*, p. 79.

25. McLuhan, *Understanding Media*, pp. 3, 50.

26. Langer, *op. cit.*, p. 172.

27. Cassirer, *The Logic of the Humanities*, p. 67.

28. Kuhn, *op. cit.*, p. 62.

29. Hannah Arendt, *Between Past and Future* (New York: Viking, 1961), pp. 8–9.

30. Heidegger, "A Letter on Humanism," p. 283.

31. Isak Dinesen, *Anecdotes of Destiny* (New York: Random House, 1958), pp. 17–20.

32. Jaspers, *The Origin and Goal of History* (New Haven: Yale University Press, 1953), p. 1.

33. Cyrus H. Gordon, *Before the Bible* (New York: Harper and Row, 1962), p. 9.

II. TIME, MYTH, AND SOCIETY

1. Ludwig Wittgenstein, *Tractatus Logico-Philosophicus* (London: Routledge and Kegan Paul, 1922), p. 37.

2. This discussion relies heavily on Nathan Rotenstreich, *Between Past and Present* (New Haven: Yale University Press, 1958), pp. 51–55.

3. Wittgenstein, *op. cit.*, p. 179.

4. Edmund Husserl, *The Phenomenology of the Internal Time-Consciousness*, trans. James S. Church (Bloomington: University of Indiana Press, 1964), p. 28.

5. Susanne Langer, *Feeling and Form* (New York: Scribner, 1956), Ch. 7. Walter Dürr, "Rhythm in Music: A Formal Scaffolding of Time," in J. T. Fraser (ed.), *Voices of Time* (New York: George Braziller, 1966).

6. J. N. Findlay, "Time: A Treatment of Some Puzzles," in Anthony Flew (ed.), *Logic and Language* (Oxford: Basil Blackwell, 1955), p. 37.

7. Cf. J. J. C. Smart, "The River of Time," in Anthony Flew (ed.), *Essays in Conceptual Analysis* (London: Macmillan, 1960).

8. For further representative discussions of these problems, see chapters by Goodman, Quine, and Taylor in J. J. C. Smart (ed.), *Problems of Space and Time* (New York: Macmillan, 1964).

9. Rotenstreich, *op. cit.*, p. 61.

10. E. R. Leach, "Two Essays Concerning the Symbolic Representation of Time," *Rethinking Anthropology* (London: Athlone, 1961), p. 133.

There is a continuing debate among scientists and philosophers of science about the reality of time in the physical world. G. J. Whitrow, *The Natural Philosophy of Time* (New York: Harper and Row, 1963), argues that in the history of natural science and natural philosophy, from Euclid to Einstein and Minkowski, a basically nontemporal view of the world has tended to prevail, and time has either been ignored or fused with space. Even Newton, who set forth an idea of time as a receptacle in which events happen, possessing an intrinsic metric, did not see the lapse of time as altering anything. Today there is general agreement that there are irreversible processes in the physical and biological world, but "the central point of dispute concerns the status of 'becoming,' or happening, and of past, present, and future; in other words, those features of time for which there are no spatial analogies" (p. 310). For Whitrow, becoming and the perception of temporal dimensions may be accounted for by the fact that "our minds are adapted to the world we live in, and this is a constantly changing world with a universal basic rhythm," and time cannot be reduced to a function of consciousness or to basically nontemporal processes in the physical world (pp. 310–311). But according to Herman Weyl, "the objective world simply *is*, it does not *happen*. Only to the gaze of my consciousness, crawling upward along the life-line of my body, does a section of this world come to life as a fleeting moment in time." *The Philosophy of Mathematics and Natural Sciences* (Princeton: Princeton University Press, 1949), p. 116. For further discussion see Adolph Grünbaum, *Philosophical Problems of Space and Time* (New York: Knopf, 1963), pp. 217–218; Max Black, *Models and Metaphors* (Ithaca: Cornell University Press, 1962), Ch. 10.

11. Norwood Russell Hanson, *Patterns of Discovery* (Cambridge: Cambridge University Press, 1958), p. 64.

12. M. Merleau-Ponty, *Phenomenology of Perception* (New York: Humanities Press, 1962), p. 411.

13. Oswald Spengler, *The Decline of the West* (New York: Knopf, 1926), p. 122.

14. Thomas Mann, *The Magic Mountain,* trans. H. T. Lowe-Porter (New York: Knopf, 1939), p. 86; Paul Fraisse, *The Psychology of Time,* trans. Jennifer Leith (New York: Harper and Row, 1963), p. 177.

15. Benjamin Lee Whorf, *Language, Thought and Reality* (New York: M.I.T. and John and Sons, 1956), p. 140. Also cf. P. Stutterheim, "Time in Language and Literature," in Fraser, *op. cit.*

16. Whitrow, *op. cit.*, p. 53.

17. Sigmund Freud, *Beyond the Pleasure Principle* (London: International Psycho-Analytic Press, 1922), p. 32; *New Introductory Lectures on Psycho-Analysis* (New York: Norton, 1933), p. 104. Joost A. M. Meerloo, "The Time Sense in Psychiatry," in Fraser, *op. cit.*

18. Norman O. Brown, *Life against Death* (Middletown: Wesleyan University Press, 1959), has seized upon the implication of the idea of a timeless unconsciousness and argues that the sense of time or history is a function of repression and that if repression were abolished and the id and ego were unified, it would mean a release from time. He concludes from this premise and

recent studies on the cultural relativity of time that what Kant understood as a necessary category of cognition is in fact an epiphenomenon of repression and that not only does the perception of time vary with the structure of repression but no universality or necessity can be attributed to the consciousness of time. Cf. Herbert Marcuse, *Eros and Civilization* (New York: Vintage, 1962), pp. 211–216.

19. For a detailed treatment of these problems see Fraisse, *op. cit.*; Whitrow, *op. cit.*, pp. 47–114; Adolf Portmann, "Time in the Life of the Organism," and Max Knoll, "Transformations of Science in Our Age," in Joseph Campbell (ed.), *Man and Time* (New York: Pantheon, 1956); H. Woodrow, "Time Perception," in S. S. Stevens (ed.), *The Handbook of Experimental Psychology* (New York: Wiley, 1931); Janet Harker, *The Physiology of Diurnal Rhythms* (Cambridge: Cambridge University Press, 1965); Erwin Bunning, *The Physiological Clock* (New York: Academic Press, 1964); Fraser, *op. cit.*, Part III, and John Cohen, "Subjective Time," *ibid.*

20. Ludwig von Bertalanffy, "An Essay on the Relativity of Categories," *Philosophy of Science*, Vol. 22, No. 2, pp. 246–247.

21. See for example, Abram Kardiner, *The Individual and His Society* (New York: Columbia University Press, 1935), p. 4.

22. See for example, Jean Piaget, "The Development of Time and Space Concepts in the Child," *Explorations*, No. 5, pp. 119–130; "Time Perceptions in Children," in Fraser, *op. cit.*

23. Edward Sapir, *Culture, Language and Personality* (Berkeley: University of California Press, 1936), pp. 7, 69.

24. Whorf, *op. cit.*, p. 140.

25. For further discussions of the relation between language, culture, and the concept of time see especially Clyde Kluckhohn, "Culture and Behavior," in G. Lindzey (ed.), *Handbook of Social Psychology* (Cambridge: Addison-Wesley, 1954), Vol. 2, Ch. 25, pp. 933–936; H. Hoijer (ed.), *Language in Culture, American Anthropological Memoir 79,* 1954; Paul Henle (ed.), *Language Thought and Culture* (Ann Arbor: University of Michigan Press, 1958); Edward T. Hall, *The Silent Language* (Garden City: Doubleday, 1959).

26. C. G. Jung, *The Interpretation of Nature and the Psyche* (New York: Pantheon, 1955), p. 28. Also M. L. von Franz, "Time and Synchronicity in Analytic Psychology," in Fraser, *op. cit.*

27. Spengler, *op. cit.*, p. 123.

28. "Let us no longer say that time is a 'datum of consciousness'; let us be more precise and say that consciousness unfolds or constitutes time." M. Merleau-Ponty, *op. cit.*, p. 414. See also Husserl, *op. cit.*, p. 23; Martin Heidegger, *Being and Time* (New York: Harper, 1962); Jean-Paul Sartre, *Being and Nothingness* (New York: Philosophical Library, 1956). For an examination of the relation between time and self-consciousness, see A. Irving Hallowell, *Explorations*, No. 2, pp. 128–139.

29. See Irving M. Copi, "The Growth of Concepts," in Henle, *op. cit.*, p. 48.

30. Sigfried Giedion, "Space Conception in Prehistoric Art," *Explorations*, No. 6, p. 38. Also Hall, *The Hidden Dimension* (New York: Doubleday, 1966).

31. Fraisse, *op. cit.*, p. 158. See Jean Piaget, *Le Développement de la notion du temps chez l'enfant* (Paris: Presses Universitaires de France, 1946).

32. Cassirer, *The Philosophy of Symbolic Forms* (New Haven: Yale University Press, 1953–1957), Vol. 1, pp. 98–99, 217–218. Also Giedion, *The Eternal Present* (New York: Pantheon, 1962), Vol. 1; H. A. Groenewegen-Frankfort, *Arrest and Movement* (Chicago: University of Chicago Press, 1931).

33. Ernst Cassirer, *The Philosophy of Symbolic Forms*, Vol. 2, p. 128. For representative discussions of the image of time in primitive societies, see Paul Bohannon, "Concepts of Time among the Tiv of Nigeria," *Southwestern Journal of Anthropology*, Vol. IX, No. 3 (Autumn, 1953); A. Irving Hallowell, "Temporal Orientations in Western Civilization and in a Preliterate Society," *American Anthropologist*, Vol. 39 (1937); P. Bourdieu, "The Attitude of the Algerian Peasant toward Time," in J. Pitt-Rivers (ed.), *Mediterranean Countrymen* (The Hague: Mouton, 1963).

34. Henri-Charles Puech, "Gnosis and Time," and Mircea Eliade, "Time and Eternity in Indian Thought," in Campbell, *op. cit.*, pp. 84, 173.

35. G. van der Leeuw, "Primordial Time and Final Time," in Campbell, *op. cit.*, p. 332.

36. Eliade, *The Myth of the Eternal Return* (New York: Pantheon, 1959), p. 5. See also *Myth and Reality*, trans. Willard R. Trask (New York: Harper and Row, 1963).

37. Cassirer, *op. cit.*, Vol. 2, p. 108.

38. See Martin P. Nilsson, *Primitive Time-Reckoning* (Oxford: The University Press, 1920); J. Eric S. Thompson, *The Rise and Fall of Maya Civilization* (Norman: University of Oklahoma Press, 1954), pp. 137–144; James H. Breasted, "The Beginnings of Time-measurement and the Origins of Our Calendar," in *Time and Its Mysteries* (New York: Collier, 1962).

39. H. and H. A. Frankfort, John A. Wilson, and Thorkild Jacobsen, *Before Philosophy* (Baltimore: Pelican, 1949), p. 32.

40. Webster Hering, "The Time Concept and Time Sense among Cultured and Uncultured Peoples," in *Time and Its Mysteries*, pp. 95, 96.

41. It should be readily apparent that the idea of time as form would be unacceptable from the standpoint of many philosophic positions—especially those associated with a speculative philosophy of history and materialism. For example, Lenin argued that "space and time are not mere forms of phenomena, but objectively real forms of being." V. I. Lenin, *Materialism and Empirio-Criticism* (London: Lawrence and Wishart, 1948), p. 176.

42. Early theories of mythology such as that set forth by Max Müller in 1856, *Comparative Mythology* (London: G. Routledge and Sons, 1909), were developed from studies in comparative philology. Müller concluded, like Herbert Spencer, that mythology was a "disease of language originally resulting from the inability of the early mind to express itself in theoretical terms and continuing in the present because of the impossibility of ever establishing a perfect correspondence between thought and expression." E. B. Tylor, the founder of the anthropological school, elaborated a positivistic notion of the myth as a prescientific stage in the evolution of the mind: *Researches into the Early History of Mankind* (London: J. Murray, 1870);

Primitive Culture (New York: Holt, 1889). The historicoanthropological approach was further developed by Andrew Lang, who interpreted the myth as a product of irrational fancies as opposed to religion which emerged from the contemplative attitude: *Custom and Myth* (London: Longmans, Green, 1884); *Myth, Ritual and Religion* (London: Longmans, Green, 1913). The same stress on developmental stages was present in Frazer's famous quarry of anthropological fact, *The Golden Bough,* where he describes mythology as a primitive attempt to explain the natural world. The boldest attempt to refute the notion of a prelogical mentality is that of Paul Radin, *Primitive Man as Philosopher* (New York: Appleton, 1927), who maintains that the primitive mind cannot be differentiated from that of modern man. As opposed to Cassirer, he asserts that the concreteness of primitive language does not impair its ability to signify abstraction which is accomplished by the addition of affixes, not unlike German, and particular philosophic systems are merely the result of certain historical conditions. The most important advance in understanding the character of mythic thought was the seminal work of Lucien Lévy-Bruhl, *How Natives Think,* trans. Lilian A. Clare (London: George Allen and Unwin, 1926), who views the mythic mind as "prelogical" but not so much as a stage in the evolution of thought as simply a different mental pattern; that is, the primitive mind simply does not adhere to certain logical forms such as the law of contradiction (p. 78). Not only do their "collective representations differ from ours through their essentially 'mystic' character" but they "are not connected with each other as ours would be" (p. 68). Rather than by laws of logic, the primitive mind manipulates symbols by laws peculiar to itself such as the "law of participation."

Recent theories concerning the origin of mythic images which have become important in the study of comparative mythology, such as Jung's speculations regarding the collective unconsciousness and the formation and development of archetypes, offer profound implications for a transcultural theory of symbolic forms. Nevertheless, such theories of origin may be separated from a study of the function which the myth performed in society and do not challenge the idea of the myth as an autonomous vision of reality and as a form under which society strives to order itself internally and relates itself to the universe at large. See C. G. Jung, *Psychological Types,* trans. H. Godwin Baynes (New York: Harcourt, Brace, 1924), and C. J. Jung and C. Kerényi, *Essays on a Science of Mythology,* trans. R. F. C. Hull (New York: Pantheon, 1949); Erich Neumann, *The Origins and History of Consciousness,* trans. R. F. C. Hull (New York: Pantheon, 1954). For applications of Freudian psychology see Otto Rank, *The Myth of the Birth of the Hero* (New York: Journal of Nervous and Mental Diseases Publishing Co., 1914).

According to Jung certain important mythological motifs or primordial images are common to all ages and cultures and are expressions of a collective unconscious: "The primordial image is a mnemic deposit, an *imprint* . . . a typical basic form of a certain ever-recurring psychic experience" (*Psychological Types,* p. 556). Or as Joseph Campbell remarks in *The Hero with a Thousand Faces* (New York: Pantheon, 1949): "Dream is the personalized myth, myth the depersonalized dream; both myth and dream are symbolic in the same general way of the dynamics of the psyche" (p. 19). Other suggestions related to the notion of the inherited image which go equally far

beyond the sociofunctional approach, although tending toward biological re-
ductionism, may be found in Campbell's theory of "innate neurological structures," *The Masks of God: Primitive Mythology* (New York: Viking, 1959),
and the speculations of Jung and Kerényi regarding mythic symbols as "a
spontaneous product of the objective psyche" (see *Essays* above).

43. Bronislaw Malinowski, *Myth in Primitive Psychology* (New York:
Norton, 1926), p. 18.

44. Owen Barfield, *Saving the Appearances* (New York: Harbinger,
1965), p. 41.

45. Although the problem of the relation of myth to ritual has been subject of considerable controversy, the weight of opinion leans toward the view
that the act preceded the word. The origin of this approach is rooted in
Tylor's theory of the myth as an explanation of social custom which survives
its original function. This theory of the ritual origin of the myth was continued in Frazer's speculations on the priesthood at Nemi and has been most
forcefully set forth in the works of Jane Harrison: *Prolegomena to the Study
of Greek Religion* (Cambridge: Cambridge University Press, 1908); *Themis*
(Cambridge: The University Press, 1912); and subsequently by Gilbert Murray, *The Rise of the Greek Epic* (Oxford: Oxford University Press, 1960),
and Francis Cornford, *From Religion to Philosophy* (New York: Harper
Torchbooks, 1957); *The Origin of Attic Comedy* (Garden City, N.Y.: Doubleday Anchor Books). In these studies, philosophy, religion, literature, drama,
and art and their mythical content are traced back to ritual and forms of
social organization. More recently, Theodor H. Gaster, *Thespis* (New York:
Harper and Row), has attempted to demonstrate that much of the literature
of the Near East was grounded in the dramatic form of the ritual and its
accompanying myths. For a discussion of the ritual approach see Edgar H.
Stanley, "The Ritual View of Myth and the Mythic," *Journal of American
Folklore*, Vol. 68, No. 270 (1955). See also Franz Boas, *The Mind of Primitive
Man*, rev. ed. (New York: Macmillan, 1938), and "Mythology and Folklore,"
in F. Boas (ed.), *General Anthropology* (Boston: Heath, 1938).

46. Susanne Langer, *Philosophy in a New Key* (New York: New American Library, 1948), p. 173.

47. *Freedom in the Ancient World* (New York: Harper, 1961), p. 44.

48. Giovanni Battista Vico, *The New Science of Giambattista Vico*,
trans. from 3rd ed. by Thomas Goddard Bergin and Max Harold Fisch (Ithaca:
Cornell University Press, 1948), No. 31.

49. Ernst Cassirer, *Language and Myth*, trans. Susanne K. Langer (New
York: Harper, 1946), p. 11. For a critique of Cassirer's treatment of myth
see M. F. Ashley Montague, "Cassirer on Mythological Thinking," in Paul A.
Schlipp (ed.), *The Philosophy of Ernest Cassirer* (Evanston: Library of
Living Philosophers, 1949). For a consideration of historical and contempo-
rary approaches to the study of myth, see David Bidney, *Theoretical An-
thropology* (New York: Columbia University Press, 1954), Ch. 10, and "Myth,
Symbolism and Truth," *Journal of American Folklore*, Vol. 68, No. 270 (1955).

50. Langer, *op. cit.*, pp. 148, 150–152; emphasis added.

51. *Ibid.*, p. 153.

52. *Ibid.*, p. 172.

53. Frankfort *et al.*, *op. cit.*, p. 11.

54. *Ibid.*, p. 16.

55. Eric Dardel, "The Mythic," *Diogenes,* No. 7 (1954), p. 44.

56. Kerényi, *op. cit.*, p. 19.

57. *Ibid.*, p. 13.

58. Eliade, *The Myth of the Eternal Return*, p. 5.

59. Van der Leeuw, *op. cit.*, p. 331.

60. Eliade, *Myths, Dreams, and Mysteries,* trans. Philip Mairet (New York: Harper, 1961), p. 23.

61. James B. Pritchard (ed.), *Ancient Near Eastern Texts Relating to the Old Testament* (Princeton: Princeton University Press, 1950), pp. 60–61.

62. Mann, *Essays of Three Decades,* trans. H. T. Lowe-Porter (New York: Knopf, 1948), p. 425.

63. I Corinthians 13:12.

64. Jerome S. Bruner, "Myth and Identity," *Daedalus,* Vol. 88, No. 2 (1959), p. 350.

65. *Ibid.*, p. 352.

66. Eliade, *The Myth of the Eternal Return,* p. 46.

67. Jung, *Psychological Types,* pp. 475–476, 555–556.

68. A. J. Wensinck, "The Semitic New Year and the Origin of Eschatology," *Acta Orientalia,* Vol. 1 (1922), p. 169.

69. Eric Voegelin, *Order and History: Israel and Revelation* (Baton Rouge: Louisiana State University Press, 1956), Vol. 1, p. 6.

70. Campbell, *The Masks of God: Primitive Mythology,* p. 146. In addition to the sources cited, the following works have been utilized: Breasted, *The Development of Religion and Thought in Ancient Egypt* (New York: Scribner, 1912); I. Engnell, *Studies in Divine Kingship in the Ancient Near East* (Uppsala: Almquist and Wiksells, 1943); C. J. Gadd, *Ideas of Divine Rule in the Ancient East* (London: Oxford University Press, 1948); Samuel H. Hooke (ed.), *The Labyrinth* (New York: Macmillan, 1935), *Myth and Ritual* (London: Oxford University Press, 1933); E. O. James, *Myth and Ritual in the Ancient Near East* (New York: Praeger, 1958); Carl H. Kraeling and Robert M. Adams (eds.), *City Invincible* (Chicago: University of Chicago Press, 1960); Samuel N. Kramer, *Sumerian Mythology* (Philadelphia: American Philosophical Society, 1944); S. Langdon, *Semitic Mythology* (Boston: Marshall Jones, 1931); Daniel D. Luckenbill, *Ancient Records of Assyria and Babylon* (Chicago: University of Chicago Press, 1926–1927, 2 vols.); A. Leo Oppenheim, *Ancient Mesopotamia* (Chicago: University of Chicago Press, 1964); A. A. Wilson *et al.*, "Authority and Law in the Ancient Orient," *Supplement to the Journal of American Oriental Society,* No. 17 (1954).

71. Campbell, "The Historical Development of Mythology," *Daedalus,* Vol. 88, No. 2 (1959), p. 236.

72. Voegelin, *op. cit.*, p. 6. The term "integral myth" is borrowed from John Wild, *Human Freedom and Social Order* (Durham: Duke University Press, 1959), p. 29.

73. H. W. Fairman, "The Kingship Rituals of Egypt," in S. H. Hooke (ed.), *Myth, Ritual and Kingship* (Oxford: Clarendon Press, 1958), p. 75.

74. Wilson in Frankfort *et al.*, *op. cit.*, pp. 72, 74–75.

75. For details of the creation stories and the credentials of the king, see chapters by Wilson in *ibid.* and Frankfort, *Kingship and the Gods* (Chicago: University of Chicago Press, 1948).

76. Breasted, *Ancient Records of Egypt* (Chicago: University of Chicago Press, 1906–1907), Vol. 3, p. 121.

77. Frankfort, *op. cit.*, p. 157.

78. Pritchard, *op. cit.*, p. 213; Breasted, *Ancient Records*, Vol. 1, p. 255, Vol. 2, p. 387.

79. *Ibid.*, Vol. 3, pp. 86, 243; Pritchard, *op. cit.*, p. 231.

80. Frankfort, *op. cit.*, p. 62; Wilson in Frankfort *et al.*, *op. cit.*, p. 95.

81. Breasted, *Ancient Records*, Vol. 2, p. 85; Pritchard, *op. cit.*, p. 431.

82. Frankfort, *op. cit.*, p. 78.

83. Frankfort, *The Birth of Civilization in the Near East* (Bloomington: University of Indiana Press, 1959), pp. 20–21.

84. S. G. F. Brandon, *Time and Mankind* (New York: Hutchinson, 1951), p. 31.

85. Frankfort, *op. cit.*, p. 79.

86. Fairman, *op. cit.*, p. 98.

87. See Gaster, *op. cit.*, pp. 383–403.

88. Breasted, *Ancient Records*, Vol. 2, p. 62.

89. Mann, *Joseph and His Brothers*, trans. H. T. Lowe-Porter (New York: Knopf, 1948), p. 292.

90. In regard to the problem of kingship in the ancient Near East, the so-called "myth and ritual school" has emphasized the cultic origin of the myth and developed considerable evidence for a common ritual-myth pattern disseminated throughout the area and revolving around the institution of divine kingship. (See works edited by S. H. Hooke cited above. The most recent group of essays, *Myth, Ritual and Kingship,* deals with some of the later developments in the ritual-myth hypothesis and contains a critical analysis of the assumptions of the school as well as a defense and clarification of the original intentions of the school.) The most severe challenge to the hypothesis has been the work of Frankfort, *The Problem of Similarity in Ancient Near Eastern Religions* (Oxford: Clarendon Press, 1951), and *Kingship and the Gods,* who has made a definitive case for significant differences in the various manifestations of kingship and the function of myth and ritual in Near Eastern cultures.

91. Frankfort, *Kingship and the Gods*, p. 6.

92. *Ibid.*, pp. 7–11.

93. Campbell, *The Masks of God: Oriental Mythology* (New York: Viking Press, 1962), p. 107.

94. Burr C. Brundage, "The Birth of Clio: A Résumé and Interpretation of Ancient Near Eastern Historiography," in H. Stuart Hughes (ed.), *Teachers of History* (Ithaca: Cornell University Press, 1954), p. 200.

95. Dardel, *op. cit.*, p. 45.

96. Thorkild Jacobsen, *The Sumerian King List* (Chicago: University of Chicago Press, 1939), p. 71.

97. Pritchard, *op. cit.*, p. 68.

98. Jacobsen, *op. cit.*, p. 77.

99. *Ibid.*, p. 84.

100. Pritchard, *op. cit.*, pp. 44–47.

101. E. A. Speiser, "Ancient Mesopotamia," in Robert C. Dentan (ed.), *The Idea of History in the Ancient Near East* (New Haven: Yale University Press, 1955), p. 53 note.

102. Brundage, *op. cit.*, pp. 206–210; Speiser, *op. cit.*, pp. 50–60.

103. Pritchard, *op. cit.*, p. 61.

104. Voegelin, *Order and History*, Vol. 1, p. 25.

105. Alexander Heidel, *The Babylonian Genesis* (Chicago: University of Chicago Press, 1951). Also chapters by Jacobsen in Frankfort *et al.*, *op. cit.*

106. Pritchard, *op. cit.*, *pp.* 164–165.

107. Voegelin, *Order and History*, Vol. 1., p. 27.

108. Pritchard, *op. cit.*, p. 337.

109. *Ibid.*, pp. 435, 440.

110. Frankfort, *Kingship and the Gods*, p. 261.

111. *Ibid.*, p. 243.

112. Pritchard, *op. cit.*, p. 382.

113. W. G. Lambert (ed.), *Babylonian Wisdom Literature* (Oxford: Clarendon Press, 1960), p. 113; Pritchard, *op. cit.*, pp. 160–198.

114. Brandon, *op. cit.*, p. 54.

115. Heidel, *The Gilgamesh Epic and Old Testament Parallels* (Chicago: University of Chicago Press, 1946), p. 69.

116. *Ibid.*, p. 70.

117. Heidel, *The Babylonian Genesis*, pp. 147–153.

118. Lambert, *op. cit.*, pp. 75, 41.

119. Mann, *Joseph and His Brothers*, p. 33.

120. S. A. Pallis, "The Babylonian Akitu Festival," *Det Kgl. Danske Videnskabernes Selskab*, Vol. 12 (November 1, 1926), pp. 42–43.

121. Gaster, *op. cit.*, p. 23.

122. Eliade, *The Myth of the Eternal Return*, p. 54.

123. Gaster, *op. cit.*, p. 17.

124. Pritchard, *op. cit.*, p. 457.

125. Niccolò Machiavelli, *The Prince and Discourses* (New York: Modern Library, 1940), p. 397.

126. Aristotle, *Politics*, trans. Ernest Barker (New York: Oxford University Press, 1958), p. 7.

127. Voegelin, *Order and History*, Vol. 1, p. 299.

128. Marcus Tullius Cicero, *On the Commonwealth*, trans. G. H. Sabine and S. B. Smith (Columbus: Ohio State University Press, 1929), p. 112.

129. Herman Hesse, *Magister Ludi*, trans. Mervyn Savill (New York: Frederick Ungar, 1949), p. 396.

130. Eliade, *The Myth of the Eternal Return*, p. 76.

131. C. N. Cochrane, *Christianity and Classical Culture* (New York: Oxford University Press, 1957), p. 11.

III. HISTORY AND POLITICAL SPACE: THE HEBREWS

1. Eric Voegelin, *Order and History: Israel and Revelation* (Baton Rouge: Louisiana State University Press, 1956), Vol. 1, p. 142.

2. The weight of evidence supports the view that several segments of the Psalms were the expression of a cultic ritual surrounding the kingship. See Sigmund Mowinckel, *The Psalms in Israel's Worship* (Oxford: Blackwell, 1962), 2 vols.

3. Henri Frankfort, *Kingship and the Gods* (Chicago: University of Chicago Press, 1948), p. 341.

4. Murray Lee Newman, Jr., *The People of the Covenant* (New York: Abingdon, 1962), p. 51.

5. *Ibid.*, pp. 55–70; Martin Noth, *History of Israel* (New York: Harper, 1960), p. 91 note.

6. *The Holy Scriptures,* Masoretic text (Philadelphia: Jewish Publication Society of America, 1955), Judges 21:25.

7. I Samuel 11.

8. *Ibid.*, 9:16.

9. *Ibid.*, 10:1.

10. *Ibid.*, 8:5.

11. *Ibid.*, 8:7.

12. *Ibid.*, 10:24; 10:19.

13. Genesis 15:18.

14. Psalms 110:4; 2:7.

15. Aubrey R. Johnson, *Sacral Kingship in Ancient Israel* (Cardiff: University of Wales Press, 1955), p. 173. Also Walter Harrelson, "Nonroyal Motifs in the Royal Eschatology," in Bernhard W. Anderson and Walter Harrelson, *Israel's Prophetic Heritage* (New York: Harper, 1962).

16. A.J. Wensinck, "The Semitic New Year and the Origin of Eschatology," *Acta Orientalia,* Vol. 1 (1922), pp. 167–170.

17. For a detailed analysis of contrasts and similarities between mythic and Hebrew conceptions of reality see Brevard S. Childs, *Myth and Reality in the Old Testament* (London: SCM Press, 1960).

18. Voegelin, *Order and History,* Vol. 1, p. 491.

19. Amos 3:7.

20. Isaiah 46:10.

21. Hosea 2; Ezekiel 16.

22. II Samuel 23:3; Mowinckel, *He That Cometh,* trans. G. W. Anderson (New York: Abingdon, 1954), Ch. 3.

23. See R. E. Clements, *Prophecy and Covenant* (London: SCM Press, 1963).

24. Isaiah 8:16–18; 7:14; 9:6, 7.

25. Isaiah 2; 11:1.

26. See Mowinckel, *He That Cometh,* for a detailed, although not uncontroversial, account of the origin and development of the Messianic idea and its relation to politics and the myth. Also Martin Buber, *The Prophetic Faith* (New York: Harper Torchbooks, 1960), p. 142; Joseph Klausner, *The Messianic Idea in Israel,* trans. W. F. Stinespring (New York: Macmillan, 1955); Ange Bentzen, *King and Messiah* (London: Lutterworth, 1955).

27. Isaiah 33:22; Ezekiel 37:24, 28.

28. Isaiah 57:15.

29. For example see Oscar Cullman, *Christ and Time,* trans. Floyd F. Filson (Philadelphia: Westminster, 1949), pp. 51–60. Cf. Christopher R. North, *The Old Testament Interpretation of History* (London: Epworth, 1946); J. Muilenberg, "The Biblical View of Time," *Harvard Theological Review,* Vol. 54 (1961); N. H. Snaith, "Time in the Old Testament," in F. F. Bruce (ed.), *Promise and Fulfillment* (Edinburgh: T & T Clark, 1963).

30. Tom F. Driver, *The Sense of History in Greek and Shakespearean Drama* (New York: Columbia University Press, 1960), p. 52.

The two basic tenses in Hebrew are the perfect and imperfect, signifying complete and incomplete action. Time was perceived from the point of view of the subject who had no present outside the past and future. The idea of being as presence—as the eternal present—belongs to Greek philosophy and cannot be fitted into the structure of Hebrew thought and language. For a comparison of dynamic versus static thinking in regard to the Hebrews and Greeks, especially as evidenced in language structure, see Thorlief Boman, *Hebrew Thought Compared with Greek,* trans. Jules L. Moreau (Philadelphia: Westminster, 1960), pp. 27–73. Cf. James Barr, *Biblical Words for Time* (Naperville: Alec R. Allenson, 1962); Arnaldo Momigliano, "Time in Ancient Historiography," *History and Theory,* Beiheft 6 (1966), *History and the Concept of Time.*

31. Robert Aron, *Jesus of Nazareth: The Hidden Years,* trans. Frances Frenaye (New York: William Morrow, 1960), p. 56.

32. Buber, *op. cit.,* pp. 28–29. The word "Yahweh" implies not only life and being but being whose manner of appearance is not predetermined. Yahweh is probably derived from the verb *hyah* which means at once "to be," "to become," and "to effect"; the action of Yahweh constitutes being or history. See Boman, *op. cit.,* pp. 38–50.

33. Deuteronomy 5:3.

34. Aron, *op. cit.,* pp. 126–127.

35. Jeremiah 23:5; Isaiah 11:1.

36. Buber, *op. cit.,* pp. 168–169.

37. Jeremiah 1:5, 10.

38. Jeremiah 31:29–34.

39. Ezekiel 11:23.

40. Buber, *op. cit.,* p. 186.

41. Isaiah 40:2; 44:22.

42. *Ibid.,* 45:1–5; 41:2, 25.

43. *Ibid.,* 41:8; 43:1; 44:1.

44. *Ibid.,* 46:13.

45. *Ibid.,* 43:14; 44:28; 45:13.

46. *Ibid.,* 43:16–19. See Bernhard W. Anderson, "Exodus Typology in Second Isaiah," in Anderson and Harrelson, *op. cit.*

47. Isaiah 42:17–19.

48. *Ibid.,* 42:9.

49. Stanley Brice Frost, "Apocalyptic and History," in J. Philip Hyatt (ed.), *The Bible in Modern Scholarship* (New York: Abingdon, 1965).

50. Whether the Songs are the work of the prophet Deutero-Isaiah or a subsequent author, possibly one of his disciples, is a point of debate in Old Testament scholarship. For example, Buber (*op. cit.,* p. 205) contends that the Songs belong to a later period of the prophet's thought, while Mowinckel (*He That Cometh,* pp. 242–245) attributes them to the work of another prophet. The answer is not decisive for the purpose here, but since there are marked differences of attitude between the Songs and the main body of Deutero-Isaiah, the latter interpretation will be assumed. For a detailed discussion of this problem as well as a summary and analysis of contemporary scholar-

ship on the question of the meaning of the symbol of the Servant see Christopher R. North, *The Suffering Servant in Deutero-Isaiah* (London: Oxford University Press, 1956).

51. Isaiah 49:1–3.

52. *Ibid.,* 52:15.

53. *Ibid.,* 42:7; 49:5; 52:13, 15.

54. *Ibid.,* 42:1.

55. *Ibid.,* 42:4.

56. *Ibid.,* 42, 49, 50, 52–53.

57. *Ibid.,* 49:6.

58. *Ibid.,* 50:4; 54:3; 52:7–12; Buber, *op. cit.,* pp. 203–204.

59. H. and H. A. Frankfort, John A. Wilson, and Thorkild Jacobsen, *Before Philosophy* (Baltimore: Pelican, 1949), p. 245.

60. Eric Dardel, "The Mythic," *Diogenes,* No. 7 (1954), p. 46.

61. Amos 5:18.

62. Jerome S. Bruner, "Myth and Identity," *Daedalus,* Vol. 88, No. 2 (1959), p. 357.

63. Erich Neumann, "Art and Time," in Joseph Campbell (ed.), *Man and Time* (New York: Pantheon, 1956), pp. 11, 14.

64. Paul Valéry, *History and Politics,* trans. Denise Folliot and Jackson Mathews (New York: Pantheon, 1962), pp. 97, 40.

ADDITIONAL BIBLIOGRAPHY

1. William F. Albright, *From the Stone Age to Christianity* (Baltimore: Johns Hopkins Press, 1957).

2. Julius A. Bewer, *The Literature of the Old Testament,* 3rd ed. (New York: Columbia University Press, 1962).

3. John Bright, *A History of Israel* (Philadelphia: Westminster, 1939).

4. George A. Buttrick (ed.), *The Interpreters' Bible* (Nashville: Abingdon, 1963).

5. Otto Eissfeldt, *The Old Testament,* trans. Peter R. Ackroyd (New York: Harper and Row, 1965).

6. Abraham J. Heschel, *The Prophets* (New York: Harper and Row, 1962).

7. Curt Kuhl, *The Prophets of Israel,* trans. Rudolf J. Ehrlich and J. P. Smith (Richmond: John Knox, 1960).

8. J. Lindblom, *Prophecy in Ancient Israel* (Philadelphia: Muhlenberg, 1962).

9. A. Lods, *The Prophets and the Rise of Judaism,* trans. S. H. Hooke (New York: E. P. Dutton, 1937).

10. Theophile James Meek, *Hebrew Origins* (New York: Harper, 1950).

11. George E. Mendenhall, *Law and Covenant in Israel and the Ancient Near East* (Pittsburgh: Biblical Colloquium, 1955).

12. Harry M. Orlinsky, *Ancient Israel* (Ithaca: Cornell University Press, 1954).

13. J. Pedersen, *Israel, Its Life and Culture* (London: Oxford University Press, 1926, 1940), 4 vols.

14. H. H. Rowley, *Men of God* (London: Thomas Wilson Sons, 1963).

15. ——— (ed.), *Studies in Old Testament Prophecy* (Naperville: Alec R. Allenson, 1957).

16. Roland de Vaux, *Ancient Israel*, trans. John McHugh (New York: McGraw-Hill, 1961).

IV. TIME, THE SELF, AND THE PROBLEM OF SOCIAL ORDER:
THE GREEKS

1. In addition to other works cited, the following sources were utilized in the discussion of Homer and early Greek civilization: C. M. Bowra, *Tradition and Design in the Iliad* (Oxford: Clarendon Press, 1930); *Homer and His Forerunners* (Edinburgh: Thomas Nelson and Sons, 1935); E. R. Dodds, *The Greeks and the Irrational* (Berkeley: University of California Press, 1951); Sterling Dow, "The Greeks in the Bronze Age," *XIe Congrès international des sciences historiques* (Stockholm, 1960); G. L. Field, *Minoan of Ancient Crete* (New York: Thomas Y. Crowell, 1965); G. S. Kirk (ed.), *The Language and Background of Homer* (Cambridge: Heffer and Sons, 1964); A. B. Lord, *Singer of Tales* (Cambridge: Harvard University Press, 1960); H. L. Lorimer, *Homer and the Monuments* (New York: St. Martin's, 1950); S. Marinatos, *Crete and Mycenae* (New York: Harry N. Abrams, 1960); F. Matz, *Minoan Civilization* (New York: Cambridge University Press, 1962); Gilbert Murray, *The Rise of the Greek Epic* (New York: Oxford University Press, 1960); G. E. Mylonas, *Ancient Mycenae* (Princeton: Princeton University Press, 1957); *Mycenae and the Mycenaean Age* (Princeton: Princeton University Press, 1966); J. L. Myres, *Homer and His Critics* (London: Routledge and Kegan Paul, 1958); M. P. Nilsson, *Homer and Mycenae* (London: Methuen, 1933); *The Mycenaean Origin of Greek Mythology* (Berkeley: University of California Press, 1932); Denys L. Page, *History and the Homeric Iliad* (Berkeley: University of California Press, 1959); Leonard R. Palmer, *Mycenaeans and Minoans* (New York: Knopf, 1962); Chester G. Starr, *The Origins of Greek Civilization* (New York: Knopf, 1961); William Taylour, *The Mycenaeans* (New York: Praeger, 1964); Michael Ventris and John Chadwick, *Documents in Mycenaean Greek* (Cambridge: The University Press, 1956); Alan J. B. Wace and Frank H. Stubbings, *A Companion to Homer* (New York: St. Martin's, 1963); H. T. Wade-Gery, *The Poet of the Iliad* (Cambridge: The University Press, 1952).

2. See especially Cedric H. Whitman, *Homer and the Homeric Tradition* (Cambridge: Harvard University Press, 1958), for an extended discussion of the relation between the *Iliad* and geometric art. Also T. B. L. Webster, *From Mycenae to Homer* (New York: Praeger, 1959). Cf. Peter Green, *Essays in Antiquity* (Cleveland: World Publishing Co., 1960) for a sharp dissent from the Whitman-Webster thesis. Green, however, criticizes what he believes to be an unfounded assumption of symmetry and does not confront the argument on its merits.

3. Susanne Langer, *Philosophy in a New Key* (New York: New American Library, 1948), p. 174.

4. Whitman, *op. cit.*, p. 14. For a perceptive and balanced discussion of the problem of unity of authorship in the *Iliad* see Kirk, *The Songs of Homer*

(Cambridge: The University Press, 1962). Kirk agrees that the structure of the *Iliad* presupposes a deliberate effort on the part of a single creative individual. But since this work was the result of the weaving of many traditional elements, there is evidence of both "unity" and "plurality" of authorship, and this has furnished the basis for an understandable yet long and futile debate between "Analysts" and "Unitarians" (p. 159). Kirk contends that the arguments for design and symmetry by such authors as Myres, Webster, and Whitman are overstated, but he concludes that the work does form a "new, self-centered, purposive and non-random organism" and thus it would be difficult to account for the structure of the work without assuming "the motive of personal design and ambition by a specially gifted and famous singer" (pp. 253–265, 280).

5. Whitman, *op. cit.,* pp. 44–45.

6. Homer, *The Iliad,* trans. A. T. Murray (Cambridge: Harvard University Press, 1925), Vol. 1, p. 497; Vol. 2, pp. 105, 173; for example, "The wrath do then say, O goddess . . . sing thou thereof from the time when . . ."; "Tell me now, ye Muses, that have dwellings on Olympus." See Bruno Snell, *The Discovery of the Mind,* trans. T. G. Rosenmeyer (Cambridge: Harvard University Press, 1953), pp. 136–137.

7. Snell, *op. cit.,* p. 20. See also *Poetry and Society* (Bloomington: University of Indiana Press, 1961).

8. *Ibid.,* Ch. 1.

9. Francis Cornford, *From Religion to Philosophy* (New York: Harper Torchbooks, 1957), p. 12; William Chase Greene, *Moira* (Cambridge: Harvard University Press, 1944), pp. 13–14. Cf. Cornford and Greene on the origin and development of *Moira* and its relation to Greek philosophy and the idea of *physis.*

10. See *Iliad,* Vol. 2, pp. 577, 601, on gods and Fates as the spinners of men's destinies.

11. *Iliad,* Vol. 2, p. 197; Greene, *op. cit.,* p. 17.

12. *Iliad,* Vol. 1, pp. 43, 49.

13. Cornford, *op. cit.,* p. 117.

14. *Iliad,* Vol. 2, p. 297.

15. *Ibid.,* Vol. 1, p. 567.

16. Arthur W. H. Adkins, *Merit and Responsibility* (Oxford: Clarendon Press, 1960), p. 25.

17. Herodotus, *The Histories,* trans. Aubrey de Selincourt (Baltimore: Penguin, 1954), p. 124.

18. *Iliad,* Vol. 2, pp. 443–477.

19. Starr, *op. cit.,* p. 183.

20. Snell, *Discovery of the Mind,* p. 22.

21. Whitman, *op. cit.,* p. 238.

22. *Iliad,* Vol. 2, p. 265.

23. Snell, *Discovery of the Mind,* p. 31. Snell correctly emphasizes, however, the limitations on any explanation of social order and disorder which does not differentiate thought and action and recognize thought as a creative force capable of holding a community together. See *Poetry and Society,* p. 13.

24. Greene, *op. cit.,* pp. 18–19.

25. *Iliad,* Vol. 2, pp. 343, 347.

26. *Ibid.,* Vol. 1, pp. 401–425.

27. *Ibid.,* Vol. 2, p. 565.

28. See note 15.

29. *The Odyssey of Homer,* trans. T. E. Shaw (New York: Oxford University Press, 1932), p. 1.

30. An integral part of the "epic illusion" in Homer was the ability to create the feeling of "continuous time," progression and movement. See Samuel Eliot Basset, *The Poetry of Homer* (Berkeley: University of California Press, 1938), pp. 28–44.

31. Webster, *op. cit.,* pp. 218–236.

32. *Iliad,* Vol. 1, p. 217.

33. Erich Auerbach, *Mimesis,* trans. Willard R. Trask (Princeton: Princeton University Press, 1953), pp. 29, 32.

34. *Iliad,* Vol. 1. p. 309.

35. Werner Jaeger, *The Theology of the Early Greek Philosophers* (Oxford: Clarendon Press, 1947), p. 13.

36. A different interpretation of Homer's sense of the temporal appears in Auerbach (*op. cit.*) in which the author, apparently assuming the unqualified coincidence of "style" and "literary representation of reality," attempts to contrast Homer with the Elohist historians of the Old Testament. Obviously the sense of time is more apparent in the Old Testament, but not only are the two hardly comparable, since the Homeric epic represents a conscious stylistic venture, but the structure of the poem and such characteristics of style as placing each piece of action in a "foreground, only a uniformly illuminated, uniformly objective present," may, for example, have been dictated more by the problems of public presentation than by an attempt to represent reality which was accomplished by the manipulation of epic formulas (p. 7). Auerbach's wish to equate style and reality leads him to such incredible assertions as the statement that the characters "have no development" or that time touches them "only outwardly" or that the "instability of fortune" appears as "a fate which strikes from without" (pp. 17, 18, 29); such an analysis belies the figure of Achilles. Cf. Harry and Agatha Thornton, *Time and Style* (London: Methuen, 1962); H. Fränkel, "The Zeitauffassung in der frühgriechischen Literatur," *Wege und Formen frühgriechischen Denkens* (Munich: Beck, 1955).

37. Langer, *op. cit.,* pp. 172, 173.

38. Jaeger, *Paideia: The Ideals of Greek Culture,* trans. Gilbert Highet (New York: Oxford University Press, 1945), Vol. 1, pp. 65, 66; see Langer, *Feeling and Form* (New York: Scribner, 1956), pp. 40, 59, 94, 212–213, for analysis of discursive and presentational symbolization; that is, the difference between philosophy and art and their respective spheres of truth. Also *Philosophical Sketches* (Baltimore: Johns Hopkins Press, 1962), pp. 84, 94.

39. On the relation between tradition and creativeness in Hesiod see Friedrich Solmsen, *Hesiod and Aeschylus* (Ithaca: Cornell University Press, 1949).

40. Jaeger, *Theology,* p. 11; *Paideia,* Vol. 1, pp. 66–67.

41. *Theogony,* p. 81. Citations in *Theogony* and *Works and Days* refer to Hesiod, *The Homeric Hymns and Homerica,* trans. Hugh G. Evelyn-White (Cambridge: Harvard University Press, 1936).

42. *Ibid.*

43. Snell, *The Discovery of the Mind,* p. 138; *Works and Days,* p. 3.

44. Solmsen, "Chaos and 'Apeiron,' " *Studi Italiani di Filologia Classica,* Vol. 24 (1950), pp. 235–248, for a further comparison of the *Theogony* and Ionian physics. Also Paul Seligman, *The Apeiron of Anaximander* (London: Athlone, 1962), pp. 89–110: Charles H. Kahn. *Anaximander and the Origins of Greek Cosmology* (New York: Columbia University Press, 1960).

45. Solmsen, *Hesiod and Aeschylus,* p. 75.

46. *Theogony,* p. 145.

47. *Work and Days,* p. 23.

48. *Ibid.,* p. 15.

49. *Ibid.,* pp. 19, 21; Solon, *Elegy and Iambus,* trans. J. M. Edwards (New York: Putnam, 1931), Vol. 1, p. 119.

50. *Works and Days,* pp. 3–17, 23–25.

51. Cf. Grace E. Cairns, *Philosophies of History* (New York: Philosophical Library, 1962), p. 196. Also see especially A. O. Lovejoy and G. Boas (eds.), *A Documentary History of Primitivism and Related Ideas in Antiquity* (Baltimore: Johns Hopkins Press, 1935).

52. *Works and Days,* pp. 13–14.

53. Cf. Frederick J. Teggart, "The Argument of Hesiod's *Works and Days,*" *Journal of the History of Ideas,* Vol. 8, No. 1 (January, 1947), pp. 51–53. Teggart makes the interesting point that the *Odyssey* also emphasizes the relation between justice and the good life, but while in the *Odyssey* justice is the result of a good king, in Hesiod the good life depends on the efforts of the people and the principle pervading the whole community. This is an indication of the progressive breakdown of integral mythic symbolism as well as an indication of the wider audience to which Hesiod's poems were addressed.

54. *Works and Days,* pp. 12–13.

55. T. A. Sinclair, *A History of Classical Greek Literature* (London: G. Routledge and Sons, 1934), p. 68.

56. *Works and Days,* p. 11.

57. Solmsen, *Hesiod and Aeschylus,* p. 83.

58. Friedrich Nietzsche, *The Philosophy of Nietzsche* (New York: Modern Library, 1954), p. 653; Kurt von Fritz, "Pandora, Prometheus and the Myth of the Ages," *Review of Religion,* Vol. 11, No. 3 (March, 1947), pp. 227–260. However, the author argues that none of the races constitute actual historical periods, but are all ways of viewing the past.

59. J. Gwyn Griffiths, "Archaeology and Hesiod's Five Ages," *Journal of the History of Ideas,* Vol. 17, No. 1 (January, 1956), p. 115. Cf. John Myres, *Herodotus, Father of History* (Oxford: Clarendon Press, 1953), p. 44.

60. *Works and Days,* p. 13.

61. Thomas G. Rosenmeyer, "Hesiod and Historiography," *Hermes Zeitschrift für Klassische Philologie,* 85. Band, Heft 3 (November, 1957), pp. 266, 267, 279. Rosenmeyer also presents several less convincing points and attempts to identify the tale too rigidly with a historical investigation.

62. *Works and Days,* pp. 15–31. For an elaboration of the parallel with the prophets, especially Amos, Hosea, Micah, and Isaiah, see Teggart, *op. cit.,* and the further distinctions made by Eric Voegelin, *Order and History: The World of the Polis* (Baton Rouge: Louisiana State University Press, 1957),

Vol. 2, pp. 159–162. Like the prophets, Hesiod describes the conditions of the present and then makes the pronouncement of doom followed by a description of the apocalypse. This is in turn followed by a declaration of the importance of justice and a promise for the future.

63. *Works and Days*, p. 31.

64. Jacques Maritain, *Creative Intuition in Art and Poetry* (New York: Pantheon, 1955), p. 21.

65. Jaeger, *Paideia*, p. 117.

66. *Lyra Graeca*, trans. J. M. Edmonds (Cambridge: Harvard University Press, 1931), Simonides, Vol. 2, p. 339.

67. *Ibid.*, pp. 295, 297. The reaction of Mimnermus, with his obsessive fear of old age and death is typical; the life of man is "like the leaves that come in the flowering Springtime when they wax so quickly beneath the sunbeams, like them we enjoy the blossoms of youth for a season but an ell long, the Gods giving us knowledge neither of good nor evil; for here beside us stand the black Death-Spirits, the one with the end that is grievous Eld, the other that which is Death. . . . And when the end of maturity be past, then to be dead is better than to live . . . there is no man in the world to whom Zeus giveth not manifold woe." *Elegy and Iambus*, Vol. 1, pp. 90, 91, 93.

68. Jaeger, *Paideia*, pp. 124–125.

69. *Elegy and Iambus*, Archilochus, Vol. 2, p. 131.

70. See Webster, *Greek Art and Literature, 700–530 B.C.* (London: Methuen, 1959), and Snell, *Poetry and Society*, for a detailed analysis of these developments. Also A. R. Burn, *The Lyric Age of Greece* (New York: St. Martin's, 1960).

71. Marshall McLuhan, *Understanding Media* (New York: McGraw-Hill, 1964), p. 43.

72. *Elegy and Iambus*, Tyrtaeus, p. 77; the same sentiments are expressed by Callinus, pp. 45–47.

73. *Ibid.*, pp. 69, 73.

74. *Ibid.*, p. 77.

75. *Elegy and Iambus*, Solon, Vol. 1, pp. 147–151.

76. Snell, *Discovery of the Mind*, pp. 65, 69.

77. *Elegy and Iambus*, Solon, p. 147.

78. *Ibid.*, pp. 133, 143–144, 151.

79. *Elegy and Iambus*, Theognis, pp. 307, 333.

80. *Ibid.*, pp. 245, 357, 367, 275, 251, 261, 281.

81. *Ibid.*, pp. 283, 351, 327, 247.

82. Xenophanes, fr. 2; translations unless otherwise specified are from Kathleen Freeman, *Ancilla to the Pre-Socratic Philosophers* (Oxford: Blackwell, 1948).

83. Jaegar, *Theology*, pp. 19, 41, 42.

84. Xenophanes, frs. 1, 10, 11.

85. *Ibid.*, frs. 8, 18, 34.

86. *Ibid.*, frs. 23–24.

87. B. A. van Groningen, *In the Grip of the Past* (Leiden: Brill, 1953), pp. 15, 74–76; Jaeger, *Theology*, pp. 20, 23–28.

88. Xenophanes, frs. 14, 25.

89. Snell, *Discovery of the Mind*, p. 128.

90. Heraclitus, fr. 78; "When you have listened, not to me but to the law (Logos)" fr. 50.

91. *Ibid.*, frs. 113, 1, 26, 34, 104, 128.

92. *Ibid.*, frs., 123, 35, 107, 14–15, 42, 57, 40.

93. Ibid. frs. 101, 32, 33, 41, 114, 45, 30; Snell, *Discovery of the Mind,* pp 144–146; Jaeger, *Theology,* pp. 115–117. The term *logos* is ambiguous and takes on different shades of meaning in Greek philosophy, but in Heraclitus it signifies not only truth as revealed in his oracular pronouncements but a universal law of the cosmos which pervades all things and is especially manifest in the human mind. All order, whether of the soul, polis, or cosmos, partakes of the *logos;* "For all human laws are numbered by one, which is divine" (fr. 114), or "The people should fight for the Law (*Nomos*) as if for their city-wall" (fr. 44). For a comprehensive treatment of the meaning of *logos* in Greek thought see W. K. C. Guthrie, *A History of Greek Philosophy* (Cambridge: The University Press, 1962), Vol. 1, pp. 420–424.

94. Heraclitus, fr. 103.

95. G. S. Kirk and J. E. Raven, *The Presocratic Philosophers* (Cambridge: The University Press, 1957), pp. 193–201.

96. Heraclitus, fr. 119.

97. See Gerald F. Else, *The Origin and Early Form of Greek Tragedy* (Cambridge: Harvard University Press, 1965).

98. Erich Neumann, "Creative Man and Transformation," in *Art and the Creative Unconscious,* trans. Ralph Manheim (New York: Pantheon, 1939), p. 168.

99. Snell, *Discovery of the Mind,* p. 100.

100. Jaeger, *Paideia,* Vol. 1, p. 255.

101. Aristotle, *Poetics,* 1450a16, 1450b5–10.

102. John Jones, *On Aristotle and Greek Tragedy* (London: Chatto and Windus, 1962), p. 45.

103. Aristotle, *op. cit.,* 1451b5–10.

104. H. D. F. Kitto, *Form and Meaning in Drama* (London: Methuen, 1956), Ch. 7.

105. Snell, *Scenes from Greek Drama* (Berkeley: University of California Press, 1964), Ch. 1. See *Aeschylus,* trans. Herbert Wier Smyth (Cambridge: Harvard University Press, 1957), Vol. 2, Appendix, for translation of the latest fragments of the *Myrmidons, Nereids* (the death of Patroclus), and *Phrygians* (Hector's ransom). Despite the acuteness of Snell's work it is somewhat marred by his enthusiasm for the idea of the unilinear evolution of consciousness. Although his thesis is generally instructive, his premise appears to lead him to neglect the degree to which self-awareness was present in the epic and to overemphasize the concern of tragedy with the psychology of the individual characters. Cf. Kitto, *op. cit.,* pp. 203–205, 207–208, 213–214. Just as Auerbach (*op cit.*) and Tom F. Driver, *The Sense of History in Greek and Shakespearean Drama* (New York: Columbia University Press, 1960), assume that the structure of a literary piece necessarily reflects society's view of reality, Snell assumes that the treatment of character necessarily reflects the author's understanding of psychology. For example, Driver maintains that the theatre "tends to reflect the assumptions of its age regarding time and history because it is on the one hand a narrative of temporal

events, and on the other hand an enactment taking place within a moment of time. . . . It becomes a miniature history in itself" (p. 6). Although the analysis of structure can be important in discerning the attitude toward time, the structure of a play may be informed by other motives than a representation of reality.

106. *The Complete Plays of Aeschylus,* trans. Gilbert Murray (London: George Allen and Unwin, 1952), *Prometheus Bound,* p. 70.

107. *Prometheus Bound,* p. 31.

108. Jaeger, *Paideia,* Vol. 1, p. 254; see Francis Cornford, *Thucydides Mythistoricus* (London: Edward Arnold, 1907), especially pp. 138–152.

109. Richard Kuhns, *The House, the City and the Judge* (New York: Bobbs-Merrill, 1962), p. 13.

110. *Prometheus Bound,* p. 25.

111. *Ibid.,* p. 20, "But he will learn pity by suffering."

112. *Ibid.,* p. 29.

113. *Ibid.,* p. 41.

114. *Ibid.,* pp. 24, 41, 46.

115. *Ibid.,* p. 31.

116. *The Complete Plays of Aeschylus: The Eumenides,* p. 236; Solmsen, *Hesiod and Aeschylus,* p. 216.

117. *The Eumenides,* p. 212.

118. *Ibid.,* pp. 226, 243; cf. G. Glotz, *The Greek City* (New York: Knopf, 1951), pp. 106–107.

119. Kuhns, *op. cit.,* p. 58.

120. Democritus, fr. 252.

121. Van Groningen, *op. cit.,* p. 24.

122. Polybius, *The Histories,* trans. W. R. Paton (New York: Putnam, 1922), Vol. 3, p. 79.

123. See van Groningen, *op. cit.*

124. Voegelin, *The World of the Polis,* p. 51.

125. R. G. Collingwood, *The Idea of History* (New York: Oxford University Press, 1946), p. 20.

126. Common interpretations of the Greek conception of history are typified in the following remarks on Thucydides: "Historical movement is understood in the same way as the cosmic movement, in which all change is simply the same thing in new constellations. History, therefore, is not regarded as a peculiar field of life distinct from nature."—D. Rudolph Bultmann, *History and Eschatology* (Edinburgh: The University Press, 1957), p. 15. "They were convinced that whatever is to happen will be of the same pattern and character as past and present events; they never indulged in the prospective possibilities of the future."—Karl Lowith, *Meaning in History* (Chicago: University of Chicago Press, 1949), pp. 4, 6. "It is clear that [Thucydides] finally adopted a cyclical view of history very much like Plato's."—J. H. Finley, Jr., *Thucydides* (Cambridge: Harvard University Press, 1942), p. 83. "Time itself, in their opinion, was a circle—a periodical resuming of the same, a cycle in which even the life of the human soul was involved."—Erich Frank, *Philosophical Understanding and Religious Truth* (New York: Oxford University Press, 1945), p. 67. The same lack of distinction between the movement of the cosmos and history is evident in Guthrie's "Cycles of Existence:

the Golden Age," *In the Beginning* (London: Methuen, 1957), and in Rein-
hold Niebuhr's contention that "history was made intelligbile by its unqualified identification with natural time," *Faith and History* (New York: Scribner,
1949), p. 37, or Oscar Cullman's statement that "time in Hellenism is not conceived in a rectilinear manner," *Christ and Time,* trans. Floyd F. Filson
(Philadelphia: Westminster, 1949). Christian philosophers have a continuing
propensity to read a cyclical theory into the classical notion of history. Cf.
Starr, "Historical Time and Philosophical Time," and Arnaldo Momigliano,
"Time in Ancient Historiography," *History and Theory,* Beiheft 6 (1966),
History and the Concept of Time.

127. Herodotus, *The Persian Wars,* trans. George Rawlinson (New York:
Random House, 1952) pp. 111, 18, 251; when it is said that "it is not possible even for a god to escape the decree of destiny" (p. 51), it refers to the
fact that Croesus was punished for the sin of his ancestors; this is the tragic
fate that pursued the characters of Aeschylus and does not imply that men
and gods were swept along in cosmic movement (p. 272).

128. *Ibid.,* pp. 6, 17, 19, 237.

129. B. L. Ullman, "History and Tragedy," *Transactions and Proceedings
of the American Philological Association,* Vol. 73 (1942), pp. 25–53; A. W.
Gomme, *The Greek Attitude to Poetry and History* (Berkeley: University
of California Press, 1954), pp. 76, 87.

130. Herodotus, *op. cit.,* p. 252.

131. *Ibid.,* pp. 202, 372. References to the gods by Herodotus are clearly
metaphorical; expressions such as the "jealousy" or "punishment" of the
gods (pp. 18, 174, 231, 435) imply only the inevitable reaction to immodera-
tion in a social context.

132. Thucydides, *The Peloponnesian War* (New York: Modern Library,
1931), pp. 3, 13–15, 110.

133. *Ibid.,* pp. 189–191.

134. *Ibid.,* pp. 1, 15. See M. J. Finley, "Myth, Memory, and History,"
History and Theory, Vol. IV, No. 3, 1965).

135. Hannah Arendt, *The Human Condition* (New York: Doubleday Anchor Books, 1958), p. 19; also *Between Past and Future* (New York: Viking,
1961), p. 42.

136. Alcmaeon, fr. 2.

137. Arendt, *The Human Condition,* p. 198. She is also correct in her
assertion that "the greater part of political philosophy since Plato could easily
be interpreted as various attempts to find theoretical foundations and practical ways for an escape from politics altogether.

138. *Ibid.,* pp. 174, 176.

139. *Ibid.,* pp. 20–21.

140. *Prometheus Bound,* p. 32.

141. Guthrie, *A History of Greek Philosophy,* pp. 205, 336–340.

142. Guthrie (*A History of Greek Philosophy,* p. 281) assumes on the
basis of statements of Eudemus and Porphyry that Pythagoreanism included
a doctrine of the "exact repetition of history," but there is little evidence
to support the notion that the Pythagoreans applied their theory of cosmic
cycles to historical events or, if they did, that this view was at all typical of
Greek thought. Pythagoreanism and the Orphic doctrines of the wheel of

time and the immortality and reincarnation of the soul, the great year and the destruction and rebirth of the world, and the escape of the soul from the cycle should not be used as a basis for interpreting the Greek understanding of history.

143. Parmenides, fr. 8.

144. *Elegy and Iambus*, Solon, p. 149; *The Odes of Pindar*, trans. John Sandys (New York: Macmillan, 1919), "Olympian Ode X," p. 115. Yet Pindar, in his tribute to the dead at Thermopylae, refers to the preservation of fame from the destruction of time.

145. Cornford, *From Religion to Philosophy*, p. 171; Pindar, *op. cit.*, pp. 19, 26–27. There is considerable evidence that might be adduced to show more than an etymological similarity between Kronos and *chronos*; in, for example, *Oedipus at Colonus* the god of the sea is spoken of as the son of time, p. 112. The idea of *chronos* as a living force is probably Orphic in origin.

146. Anaximander, fr. 9.

147. Cf. *Euripides*, trans. Arthur S. Way (Cambridge: Harvard University Press, 1953), Vol. 4, *Alcestis*, pp. 437, 497. Alcestis and Hercules assure Admetus that time heals sorrow.

148. Heraclitus, fr. 52; Snell, *Discovery of the Mind*, p. 218. Although there are allusions to *aion* as a god—maybe Dionysus—Guthrie (*A History of Greek Philosophy*, p. 428) states that in regard to this fragment "I can only say with Gigon that it is one of those "vor denen wir kapitulieren müssen.'" But see A. J. Festugière, "Le Sens philosophique du mot Aion," *La Parole de Passato*, Vol. 4, No. 11 (1949). *Aion* at first meant the duration of the life of any living individual, while *chronos* signified time in the generic sense. Each *aion* took place within the scope of *chronos*. But when this particular duration was applied to a god or later to *apeiron* it meant a duration of life without end. Eventually, as with Plato, it came to mean the life that is self-sufficient, *Autozoon*, and within which all other forms are contained. Here *aion* signifies eternity—the eternal present—and all lesser forms of duration are merely images; *chronos* becomes an image of *aion*.

R. B. Onians, *The Origins of European Thought* (Cambridge: The University Press, 1951), notes that *aion* was associated with *psyche* and that before it came to mean "period of existence" or "lifetime" it denoted life-force or fluid of life, that is, essence of life, often connected with body fluids (pp. 200–228). See W. von Leyden, "Time, Number, and Eternity in Plato and Aristotle," *Philosophical Quarterly*, Vol. 14, No. 54 (January, 1964).

One version of Orphic cosmogony relates how the world egg was produced by a serpent which emerged from the primeval waters. The serpent was called *chronos*. Also Phrekydes, a contemporary of Thales, taught that it was from the seed of *chronos* that the other elements of the universe were derived. In early Greek cosmology Okeanos, the primeval water, was conceived as a serpent wound around the earth. There was a close connection between this procreative liquid and *psyche* and *aion*. *Chronos* and *aion* were both understood as creative life forces and were closely associated with the ideas of fate and destiny (pp. 251–253). For further discussion see E. R. Leach, *Rethinking Anthropology* (London: Athlone, 1961) Ch. 6.

149. Euripides, *op. cit.*, *Children of Hercules*, Vol. 3, p. 325. "Many blessings fate cometh on-bearing, with whom Time [aion] paceth on, bringing

healing, *Kronos'* offspring divine." See Onians, *op. cit.*, pp. 413–415, on the relations between fate and time.

150. Sophocles, *Antigone*, in *The Complete Greek Tragedies*, Vol. 2, David Grene and Richard Lattimore, (eds.) (Chicago: University of Chicago Press, 1959), p. 178.

151. *Ajax*, p. 219.

152. *Ibid.*, p. 240; "By the time of Sophocles the verb 'assuage' or 'dim' had generally come to mean 'destroy,' 'make wither.' So even the built in healing power of great time is not respectful of substance. It cancels out the end; but it cannot be expected to put anything in its place. Softening is not transformation, but deprivation." Thomas G. Rosenmeyer, *The Masks of Tragedy* (Austin: University of Texas Press, 1963), p. 161. Ajax had stated that "the long and countless drift of time brings all things from darkness into light" and that he would "give way to Heaven, and give way before the sons of Atreus" and give way to rulers like the passing of the seasons (pp. 357–358).

153. For an interesting discussion of the similarities and contrasts between the figure of Ajax in Homer and Sophocles, see G. M. Kirkwood, "Homer and Sophocles' Ajax," in M. J. Anderson (ed.), *Classical Drama and Its Influence* (New York: Barnes and Noble, 1965).

154. *Ajax.*, pp. 264, 266.

155. *Ibid.*, p. 268.

156. For a detailed analysis of the pessimistic element in Sophocles see J. C. Opstelten, *Sophocles and Greek Pessimism*, trans. J. A. Ross (Amsterdam: North-Holland Publishing Co., 1952).

157. John Finley, Jr., *Four Stages of Greek Thought* (Stanford: Stanford University Press, 1966), p. 36.

158. *Oedipus at Colonus*, p. 91.

159. *Philoctetes*, pp. 450, 420; *Electra*, pp. 376, 392; *The Women of Trachis*, pp. 283–284.

160. *Oedipus at Colonus*, pp. 107–108. Cf. his attitude toward time in the opening lines of the play. The optimistic attitude of the chorus toward time is often apparent: *Oedipus at Colonus*, p. 142; *Electra*, p. 339. But not always: *Antigone*, p. 180, *Oedipus the King*, pp. 64, 65. See Bernard M. W. Knox, *The Heroic Temper: Studies in Sophoclean Tragedy* (Berkeley: University of California Press, 1964), pp. 25–26.

It could be argued that "time as a tragic factor in Sophocles goes through three successive aspects, from the general force which breeds and withers the obscure lives of this world, through the all-destructive enemy by which we are discovered and rudely awakened, to the almost benign medium through which man may substantiate his morality and claim dignity." Cedric H. Whitman, *Sophocles* (Cambridge: Harvard University Press, 1951), pp. 170–171.

161. Cf. Kitto, who argues that in Sophocles human affairs are bound up with cosmic movement and that "an eternal rhythm pervades the universe, and man is part of it . . . a universal rhythm, ruling in the physical world and in human affairs alike." *Greek Tragedy* (London: Methuen, 1950), p. 143.

162. *Electra*, p. 361.

163. Victor Ehrenberg, *The Greek State* (Oxford: Basil Blackwell, 1960), pp. 9, 44, 90.

164. Adkins, *op. cit.*, p. 7.

165. For a perceptive study of this transition see Ehrenberg, *The People of Aristophanes* (New York: Schocken, 1962).

166. Thucydides, *op. cit.*, pp. 107–109, 118–119.

167. Ehrenberg, *Sophocles and Pericles* (Oxford: Basic Blackwell, 1954), p. 164.

V. THE IDEA OF THE POLITICAL: PLATO

1. *Republic*, 606e. Unless otherwise indicated, all references to Plato are from Edith Hamilton and Huntington Cairns (eds.), *The Collected Dialogues of Plato* (New York: Pantheon, 1961).

Although not footnoted, the following works were helpful in the discussion of Plato. John F. Callahan, *Four Views of Time in Ancient Philosophy* (Cambridge: Harvard University Press, 1948); George S. Claghorn, *Aristotle's Criticism of Plato's Timaeus* (The Hague: Nijhoff, 1954); Robert E. Cushman, *Therapeia* (Chapel Hill: University of North Carolina Press, 1958); Perceval Frutiger, *Les Mythes de Platon* (Paris: Librairie Félix Aléon, 1930); Ronald B. Levinson, *In Defense of Plato* (Cambridge: Harvard University Press, 1953); Joseph P. Maguire, "Plato's Theory of Natural Law," *Yale Classical Studies* (New Haven: Yale University Press, 1947), pp. 151–178; Glenn R. Morrow, "Plato and the Law of Nature," *Essays in Political Theory,* Presented to George Sabine, Milton R. Konvitz, and Arthur E. Murphy (eds.) (Ithaca: Cornell University Press, 1948); J. E. Raven, *Plato's Thought in the Making* (Cambridge: Cambridge University Press, 1965); Culbert Gerow Rutenber, *The Doctrine of the Imitation of God in Plato* (Philadelphia: King's Crown Press, 1946); Pierre-Maxime Schuhl, *La Fabulation Platonicienne* (Paris: Presses Universitaires de France, 1947); John Alexander Stewart, *The Myths of Plato* (London: Centaur, 1960); Alfred E. Taylor, *A Commentary on Plato's Timaeus* (Oxford: Clarendon Press, 1928); Raymond Weil, *L' "Archéologie" de Platon* (Paris: Klincsieck, 1959); John Wild, *Plato's Theory of Man* (Cambridge: Harvard University Press, 1946).

2. *Republic*, 476c, 520c.

3. *Ibid.*, 514–515.

4. *Gorgias*, 521d, 522d.

5. *Phaedrus*, 259e.

6. Diogenes Laertius, *Lives of Eminent Philosophers*, trans. R. D. Hicks (Cambridge: Harvard University Press, 1925), Vol. 1, p. 281.

7. Helmut Kuhn, "The True Tragedy," *Harvard Studies in Classical Philology*, Vol. 53 (1942), p. 37.

8. The nature of the dialogue is problematical. Its form is artistic, but much of its content is essentially discursive. Maybe David Grene describes it best: "They are not philosophy, as philosophy has since been understood, but the artistic correlative of the experience that makes philosophy." *Man in His Pride* (Chicago: University of Chicago Press, 1950), p. 139.

9. *Phaedrus*, 275d–277a; *Letters: VII*, 314c; *Letters: VI*, 323d; J. Huizinga, *Homo Ludens* (Boston: Beacon, 1950), pp. 149–151; on the nature of serious play, p. 5.

10. *Protagoras*, pp. 347–348.

11. Paul Friedländer, *Plato*, trans. Hans *Meyerhoff* (New York: Pantheon, 1964), Vol. 2, p. 217.

12. *Menexenus*, 235a–c; Plato's description of Pericles' speech: "O Menexenus! Death in battle is certainly in many respects a noble thing. The dead man gets a fine and costly funeral, although he may have been poor, and an elaborate speech is made over him by a wise man who has long ago prepared what he has to say, although he who is praised may not have been good for much. The speakers praise him for what he has done and for what he has not done—that is the beauty of them."

13. Friedländer, *op. cit.*, p. 136.

14. *Ion*, 530c.

15. *Ibid.*, 533d–536a; 540–542b.

16. *Republic*, 492b.

17. *Gorgias*, 502e.

18. *Protagoras*, 316d.

19. *Republic*, 379d.

20. *Ibid.*, 607b.

21. *Ibid.*, 496c.

22. Eric A. Havelock, *Preface to Plato* (Cambridge: Belknap Press, Harvard, 1963), pp. 9, 12, 13. This book is invaluable in understanding the significance of Plato's rejection of the tradition, and the discussion above relies heavily on his interpretation. However, despite his brilliant thesis, the author fails to draw out the political implications of this transformation.

23. *Ibid.*, 595c, 607a, 598d, 600e, 605c.

24. *Sophist*, 242c.

25. Havelock, *op. cit.*, p. x.

26. *Republic*, 595b.

27. *Ibid.*, 603c.

28. Havelock, *op. cit.*, p. 38.

29. *Ibid.*, p. 27.

30. Bruno Snell, *Poetry and Society* (Bloomington: University of Indiana Press, 1961), p. 10.

31. Havelock, *op. cit.*, p. 57.

32. *Gorgias*, 502c.

33. *Protagoras*, 326a–b.

34. Havelock, *op. cit.*, p. 200.

35. *Apology*, 22a–c.

36. *Republic*, 392d.

37. *Ibid.*, 533d.

38. *Symposium*, 203b–c.

39. *Ibid.*, 206.

40. *Ibid.*, 202e.

41. *Ibid.*, 208a–c.

42. *Ibid.*, 209a.

43. *Ibid.*, 209b–c.

44. *Ibid.*, 209d–e.

45. *Ibid.*, 210–212a.

46. *Republic*, 376 *ff.*, 399e.

47. *Ibid.*, 379a.

48. *Ibid.*, 377e, emphasis added.

49. *Ibid.*, 387b, 398b.

50. *Ibid.*, 377d–378, 392b.

51. *Ibid.*, 391e.

52. *Ibid.*, 380d ff., 382 ff.

53. *Ibid.*, 392c.

54. Marshall McLuhan, *Understanding Media* (New York: McGraw-Hill, 1964), pp. 7, 9.

55. *Republic,* 393c, 392d.

56. *Ibid.*, 394c.

57. *Ion,* 535b–e.

58. *Republic,* 394d.

59. *Ibid.*, 395d.

60. *Ibid.*, 395b.

61. *Ibid.*, 397b, 398a–b.

62. *Ibid.*, 521c–522c.

63. The lengthy discussion of *mimesis* in Book III implies that this use of the word with regard to epic and drama was not entirely familiar. *Mimeisthai* originally meant a mimicking of voice or gesture, usually in music and dancing. In the fifth century it came to mean the imitation of a person and action in general, and the concept was soon transferred to actual images as in pictures or statues—*mimema*. *Mimesis* appears in the late fifth century and denotes all of the above. By the fifth century the Pythagorean notion of the relation between the soul and music was also accepted. On this foundation Plato developed his idea of mimetic identification. "The thing which dramatic imitation (in Plato's sense, i.e., impersonation) and musical imitation have in common is assimilation of one's soul to the character of the person or 'life' which is imitated." Gerald F. Else, " 'Imitation' in the Fifth Century," *Classical Philosophy*, Vol. 53, No. 2 (April, 1958), p. 85.

The pejorative use of *mimesis* was apparently a creation of Plato. "One concludes that when Plato chose *mimesis* as his all-inclusive term for 'poetry' his readers would have little difficulty in following him, but would have been shocked indeed when in Book 10 he demoted poetry to a status *below* that of a skilled craft." Havelock, *op. cit.*, note 22, pp. 57, 60. This elevated thought above action; the poetic tradition was inseparable from the Homeric idea of *arete* as the speaking of words and the doing of deeds. The idea that virtue is knowledge is a challenge to the tradition.

Havelock (*op. cit.*, note 37, pp. 33–35) is correct in criticizing those who imply that Plato was developing a theory of art in the sense of aesthetics in Book X, that is, that for example the carpenter by making a physical replica was a truer "artist." Cf. R. C. Lodge, *Plato's Theory of Art* (London: Routledge and Kegan Paul, 1953), Ch. 9, especially pp. 171–175; also W. J. Verdenius, *Mimesis* (Leiden: Brill, 1949), p. 21. In fact, "in the Platonic corpus, there is no theory of art purely as such. This fact is undoubtedly significant; it probably means that Plato was not interested in aesthetic theory *per se*." Catherine Rau, *Art and Society* (New York: Richard R. Smith, 1951), p. 14. As Rau again states, "It cannot be repeated too often that in the *Republic*, he is not offering a general theory of art, . . . not aesthetics at all, but politics"

(p. 30). However, Rau goes on to argue that "his criticisms are not a rejection of art, especially drama, in general, of art or drama as such; they are a protest against the particular drama and other arts of his time. . . . He is not condemning art, but abuses of art" (p. 31). But what Plato was condemning was what today might be understood as the artistic experience as such: communication by feeling. Poetry must be replaced by discourse and painting by craft. It is not that the carpenter is a better "artist" or that the dialogue is better "poetry."

In Book X Plato is not talking aesthetics but education. Plato's attack is directed against poetry as a process of indoctrination; poetry was functional in Greek culture; that is, it held the community together, preserved the group memory, and provided a means of social and political education. Thus it did not fall into the realm of aesthetics; the poetic experience was not an aesthetic experience, but an educational one. Plato's rejection of poetry for conceptual thought and his rejection of the traditional *paideia* and culture were intimately connected. Only at the point where discursive symbolization was accepted could poetry be readmitted into cultural life as aesthetic or a separate realm of study as with Aristotle; only when it became essentially nonfunctional did it become "art."

For a critical review of the literature on the problem of a theory of art in Plato see Havelock, *op. cit.*, pp. 33–35, note 57; also pp. 15–16, note 12; p. 32, note 28. Havelock argues cogently that those who attribute a theory of art or aesthetics to Plato assume "(i) that 'art' must have meant to Plato much what it means to us, and consequently must be accommodated within the Platonic system, (ii) that Greek 'art' must include Greek poetry. These are held in defiance of the fact that neither 'art' nor 'artist,' as we use the words, is translatable into archaic or high-classical Greek" (p. 33). Plato simply did not treat the poet as an "artist" and his product as "art." "Plato writes as though he had never heard of aesthetics, or even of art" (p. 29).

Havelock believes that the introduction of the painter in Book X was "purely *ad hoc* [and] the ultimate target remains not the 'artist' (in our sense) but exclusively the 'producer of words,' that is, the 'poet.'" In a sense this is true since the role of the painter was essentially nonfunctional, but Plato was making a broadside attack on artistic communication as such and although the painter was not an educator the experience of viewing a painting was not qualitatively different than listening to poetry. Both were nondiscursive modes.

For further background see T. B. L. Webster, *Art and Literature in Fourth Century Athens* (London: Athlone, 1956).

64. *Republic*, 595c.
65. *Ibid.*, 597e.
66. On tragedy see *Phaedrus*, 268c–269a.
67. *Republic*, 398c.
68. *Ibid.*, 599d–e.
69. *Ibid.*, 600a–b.
70. *Ibid.*, 600c–e.
71. *Ibid.*, 600c–601c.
72. *Ibid.*, 602b.
73. *Ibid.*, 475d–477.

74. *Ibid.*, 602d, 603a, d.

75. *Ibid.*, 605a–b.

76. *Ibid.*, 606e–607a, emphasis added.

77. *Ibid.*, 607b–608b.

78. Hannah Arendt, *The Human Condition* (New York: Doubleday Anchor Books, 1958), pp. 156–186, 201–203.

79. *Ibid.*, pp. 275–277.

80. Aristophanes, *The Comedies of Aristophanes*, trans. William James Hickie (London: Bell and Daldy, 1872), Vol. 2, *The Frogs*, p. 564.

81. *Ibid.*, Vol. 1, *The Birds*, p. 349.

82. *Ibid.*, pp. 582, 585.

83. For an elaboration of this theme see the discussion of the *Frogs* in Cedric H. Whitman, *Aristophanes and the Comic Hero* (Cambridge: Harvard University Press, 1964).

84. *Frogs*, p. 583.

85. Werner Jaeger, *Paideia: The Ideals of Greek Culture*, trans. Gilbert Highet (New York: Oxford University Press, 1945), Vol. 2, p. 199.

86. *Republic*, 612b, 617e.

87. *Ibid.*, 608.

88. *Letters: VII*, 341c.

89. *Republic*, 377a; *Euthyphro*, 6a.

90. *Protagoras*, 320c.

91. Paul Friedländer, *Plato*, trans. Hans Meyerhoff (New York: Pantheon Books, 1958), Vol. 1, p. 176.

92. *Phaedrus*, 265b.

93. *Statesman*, 268c–d.

94. *Ibid.*, 274e. As Friedländer says, the "Socratic myths are found in the middle or at the end of the dialogue, but not at a place where the dialectical method has not yet begun" (*op. cit.*, p. 176).

95. *Ibid.*, Vol. 1, p. 189.

96. *Phaedo*, 114d; *Meno*, 86b.

97. *Republic*, 621c; *Gorgias* 493c, 523a, 527a.

98. *Ibid.*, 330d.

99. *Phaedrus*, 229b–230a.

100. *Ibid.*, 275b–c.

101. *Philebus*, 16c.

102. *Phaedrus*, 245–246a.

103. *Republic*, 509c.

104. *Ibid.*, 612b.

105. Cf. Ludwig Edelstein, "The Function of the Myth in Plato's Philosophy," *Journal of the History of Ideas*, Vol. 10, No. 4 (October, 1949), pp. 463–481, especially p. 467.

106. Erich Neuman, "Creative Man in Transformation" in *Art and the Creative Unconscious*, trans. Ralph Manheim (New York: Pantheon, 1939), p. 172.

107. Eric Voegelin, *Order and History: Plato and Aristotle* (Baton Rouge: Louisiana State University Press, 1957), Vol. 3, p. 185.

108. Huizinga, *op. cit.*, p. 130.

109. Voegelin, *Plato and Aristotle*, Vol. 3, p. 185.

110. Friedrich Nietzsche, *Beyond Good and Evil*, trans. Marianne Corvan (Chicago: Henry Regnery, 1955), p. 77.

111. *Letters: VII*, 324b–326c.

112. Neumann, *op. cit.*, p. 186.

113. Critias, Fr. 1.

114. The development of the *physis/nomos* antithesis is a complicated philological problem, but it will suffice to say that this opposition could occur only after it became evident that there was not a divine *nomos* that nourished all other *nomoi*. *Physis* was transformed into a reference for action only when the problem of man in society had become acute.

115. *Letters: VII*, 330d–331d.

116. *Republic*, 449b; *Gorgias*, 507e.

117. Henry G. Wolz, "Philosophy as Drama: An Approach to Plato's Dialogues," *International Philosophical Quarterly*, Vol. 3, No. 2 (May, 1963).

118. *Republic*, 368d–e.

119. Jaeger, *op. cit.*, pp. 354, 259.

120. For example, *Republic*, 435e, 544d–e.

121. *Letters: VII*, 328c.

122. *Republic*, 369c.

123. *Ibid.*, 369c.

124. *Ibid.*, 376d.

125. *Ibid.*, 433b–444a.

126. *Ibid.*, 449a.

127. *Ibid.*, 424a.

128. *Ibid.*, 450c–d.

129. *Ibid.*, 452a.

130. *Ibid.*, 453a–457c.

131. Leo Strauss, *The City and Man* (Chicago: Rand McNally, 1964), p. 116.

132. *Republic*, 457d–462c.

133. *Ibid.*, 466c–e.

134. *Ibid.*, 471c–e.

135. *Ibid.*, 472c–d.

136. *Ibid.*, 473a.

137. *Ibid.*, 472e.

138. *Letters: VII*, 327a–b.

139. *Republic*, 473.

140. *Ibid.*, 493c.

141. *Ibid.*, 496a–497b.

142. *Ibid.*, 497b–d.

143. *Ibid.*, 499b–d.

144. *Ibid.*, 500–501c.

145. It should be noted that in the allegory of the cave the return of the Philosopher is directly related to the problem of actualization.

146. *Republic*, 501c–502c.

147. *Ibid.*, 502d.

148. As the *Seventh Letter* demonstrates, this concerns the question of possibility and is not Plato's recommendation.

149. *Republic*, 540–541a.

150. *Ibid.*, 591c–592d.

151. Certain interpretations, however, such as that of Karl Popper, are too extravagant to deserve comment, and although to interpret these sections as attempts at "theoretical model building" such as "A Day in the Life of an Atom" (W. H. Walsh, "Plato and the Philosophy of History: History and Theory in the *Republic*," *History and Theory*, Vol. 2, No. 1 [1962], p. 10) is more relevant, it is not very meaningful in terms of Plato's metaphysics.

152. *Republic*, 543c–544b.

153. It is not entirely meaningless to speak of this as a "philosophy of history." See R. L. Nettleship, *Lectures on the Republic of Plato* (New York: Macmillan, 1901), p. 299. "Philosophy" and "history" are not unrelated in Plato's thought; philosophy is the manifestation of the Idea in history.

154. *Republic*, 546a.

155. *Ibid.*, 545d–e. Nowhere does Plato's understanding of myth emerge more clearly. Myth is consciously employed as a tool of speculative thought.

156. *Statesman*, 303c.

157. *Ibid.*, 259b; *Letters: II*, 310e; *Letters: VII*, 335d.

158. *Statesman*, 269b–275e. The chronological relation between the *Statesman* and the *Timaeus* is obscure and can hardly be determined by an analysis of their content since neither actually constitutes a refinement of the other. The decision to consider the *Statesman* first is arbitrary and governed entirely by the decision to treat the *Timaeus* and the *Laws* together. Actually much of the myth in the *Statesman* presupposes information included in the Timaeus myth. Because of the difficulty in interpreting the myth in the *Statesman* three translations were used simultaneously: J. B. Skemp, *Plato's Statesman* (London: Routledge and Kegan Paul, 1952); A. E. Taylor, *Plato: The Sophist and the Statesman* (New York: Thomas Nelson and Sons, 1961); B. Jowett, *The Dialogues of Plato* (New York: Random House, 1937), Vol. 2.

159. *Statesman*, 268d.

160. *Ibid.*, 268e.

161. *Ibid.*, 269b.

162. *Ibid.*, 269c, 270a. Skemp's translation implying that God reversed the rotation himself is misleading and has no foundation in the Greek text (269e.).

163. *Ibid.*, 273d–e.

164. *Ibid.*, 269d.

165. *Ibid.*, 270b.

166. *Ibid.*, 269c–e, 272e.

167. *Ibid.*, 269b, 270b.

168. *Ibid.*, 272a.

169. *Ibid.*, 272b–d.

170. *Ibid.*, 273a.

171. *Ibid.*, 273a–b.

172. *Ibid.*, 273c–274d.

173. *Letters: II*, 311b.

174. *Statesman*, 274e–275a, 290d.

175. *Republic*, 619b–c; *Statesman*, 276c, 301b–e.

176. *Statesman*, 273b.

177. *Ibid.*, 273b–c.

178. *Ibid.*, 273e.

179. *Ibid.,* 273c–d.

180. *Ibid.,* 303c.

181. Martin Heidegger, *Holzwege* (Frankfurt am Main: Vittorio Klostermann, 1950), p. 243.

182. In a sense there is a cycle or recurrence—the recurrence of the idea as it is lost and recovered in history. This is Plato's doctrine of *anamnesis* writ large. The recovery of the idea constitutes a regeneration of the spirit and consequently of political order.

183. *Statesman,* 259b, 292e.

184. Platonic irony is evident in the remark, "If both sides turn out to be quite unreasonable, we shall merely look foolish if we suppose that nobodies like ourselves can make any contribution after rejecting such paragons of ancient wisdom." *Theaetetus,* 181a–b.

185. *Sophist,* 249c–d.

186. *Ibid.,* 235d–236b.

187. *Ibid.,* 265e–268d.

188. *Statesman,* 279b–290e.

189. *Ibid.,* 291c, 292c.

190. *Ibid.,* 293e.

191. *Ibid.,* 293b, 293d. Plato argues that the qualification of a doctor cannot be assessed by the willingness of the patient to submit.

192. *Ibid.,* 297e, 294a–b, 295a–b, 297b.

193. *Ibid.,* 299b–c, 301a, 297c.

194. *Ibid.,* 303e–304a.

195. *Ibid.,* 305d–e.

196. *Ibid.,* 308b–e.

197. *Statesman,* 309c–311a.

198. *Ibid.,* 301c–302a.

199. *Ibid.,* 292e–293a, 300e.

200. For an analysis of this problem which takes account of earlier research, the following works are suggested: Norman Gulley, *Plato's Theory of Knowledge* (New York: Barnes and Noble, 1962); I. M. Crombie, *An Examination of Plato's Doctrines* (London: Routledge and Kegan Paul, 1962). Also G. E. M. Anscombe, "The New Theory of Forms," *Monist,* Vol. 50, No. 3 (July, 1966).

201. *Letters: VII,* 335c–336a, 328c, 326d. Although it is questionable to what extent Plato ever envisaged an embodiment of the *Republic* at Syracuse, it is tempting to equate the attempt to convert Dionysius, the hope that Dion could establish a successful rule, and the messages to Dion's party after his death with the *Republic, Statesman,* and *Laws,* respectively, and to understand each as successive concessions to "reality." This implication is certainly present (see especially *Letters: VII,* 337d). The manifold references in the *Letters* to a regime under law in regard to both Dionysius and Dion do not necessarily imply a rejection of the *Republic* and *Statesman* for in both instances there would not have been an absence of law; the opposition in the *Statesman* is not between law and not-law, but between the sources of law, and in the *Laws* it is still the philosopher (Plato) who authors the laws. When Plato argues that no city should be subject to "human masters . . . but to laws" (*Letters: VII,* 334c) he is condemning the tryrants, not renouncing the ideal of the *Republic*

and *Statesman,* since there law grounded in true knowledge was the true ruler. However, there is little to support the argument that Plato conceived of precisely reproducing the schema of any of these dialogues in Sicily. Although the recommendations to the friends of Dion, especially in the *Eighth Letter* (355a–357), are unmistakably akin to the *Laws,* it is by no means an exact replica.

202. *Timaeus,* 17c. Francis Cornford, *Plato's Cosmology* (New York: Liberal Arts Press, 1957). All references to the *Timaeus* will be from this translation.

203. *Ibid.,* 26c–d.

204. *Ibid.,* 17a–19b.

205. *Ibid.,* 19b–c.

206. *Ibid.,* 19d–e.

207. *Ibid.,* 19e.

208. *Ibid.,* 27a. Hermocrates' role in this "entertainment," this "banquet of discourse," remains unstated, but it can only be assumed that he is somehow related to the history of Athens. Although Cornford's suggestion that Book III of the *Laws* contains the intended content of the *Hermocrates* seems intriguing (*Plato's Cosmology,* p. 8), there is a question whether Plato actually intended to write the *Hermocrates* (or finish the *Critias* which breaks off at the point of the beginning of the conflict between Athens and Atlantis) since nothing of its content is mentioned in the *Timaeus.* Hermocrates, who was responsible for the defeat of Athens at Sicily, all too obviously symbolizes the final stage in Athenian history; there is no apparent reason why he would have been especially qualified to relate the history that appears in the *Laws.*

209. *Republic,* 532b–533d.

210. *Timaeus,* 20e, 21a, 21d, 26e.

211. *Ibid.,* 20e, 21d.

212. It is possible that the unfinished state of the *Critias* can be explained by the remarks that "if only [Solon] had taken his poetry seriously like others, instead of treating it as a pastime, and if he had finished the story he brought home from Egypt and had not been forced to lay it aside by the factions and other troubles he found here on his return, I believe no other poet—not Homer or Hesiod—would have been more famous than he" (21c). It is tempting to interpret this passage as Plato's own dilemma. He abandons the epic of the ancient Athens, gives up the poetic Muse, to become the lawgiver of the *Laws.* Rather than become a poet like Hesiod or Homer he, like Solon, is forced to become a more serious *poietes.*

213. See also the reference to the oriental origin of names in Greek mythology in the *Critias* (110a–b, 113a–b).

214. *Timaeus,* 22b–c. Destruction "by fire and water" is a continually recurring symbol in Greek literature for wars and invasions as well as natural catastrophies. For example, in the *Iliad* the siege of Troy is metaphorically described as the battle of fire and water.

215. "We have the Nile, who preserves us in so many ways" (22d).

216. *Ibid.,* 23a–c.

217. Friedländer, *op. cit.,* Vol. 1, p. 203; Voegelin, *op. cit.,* Vol. 3, p. 205; Cornford, *op. cit.,* pp. 361–364. As Cornford points out, the dialogue takes place on the day of the Panathenaic festival in which Athens' leadership in the victory over Persia was an integral theme.

218. Cornford calls attention to the Aeschylean influence in the dialogues. The irreducible element of fate and destiny which was present in the Homeric epic became the central problem of the *Oresteia* where Athena, representing the divine wisdom Zeus, effects a reconciliation with the Furies through persuasion. Cornford speculates that had Plato written the *Hermocrates,* the three dialogues would have constituted a parallel trilogy in which there would have been a rebirth of the state organized around the reconciliation of the Idea and the nature of man. However, it would seem that such a reconciliation is exactly what Plato *has* effected in the *Laws.*

Voegelin, *op. cit.,* Vol. 3, pp. 203–204, 206–208, relying on Cornford's remarks, also emphasizes the Aeschylean influence and extends the argument by interpreting Athens and Atlantis as "being" and "becoming," respectively, and the outcome as the incarnation of the Idea; the deluge becomes the inevitable decline of every such incarnation. He also draws a parallel between the symbol of persuasion in the *Eumenides* and *Timaeus* as that which overcomes necessity and between the Persians and the defeat of Atlantis where empires fall because of *hybris.*

219. K. T. Frost, "The *Critias* and Minoan Crete," *Journal of Hellenic Studies,* Vol. 33 (1913), pp. 189–206; S. Marinatos, "The Volcanic Destruction of Minoan Crete," *Antiquity,* Vol. 13 (1939), p. 425; Glenn D. Morrow, *Plato's Cretan City* (Princeton: Princeton University Press, 1960), pp. 18–19, note 8. Recent archaeological discoveries have substantiated the existence of a Minoan empire in the Aegean and lend credence to the historical ground of the Athenian myth of Theseus and the Minotaur. Although the Minoans probably captured Athens toward the end of the sixteenth century, the empire was of limited power and its penetration of the mainland was not extensive; its activities and resources were apparently limited largely to trade and the exacting of minor tribute, but this serves to explain the wealth of Knossos.

However, despite the new evidence of the existence of the empire there has been little or no attempt to re-evaluate Plato's myth in light of these findings. It is not so important whether Plato's myth conforms exactly to what is now known but that it conforms to the information that was available to him.

220. *Critias,* 110a.

221. *Ibid.,* 107b.

222. *Ibid.,* 107c–108d.

223. Friedländer, *op. cit.,* Vol. 1, pp. 203, 319–321. A much more extended parallel could be drawn between Atlantis and typical Near Eastern states than Friedländer has attempted.

224. See C. Seltman, "Life in Ancient Crete," *History Today,* 1953, p. 332. Also R. W. Hutchinson, *Prehistoric Crete* (Baltimore: Penguin, 1962), and Emily Verneule, *Greece in the Bronze Age* (Chicago: University of Chicago Press, 1964).

225. *Critias,* 109c.

226. *Ibid.,* 109c–d.

227. In Aeschylean drama it is Hephaestus and Athena who represent the new rule of Zeus according to wisdom and justice, and in *Prometheus Bound* it is the Ocean who sympathizes with Prometheus' revolt against Zeus.

228. *Critias,* 109d–e.

229. *Ibid.,* 112c–e.

230. *Ibid.,* 121b–c. Atlantis even made a bad job of its spatial layout. If

the plan of Atlantis is compared with the structure of the civic plan in the *Laws* there are apparent structural defects which break the symmetry and may be intended to symbolize, in part, the reason for decline. For example, the structure of Atlantis is symbolized by odd numbers, and the polity of the *Laws* by even. The capital city is not located at the center of the territory, and there are other dysfunctional features and mathematical irregularities in the city planning. Also, unlike the *Laws*, the Atlantean state apparently contained no notion of mathematical limit, and this corresponds historically with the overexpansion of the Minoan empire. For a discussion of the arithmetical design of Atlantis see Robert S. Brumbaugh, *Plato's Mathematical Imagination* (Bloomington: University of Indiana Press, 1954), pp. 47–59. His discussion also supports the relation of Atlantis to the Minoan empire.

231. *Critias*, 121a–b.

232. *Laws*, 683e–684a.

233. No attempt is made here to analyze in detail the literary structure of the *Laws* or the entire range of symbolization which gives meaning and unity to the dialogue. For the most complete treatment available on the *Laws* see Maurice Vanhoutte, *La Philosophie politique de Platon dans les Lois* (Louvain: Publications Universitaires de Louvain, 1953).

234. It should be noted that for Plato *eidos* still retains much of its earlier meaning as external form or shape, but its principal meaning is internal structure apart from sensible appearance. In the *Timaeus*, the form that god imposes on the universe and the appearance of the best society in history necessarily carries with it a certain external manifestation, but the *eidos* of order is the immanence of *nous* in *psyche*. Likewise, in the *Laws* the political order is achieved partially through a proper balance of external institutions, but the substance of the polity is the psychical imitation of god.

235. *Laws*, 683e. In addition to Taylor's translation of the *Laws* that of R. G. Bury is also utilized (Cambridge: Harvard University Press, 1926).

236. *Ibid.*, 676b–c.

237. *Ibid.*, 677a. That Plato raises such a question after assuming the answer in the previous dialogues indicates that he is not entirely satisfied with the explanation but that it must serve as a starting point in tracing the evolution of a culture. For the Greek mind the idea of the collapse of a civilization and the beginning of a new one was an event that was far from amenable to conceptualization, and even in the modern age it can hardly be said that the difficulty has been resolved.

238. Plato admits the poet as a source of historical truth (*aletheia gignomenon*). It is significant that Plato uses the same word for "history" and "becoming." *Laws*, 682a.

239. *Ibid.*, 679c.

240. This type of city, like the democracy of the *Republic*, is a "bazaar of constitutions" (557d). This is necessary for Plato's schema so that numerous possibilities would be open to the Dorian states.

241. *Ibid.*, 683b. For an evaluation of Plato's Peloponnesian history see Morrow (*op. cit.*, pp. 63–73), who concludes that there are no "important instances in which Plato has distorted facts in the interest of theory. In most cases he relies on traditions generally accepted, or accepted by the most competent of his contemporaries; and when he departs from these generally

accepted traditions he is moved by critical considerations that were decisive also for Aristotle." Precisely the same conclusion must be reached in regard to Plato's attempt to illuminate the primitive history prior to the Dorian invasion.

242. *Laws*, 692a. Plato implies that if a state, like the individual soul, is constructed with a view toward peace and self-sufficiency rather than war not only will internal faction be prevented but external conflicts as well. This was the possibility he saw in the Doric federation.

243. The legislative criteria which Plato sets forth at this point differ from those listed in the first book of the *Laws* which included such features as sobriety, valor, and so on and from the two principal characters (moderate and courageous) with which the royal weaver was concerned in the *Statesman*. Plato states that one must not be surprised that "we have already more than once proposed certain ends as those to which the legislator must look, and that our principles have not always appeared to be identical" (693b–c). What Plato means is that the variety of expressions all amount to the same thing; that is, the establishment of due proportion, measure, or limit.

244. *Laws*, 698a, 699e.

245. *Ibid.*, 693a.

246. *Ibid.*, 906c–e, 901e.

247. *Ibid.*, 692b–c, 693a–b.

VI. THE PLATONIC RESTORATION: THE *Laws*

1. *Laws*, 753e–754a, 690e. The symbol of the beginning runs through the entire dialogue; for example, 752d.

2. *Ibid.*, 775e.

3. *Ibid.*, 691a–d.

4. *Ibid.*, 708d.

5. It is possible that such a distinction was never rigidly posed.

6. See I. M. Crombie, *An Examination of Plato's Doctrines* (London: Routledge and Kegan Paul, 1962), Ch. 1, for a detailed argument on this point.

7. See Gregory Vlastos, "The Degrees of Reality in Plato," in Renford Bambrough (ed.), *New Essays in Plato and Aristotle* (New York: Humanities Press, 1965), and R. E. Allen, "Participation and Predication in Plato's Middle Dialogues," in R. E. Allen (ed.), *Studies in Plato's Metaphysics* (New York: Humanities Press, 1965).

8. *Sophist*, 246–261.

9. *Ibid.*, 248a.

10. Crombie, *Plato, The Midwife's Apprentice* (New York: Barnes and Noble, 1965), p. 26.

11. *Republic*, 509–511, 533–534; the difference between the two sections is the use of the terms *episteme* and *noesis*, which are apparently interchangeable.

12. *Philebus*, 58–59.

13. *Ibid.* 16c–d.

14. *Ibid.*, 23c–d.

15. *Ibid.*, 26b–d.

16. *Ibid.*, 26e–27d.

17. *Ibid.*, 29d–30e.

18. *Ibid.*, 62a–b. This corresponds to the arguments of the *Seventh Letter* (341–344) where he lumps together *episteme,* intelligence, and true belief (*aletheia doxa*).

19. *Ibid.*, 64b.

20. *Ibid.*, 64d–65a.

21. *Timaeus,* 27d–29c. Cornford's translation of this distinction in terms of "real" and "unreal" is unfortunate because, even in the *Republic,* Plato does not deny reality to things that are becoming. See N. R. Murphy, *The Interpretation of Plato's Republic* (Oxford: Clarendon Press, 1951), p. 200.

22. Plato states that the "maker and father of this universe it is a hard task to find, and having found him it would be impossible to declare him to all mankind." The symbol of the demiurge means simply that order is the result of creative intelligence and beyond this it is impossible to go.

23. Cornford argues that Plato believed that there could be no self-consistent science of nature, no precise knowledge of natural things is possible, and that to "find reality you would do better to shut your eyes and think." Plato seems to be applying the division between being and becoming, but the *Philebus* has demonstrated that these are not mutually exclusive; the cosmos must be understood as *ousia* created from *genesis* by the application of limit. Although it is not susceptible to the same degree of truth as ultimate being, neither does Plato relegate it to the lowest division of the line which is mere conjecture. The physical world cannot be comprehended with the same degree of truth as the forms, but it is an object of *pistis* (faith, trust, or true belief), and just as *genesis* may lead to *ousia, pistis* points toward *aletheia.* If it were otherwise, the cosmos could hardly be a guide for the guardians in the *Laws.* The becoming of the universe is informed with being, and although astronomy is no substitute for the dialectic which leads to the "very essence of each thing" and even to the "good in itself which is the limit of the intelligible," the heavens were fashioned "in the best possible manner for such a fabric" and can aid in the study of ultimate reality (*Republic,* 529b–532b); since the craftsman was good, he made the world like himself, and the sensible characteristics are good copies (for example, *Timaeus,* 30a–b). Plato states in several places (*Phaedrus,* 250b; *Statesman,* 285e–286a) that certain of the most important forms such as beauty are clearly manifest in the physical world as well as a host of lesser ones that have clear sensible images; others, however, such as justice have no clear visible manifestation.

Appearances such as fire are not ultimate objects of knowledge and cannot be described as "this" or "that" which implies permanence, but they are continually manifest as the same quality, and thus even here the universe is far from devoid of determinate characteristics apprehendable by perception (49b–e). These characteristics point beyond themselves toward the forms. To a large extent what is meant by "likely" is that the constitution and action of particles cannot be understood exactly and must be stated in terms of probabilities that conform to what is observable (59c–e).

Cornford's argument—that the "intelligible living creature" or system of forms which provided the demiurge with a model does not constitute the entire realm of forms—is not convincing. Plato seems to say that this is precisely the case (30c–31b, 92c). Some of the forms are, as mentioned above, clearly visible, but others are nevertheless manifest in the cosmos. Although not directly visible to sight by their appearance in a particular object, the motions of the universe provide images of justice, order, goodness, wisdom, and so on, which if apprehended turn the mind toward being itself. It is for this reason that the state proposed in the *Laws* can take its cue from the heavenly measure. The model of the physical world must be the whole body of transcendent forms, both those whose images are concretely visible and those whose images are discernible if not clearly visible.

24. *Timaeus*, 51c–e, 52a–b.

25. To argue at this point that Plato's symbols are drawn from nonpolitical sources seems irrelevant. Analyses such as that typified by the work of Renford Bambrough, "Plato's Political Analogies," in Peter Laslett (ed.), *Philosophy, Politics, and Society* (New York: Macmillan, 1956), pp. 98–115, fail to take account of the symbolic content of the analogies.

26. *Symposium*, 206e.

27. *Timaeus*, 29e–30a.

28. *Ibid.*, 51e.

29. *Laws*, 739a ff.

30. *Ibid.*, 735d–736c.

31. *Ibid.*, 740a.

32. T. S. Eliot, "Burnt Norton" *The Complete Poems and Plays* (New York: Harcourt, Brace, 1952), p. 118.

33. *Laws*, 739e, 732e, 853c.

34. *Ibid.*, 757.

35. *Ibid.*, 742e.

36. *Ibid.*, 740a, 807b, 875d.

37. *Philebus*, 55d–56d. This is not far removed from Aristotle's comments on the preciseness of the political art.

38. *Ibid.*, 616.

39. *Laws*, 736b.

40. *Ibid.*, 739b. The *Laws* does not pretend to give more than an "outline" of a legislative code (734a, 800b), and it is assumed that the laws described presuppose "ideal" conditions and may be altered to fit particular circumstances (for example, 746a–c, 841). Cf. David Grene's argument that the *Laws* is not concerned with actualization: *Man in His Pride* (Chicago: University of Chicago Press, 1950), pp. 146, 155, 176.

41. *Laws*, 739b, 739e, 710e.

42. Throughout the *Laws* what Plato refers to as god (*Theos*) is the cosmos or manifest intelligence. In the last paragraph of the *Timaeus* he refers to the world (*kosmos* or *ouranos*—he uses the words interchangeably) as "an image of the intelligible, a perceptible god, supreme in greatness and excellence, in beauty and perfection, this Heaven single in its kind and one" (92c; also 55d, 68e).

43. *Laws*, 709a–712a.

44. Arthur W. H. Adkins, *Merit and Responsibility* (Oxford: Clarendon Press, 1960), p. 348.

45. *Timaeus*, 69e.

46. For a similar thesis see Lewis Mumford, "Utopia, the City and the

Machine," *Daedalus* (Spring, 1965). "What Plato did . . . was to rationalize and perfect the institutions that had come into existence as an ideal pattern before, with the founding of the ancient city" (p. 214).

47. *Laws*, 713e, 739e.

48. *Ibid.*, 712d–e.

49. *Ibid.*, 681d, 711e.

50. *Ibid.*, 713a.

51. *Ibid.*, 713c–e.

52. *Ibid.*, 713b, 950d. Explicit references to Egypt; 656d, 657b, 660c, 799a, 819b. The meaning of the sun as a symbol in the allegory of the cave is more than a simile; the sun is to the cosmos as the Good is to the forms because the Good and the forms are manifest in the cosmic order.

53. *Arche,* implying beginning, essence, and rule.

54. *Ibid.*, 714a.

55. "A double word-play: *nous* = *nomos,* and *dianomas* = *daimonas.* Laws being 'the dispensations of reason,' take the place of the 'daemons' of the age of Cronos: the divine element in man (*to daimonion*), which claims obedience, is reason (*nous*)." R. G. Bury, *Laws* (Cambridge: Harvard University Press, 1926), Vol. 1, pp. 286–287.

56. *Laws*, 715e–716a, 714a–d, 716c–d.

57. "Reason overruled necessity by persuading her to guide the greatest part of things that become towards what is best" (*Timaeus,* 48a).

58. It could be argued that order is achieved by a more "political" process. The idea of *techne* as the art of the craftsman or maker who performs an operation on an inert substance with the attending connotations of violence receded in the *Statesman* in favor of the ameliorated *techne* of the weaver who gives all the strands their due and now appears, as in the *Eumenides,* as the force of reason linked with persuasion (*peitho*).

59. *Timaeus,* 48a.

60. *Ibid.*, 48e–49a, 52a–c.

61. *Ibid.*, 49e, 50b–c, 51a, 52b.

62. *Ibid.*, 52d–53c.

63. It appears that *genesis* is often used as a generic term for becoming, and although in the earlier sections of the dialogue *genesis* and *gignesthai* are sometimes used interchangeably or ambiguously, the term is generally reserved in the later sections for chaotic becoming as opposed to cosmic becoming (*gignomenon*). What is important is that plato makes a qualitative distinction between the two types of becoming which is not readily apparent in translation.

64. *Timaeus,* 50c–d.

65. The argument is not that Plato was consciously constructing an exact analogy between human time and *genesis* and *chora* and political space, but rather that in the pattern of his thought these must be understood as symbolic equivalents.

66. *Laws*, 718c.

67. *Timaeus,* 51e.

68. *Laws*, 718d–722c. It is worth while noting that one should guard against reading Aristotle into Plato as Leo Strauss appears to do. Strauss argues that order is "the work of nature as distinguished from art," *Natural*

Right and History (Chicago: University of Chicago Press, 1953), p. 92, but the situation is quite the opposite. For Plato what is natural or primary, as opposed to the materialistic thesis, is *nous* in *psyche* that through *techne*, whether divine or human, creates *taxis* and *kosmos* which is the aim of all art.

69. In the structure of the dialogue it is at this point (722c–d), when the participants stop to rest, that the Stranger notes that the conversation that had begun at daylight on this day of the summer solstice has lasted until noon; the journey from Knossos to the cave and shrine of Zeus on the mountain, where tradition states that Minos received the laws every ninth year, is half completed. And the Stranger remarks, halfway through this particular discussion of preambles and persuasion, that all that has gone before is not after all a casual argument but part of a prelude to the actual consideration of the laws. This is because "all utterance and vocal expression have preludes and tunings-up . . . which provide a kind of artistic preparation which assists toward the further development of the subject."

70. *Laws*, 718b, 832b.

71. *Ibid.*, 723a.

72. *Ibid.*, 722d–e.

73. The citharoedic nome as a musical form carried the name of law because it did not permit change in tone and rhythm— " 'On les avait appelés ainsi parce qu'il n'était pas permit d'enfreindre la tension des cordes reconnue légale pour chacun d'eux.' " See Evanghelos Moutsopoulos, *La Musique dans l'œuvre de Platon* (Paris: Presses Universitaires de France, 1959), pp. 274–279.

74. *Laws*, 627d.

75. *Ibid.*, 626e, 714e, 731e, 732c.

76. *Ibid.*, 627e–628a.

77. *Timaeus*, 57c.

78. *Ibid.*, 32c.

79. *Laws*, 747a. Robert S. Brumbaugh provides an excellent and indispensable discussion of Plato's application of mathematics in the *Laws* as well as in his other works. *Plato's Mathematical Imagination* (Bloomington: University of Indiana Press, 1954).

80. *Laws*, 771e–785, 721a, 704b ff., 836 ff.

81. *Ibid.*, 738d, 739c ff., 743c.

82. For a complete analysis of the extent to which the concept of mixture permeates the entire structure see Glenn R. Morrow, "Plato and the Law of Nature," *Essays in Political Theory* (Ithaca: Cornell University Press, 1948), Ch. 10.

83. *Laws*, 628a–632c, 726–734e, 743e–745a.

84. *Timaeus*, 33a–d, emphasis added.

85. Grene's thesis (*op cit.*, p. 158) that Plato, despairing of bringing the best state into existence, reverts in the *Laws* to an expanded version of the "mechanical-toy state" of the *Republic* has much to recommend it for there is indeed a striking resemblance, and necessarily so, between the *Laws* and the "purified" polis; Grene argues that the *Laws* is the intellectual play of the philosopher who, failing to actualize the paradigm, constructs a frozen "realistic model" equally unrealizable. But this argument ignores the cosmic

symbolism in the *Laws* and the attempt to overcome the flaw of the *Republic* by fitting the state into the system of the universe. Grene is largely correct when he states that "the crucial value of the state is not in the understanding of its governing class or of the rest of the population but in the virtually ritualistic organization and functioning of the state as a whole" (p. 159), but he fails to consider why this is true.

86. If the individual has chosen a good life, the soul returns to its daemon or planet at death; otherwise it suffers successive and lower reincarnations until it gains control of itself, at which time it returns to its original and best condition.

87. *Timaeus*, 39e, 40d–44d.

88. *Ibid.*, 87b, 90c–d.

89. See Brumbaugh, *op. cit.*, p. 58, for a composite diagram of the civic plan.

90. *Timaeus*, 34a–b; *Laws*, 897c–e.

91. *Timaeus*, 36d, 34c; *Laws*, 896c.

92. *Ibid.*, 632c, 960b.

93. *Timaeus*, 35a. These terms are derived from the *Sophist* where the argument concerned existence itself, rest, and motion and how true existence can be blended with the latter two to create *ousia*. Each is different from the other and the same as itself so both motion and rest partake of existence, sameness, and difference.

94. For further discussion of the composition of the soul see Francis Cornford, *Plato's Cosmology* (New York: Liberal Arts Press, 1957), pp. 59–66. The important point here is that the soul symbolizes the intermediary between being and becoming.

95. The predominance of the geometric metaphor in the *Republic* evidences the lack of concern with the realm of necessity, while in the *Timaeus* and *Laws* the concurrence of geometric and arithmetical proportions as producers of harmony symbolizes the limitation inherent in the material on which form or being is imposed. For a full discussion of the mathematical structure of the world soul see Cornford, *Cosmology*, pp. 66–72, and Brumbaugh, *op. cit.*, pp. 220–229.

96. *Timaeus*, 36b–37c, and Cornford's commentary, *op. cit.*, pp. 72–97.

97. *Timaeus*, 37c.

98. *Ibid.*, 37d, 38c.

99. Cornford argues that the movement of chaos is due to the irrational motion of the soul, but chaos is coeternal with the forms and prior to soul. See Gregory Vlastos, "The Disorderly Motions in the *Timaios*," *Classical Quarterly*, Vol. 33, No. 1 (January, 1939). In Book X of the *Laws* Plato is speaking of "created" motion, motion in time, that is, "is, has been, and shall be" (896a); the soul is the cause only of created motion. Vlastos has also pointed out that although the demiurge created uniform motion and measurable time or *chronos*, he did not create time as flux in the sense of mere change. "This is precisely Plato's primitive chaos . . . irreversible temporal succession." See "Creation in the *Timaeus*: Is It a Fiction?" in Allen, *op. cit.*; Edward N. Lee, "On the Metaphysics of the Image in Plato's *Timaeus*," *Monist*, Vol. 50, No. 3 (July, 1966).

100. *Timaeus*, 39b–e.
101. *Ibid.*, 69d.
102. *Ibid.*, 41c–42b.
103. *Ibid.*, 44d.
104. *Ibid.*, 80b, 47a–d.
105. *Ibid.*, 73b–d.
106. *Ibid.*, 69d–71b.
107. *Ibid.*, 86b–e.
108. *Laws*, 951a–c.
109. *Ibid.*, 964–965a; *Timaeus*, 37b–c.
110. Note the play on words when the Athenian, at the beginning of his discussion of the guardians, states that in the telling of this "fanciful tale . . . I should not like to leave it without its head" (*Laws*, 752a).
111. Taylor translates *nomophylakes* as "curators of the laws," but this is misleading since in the sections on the Nocturnal Council he translates *phylakes* as "guardians." This tends to obscure the essential functional identity of the two bodies.
112. *Laws*, 752a–755b. There is no need here to present in detail the duties of the guardians. An exposition of the content of the *Laws* has been avoided wherever possible since this task has been admirably accomplished by Morrow.
113. *Ibid.*, 945c–d; *Timaeus* 73e–74e.
114. *Ibid.*, 69c–70b.
115. *Ibid.*, 70d–71a; *Laws*, 846d. The parallels between cosmos, state, and individual might be more exhaustively pursued, but the above is sufficient to establish the nature of Plato's symbolization.
116. See Morrow's note (*op. cit.*, p. 500, note 2) on those commentators who argue that the Council does not articulate with the other institutions of the state.
117. *Laws*, 769a–770b.
118. *Ibid.*, 951c–952a.
119. *Ibid.*, 964e–965a.
120. *Ibid.*, 960c–d; *Republic*, 620a–621b.
121. *Laws*, 961c–962a.
122. *Ibid.*, 962b–c.
123. *Ibid.*, 963a–967d; *Epinomis*, 970a.
124. *Timaeus*, 47a–c.
125. *Laws*, 967d–968b.
126. *Timaeus*, 38c.
127. *Laws*, 969b.
128. *Epinomis*, 977d.
129. *Ibid.*, 991d–e.
130. Cornford finds it suitable to omit such passages, while an extreme example of the search for esoteric doctrine may be found in Andrew Efron, *The Sacred Tree Script* (New Haven: Tuttle, Morehouse and Taylor, 1941).
131. Brumbaugh, *op. cit.*, p. 5.
132. *Republic*, 443d–e, 432a.
133. *Laws*, 737e–738a, 771b.

134. Cf. Brumbaugh, *op. cit.*, p. 61, and Morrow, *op. cit.*, p. 130, who argue that the choice is essentially one of convenience.

135. *Laws*, 737e–738a, 744c, 745b, 756b–e, 758b–e, 760a–764a, 828b–c, 848, 946a–d.

136. *Ibid.*, 897d.

137. *Ibid.*, 771b, emphasis added.

138. *Ibid.*, 809d.

139. *Ibid.*, 828d.

140. *Timaeus*, 40d; *Epinomis*, 984d.

141. *Laws*, 886c–e.

142. *Ibid.*, 888a, 903b, 892c.

143. *Georgias*, 503e–504e.

144. *Ibid.*, 508a.

145. *Laws*, 903b–c.

146. *Ibid.*, 905d.

147. *Ibid.*, 904a–e, 901e.

148. *Ibid.*, 906a–b.

149. *Ibid.*, 635d–e, 731e; *Timaeus*, 64a–65b.

150. *Laws*, 732e.

151. *Ibid.*, 644c–645c, 653b.

152. *Ibid.*, 643b–644a.

153. *Ibid.*, 645d–650b, 665d–672e.

154. *Ibid.*, 653c–654b.

155. *Timaeus*, 47c–d.

156. *Laws*, 700a–701b; *Republic*, 424b–425c.

157. *Laws*, 665a; Werner Jaeger, *Paideia: The Ideals of Greek Culture*, trans. Gilbert Highet (New York: Oxford University Press, 1945), Vol. 1, p. 126.

158. *Laws*, 656d–657b, 659b.

159. *Ibid.*, 659e, 840c.

160. *Ibid.*, 663b–c; *Protagoras*, 356b–c.

161. *Laws*, 663c–664a.

162. *Ibid.*, 665c.

163. Herman Hesse, *Magister Ludi*, trans. Mervyn Savill (New York: Frederick Ungar, 1949), pp. 30–31, 42. For an exhaustive study of the place of music in Plato's work see Moutsopoulos, *op. cit.*

164. *Laws*, 816a.

165. Eliot, *op. cit.*, p. 119.

166. *Laws*, 797a–798d.

167. *Ibid.*, 793a–d.

168. *Ibid.*, 799a–800a, 814d–816d.

169. *Ibid.*, 802a–d.

170. *Ibid.*, 811b–812b.

171. *Ibid.*, 818a–822c.

172. *Ibid.*, 802b–803b, emphasis added.

173. *Ibid.*, 803b, 685a; *Letters: VII*, 344c.

174. *Laws*, 804b.

175. *Ibid.*, 803b.

176. *Ibid.*, 803c.

177. *Ibid.*, 817b.

VII. CONCLUSION

1. Whether Aristotle understood Plato or misrepresents his position need not be explored here. See Harold Cherniss, *Aristotle's Criticism of Plato and the Academy* (New York: Russell and Russell, 1962).

2. *Politics*, 1276a–b. All references to Aristotle are from W. D. Ross (ed.), *The Works of Aristotle* (Oxford: Clarendon Press, 1927).

3. Martin Heidegger, *An Introduction to Metaphysics*, trans. Ralph Manheim (New York: Doubleday, 1961), pp. 155–156.

4. *Ibid.*, p. 128.

5. *Physics*, 223b.

6. *Ibid.*, 221b.

7. *Problemata*, 916a.

8. *Metaphysics*, 1018b.

9. *Meteorologia*, 339b; *De Caelo*, 270b; *Politics*, 1264a, 1329b.

10. *Metaphysics*, 982b, 1074b.

11. *Physics*, 219a.

12. *Ibid.*, 217b–218a.

13. Heidegger, *op. cit.*, p. 172.

14. *Physics*, 221b–222a.

15. *Ibid.*, 222b.

16. *Politics*, 1289b.

17. *The Confessions of St. Augustine*, trans. J. G. Pilkington (New York: Liveright, 1943), Bk. XI, Chs. XII–XXXI.

18. Niccolò Machiavelli, *The Prince and Discourses* (New York: Modern Library, 1940), p. 103.

19. *Ibid.*, pp. 105, 208, 216, 530.

20. *Ibid.*, p. 397.

21. *Ibid.*, pp. 129, 272.

22. *Ibid.*, p. 114.

23. *Ibid.*, pp. 3, 104, 383.

24. *Ibid.*, pp. 138, 139.

25. *Ibid.*, p. 141.

26. *Ibid.*, pp. 105, 397–398, 402.

27. Thomas Hobbes, *Leviathan* (New York: Collier, 1962), p. 478.

28. *Ibid.*, p. 158.

29. *Ibid.*, p. 30.

30. *Ibid.*

31. *Ibid.*, pp. 236–237.

32. *Ibid.*, pp. 87, 100.

33. *Ibid.*, pp. 237, 270.

34. Jean-Jacques Rousseau, *The Social Contract and Discourses*, trans. G. D. H. Cole (New York: E. P. Dutton, 1950), p. 231.

35. *Ibid.*, p. 211.

36. *Ibid.*, pp. 238, 244, 247.

37. *Ibid.*, p. 189.

38. *Ibid.*, p. 270.

39. Rousseau, *The Confessions of Jean-Jacques Rousseau* (New York: Modern Library, 1945), p. 417.

40. Rousseau, *Rêveries,* quoted in Georges Poulet, *Studies in Human Time,* trans. Elliot Coleman (New York: Harper, 1959), p. 163.

41. Rousseau, *Social Contract and Discourses,* p. 281.

42. *Ibid.,* pp. 84, 88.

43. Ortega y Gasset, *Concord and Liberty* (New York: Norton, 1946), pp. 50, 95.

44. F. Nietzsche, *The Use and Abuse of History* (New York: Liberal Arts Press, 1957), p. 56.

45. Heidegger, *What Is Philosophy,* trans. William Kluback and Jean T. Wilde (New York: Twayne, 1958), pp. 71–73.

INDEX